RISK IN PROBATION PRACTICE

Risk in Probation Practice

HAZEL KEMSHALL

Ashgate

Aldershot • Brookfield USA • Singapore • Sydney

Published by
Ashgate Publishing Limited
Gower House
Croft Road
Aldershot
Hampshire GU11 3HR
England

Ashgate Publishing Company
Old Post Road
Brookfield
Vermont 05036
USA

British Library Cataloguing in Publication Data
Kemshall, Hazel
    Risk in probation practice
    1. Probation - Great Britain 2. Risk assessment - Great
    Britain 3. Risk management - Great Britain
    I. Title
    364.6'3'0941

Library of Congress Catalog Card Number: 98-73401

ISBN 1 85972 318 7   19874804

Printed and Bound by Biddles Short Run Books, King's Lynn

Contents

Acknowledgements

Many people have supported my work on risk and stimulated my thinking over this four year period.

Particular thanks must go to Gillian Hundt for starting me on the research process, Liz Ross for much patient mentoring on methodology, and Paul Holt for assistance with the analysis. My thanks are extended to Eric Morrell, Chief Probation Officer, and to Liz Stafford, Research and Information Officer for facilitating research access in the West Midlands Probation Service; to Sue Roberts of the Home Office Probation Training Section for entrusting me with the training brief; and to Gill MacKenzie, Chief Probation Officer of Gloucestershire for ensuring Association of Chief Officer support at crucial moments. Gratitude is expressed to my colleague Jacki Pritchard who provided key advice and editorial comment, and to Ann Lane and Sue Gilbert who provided excellent secretarial advice and support. The project was sponsored by the Economic and Social Research Council's 'Risk and Human Behaviour' programme grant number L211252018.

However, this work would not have been completed without the unstinting support of all staff in the study. Their trust and frank co-operation are deeply appreciated.

List of abbreviations

A list of abbreviations is provided to assist readers.

PSA: Probation Service Assistant.

ASW: Assistant Warden (Hostels).

PO: Probation Officer.

SPO: Senior Probation Officer.

ACPO: Assistant Chief Probation Officer.

NAPO: National Association of Probation Officers.

ACOP: Association of Chief Officers of Probation.

HMIP: Her Majesty's Inspectorate of Probation.

NPRIE: National Probation Research and Information Exchange.

An Introduction

> ...Who performed this screening? How does it work? Who is the man or woman who made the final and fateful decision that the crime-sodden Compton was suitable company for the most vulnerable section of society? The ...Probation Service must answer these questions. Until we get the fullest of explanations, we mustn't trust their judgement further (Maureen Messant, Birmingham Evening Mail, 1996).

On October 25th 1996 the Birmingham Evening Mail published an editorial entitled: 'We're sick of these outrageous decisions' (p.15), in which the risk assessment practice of the Probation Service was severely criticised. The case concerned the brutal murder of a recipient of community service by an offender who had made contact with the victim during the completion of his community service order. The 'outrageous decision' reflected media and public perceptions that the Probation Service had placed a vulnerable person at risk through the failure of its risk assessment procedures.

Whilst a subsequent editorial less virulently apportioned blame for the failure of the risk assessment to the poor communication between Probation and the Crown Prosecution Service (Evening Mail 16th July 1997, p.6); both editorials illustrate the centrality of risk practice to probation work, and the high costs to individuals and the agency when 'something goes wrong'.

Assessing the riskiness of offenders for whom it has a statutory responsibility is now the core business of the Probation Service. Establishing and responding to the risk levels of offenders requires new and reliable techniques of risk assessment, risk analysis, and risk management. Staff and managers in Probation face daily decisions and dilemmas in these areas, most often about individual risk levels and how to avoid, control or minimise risk. Risk has become the dominant raison d'être of the Service, supplanting ideologies of need, welfare or indeed rehabilitation as key organising principles of service provision (Kemshall et al 1997). Risk is now the central focus of practitioner activity and a key area of scrutiny and accountability for managers.

As risk becomes the primary principle for the organisation and delivery of probation work, the Service is undergoing rapid change in both its key concerns and its fundamental relationships with offenders. Risk is the key strategic mechanism for the allocation of resources and as such it entails a differing categorisation of offenders than the more traditional ones of need and rehabilitation. An analysis of risk in probation practice provides an important insight into the changing nature of probation work and of the impact of this change upon the daily practices of staff and managers.

Scope and structure of the book

The book has its origins in research conducted under the Economic and Social Research Council's (ESRC) 'Risk and Human Behaviour Programme' (grant number L211252018), launched in 1993. The Programme initiative reflected increased societal concern with risk (Beck 1992), particularly with the accurate identification of hazards and their reduction. The programme objectives relevant to the present study were:

- The extent to which perceptions of risk vary.

- The extent to which risk assessments are influenced by value judgements and biases.

- How different understandings of risk and methods of risk assessment are reconciled in policy-making and implemented by frontline risk assessors.

- The impact of conditions of uncertainty upon risk decision making, in particular upon individuals' capacity to understand and use probability data on risk.

In 1993 the Probation Service was beginning to digest and adapt to its growing role in the assessment and management of offender risk. The Home Office instruction to Chief Probation Officers to set up and maintain registers of Potentially Dangerous Offenders (Home Office 1988), began to focus the Service's attention on the issues of credible identification and management. In addition, the risk reduction and public protection themes of the Criminal Justice Act 1991 (Wasik and Taylor 1991) gave legislative impetus to the Service's risk agenda. This presented an opportunity to investigate the ESRC's major objectives in the context of both local and national efforts to frame and implement policies on offender risk. The research study followed this challenging period (1993-1997), and the contents of the book reflect this time of change, tension and the daily reality of grappling with risk 'on the ground'. In capturing what has been to some extent the 'moveable feast' of risk, the book imposes a logic and structure on the material which was not always apparent either in the activities of the researcher or in the activities of service managers and staff. However, for ease of access and presentation the book is divided into three parts.

Following an outline of the research study and presentation of methodology in chapter one, Part One addresses issues of method and measurement in risk assessment in addition to placing offender risk within a wider penal policy context. The origins of risk within recent probation history are also reviewed, in addition to the impact of risk concerns on the work of the service.

This is followed in Part Two by presentation of the research findings with particular reference to the values influencing risk practice; the knowledge base used by staff and managers in their assessment and management of risk; the current state of staff and management practice on risk and the reasons for this; and the extent of 'fit' between policy expectations and daily practice.

Part Three of the book addresses the implications of the research findings for policy and practice; including issues of policy formulation and implementation; agency risk management strategies; resource allocation for risk; and staff development and training to ensure improved decision making on risk.

Whilst aimed at a broad readership of all probation staff involved in risk work, probation managers, policy makers and criminal justice academics, the book is not a handbook of 'good practice' or a review of the most effective methods for risk assessment. Both areas have been adequately addressed elsewhere (for example Kemshall and Pritchard 1996, 1997, Kemshall 1996). Rather the book investigates the complexities of working with risk and adopts a critical stance towards the possibility of certainty in risk practice in marked contrast to those texts which focus upon the generation of risk indicators (Andrews 1995, Copas et al 1994). Whilst acknowledging that the Probation Service has a pragmatic need to assess risks as credibly as possible, the emphasis in this book is upon understanding and improving the decision making processes of staff rather than upon advocating any particular assessment method.

Matters of definition, concept and theory

Whilst policy makers may weary of academic preoccupations with defining risk and wish to resort to 'commonsense' resolutions of such difficulties, what risk is remains a perennial question. For the purposes of this book risk is understood as the probability that an event or behaviour carrying the possibility of an adverse or negative outcome will occur. However, it is accepted that any definition of risk can be construed as a heuristic device, that is as a cognitive construct in order to achieve conceptual clarity and certainty in dealing with information and events. The reader will see a number of other definitions in the text, not least the heuristic devices of frontline risk assessors, their managers, and those responsible for policy formulation at central government level.

The research study was particularly interested in the risk definitions used by participants and how these might differ and indeed clash. Such differences may or may not be articulated, however the potential for conflict and indeed managerially undesirable decisions remains. The book has attempted to foreground these various definitions, to place them within their context of use, and to compare them to the definitions of central policy makers and experts on offender risk. Again the author recognises the severe imperative upon the service to reliably assess risk, and the natural resistance to 'getting bogged down' in issues of definition. However, what is understood by the term risk cannot be taken for granted as Part Two will illustrate. Clarity and consensus about the term are essential to successful policy implementation and practice.

A major theme of the book is that risk cannot be understood outside its context of use. The risk concerns of bungee jumpers are not the same as those of Probation Service employees. This is not to suggest that risk is bedevilled by an unresolvable relativism. Rather it is to suggest that definitions, understandings and perceptions of risk are rooted in value frames and contexts of use. A critical appraisal of such value frames and contexts is offered with consideration of their impact on policy and practice. Readers can use this as a knowledge base to inform their own policy and practice choices, and to gain greater understanding of why and how those choices on risk are made. Risk can be conceptually difficult to grasp, open to varying definitions and understandings. However, some key components can be identified. It is concerned with future activities and represents what Kemshall et al (1997) have defined as an attempt to colonise the future to present concerns and certainties. Ironically the major instrument of this colonisation is information from the past, with information on past adversities central to the probability calculations of future ones. The limitations of such an approach to risk assessment is explored in Part One. Concerns with future adversity, particularly of high impact in a context of media scrutiny and public accountability tends to result in a pursuit of methods which can guarantee ever increasing levels of certainty, and methods to limit the impact of adverse events once they have occurred. Efforts to control the future can also result in greater control of the present, in this case the present activities of those deemed to pose a future risk, and those managers and practitioners responsible for them.

In addition to being future orientated, risk is now conceptualised almost entirely in negative terms; the possibility of adversity which in turn should be reduced, controlled and avoided. Traditionally risk was a neutral concept, allowing for risk taking as well as risk avoidance (Douglas 1992, Parton 1996). However, the current risk frame is almost totally in terms of hazard, threat, and negative outcome (Beck 1992, Douglas 1992). The framing of events or behaviours as adverse or negative can be highly subjective involving choices and the value placed upon particular outcomes. This can result in contrasting positions between experts and policy makers on the one hand, and individual risk assessors at the frontline. Assessors consider both issues of probability and desirability of various outcomes, literally weighing up and trading off the merits of various options. This is well illustrated in the analysis of the responses to the case scenarios in chapter five. Here the risk analysis processes used by staff are presented in some detail.

Processes of risk analysis can impact upon the acceptability and use of formal risk assessment methods.This cannot be explained by sole reference to the malicious, negligent or ignorant activities of risk assessors; rather it requires a consideration of how risk choices are calculated and made, how differing priorities of risk may be produced, and how conflicts over varying perceptions of risk occur and can be resolved. Social theories on risk provide insight into the cultural context of risk concerns; how risks gain currency, legitimacy and priority (Douglas 1992, Douglas and Wildavksy 1983). Such an approach to risk focuses attention on the selection of risks for assessment and prevention, and the classificatory mechanisms used to identify and measure them. This theoretical approach is reviewed in Part

One and contrasted to the positivist response in which risk is conceptualised as an objective, static phenomenon amenable to routine measurement and control. The social constructivist approach to risk is also used in Part Two to explore the activities of staff and managers in their daily practice with risk.

These daily practices have implications for risk management, that is, for how risk can be managed by the individual intervention strategies of staff, and for how managers manage the process and practice of risk in the agency. A key issue for practitioners assessing risk is the compatibility of formal risk assessment methods with professional values as exemplified in chapters five and six. Practitioners are also concerned with the outcomes of varying interventions on risk and their consequences for key individuals. This is most often expressed as dilemmas about risks, rights and responsibilities (Kemshall and Pritchard 1997).

For managers, risk management is about 'getting it right' and the high consequences should something go wrong. A key issue for senior managers is how risk practice should be organised and managed, in particular which type of management processes are likely to enhance the risk decision making of staff. To answer this it is important to recognise the type of decisions being made, about what and in what context, and which management process is suited to the regulation of decisions. An incongruity between regulatory process and decision type may have disastrous consequences by lowering the efficacy of decisions. Recent disaster inquiries and Health and Safety reports more often indict management processes than the activities of individuals (Cullen Report 1990, Health and Safety Executive 1988, Hidden Report 1989). Prescriptive procedures can degrade over time, for example in the Piper Alpha north sea oil rig disaster (Cullen 1990), and in the absence of correct paper work safety is presumed in order to maintain production. Alternatively procedures are adapted to existing belief systems and work practices, for example in the Challenger shuttle disaster. In this situation NASA officials had known for sometime about the O-ring erosion but interpreted it as a low level non-fatal risk in line with previous incidents (Clarke 1995, Starbuck and Milliken 1988). Both their belief system and assessment procedures had reduced their decision making to a 'ritual' (Clarke 1995), within which they were able to justify their decision at the subsequent inquiry by stating that because it had been made according to the 'right' procedures it was correct despite the negative consequences. This is clearly a situation which probation managers should seek to avoid.

The differing approaches to regulating risk decisions are reviewed in Part One, and Part Two provides an insight into how staff and managers are routinely adapting management processes on risk to their own value frames and practice concerns. This forms the context within which any management process for regulating the risk decisions of staff must operate. Part Three addresses the issue of gaining greater congruity between management regulatory processes and practitioner activities on risk.

Alarms and scares: doing risk in the 'Risk Society'

Increasingly those in the risk business have to account publicly for their decisions in a climate where experts are not necessarily trusted (Adams 1995, Kemshall et al 1997, Parton 1996). Professional judgement is increasingly questioned (Parton 1996) and the monopoly of power and expertise traditionally held by professionals is perceived as uncertain and open to challenge (Lupton 1993,1994). Users dispute the expertise of the professional, for example in health care (Heyman 1997), and experts are often seen to be in disagreement with policy makers and with each other (for example in the Bovine spongiform encephalopathy (BSE) scare, Independent 4th December 1997, Miller and Reilly 1996).

In addition to this fracturing of trust there is a keenness to apportion blame. As Douglas (1992) expresses it we are now in a blaming culture which:

> ...is ready to treat every death as chargeable to someone's account, every accident as caused by someone's criminal negligence, every sickness a threatened prosecution (p.15-16).

Holding to account has replaced the trust which professionals and experts long enjoyed, and risk is the main topic of both accountability and blame allocation (Kemshall et al 1997).

The public may not necessarily have access to risk information, and are often confronted with risk as an intangible concept expressed as a range of probabilities (such as the range of possible deaths from human form of BSE). Both the range of risks, their uncertain nature, and difficulty in assessing probabilistic information even when presented, diminish public understanding and acceptability of risks (Slovic et al 1980, Slovic 1987). In this situation, risk performance is most often judged with hindsight bias once something has gone wrong. In these circumstances, professionals and their agencies are left to account for their decision making in a negative climate. It is the process of decision making and how that process was managed which will be called into account. Crucial to judgements of that accounting will be the perceived trustworthiness of those providing the account. This is not only an issue of whether defensible decisions are made which can withstand both public scrutiny and litigation (Carson 1996), it is also a matter of organisational credibility with the public and other primary stakeholders.

The end of the century sees us facing ever more risks: pollution, contamination of the food supply, shortages of key resources such as water, incurable diseases, war, famine and crime to name but a few. The benefits of modernisation are questioned as the ills begin to outweigh the gains (Beck 1992). Risks grow as benefits fall, coupled with the weakening of social bonds and the isolation of the individual. In this context not only has awareness of risk risen but it is also perceived as an individual threat from which traditional support structures, experts and professionals can no longer protect us. All hazards become highly personalised, and the professional expertise of those working with risk is viewed sceptically and as rooted in self-interest (after all it is what these professionals get paid for). Offender risk is no exception. Whilst the British Crime survey concluded that there is little to fear other than fear itself (Mirlees-Black and Maung 1994), public fears over crime have continued to grow (Sparks 1992). Both central government penal policy makers and those who implement such policies are increasingly held to account for the alleviation of such fears.

Risk is a risky business conducted largely in a 'climate of uncertainty' (Brearley 1982). Public and personal harm is at stake, as is individual blame, organisational censure and loss of agency credibility. Dealing with risk is now central to professional life in the Probation Service. This book addresses what it is *to do risk* in Probation.

Part One: Methodology and Context

Risk is an everyday preoccupation as well as a criminal justice one. As Adams expresses it, we are all experts on risk to some degree (Adams 1995), and there are moments of uncertainty, choice and 'gambling' in the conduct of our everyday lives. How then should we understand and investigate this thing called 'risk'? Is it a matter of commonsense lay experience or a matter of formal expertise? These are key questions as to how risk is to be conceptualised and understood, and to a large extent involve questions on how risk is to be identified, measured and controlled. The following chapters outline a distinct theoretical and methodological approach to risk rooted in social constructivism. In essence, a pre-occupation with how risk gains particular meanings and usage, how particular assessment and measurement methods gain currrency, and how those dealing with risk (in this case probation staff) confer meaning and use on the term.

Chapter one outlines this approach to the research enterprise in some detail, including some attention to the difficult issues of validity and claims to knowledge within a research approach which foregrounds the contingent and uncertain nature of risk. This 'nature of risk' is further pursued in chapter two, and current approaches to method and measurement in offender risk are reviewed, including the problem of probability and the social construction of measurement tools.

The implications of social constructivism and social theories of risk for understanding and managing risk in the Probation Service are reviewed in chapter three, in particular the social and organisational dynamics which result in differing and at times competing views of risk. The issues for the effective organisational management of risk work and the current managerial responses, for example of prescriptive guidance, are briefly reviewed. This is followed in chapter four by a more in-depth and extensive exploration of the historical and policy precursors of risk based work in the Service. Whilst many readers will be well versed in such a history of the Service from other sources (primarily the McWilliams quartet, 1985,1986, 1987, 1989); nevertheless, a recognition of the origins of risk and the cumulative policy journey to a risk based penality are worth re-stating in the face of some temptation to view risk as solely the product of 'Howardism' or a rather recent 'flavour of the month'.

1. Researching Risk in Probation Practice: Methodology

The concern with offender risk prediction is not entirely new. Burgess (1928, 1929, 1936), for example pioneered parole risk prediction in the late 1920s, a technique emulated subsequently by Ohlin and Duncan (1949), Mannheim and Wilkins (1955) and the Gottfredsons (Gottfredson and Gottfredson 1985, 1986,1993). The principles utilised by Burgess (1928, 1936) still form the core of actuarial (i.e. statistically based) parole risk prediction today (Copas et al 1996), and were utilised in Nuttall's prediction model in England (1977), and Nuffield's (1982) model in Canada.

However, the Carlisle Committee (1988) found that the risk of reoffending and the risk to public safety were not integral to parole decision making. Rather ideals of rehabilitation coupled with satisfactory reports of institutional behaviour were central to the largely subjective and anecdotal decision making of local review committees (Flynn 1978, Glaser 1973). The demise of the Nuttall predictor (1977) is well documented by Polvi and Pease (1991) and illustrates the difficulty in both locating risk as central to decision making, and in moving decision makers away from case-based highly subjective information (Carroll and Payne 1976, Glaser 1962, 1973).

Risk prediction in probation supervision has a more recent history. Originally concerned with classifying those 'most amenable to resocialisation' (Flynn 1978), the risk assessment methodologies often have as much to do with rationing the use of supervision and allocating costly community resources as with the prediction of risk per se (Andrews and Bonta 1994, Harris 1994). Their overt link to issues of evaluating practice performance and the effectiveness of service delivery has sometimes hindered their acceptance by both practitioners and managers (for example Association of Chief Officers of Probation 1995, Fletcher 1995, National Probation Research and Information Exchange 1995). The challenge to professional autonomous decision making is particularly resented (Fletcher 1995).

The response of users to both the parole and probation risk predictors also illustrates a major gap between research and practice. Whilst criminology has become increasingly concerned with risk, predominantly with questions of risk distribution, perception and management (Box 1987, Clark et al 1993, Cornish and Clarke 1986, Farrington and Tarling 1985, Flynn 1978, Gottfredson and Gottfredson, 1985, 1986, 1993), research into how criminal justice workers assess and respond to risk is less prevalent (Glaser 1973). Studies of offender risk in both the United States and more recently in Britain have concentrated upon either the production of risk predictors for recidivism (Copas et al 1994), or upon offender responses to getting caught and the types of calculations offenders make in deciding to desist (Cornish and Clarke 1986). However, a key question must be the extent to which such studies have impacted upon the knowledge base and practices of those criminal justice personnel responsible for offender risk assessment, in this case probation staff. It is these personnel who have a key role on behalf of their organisation for the assessment and management of offender risk at point of sentence, during community supervision and at point of parole release. There has been little investigation into how those responsible for offender assessment and supervision receive and process information on risk. For example:

- Do probation risk assessors see risk in the same terms as academic criminologists?

- Are the calculations of risk by frontline staff similar or different to the statistical calculations of experts?

- What risk assessment indicators and methods do staff rely upon in their daily practice with risk?

- What is it that frontline workers and their managers actually do when they assess offender risk?

Answering these questions has been the main concern of this study.

Purpose of the study

The study was funded under the Economic and Social Research Council's (ESRC) Risk and Human Behaviour Programme, originally for a two year period from 1994-1996, with the author as the sole researcher.

This period was extended by one year to allow for an increased period of dissemination which included training for Probation senior managers, the production of training materials, training of in-service trainers, and training of main grade probation officers (funded separately by the Home Office Probation Training Unit), and a review of assessment methods for the Home Office Research and Statistics Directorate (Kemshall 1996).

The research has examined how Probation managers and staff understood and applied the term risk in their daily supervision and management of offenders. Of particular interest was how staff and managers assessed offender risk and risky situations, how information on risk was acted upon, what was determined as risky and how risk decisions were actually made. In addition to these concerns, the research has attempted to develop an analytic framework for understanding how risk decisions are actually made 'in the field' in order to inform policy development, practice guidance and training. In this sense the research has had an increasing action bias, with particular attention to enhancing risk decision making by staff and managers.

In particular a key theme has been how best to achieve effective risk decisions, and the respective roles of professional judgement and prescriptive procedures in improving decision making. In effect:

- What types of decision making results in the most accurate risk assessments and the most effective risk management strategies?

- And what types of policies, procedures and practice guidance best facilitate these decisions?

This necessarily leads into the fraught area of evaluating risk practice and assessing the quality of risk decisions in the field where the negative performance indicators of false negatives resulting in harm can be highly visible. However, evaluating the type of practice and management which not only contributes to true positives and true negatives but also reduces risk can be more difficult. This led to an increasing preoccupation with the following questions:

- Can the characteristics of an accurate risk assessment be identified and consistently replicated across the Probation Service?

- Given the difficulties inherent in risk prediction what levels of accuracy can be achieved and how accurate is accurate enough?

- Are risk management strategies reducing risk or are they merely mis-targeted at those falsely classified as risky by poor assessment procedures?

These are key questions for Service personnel as they attempt to respond to the risk agenda with credibility and within shrinking resources. Whilst no study should claim to definitively answer such complex questions, this book does attempt to constructively add to the debate.

Research methods and theoretical framework

Research on offender risk has predominantly been undertaken from a positivist and normative position, concerned with the identification and dissemination of those factors most likely to assist practitioners in the accurate prediction of risk. Research inquiry has framed the problem of risk as one of more accurately defining the phenomenon of offender risk and uncovering the factors which can indicate that risk is likely to be present or not. For example the work of Copas et al (1994) in establishing the factors most likely to predict the risk of reoffending, or the work of Andrews (1995) in identifying those risk factors most associated with future criminal conduct. Accurate risk prediction is then viewed as a matter of communicating such research findings to policy makers, managers and workers, and regulating the degree of fit between practice and research. However, this approach to risk research does not necessarily tell us how frontline workers assess and respond to risk, nor how research information and risk indicators are incorporated into worker judgements.

Attention to what practitioners and managers actually do when working with risk invites a different theoretical and research position. This position assigns '...a significant role to the organisational members' own subjective ideas about the phenomena in question' (G. Smith and Harris 1972, p. 27). This view takes the construction, understanding and use of the phenomena by participants as the focus of research inquiry. This is not to assert the totally relative position that offender risk has no existence outside the meanings conferred upon it by practitioners, but that exploring such meanings are essential to understanding how workers assign certain factors as risky and others as not. The purpose is to identify what people do in order to assess and manage risk, and not necessarily to evaluate these activities or to state what ought to be done.

Methods

Research which priotitises the views of its participants requires methods designed to gather them. As Dey (1993) expresses it, methods designed to deal with meanings. Such meanings are not merely the subjective thoughts of individuals, but are also embedded in social practices (Dey 1993) and the contexts within which they are daily used. The research study therefore used a range of qualitative methods particularly designed for accessing meanings.

The study took place in a large, diverse Probation Service covering a range of offender types and geographical area. Six probation teams and their relevant managers were chosen as a purposively constructed sample to represent the range of probation tasks and settings (with the exception of community service and family court welfare). In total 31 probation officers, 7 senior probation officers, and 6 assistant chief officers took part in the study over a two year period. Despite staff changes, the six teams remained in the study for the full period and the co-operation of all staff remained very high.

In any qualitative study the representativeness of the sample and the ability to draw general conclusions from it have been the subject of long-term debate (Patton 1980). However, Dey (1993) usefully distinguishes between two kinds of generalisation: the first are generalisations derived from induction and based upon our empirical observations; and the second, which is about the application of our generalisations to the population as a whole. The primary role of qualitative research is to establish the generalisations which the data will support and the conditions '..under which our generalisations may hold true'. (Dey 1993, p.263). In this sense the sample is representative of the various settings typifying work in probation practice, and the conclusions drawn, whilst suggestive, could be tested for applicability in other probation and similar settings.

The study employed a range of qualitative data collection methods: avignette survey, semi-structured interviews, observation and collection of field notes, and critical path analysis workshops, with each stage of the project utilising differing methods to collect specific data. In addition, each stage was designed to provide verification of the data collected previously (Denzin 1978). The detail of the methodology is presented stage by stage.

Stage One In stage one the objective of the research was to gather data on the current definitions and meanings on risk within the agency; and to assemble initial data on the knowledge base, value system and concepts of risk which staff routinely drew upon in order to accomplish their risk assessments. This was done by the use of the vignette technique (Finch 1987, Finch and Mason 1993); a technique in which interviewers ask interviewees to consider a range of hypothetical situations and to provide choices of actions and outcomes and reasons for these. Finch (1987) argues that this technique assists in the study of normative issues and assists in the uncovering of contextually specific material particularly around respondents' beliefs and values. Whilst this technique will not tell us what people actually do, it has the potential to survey the beliefs on risk current in the agency and the type of knowledge workers (including managers) are using in their risk assessments. Vignettes can also be of use in situations where data collection is sensitive, for example in situations where staff may believe that their performance is being evaluated. Analysis can subsequently produce an initial schema of the value system and knowledge base utilised by staff in their risk assessments.

The design of the vignettes originally proved problematic. Which hypothetical case situations were to be chosen and why? This was resolved by selecting recent or 'live cases' typical of the range of the agency's work which could be anonymised and used for data collection. This communicated a crucial realism to staff, and assisted the researcher in avoiding the communication of implicit or explicit definitions of risk and 'acceptable' courses of action. The vignettes were piloted with one team and then applied to the sample as a whole after minor revision. The vignettes are reproduced as appendix one.

Stage Two This stage aimed to collect data on the operationalisation of risk in practice, and to determine the situational factors affecting risk assessment, risk decision making and risk management decisions. Semi-structured interviews were used to illicit further clarification of the beliefs, values and knowledges of risk being used; and to explore in depth thefactors which participants felt impinged upon their decision making. Semi-structured interviews use a topic guide rather than fixed word questions in order to facilitate a conversational format and greater flexibility (the topic guide is reproduced as appendix two). This approach is designed to gain data on participants' views of the world in their own words, thus avoiding the impingement of the researcher's meanings.

This was supported by approximately 120 hours of observation of managers and practitioners across the various settings in discussions, team meetings and direct work with offenders. The observations were recorded in field notes which also contained a record of conversations both formal and informal, observation of procedures, and the daily activities of participants. Field notes also included the researcher's reflections both upon the process of the study and the data collected in line with the principles expressed by Burgess (1982), Webb (1982) and Minichiello et al (1990). By the end of stage two a detailed ethnography of risk in probation practice had been assembled.

Stage Three This stage aimed to formulate an explanatory model of risk decision making on risk in probation practice which could be shared with practitioners and managers and inform policy, practice and training. This was done through a series of workshops run by the researcher with participants, workshops with staff outside the sample group for comparison (including another probation area), workshops with policy makers, and the design and pilot of training material. The applicability of the explanatory model was 'tested' with a sub-sample of staff and their cases by the use of critical path analysis in which staff were asked to identify the critical factors in their risk decision making.

Critical path analysis is a method for systematically analysing decision making processes. Whilst it has its roots in engineering (Battersby 1964), its most recent use is in the evaluation of nursing clinical judgements (Minghella and Benson 1995, Norman et al 1992, Orme and Maggs 1993, Sims 1976). In effect, the method enables practitioners to trace the critical factors involved in their decision making, and to identify the variables which have resulted in particular decision outcomes, hence the notion of criticality, and the use of the term path. The technique accepts that practitioners are presented with choices as cases progress, and that there are differing decision pathways probable in any one case. Path analyses can uncover which paths were chosen and why. This data could then be compared for 'fit' against the material generated by the explanatory model of the ethnographic material. Path analyses also provided data on what participants perceived to be the characteristics of 'good' and 'poor' risk assessments, and what factors they consider contribute to such decisions being made. The technique of critical path analysis and the material used in the critical path workshops is presented in more detail in chapter seven.

Critical path analysis has also been used to encourage a more reflective approach to decision making and clinical risk assessments by practitioners (Minghella and Benson 1995). This is crucial to risk decision making as such decisions are characterised by high levels of uncertainty (Brearley 1982) where more than one possible outcome can occur and where the penalties for 'getting a decision wrong' can be severe. This approach may assist practitioners not only in pursuing decisions which are more 'managerially desirable', but perhaps more importantly, in making the decision choices taken transparent and in rehearsing the desirablility of the various decision choices before them. The training potential of critical path analysis was considered in stage four and is presented in chapter seven.

Stage Four The final stage of the research had an action and dissemination orientation, and involved key users such as the Association of Chief Probation Officers, the Home Office Probation Unit, The Home Office Probation Training Section, senior probation managers, and of course frontline practitioners. Part of this stage was also the subject of separate funding from the Home Office Research and Statistics Directorate and the Home Office Probation Training Section. This stage produced the following material:

- A review of risk assessment methods (Kemshall 1996).

- A framework for risk decision making (Kemshall 1995, 1996, 1996a).

- Recommendations for the content of policies for the assessment and management of risk and dangerousness (Kemshall 1997).

- A national survey of Probation Service risk training provision (Kemshall 1997a).

- Training materials for frontline risk assessors (Kemshall 1997b).

- Training for senior probation officers (i.e. middle managers) piloted in Inner London Probation Service, Berkshire, and Durham.

The study was completed over a three year period integrating the data into the analysis stage by stage. The next section will consider the more complex issue of validation in research.

Validation

Validation is often regarded as a problematic issue in qualitative research (Dey 1993, Strauss and Corbin 1990, Minichiello et al 1990). Dismissed by its critics as prone to researcher bias, and dependent upon relationships of inference between the data and subsequent explanations, rather than the testable causal relationships of science. Such 'inferences' are seen as invalid because propositions generated cannot be tested. Silverman (1993) has refuted the notion that the canons of scientific validity are necessarily sacrosanct and free from defect, or indeed appropriate to the research process of qualitative research. Rather, qualitative researchers can gain a 'warrant for their inferences' (Fielding and Fielding 1986, p.12) by considering issues of plausability and credibility of the knowledge claims they are making (Hammersley 1990, Silverman 1993).

In addition, some testability may be possible. Bloor (1978, following Frake 1964) has suggested the use of structured respondent validation by predicting 'participants' classifications in actual situations of their use' and by preparing 'hypothetical cases' and predicting 'respondents' responses to them' (cited in Silverman 1993 p.159). The critical path method of stage three of this study was an attempt to do just this, coupled with active involvement of participants in research feedback.

Stanley (1990) has suggested that the documentary/interpretative method of analytic induction is shared in common by lay person and researcher alike, and advocates respondent validation. The contextual particulars derived from the realm of study can be used as indicators of an underlying pattern, providing conceptual tools for the explication of behaviour in other settings, and for theorising on the social phenomenon discovered not only in that milieu, but also relating to the wider social structure. In these terms, those who are 'of the setting' are the best judge of the explanatory model proposed. Participants should therefore be involved in quality assuring the content, process and outcomes of research. This study incorporated a steering group of participants including the local research and information officer and the assistant chief officer responsible for the risk policy, and involved all participants in regular feedback through the use of team presentations and workshops. In this way the explanation of data could be systematically checked against participants' own understanding of their activities.

Minichiello et al (1990) argue that validity is also achieved in social science research by the researcher 'staying close to the empirical world in order to ensure a close fit between the data and what people actually say and do.' (p.209). Constant cross checking of the data and the pursuit of negative cases to confirm or deny hypotheses is the hallmark of the analytical method of qualitative research. The statements of participants are considered as accounts of their activities and are not assessed for either their accuracy or bias, however they are considered to be real (Silverman 1985). This constructivist understanding of the world also extends to the role of the researcher. The researcher is not involved in the 'testing of theory' but in the 'generation of theory' through the analysis of empirical data. This has been termed the 'double subjectivity' of respondent and researcher (Minichiello et al 1990). This view accepts that both respondent and researcher have a 'position', or view, and account for their social activities from this position. Such subjectivities are not necessarily problematic if they are explicitly stated and the perspectival nature of the enterprise is acknowledged. This is distinct from positivist research enterprises which purport to a unitary view of the social world and researcher objectivity. Kuhn however has argued that the criticisms which are applied to the lack of objectivity of social science can be applied to all science (1970), and that objectivity per se is not an achievable goal.

Other commentators have argued that objectivity is better understood as reliability, validity and shareability of research knowledge (J. D. Douglas 1976, Kirk and Miller 1986, Minichiello et al 1990, Silverman 1993). Reliability is safeguarded by the adoption of established methods of data collection and clear analytical procedures in interpreting the data which could be replicated by other researchers. Validity is assured by the use of mixed strategies of data collection to facilitate cross-checking (Burgess 1984) sometimes referred to as 'triangulation (Denzin 1978), and by remaining close to the empirical data when formulating hypotheses. This is most often accomplished through the use of 'Grounded Theory' techniques of data analysis (Glaser and Strauss 1965, 1967, 1968, Strauss and Corbin 1990).

Analysing the data: the application of Grounded Theory

Championed extensively by Glaser and Strauss (1965, 1967, 1968, Strauss and Corbin 1990, Strauss and Corbin 1997), grounded theory is in essence the systematic application of the analytic induction method of data analysis and theorising. The method has two key features: constant comparison across the range of data, and the search for negative cases to confirm or deny hypotheses. In effect the researcher hypothesises as data is collected and constantly tests initial propositions by actively seeking data which does not fit.

The principle procedures of analytic induction are:

(1) An initial definition of the research problem is formulated.

(2) Data is collected and then classified for common features and conditions. An initial hypothesis about the data is formulated.

(3) Negative cases which do not fit the initial classification are scrutinised. The hypothesis is revised; or the classificatory system is re-scrutinised, expanded and reapplied; or the case is excluded on the grounds that it is not relevant to the phenomenon under study.

(4) This technique is repeated until 'saturation' is achieved, that is there are no further negative cases and a theoretical explanation of the data is proposed.

(Derived from Dey 1993, Minichiello et al 1990, Silverman 1993)

Analytic induction requires an approach to research which actively encourages the simultaneous collection and analysis of data. The present study was constructed as a staged process in order to deliberately facilitate this.

In the early stages of the research process analysis tends to be general and descriptive and initial hypotheses are largely tentative. Analysis gains greater clarity and explanatory power as negative cases are tested and saturation is achieved. However, analytic induction should not be conceptualised as a neat linear progression towards theoretical illumination. Rather the researcher operates under some uncertainty for most of the project, pursuing a number of analytical 'red herrings'. Staying 'close to the data' enables constant checking and thereby greater certainty in the final explanatory model. This technique as applied to the present study is represented in figure one.

Analytic induction is better conceptualised as a spiral between the data and hypothetical propositions in which inductive thinking becomes increasingly deductive. That is, reasoning moves from a process of inferring general statements from singular ones, to finally deducing singular statements from general ones. Bulmer (1979) has referred to this as a process of *retroduction* in which there is a '...constant inter-play between observation of reality and formulation of concepts, research and theorising..' (Sheppard 1995, p.274).

In the present study the initial proposition was that the values held by risk assessors would impact upon their assessment of risk. Stage one of the research in effect surveyed the range and type of these values in relation to a number of risky scenarios. This was a broad and somewhat speculative focus, in which the type of values, how, why and under what conditions they impacted upon risk assessment was unknown. Analysis at this stage showed no single value base in operation, but rather a range of expressed values which could be grouped together under two basic typologies; rehabilitative values and public protection ones. The classification of these value types was checked through the collection of further data in stage two, and the initial hypothesis about the relationship between these values and risk assessment was further explored in stage two and tested in the critical path workshops in stage three.

Data was analysed using the now well established techniques of coding, categorising and conceptualising (Coffey and Atkinson 1996, Dey 1993, Huberman and Miles 1994). Data was initially coded for recurrent themes and then grouped under higher order categories of similarity. For example, the vignette data was coded for any expression of value by respondents, (the term value is further explored in chapter five), initially using respondents' own language. From an initial total of 124 such 'in vivo' codes, the data was then grouped into categories of similarity. For example, the following statement was ascribed the code 'trust':

> PSO 1 ...Other ladies that I have met have genuinely been in trouble, they have done the fraud, they don't know how they have got in the situation and they are so remorseful that yes, we do trust them but people like the one I described previously you just can't trust them...Its how they come over to you. I don't know, I think I have a knack of sussing them out very quickly...

Figure 1.1 Proposed Analytical Model for Risk in Probation Practice

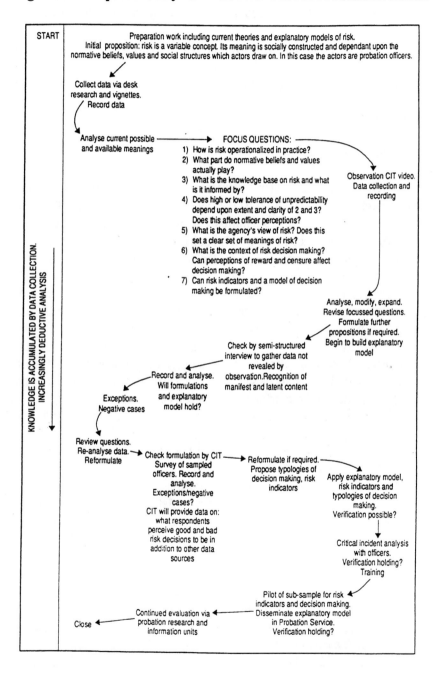

Similar statements were also ascribed this category. Categories were then analysed for links and inter-connections, by asking the following questions.

- What category is present with which other categories?

- Why are they present together?

- How do they interact?

- Why and with what results?

The NUDIST 3.1 computer software package facilitated these simple Boolean searches of association (Dey 1993), and also related them to particular respondents or case scenarios. In addition, NUDIST enabled a search of the text for other links which could be inferred from the context, for example statements of the type: " I do this because of that", and how often such statements could be collaborated by other pieces of data. In this way the researcher can gain quantitative validation of the volume of particular categories and their connections prior to formulating hypotheses. It is at this point that conceptualisation of the data takes place and explanatory theories begin to be built. At this stage the researcher is less concerned with classifying data through categorisation but is focused upon the conditions and circumstances within which certain categories occur, and the conditions under which connections between categories take place.

In the present study, the case scenarios generated various categories of value and various categories of knowledge used by officers in their risk assessments. The key question was if and how they might interact in the process of risk assessment (this is the subject of chapter five). NUDIST can display these categories visually, and relationships between any part of the 'tree' can be sought, for example: the relationship between *either* rehabilitative values *or* public protection values and the knowledge base used by staff to assess risk, in particular formal risk indicators. This is represented in figure two.

This represents a small example of the immense detail involved in the lengthy process of analysis. No research study can reproduce this process to its full extent. The relationship between the presentation of research and the process of the research itself is therefore always representational (Garfinkel 1967, Garfinkel et al, 1981), in which narrative structures are imposed and material is précised around selected themes. This is not however a recipe for the arbitrary imposition of meaning by the researcher.

Figure 1.2 Nudist Categorisation 'Tree'

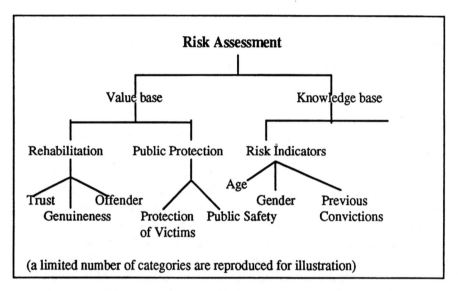

(a limited number of categories are reproduced for illustration)

Dey (1993) has posed useful criteria for the production of research accounts which include:

* Credibility and coherence of the explanation.

* Relevance to participants.

* Practical import.

* Conceptual rigour.

* Empirical weight.

Garfinkel (1967, Garfinkel et al, 1981) expressed this as the acceptance of findings based upon reasonable grounds of proof, and our acceptance of them as a co-member of the social world. Both researcher and reader are involved in an interpretive process of ordering the data, hypothesising 'knowable facts' which are confirmed or denied, subsequently

Garfinkel labelled this 'fact production in flight' (1967). In other words, establishing through researching *and reading* whether the account makes sense. Giddens (1976, 1984) has argued that it is the job of the social researcher to investigate the frames of meaning used by social actors in the conduct of their social life and to 'generate descriptions of them that are potentially available to those who have not directly participated in them' (1976, p.145). In this case the reader will be experiencing the meaning frames of our probation risk assessors through the researcher's account.

Theoretical position

In penetrating and reproducing for readers the meaning frames of the research participants, the researcher must inevitably adopt a 'position'. This is not necessarily the subjectivity of bias (Minichiello et al 1990), but is an acceptance that the researcher inevitably brings a particular perspective and frame of meaning to the research inquiry. This research study has been informed by an explicit rooting in social constructivism.

A constructivist position owes much to the sociology of knowledge (Berger and Luckmann 1967, Mannheim 1970, 1976, 1982, Schutz, 1970, 1976), and investigations into the commonsense knowledge of the every day by Garfinkel (1967). The focus of attention is upon the *production* of knowledge and knowledge claims in particular social settings, and more recently the sense making practices used by social actors as they navigate their social world (Garfinkel 1967). Importantly this theoretical view recognises that every actor in the social world intimately knows the social system of which he/she is a part, and is intrinsically involved in producing and reproducing that system through his/her conduct. More recently Giddens (1979, 1984) has described this as '*structuration*', a concept which recognises the duality of social structure; that is, that structure is the medium by which action is produced and is, in turn, the outcome of this production. In this study the practices of social actors (i.e. risk assessors) is key to understanding how they make sense of offender risk.

Social constructivism also poses risk as an essentially multi-dimensional and often contested concept (Adams 1995). The difficulty in forming an operational definition of risk for use in the field, (the 'definitional fallacy') has been noted by many researchers (Adams 1995, Douglas 1986, Kemshall 1996, Parton et al 1997). In child protection this has led to what Dingwall (1989) has called 'definition inflation', that is, the definition literally grows to encompass more and more risk concerns and characteristics. Checklists expand and workers are required to look for and recognise more and more factors. He notes the long struggle of child abuse research to produce a 'persuasive operational definition of abuse or neglect'. (p.42).

Whilst this may reflect societal, policy and agency concerns with risk at any particular point in time, it does not necessarily enhance accurate targeting of 'high risk' (Parton et al 1997). The prioritising of certain definitions and indices is more often a reflection of societal concerns and value choices than an indication that the objective reality of risk has been 'discovered' (Dingwall 1989, Douglas 1986).

The correlation between indicators and risk can also be understood as a matter of construction. As Cicourel (1964) has expressed it concepts are often translated into specific properties in order to facilitate both research measurement and field operation. However, these properties can be understood as a research construction and not necessarily as endemic to the concept itself. Like the measurements they facilitate, they bear a metaphorical rather than a literal relationship to the concept under investigation. In addition, such constructions contribute to classifications of persons and as such are morally weighted and convey orientations towards further action (Jayyusi 1984, Wattam 1992). For example access to a service (or not), or more crucially restriction of liberty. Research methodologies may obscure these issues and technical instruments hide moral evaluations, however they are present. As Dingwall et al express it:

> What matters is that we should not disguise this and pretend it is all a matter of finding better checklists or new models of psychopathology - technical fixes when the proper decision is a decision about what constitutes a good society (Dingwall et al 1983, p.244).

The applicability of social construction to risk research

Brearley (1982) has argued that risk assessments are carried out in a 'climate of uncertainty' and that a complex inter-play of knowledge base and value system influence any risk decision. In his work Brearley (1982) draws attention to the actual processes of assessment and contends that assessment is:

> ...not a neat and tidy clinical process in social work, with the knowledgeable and authoritative social worker making clear-cut and well-

founded decisions. It is often a haphazard, and necessarily uncertain, series of pragmatic and sometimes expedient decisions... (Brearley 1982, p. 76).

Schon (1987) expressed similar views in respect of professional practice and the knowledge it utilises. Schon argues that practitioners construct the problem 'from the materials of the situation' especially in situations where 'there is no obvious fit between the characteristics of the situation and the available body of theories and techniques.' (Schon 1987, p.4). Whilst describing a range of professional assessments, Schon's description well applies to practice on risk. He further argues that in constructing assessment problems practitioners 'choose and name the things they will notice', and that it is this, rather than technical problem solving which converts problematic situations into well-formed problems which can then be solved (Schon 1987, p. 4-5). Schon labels this type of practice as practice in the 'indeterminate zone', comprising 'uncertainty, uniqueness and value conflict' (p.6) It is situations of value conflict in which objectives and goals are often unclear that create the most difficulties for practitioners. This raises the issue of what constitutes practice knowledge and how the theoretical knowledge which may inform it is constructed and applied.

The context of professional practice

Professional practice is carried out by a 'community of practitioners' who share distinctive practices, actions, and language, and who operate in distinct institutional settings (Dewey 1933, Schon 1987). Practice can be characterised as a socially and institutionally regulated activity, familiar to those regularly engaged in it. In addition, practitioners share a more or less explicit body of professional knowledge, although the extent to which this is explicit, systematic, articulated and uncontested may vary (Carew 1979, Hardiker 1977, Sheppard 1995). Vickers (1978) has also argued that practitioners share an 'appreciative system', that is a set of values through which they make sense of practice situations and which orientate intervention goals and objectives. It is this 'appreciative system' which determines acceptable professional conduct (both practice and theoretical), and along with the value system acts to both facilitate and constrain practice. In effect, this is to conceptualise these key components of professional practice as the rules and resources which practitioners within their institutional community draw upon in order to achieve the activity of practice. Practice can be understood as a 'practice accomplishment' or 'situated activity' (Garfinkel 1967) within the socially organised professional world of probation work.

Practice is a product of the context within which it is organised and accomplished. However, this is often a reciprocal relationship with practice activities solidifying organisational forms and patterns of service delivery (for example social casework dominating most models of service delivery in the post-war period). Practice can also initiate change in organisational form, service delivery and practice knowledge (Smith and Harris 1972). The history of probation has a number of such examples, one of the most recent is work with sex offenders which has provided a comfortable vehicle for the service's public protection role and effectively reconfigured the offender as the perpetrator of risks (McEwan and Sullivan 1996).

Payne has argued that this is to understand practice as an essentially reflexive process (1997), in which the interaction between service user, worker and context all play their part in constituting the practice activity. This is in contrast to a positivist understanding of practice as the worker's expert implementation of empirically proven theories to the uncontested problems of clients. Alternatively, a reflexive/constructivist view sees practice as dynamic, interactive, processual, and often contested as worker, user, (and sometimes managers) struggle for the right to define and resolve the problem. This suggests that practice is a negotiated reality between differing participants in a particular context.

As 'uncertain practice' in the 'indeterminate zone' risk assessment in probation practice can be characterised as a negotiated and situated reality. In formulating and implementing policy, practice guidance and training for offender risk assessment it is essential to understand how workers (including managers) construct and use the phenomenon risk, why and under what circumstances. This is to take seriously both the meanings and usage of the term risk operationalised by practitioners, and the context within which it is routinely applied. In effect, this is to engage with what Schon (1987) has called the reflective conversations of practitioners:

> When practitioners respond to the indeterminate zones of practice by holding a reflective conversation with the materials of their situations, they remake a part of their practice world and thereby reveal the usually tacit processes of worldmaking that underlies all of their practice (Schon 1987, p.36).

This research study has attempted to engage with those reflective conversations and to make them explicit. The study represents an ethnography of the 'worldmaking' of risk.

The place of knowledge in offender risk assessment

The relationship between theoretical knowledge, and more recently empirically proven research, and practice in the field has long taxed social work commentators (Carew 1979, Payne 1997, Sheldon 1978, 1982, Sheppard 1995). In particular the lack of transferability of theoretical and scientific knowledge to practice (Bartlett 1970, Meyer 1959, Sheldon 1978). The practice knowledge of practitioners has been dismissed as less rigorous than that of academically produced theorising, and rejected as largely 'commonsense concepts and judgements' (Karpf 1931). Whilst on the other hand, 'the prescriptions of theory have, for many practitioners, often appeared distant, esoteric and hardly relevant for the complex and pressured world of practice.' (Sheppard 1995, p. 265).

In the field of offender risk assessment the failure of practitioners to implement either theoretical knowledge or empirically proven (usually by statistical methodologies) risk indicators has led to claims of anecdotal and ineffective practice (Glaser 1962, 1973, Monahan 1981). Monahan's study (1981) noted the high error rates of individual clinical assessments, a fact which both violence and mental health prediction have had to work hard to dispel (Limandri and Sheridan 1995, Monahan 1993, Steadman et al 1994). Carroll (1977, Carroll and Payne 1976) drew attention to practitioners' preferences for case based information over statistical base rates, and the cognitive biases of risk assessors in many fields is well documented (Combs and Slovic 1979, Kahneman and Tversky 1973, Kahneman et al 1982, Kahneman and Tversky 1984, Slovic 1987, Slovic et al 1980). This has led to numerous attempts to assert the experts' view over the practitioners', usually through the use of formal assessment methods and checklists. In effect, to either aid professional judgement, structure it, or replace it. This can result in heated debates between practitioners and experts as to whose view is the most reliable (for example see Fletcher's reaction to the Offender Group Reconviction Score in the National Association of Probation Officers News 1995, The Independent 1995); to practitioner circumvention of tools they distrust; or managerial imposition of formal methodologies against the wishes of practitioners.

However, this psychometric tradition of risk assessment has been criticised for failing to incorporate a social dimension into its approach. In brief, the position presumes a formal normative rationality in the cognitive processes of risk assessors. When errors occur it is presumed that this is due to irrational behaviour in the face of formal knowledge, lack of competence, or an inability to access and process the relevant probabilistic data. This position is easily rectified by increasing the knowledge and information base of risk assessors and removing irrational behaviours. Many public educative campaigns on risky behaviours are based upon this premise. However, the success of such campaigns in changing risky behaviours is questionable; for example smoking, drinking and driving, condom use and safe sex (Douglas 1986, Nelkin 1974, Roder 1961, Slovic et al 1985). This suggests that 'misperceptions' of risk cannot be understood simply as errors in the face of experts' prespecified norms, but rather as choices made by individuals in particular circumstances for particular reasons. These choices can be both strategic and well informed, for example amongst drug users who continue with 'risky' behaviours not from ignorance but because other choices are severely constrained. They lack the power to operate differently, or certain risky activities have become routine and habitual (Bloor 1995, Rhodes 1997). This perspective moves the unit of analysis from the individual risk assessor to that of context and social interaction (Rhodes 1997).

Risk assessment as a situated activity has already been posed, along with the possibility of differing perceptions and understandings of risk. In addition to a plurality of risk rationalities, emphasising the social foregrounds the reflexive interaction or social dynamics of the user - worker- context triad outlined by Payne (1997). This is the context within which knowledge of risk is both acquired and used.

Practice wisdom and risk

Practice use of knowledge in the field has attracted a high degree of attention (for example: Bartlett 1970, Carew 1979, Hardiker 1977, Hardiker and Webb 1979, Sheldon 1978, Sheppard1995, Stevenson 1970). More recently attention has turned to how theoretical knowledge is applied in social work (Payne 1997) and whether the theory-practice divide is real or illusory (Sheppard1995). Hardiker for example (1977, Hardiker and Webb 1979) whilst investigating social work ideologies rather than knowledge, found that workers 'rarely carry out their ideologies in pure form in practice...' (p.147), and posed the notion of 'operational philosophy' to account for this. In effect, operational philosophies are mediated and constrained by administrative procedures, resources, systems of accountability, and a situated case by case reasoning in order to achieve strategic outcomes in court. Hardiker posed the social inquiry assessments of probation officers as situated practical accomplishments negotiated around offence, offender and social control factors. Presumably a notion of 'operational knowledges' could similarly be posed for risk assessment.

Social constructivist theorists of social work (Howe 1994, Parton 1994, 1994a) stress this social aspect of knowing, and the role of social, cultural, economic and political conditions on the production of knowledge. Influenced by post-modern thinking, knowledge is viewed as a reflection of social forces and embedded in social relations. Knowledge claims are 'deconstructed' in order to uncover these social relations, and to establish how a particular social reality is being presented. Such realities, rather than being highly relative, are shared through social processes and 'typifications'. Social activities are routinised and habitual, as are our perceptions and assumptions of them. Activities become institutionalised and acquire a facticity beyond our perception of them. Language enables these institutionalised activities to become shared and legitimised, and perceived as a reified social structure beyond the activities of individual social actors (Berger and Luckmann 1967).

Such a view relocates attention away from the outcomes of knowledge to the process of its construction and use. Sheppard (1995) has argued that if process issues are considered then the divide between theoretical knowledge and 'practice wisdom' is less pronounced. He argues that the 'linking factor' between the theoretical knowledge products of social science and the practice wisdom of the field is 'the common methodology for understanding and reflecting upon situations..' (p.269). He poses the 'heuristic device' of analytic induction as this common methodology, derived from qualitative research into social interaction (Garfinkel 1967). The privileged position of positivism's expert researcher is rejected because '...as human beings social researchers are necessarily part of the human world they study....and are captured by their common human status.' (p.270). Sheppard argues that as such, social researchers must rely upon their 'common sense' knowledge of the world, and that the methodologies employed are '...merely refinements of those used in everyday life.' (p.271). He posits that the interpretative methodology of the social researcher utilising analytic induction and the worker assessing case materials has numerous similarities, not least the search for meaning in data:

> Practice wisdom...is optimally developed through a retroductive process of hypothesis testing and reflection, involving an approach to evidence which is sceptical, and a principle of adopting hypotheses which are least likely to be wrong (Sheppard1995, p.282. Reproduced with the permission of Oxford University Press and the British Association of Social Workers).

For Sheppard the issue is not the credibility of practice wisdom per se, but the extent to which practice routinely adopts these principles. Practitioners can be guilty of 'jumping to conclusions', failing to test, ignoring evidence, and mis-calculating the probability of an hypothesis being correct. This is compounded by much practice wisdom which is highly personalised and undisseminated to the practice community, and practice knowledge which is developed and applied unsystematically. For Sheppard this can undermine precision and the 'accurate identification of relevant variables which may be subsequently built upon.' (p. 283).

This suggests that practice knowledge does not necessarily have to lack rigour, testability or validity, and that it does have the potential to negotiate complex and varying assessment situations. However, it must demonstrate key components such as: critical awareness, routine scepticism, ability to check and validate hypotheses, and avoidance of idiosyncratic practice. As Sheppard expresses it: '..critical awareness distinguishes mere experience from its intelligent use.' (p.285).

In the area of offender risk assessment the enhancement of practice wisdom has received rather less attention than the development of technical assessment instruments although it is recognised in most quarters that professional judgement cannot be entirely replaced (Kahneman et al 1982, Kahneman and Tversky 1984, PC 63/96, Tversky and Kahneman 1973). Carson (1996) has suggested that neglect of practitioner decision making processes is managerially inexcusable, and that it is exactly the credibility and validity of these processes which come under scrutiny 'when things go wrong'. The scrutiny of 'hindsight bias', especially in situations of litigation (but not exclusively so), is essentially concerned with the demonstrable rigour, credibility and grounding of professional decisions. Adherence to the 'right' procedures will not necessarily be a saving grace. The Challenger Shuttle disaster demonstrated that the 'right' procedures do not necessarily lead to the right decisions (Starbuck and Milliken 1988).   In these circumstances attention to the current state of practice wisdom on offender risk is crucial.

2. What is Risk?

Risk of nuclear discharge, risk of falling on icy paths, risk of motoring accidents, risk of serious illness, risk of falling the victim of crime. The range of possible future events we label as risky is wide-ranging and far from uniform. The word 'risk' has begun to encompass numerous events and behaviours whose outcomes we perceive as unpredictable and often as unwanted. In our daily life we may ponder the likelihood of winning the lottery and the likelihood of becoming the victim of violent crime. Despite the low odds (estimated at 14 million to one) we may regularly buy a lottery ticket and perceive this as a risk worth taking. Alternatively we may over-estimate the likelihood of becoming a victim of violent crime (Mayhew and Aye Naung 1992) and take unnecessary steps (like investment in high security measures) to reduce the odds. At one extreme we are prepared to be risk-takers despite the odds, and at the other risk-avoiders in the face of low probability.

This example illustrates the complexity of risk decision making, and that risk assessment is not merely about 'calculating the odds'. The great gain of the lottery win is deemed to be worth it despite low odds of a satisfactory outcome. The odds of being a victim can be substantially less, but the perception of a harmful outcome outweighs concerns of likelihood. Impact, particularly of negative outcomes, is weighed in addition to probabilities, and potential gains against likely losses. The consequences of risks and their desirability is a key consideration in the acceptability of 'the odds'.

Risk can have both positive and negative outcomes, gains and losses, desirable and undesirable consequences, be worth running on the one hand and avoided at all costs on the other. Numerous activities and situations are deemed risky, but what risk is, is often a matter of dispute, challenge and negotiation. An older person living alone may be deemed to be at risk by other members of the family concerned for their well-being. However, the older person may view these 'risks' as the inevitable consequences of ageing and the acceptable price of independent living. In many aspects of social care the views of risk held by informal carers, service users and professionals may not necessarily coincide (Kemshall and Pritchard 1997).

The nuclear industry presents its risks as minimal, projecting risk control as a matter of waste management (Sellafield visitor centre 1997), and the benefits of its fuel source as far outweighing the hazards (British Nuclear Fuel advertisement Ch. 4, 1997). This is in sharp contrast to the concerns expressed by environmental activists. Such differences are not merely about matters of degree (the level of risk), or whether risk is present or not. They are often about whether a particular event or behaviour should be categorised as risky or not. The lottery ticket purchaser may think in terms of minimal investment rather than risk, our older person in terms of quality of life, Sellafield in terms of waste, and our potential crime victim in terms of fear. They are all instances of categorising or classifying a behaviour, incident or event. Sometimes as risky, sometimes as not.

Classifying risks

Classification of risk raises a number of interesting issues, not least which activities are classified, how and why, and how such classifications gain legitimacy over other options. As well as the site of negotiation this can also be the site of conflict and power. In social care, professionals have often dominated the risk agenda rather than service users (Davis 1996, Kemshall and Pritchard 1997), and medical risks have been almost entirely professionally defined (Heyman 1997). Increasingly this professional prerogative has been challenged by service users and the expertise of the professional has been questioned (Howlett for the Zito Trust 1997). Paradoxically this has been coupled with a growth in the risk industry and increased attempts to objectify every situation of risk in order to calculate both the probability of an event occurring and the resulting damage should it occur (Green 1997). Risk assessment is increasingly presented as an activity of both expertise and formal risk assessment methods somewhat at odds with the lay perceptions of risk held by the public.

In this scenario the professional worker with risk occupies a position in which their judgement can be challenged by lay public and experts alike (Birmingham Evening Mail 1996). Accountable to all and distrusted by many, it is the professional risk worker who daily encounters the contested and negotiated nature of risk. Part of their risk task is to interpret and balance the various and at times competing claims of service users, public, managers, funders and experts. How risk has been defined, classified and legitimated can be both revealed and re-asserted by the activities of such workers (Parton et al 1997). Risk in the professional life of workers provides an excellent site of study not only of these intriguing process issues but also of the nature of risk itself.

Risk and the colonisation of uncertainty

The concept of risk emerged in its original form in the seventeenth century and was rooted in the context of gambling, literally risking great gain or loss through the throw of the dice (Parton 1996). As Parton notes, with great gains and losses at stake, sophisticated methods for assessing risk were developed, given added impetus by the growth of the marine insurance industry in the seventeenth and eighteenth century. As mathematically based statistical methods for the assessment of risk became formalised into actuarial methods of risk prediction, risk assessment became the preserve of the expert (Brearley 1982, Kemshall 1996).

Whilst in its original form risk was neutral, involving the possibility of either gain or loss (Parton 1996, Rowe 1977), risk is now understood in terms of its potential negative outcomes. These outcomes are most often expressed in the language of loss, harm or damage. The Royal Society Study Group encapsulated this in their definition of risk as:

> ...the probability that a particular adverse event occurs during a stated period of time, or results from a particular challenge...(Report of a Royal Society Study Group, 1992, p.2).

Adversity frames risk negatively, particularly in terms of its likely impact. Whilst greater efforts are made at the calculability of risk in terms of probabilities and impact, its unpredictability raises the spectre of uncertainty. The more refined our identification processes become the more risks we have to worry about, avoid and insure ourselves against. As a result the world looks more hostile, hazardous and uncertain. As Beck expresses it:

> There occurs, so to speak, an over-production of risks, which sometimes relativise, sometimes supplement and sometimes outdo each other. One hazardous product might be defended by dramatising the risks of others (for example, the dramatisation of climatic consequences 'minimises' the risk of nuclear energy). (Beck, 1992, p.31. Reproduced with the permission of Sage Publications Limited)

Risk and uncertainty

Hierarchies of risks are produced as fears, concerns and uncertainties shift. The key underlying issue is a concern with the unpredictable and contingent nature of the future. Exposure to risks increases uncertainty and the possibility that one's future may contain dangerous hazards. Hence the desire to predict future risks and their potential negative outcomes. Prediction also carries with it the promise of risk management and control, in essence the promise of risk reduction and risk avoidance. These are the major preoccupations of Beck's risk society (1992). Risk assessment and prediction can therefore be understood as mechanisms for the colonisation of the future and for managing the uncertainty of contingency (Kemshall et al 1997, Parton 1996).

Uncertainty brings with it a number of consequences. Not least increased anxiety, scepticism of expert opinion, and diminished trust in both professionals and established institutions (Beck 1992). This was expressed in both media coverage and public response to the BSE food scare (Miller and Reilly 1996). The price of pluralism and diversity is uncertainty, and the more difficult it becomes to hold people to account. In a world of competing views and plural knowledge bases literally nothing can be taken on trust. How then do we hold 'experts' to account for their activities when no-one can guarantee a certain outcome and the criteria for evaluating one set of activities against another are often unclear? This is most easily resolved by recourse to the 'hindsight bias' of risk (Carson 1995), to investigations of what went wrong and to the allocation of blame.

The trustworthiness of decisions can no longer be taken for granted but must be thoroughly accounted for either against pre-specified quality standards or by fiscally driven performance indicators (Clarke et al 1994, Power 1994, 1994a, Rose 1993). Decisions not only have to be made but have to be accountable and legitimate, in effect open to scrutiny and seen to be 'defensible' and 'reasonable' (Carson 1996, Kemshall 1996b). Current responses to crime risks are part of this wider 'cultural dialogue' (Douglas 1992) about which sorts of actions will be legitimated and supported. In the 'risk society' the normative basis of actions is towards safety and risk avoidance (Beck 1992, Kemshall et al 1997, Parton 1996). Recent penal policy preoccupations with offender risk can be understood within this context, in particular the foregrounding of public protection and risk reduction.

The rise of offender risk

The concept of offender risk has become increasingly central to penal policy and probation practice. Hudson (1996) describes this 'risk penality' as characterised by a move away from concerns with justice and the equitable distribution of social goods, to a concern with the actuarial calculation of risks. The former approach is principally concerned with the regulation of property distribution and the 'fair distribution of the rights and responsibilities of citizenship...' (Hudson, 1996, p.152). The focus of attention is the offender who is deemed to be in need of discipline, regulation and where possible treatment. Risk penality has somewhat different concerns. Primarily to identify and manage risks, and to use risk as a basis for the efficient use of limited criminal justice resources. The focus of attention is now victims, either real or potential, including the more nebulous category of the 'public' who are deemed to require 'protection'.

Feeley and Simon (1992) have noted that this approach abandons the notion of the offender as the site of either treatment and change, or of punishment on a strictly just deserts basis. Rather it categorises the offender as a person to be managed at a level commensurate with their risk, a level most usually established by comparing their similarity to others profiled as risky. The offender is treated as a repository of risk factors which can be reliably uncovered through the correct application of risk assessment instruments. In essence, such instruments are designed to produce inventories of risk factors upon which offenders can be classified for risk management strategies of varying levels of control and intrusiveness.

Key components of an actuarial approach to justice are the foregrounding of the victim and the prioritising of public protection. These two components have made the centrality of risk to criminal justice increasingly acceptable. As Hudson expresses it: 'Who could argue against policies and practices designed to help people avoid suffering from criminal victimisation?' (Hudson, 1996, p.154). Risk penality is presented as self-evidently beneficial and unquestionably desirable. However, there are a number of issues in this approach which require further exploration.

Risk and justice

There is the possibility that the pursuit of risk reduction may eventually outweigh the pursuit of justice. In effect, the delicate balance between rights and responsibilities may be irrevocably shifted. This moral and ethical debate can be difficult to raise, particularly where it appears to diminish the hard won rights of victims and to inadvertently prioritise the rights of offenders to continue to perpetrate risks (see for example 'Megan's Law' Inside Story, 4/2/97). This tension between victim protection and offender rights has been particularly acute in respect of sex offenders where the obvious heinous nature of the crime makes the discussion of offender rights and justice appear superfluous (Hebenton and Thomas 1996). Victim protection has been prioritised above false positives in the new Crime Sentences Act (Home Office 1997a) and the proposed Crime and Disorder Bill (Home Office 1997b). Both the ethical issues and the potential for abuse or extension of risk based systems to other activities have yet to be subjected to full public scrutiny (Hebenton and Thomas 1996).

Risk and ethical issues

Moral and ethical issues can be obscured by the presentation of risk as merely a question of appropriate mechanisms of classification or instruments of assessment. The risk question is turned into one of technical ability, but such technical instruments carry ethical and moral consequences, not least in their inability to guarantee accuracy and avoid false positives (Floud and Young 1981). In addition, the purpose of such instruments is to identify segments of the population for increased surveillance and control. These offenders are viewed as 'intransigents' or career criminals (Blumstein et al 1986) not amenable to either treatment or resocialization, or so likely to present future harm to the public that preventative sentencing is justified (von Hirsch and Ashworth 1996, Wasik and Taylor 1991). Simon (1988) has argued that actuarial justice segregates and manages rather than normalises and reintegrates. There is the potential for this to result in the reinforcement of a criminal underclass (Hudson, 1996) and the exacerbation of the social and legal disadvantages which already exist (Christie 1993, Tonry 1995), as risk factors justify more extreme measures. In addition, risk assessment instruments reduce the offender to a catalogue of risk indicators contributing to the objectification and social distancing of offenders noted by Christie (1993) as a by-product of the commercialisation of crime control.

Segregation of offenders can also result in a 'fortress' response to crime control (O'Malley 1992) with those least likely to experience repeat victimisation most able to take preventative measures, and those most victimised least able to manage the crime in their midst (Cohen 1979, 1985). The Victims Charter (Home Office 1990, 1996) may promise service standards to victims in their use of the criminal justice system but it does not promise, nor can it deliver, safety.

Risk and resource prioritisation

The centrality of risk to current penal policy also raises the issue of how risk is to be adopted and used by the various criminal justice agencies and their personnel. Within the Probation Service for example, risk is now the key organising principle for both practice activities and resource allocation. Traditionally offender need and the rehabilitative ethic characterised service activity (McWilliams 1987, 1990, 1992, 1992a), with the primary objective of intervention being the reintegration of the offender into society as a well functioning citizen (Kemshall et al 1997). The increasingly managed approach to criminal justice (Raine and Wilson 1993) has contributed to the centrality of risk as the organising principle for probation work. Fiscal constraint, value for money and cost-benefit analyses have exacerbated the twin-track approach to sentencing noted by Bottoms in 1977 in which there is an increasing distinction between:'...on the one hand, the so called 'really serious offender' for whom very tough measures are typically advocated; and on the other hand, the 'ordinary offender' for whom ...we can afford to take a more lenient line.' (Bottoms, 1977, p.88). This twin-track approach requires increasingly more accurate and consistent measures to identify risky offenders, changing the language of need and rehabilitation to that of risk and management.

Risk is becoming the key organising principle for the delivery of services within criminal justice, and this is reflected in other agencies of social care (Kemshall et al 1997, Parton 1996). Policies and practices within the personal social services are increasingly concerned with the identification, regulation and prevention of risk (Feaviour et al 1995). Risk is the mechanism through which agency priorities are identified, clients managed, and the raison d'être of social care agencies is expressed. Risk in these varying contexts and across these varying client groups is the central focus of professional activities (Kemshall and Pritchard 1997, Kemshall et al 1997), leaving both practitioners and managers literally 'running the risk' (Kemshall and Pritchard 1996) as they struggle to interpret and implement the new rationality of risk, often in the absence of clearly articulated criteria and without appropriate methods for the calculation of both risk probabilities and impact (Brearley, 1979, 1982).

Risk distribution and societal concerns

Why is risk currently fundamental to the organisation and provision of services in social care and justice?   Beck (1992) amongst other commentators (such as Giddens 1990, 1991; Beck, Giddens and Lash, 1994) has argued that we are moving from a society concerned with the distribution of social goods to the distribution of risks. Such risks are now global, often involuntary and can carry high impact (for example nuclear risks or toxic waste). Beck argues that access to and control over goods is now of less importance than inequitable and undesirable exposure to risks, especially those caused by others. Policy at all levels is concerned with the identification, limitation and control of risk impingement. Criminal justice has already become an important arena for the development of strategies to control and minimise the inequitable and undesirable distribution of crime risks. This is expressed through the development of penal policy strategies for the proactive identification of the posers of risks, and for their effective regulation and control. Offenders are classified solely as the presenters of undesirable risks and policy is increasingly framed for the benefit of those 'at risk', with an acceptance that rights can be diminished if outweighed by potential risks (e.g. the preventative sentencing allowed for by section 2 (2) (b) of the CJA 1991).

Sparks (1992) has also noted that some risks gain greater public and social importance than others and thereby receive greater attention. Crime risks are '...more publicly salient than...the risks of domestic accidents: and some crimes are more salient than others' (p.12). He also notes that this saliency of certain risks may be at odds with the probability of their likely occurrence. However, this does not necessarily make such risks and their attendant fears irrational. Whilst the estimation of such crimes might be excessive and 'out of step' with the actual probability of their occurrence this does not necessarily reduce the fear of crime or perceptions of its likelihood.

Douglas (1992) argues that the importance given to certain 'dangers' should not be dismissed if this importance appears to be at odds with expert opinion. Rather it is important to establish the particular societal or cultural functions which those risk concerns are fulfilling. As Douglas (1992) expresses it: '...dangers (real dangers) are being used to give automatic, self-validating legitimacy to established law and order' (p.29). Douglas also notes that risk is used to create opponents from whose harm we seek protection: 'Risk is unequivocally used to mean danger from future damage, caused by the opponents'. (p.30). In the area of crime risks the 'opponents' are the 'intransigient criminals' (Blumstein et al 1986) or 'dangerous' criminals who present the risk of serious harm to others. In effect, Douglas (1992) argues that risk is not a neutral term but serves a particular purpose in the society within which it is deployed.

Garland (1990) has argued that punishment fulfils a cultural role as well as those of power and order, and that penal practices can carry particular meanings not least in the depiction of social authority:

> In the acts and institutions of punishment, the state - or ruling elite of whatever kind - self consciously constructs its own public image and, in part, its own reality. The forms which punishments take, the symbols through which they claim legitimacy, the discourses in which they represent their meaning, the organisational forms and resources which they employ, all tend to depict a particular style of authority... (Garland 1990, p.266. Reproduced with the permission of Oxford University Press).

In an examination of the penal practices of the twentieth century Garland notes a depiction of punishment as one of 'normalisation' and 'rehabilitation' representing an authoritative style of state 'welfarism'. However, Christie (1993) in his analysis of the 'commercialisation of crime control' depicts a less benevolent penalty in which the 'rehabilitative ethos' (McWilliams 1992a), with its focus on 'social inadequacy' (Sumner 1994), is rapidly being replaced with an over-riding concern to identify and manage risk (Feeley and Simon 1992, 1994). In this scenario the state is no longer 'welfarist' but concerned with overt social regulation, placing an emphasis upon freedom from risks rather than upon social integration.

The pursuit of certainty: The search for risk prediction

The increased societal and penal preoccupation with risk identification and avoidance has led to a proliferation of risk prediction tools and material on risk management (Royal Society 1992). In the area of offender risk, the accurate identification and prediction of risk has begun to seriously tax the Home Office Probation Unit and Her Majesty's Inspectorate of Probation (HMIP 1995, Home Office 1997). Interestingly, the Home Office statement on the tools available for offender risk assessment in the Risk Management pack (Home Office 1997) does not promote one method but draws attention to a range of models and proposes further evaluation. In effect, drawing attention to the difficulty of having certainty in the uncertain world of risk. This also highlights the difficulty in selecting a method which can guarantee the high levels of predictive accuracy sought by policy makers, and in developing a method which can encompass the range of risks likely.

Whilst such official documents seem to 'hedge their bets' over predictive tools, they do provide official definitions of offender risk. Within criminal justice a risk assessment is now defined as a:

> ...statement about how likely a person is to harm whom, in what circumstances...A risk assessment in this context is distinct from an assessment of the risk of re-offending though there are links between the two (Her Majesty's Inspectorate of Probation 1997 pt 4. p.11 in Home Office Risk Management pack 1997. Crown copyright is reproduced with the permission of the Controller of Her Majesty's Stationery Office).

However, the introductory document to the Home Office Risk Management pack (Home Office 1997) reviews risk assessment methods predominantly developed for the prediction of the risk of re-offending, and acknowledges that such tools: '...will not be enough in themselves to enable an accurate assessment of the danger that a person poses.' (pt.1, p.3. Crown copyright is reproduced with the permission of Her Majesty's Stationery Office).

Difficulties of definition

In practice, official responses to offender risk experience problems in distinguishing adequately between the risk of re-offending and the risk of harm (or dangerousness); and indeed other risks which present to practitioners such as: risk of parole violation, risk of prison absconding, risk to staff, and risk of self-harm. Risks may also vary from offender to offender. In addition, there is the expectation that individual offenders and their propensity to commit harmful acts on others will be identified and controlled prior to their commission (Feeley and Simon 1992, 1994, Flynn 1978, Hebenton and Thomas 1996, Kemshall 1995, Prins 1995). However, there is little practical guidance forthcoming on how this can be done other than to advise services that they will: '... need to produce in tandem a policy and practice framework for identifying and handling dangerous offenders.' (Home Office 1997, pt. 1, p.3).

These examples from official documents contained within the same Risk Management pack, and ostensibly emanating from the same source, illustrate the problems of both defining and classifying offender risk as a straight forward and self-evident phenomenon. The process by which certain activities perpetrated by offenders are classified as risky is a complex one, involving the definition and prioritising of certain risks over others, policy priorities, resource decisions, interpretation by local managers and frontline assessors, and finally the types of classificatory and assessment tools which can be developed to facilitate policy intentions. This is not to suggest that offenders do not commit acts which harm others 'in reality', rather it is to suggest that some activities are selected as more harmful than others and '...that there is nothing inevitable about this classification' (Green 1997, p.6).

The recent Protection from Harassment Act 1997 for example, illustrates how an activity can be re-classified as both more serious and more harmful (Lawson-Cruttendsen and Addison 1997), and hence its perpetrators as more risky than was traditionally the case.

Risk assessment instruments

Penal policy expectations as set out in 'Crime, Justice and Protecting the Public' (Home Office 1990a), and 'Protecting the Public - The Government's Strategy on Crime in England and Wales' (Home Office 1996b), plus legislation such as the Criminal Justice Act 1991, have all given impetus to the development and refinement of risk assessment instruments, particularly of recidivism. These instruments have their roots in the statistically based methodology of Burgess's parole predictor (1928, 1929, 1936).

Burgess' methodology still forms the core of actuarial parole prediction today. From a study of a large number of parole cases certain factors which statistically relate to the violation or success of parole are selected. Burgess selected twenty-two factors of which the following have been the most replicated in subsequent studies (Ohlin and Duncan 1949; Mannheim and Wilkins 1955; Gottfredson and Gottfredson 1993):

• Nature of the offence.

• Nature and length of sentence.

- Age at conviction.

- Number of previous convictions.

- Personality type.

- Social factors such as accommodation, marital status, social background.

Cases are then re-examined to determine which of the above factors relate to success or failure on parole, and then the generation of sum probabilities for success or failure in each case studied. This technique produces an 'experience table' of expected violation rates, and this is applied to both those cases with a low expectancy of violation and to those with a high expectancy of violation (Burgess 1936, p.228-229). In this way predictors for success or failure on parole can be retrospectively applied and validated in terms of statistical probabilities. This technique is still applied today with some adaptation of the indicators (Copas et al 1996).

This actuarial or statistical probability approach to parole risks has been extended to the risk of reconviction generally (Copas et al 1994). The pursuit of recidivism prediction has dominated much criminological research, policy and practice in recent years (for example: Copas et al 1994, Farrington and Tarling 1985, Humphrey et al 1992, Lloyd et al 1994, Wilkinson 1994). Such studies have attempted to develop and evaluate predictive instruments for the risk of recidivism, either to aid the decision making of staff (Copas et al 1994, Humphrey et al 1992, Wilkinson 1994), or to assist in the evaluation of sentencing practices and probation interventions post court (for example Copas' model allows for retrospective evaluation of disposals and interventions, and Wilkinson's facilitates evaluation of practitioner performance).

A primary objective of such instruments, as with the Cambridge Risk of Custody scale of the 1980s (Bale 1987, 1990), is the achievement of consistent and reliable decision making about assessments, particularly pre-court, based upon the use of actuarially based checklists. In addition to the pursuit of predictive utility, such instruments are increasingly advocated and used as a mechanism for the allocation of resources (Audit Commission 1989), and for the effective matching of supervision programmes to offenders (Andrews 1995, Andrews et al 1990, Harris 1994, McIvor 1990, Turner et al 1992).

Normative risk and risk management systems

Both the instruments developed for parole violation and risk of recidivism have a common approach to offender risk. Risk is understood as an objective phenomenon amenable to measurement and statistically calculated probabilities of its occurrence (Ansell and Wharton 1992). This view of risk is usually accompanied by a desire to produce criteria for risk which can be weighted and systematically used to produce actuarial tables which can ensure accuracy if properly applied by assessors. Risk assessment literally becomes a question of putting the correct information over to those 'doing the job' and ensuring that they apply it correctly. This type of risk assessment is most often found within the engineering industry, where risk is perceived as lack of safety. Ensuring safety, that is reducing risk, is viewed as a matter of correct functioning against pre-specified criteria. Performance is rigorously monitored to ensure that deviations from specified criteria do not take place or are quickly corrected. Risk assessment and risk management are viewed as matters of technical functioning with risk control achieved through the correct application of technical expertise and prescriptive decision making.

Homeostatic risk management

This approach to risk has been characterised as 'homeostatic' (Hood et al 1992) and is dependent upon an understanding of risk as a quantifiable phenomenon reducible to step-by-step decision rules, and poses risk as entirely a matter of probability calculation. Errors are viewed as the result of the mis-calculations or 'human error' of staff, prone as they are to subjective and irrational decision making (Carroll and Payne 1976, Fischoff et al 1978, Slovic 1987, Slovic et al 1985). Agencies specify goals and desired outcomes in advance, and translate such goal outcomes into rules and prescriptions for decision making which should be routinely applied by all staff. This view is usually evidenced by an investigative and correctionalist stance to risk assessment which seeks to establish 'what went wrong', and to implement policies and management systems which will in effect regulate the activities of frontline workers away from risky mistakes (for example the Beckford Report and its aftermath in child protection London Borough of Brent 1985).

Whilst the homeostatic and corrective approach to risk has predominance in engineering risks, particularly in the nuclear industry, it has its limits. It is highly dependent upon an agreed view of the nature and likelihood of the risk in question (for example the risk of radioactive discharge in the nuclear industry), and agreed goals and objectives for its regulation (the prevention of discharges for example). Transferability to contexts where the nature and likelihood of risk is uncertain, and goals and objectives contested can be problematic (Kemshall et al 1997, Parton 1996). Risk decisions within these contexts are not merely matters of technical expertise. Rather risk is viewed as situationally specific, highly variable and subject to a number of 'it depends' (Adams 1995). In these contexts, risk assessment is more often a matter of weighing up differing variables and evaluating the impact and acceptability of competing risks. Risk management can involve a consideration of the range of possible outcomes and their relative desirability. Risk is viewed as a more contested and conditional phenomenon, rooted in a complex inter-play of individual subjective views, cultural belief and the specific context within which it is operationalised (Adams 1995, Beck 1992, Douglas 1986, 1992, Douglas and Wildavsky 1983).

Collibrationist risk management

In these contexts, a 'collaborationist' approach to risk has been advocated as more likely to have greater efficacy (Hood et al 1992). The approach operates in a climate of greater uncertainty within which all risks cannot necessarily be anticipated or accurately calculated. Risks can arise which are not necessarily breaches of performance standards but which arise because circumstances, conditions or contexts have changed.

This approach views risk as being not only a more dynamic phenomenon, but also as multi-dimensional, in that it takes many forms (Adams 1995). Most situations comprise competing risks with varying cost-benefit outcomes. A useful example is provided by the debate over the compulsory wearing of seat belts (Adams 1995). In this debate, decisions on risk were not concerned with threats to safety and corrective action per se, but were also concerned with weighing and evaluating competing risks such as risks versus rights where risk reduction could only be achieved by increased control and restriction. The risk of infringing rights was viewed as less problematic than diminishing the risks of death and injury in road accidents (Adams 1995). The presumption that seat belts would reduce risk and enhance safety was overwhelming and the risk decision was taken within this frame. Such trade-offs are not uncommon in dealing with risk.

Whilst they can and should be informed by sound information, they are also a matter of judgement, and risk assessors have to decide which is the most desirable outcome. This is often a question about which risks are acceptable (Douglas 1986), which can be tolerated, and which risks are worth running and which are not. Such decisions are as much matters of value and belief as they are matters of calculation (Douglas 1986, 1992, Douglas and Wildavsky 1983).

Varying risks

In effect, one person's risk is another person's thrill, with perception of and responses to risk varying across contexts and situations (Thompson 1980). This is not to suggest that risk is entirely a relative concept rooted in the eyes of the beholder, but rather that perception, definitions and categorisations of risk are embedded in their contexts of use and that they can vary. Within Probation this is most often demonstrated by differences with external agencies such as sentencers over the seriousness of offending and the likelihood of its recurrence (Cavadino and Wiles 1994), with prisons and parole boards over home leave and early release, and with local residents over the siting of hostels. Internally there are differences over 'Schedule One' registration, registration of Potentially Dangerous Offenders (Shaw 1996), and definitions and use of the term risk (ACOP 1994). However expressed they are all arguments about the definition, perception and tolerance of risk.

These approaches to risk demonstrate the important difference between the normative definition of risk provided by experts, penal policy makers, and managers of services; and the way in which risk is defined and used 'on the ground' by frontline risk assessors.

Normative risk and the new penology

Normative definitions of risk are usually the definitions of service providers or the research experts whom they employ. Studies on risk and the risk assessment instruments which they subsequently produce are usually informed by a desire to rationalise or improve existing services, and as such adopt definitions of risk which reflect the concerns of policy makers and service managers. The Offender Group Reconviction Score (OGRS, Copas et al 1994) for example has a dual function: firstly as a predictor to guide the pre-sentence report assessments of staff and to facilitate both greater consistency and more effective targetting of penal resources; and secondly to facilitate monitoring of targetting strategies and evaluation of probation interventions (Bewley 1996). This reflects current Home Office concerns with comparing and evaluating community and custodial sentences upon reconviction rates and how these break down in terms of 'league tables' across services (Home Office Special Conferences 1995, Sutton and Davies 1996). In effect, decisions are made about what is desirable practice and policy on risk, and technologies of risk assessment and risk management are developed in order to facilitate its effective delivery.

Normative risk and predictive instruments

The pursuit of offender risk prediction through the development of various predictive instruments illustrates this normative framing of risk current in present penal policy. The development of such instruments frames the issue of risk prediction as an issue of accurate definition and measurement, concerned with the discoverability of risk as an empirical fact and with the most effective and efficient ways of identifying it. Risk prediction is expressed as a problem of clarification, that is of accurate definition and competent measurement systems which if applied correctly by assessors prediction difficulties will be eradicated. This view is exemplified by much of the work on actuarial risk predictors such as that developed by Copas on the risk of recidivism or the risk of parole violations (Copas et al 1994, Copas et al 1996). In this work Copas et al utilise the 'experience table' methodology of Burgess (1928, 1929, 1936) in order to formalise and validate statistical calculations of the risk of reconviction and the risk of parole violations. Risk is translated into a quantifiable form by reducing it to a few key characteristics of history and demography which are weighted to produce a statistical calculation of a future eventuality. The diagnosis of risk is translated into the sum probability of the weightings. However, this approach cannot predict the possible seriousness of the offence, its nature or extent. In effect OGRS calculates the chances of reconviction for offenders with similar characteristics, the probability score is a measure of expected similarity to an existing profile. OGRS does not measure actual or potential reoffending.

The problem with probability

This difficulty with OGRS well illustrates the problems with the heuristic reasoning of probability in risk assessment. Heyman (1997) has argued that probability reasoning reduces the uncertainty of risk by: '...attributing aggregate properties of a category to individuals within that category..' (p.8). This systematic flaw of probability reasoning is more commonly known as the 'statistical fallacy' (Dingwall 1989). Whilst it has some predictive utility, it does not measure 'real' events but only similarities of profile to the aggregated knowledge of past events. Classificatory profiles can change as what is known changes over time, thus classifications of risk could change as aggregates do. Hence insurance companies revise their premiums over time. In addition, aggregates and their subsequent classificatory systems have to be selected. Within offender risk, the selection has usually been to establish aggregated knowledge about easily accessible male prisoners, for example the generation of parole predictors.

When used as the basis for 'screening instruments' statistical methods can generate severe problems, not least when the event or behaviour to be screened is rare within the population as a whole (for example violence or child abuse). To be valid such an instrument must be able to detect instances of the behaviour or event of concern, (thus avoiding 'false negatives'), but also operate with a minimum of 'false positives'. However, as Dingwall (1989) notes, the pursuit of minimum 'false negatives' is often at the cost of increasing to unacceptable levels the number of 'false positives'. The prediction of ever more cases is at the cost of considerable net-widening. The acceptable balance between false negatives and false positives is often a matter of social and political acceptability rather than a matter of methodology. In the case of criminal justice, this is most often expressed as a balance between the preservation of offender rights and the protection of the public.

In addition, offenders can be classified in a number of ways. As posing a risk of re-offending, posing a risk of harm, posing a risk of self-harm, posing a risk of harm to children, a risk of parole violation, a risk to staff. It is possible for the same offender to experience differing probabilities and therefore differing risk levels depending upon the classification used. The selection and prioritising of risk classification is often a matter of policy choice rather than probabilistic utility. In Home Office documents on risk assessment methods, risk of self-harm for example is only mentioned in order to be sidelined:

...Other types of risk assessment include the likelihood of the person harming themselves, but this is not addressed in this pack' (Home Office Risk Management Pack, 1997, pt. 4, p.11. Crown copyright is reproduced with the permission of the Controller of Her Majesty's Stationery Office).

Risk, probability and underpinning assumptions

Probability approaches to risk assessment are also characterised by the following assumptions:

- Firstly, that risk is an unambiguous and objective phenomenon, free from value or theoretical orientations.

- Secondly, that risk can be objectively and consistently identified through the application of the correct measurement systems.

- Thirdly that risk is a characteristic of an individual offender or offender group.

Without these assumptions probabilistic risk assessment could not be presumed to work.

However, risk is not a neutral concept, it has to be recognised and responded to by policy makers, service managers and frontline assessors. In this sense, like need before it, risk is a product:

...of the organisational milieu within which the interaction between professionals and clients or potential clients takes place (G. Smith, 1980, p.66).

At its simplest this can literally mean that an offender is not risky until officially designated as such by individual workers or agency procedures. The particular organisation of the agency and the definitions of risk which it has chosen to utilise effectively define the categories of risk which a worker can attribute to offenders. Shaw (1991, 1996) in a study of probation service policy and practice on risk and dangerousness found that one third had no specific policy, and that where policies did exist there were 'considerable differences in the various statements' (Shaw 1996, p.157).

For instance, some policies referred only to the protection of staff, or only to people released from prison, or only to the mentally disordered. Many policies ignored individuals subject only to probation orders, whatever their past history might have been, and considered only those on parole, life licence or released from special hospitals (Shaw 1996, p.157).

Registration of dangerous offenders was similarly variable, and discussions with practitioners also revealed that Home Office Probation Circulars on Risk and Dangerousness were seen as concerned with:

...the protection of government departments and the avoidance of embarrassment to ministers when disasters occur, as well as engendering a feeling in the public that supervision in the community is punishment rather than treatment (Shaw 1996, p.161).

The characteristics of offender risk are not merely endemic to individuals, but are also the products of risk policies and agency risk procedures. For example, a brief resume of the policies and procedures current in probation services demonstrates varying definitions and categories of risk, from the equating of risk primarily with offence seriousness (South East London Probation 1996), to attempts to identify risk through a combination of offence patterns and behavioural traits (Hampshire Probation 1995). In addition, policies and procedures have to be understood and interpreted by staff. The discrepancy between the desired outcomes of such policies and the actual practices of staff reveals the complex relationship between the subjective views of frontline workers and the expressed goals of the organisation. In effect, these subjective views mediate the normative framing of risk presented by experts, policy makers and service managers and should therefore be taken seriously. Smith and Harris (1972), in discussing need have suggested that we must:

...assign a significant role to the organisational members' own subjective ideas about the phenomena in question (G. Smith and Harris, 1972, p.27).

In the pursuit of risk classification and prediction a similar significance should be given to the views of assessors. This can assist in understanding the resistance of assessors to the implementation of risk assessment and risk management instruments, without dismissing them as either irrationalities or examples of 'poor' practice requiring correction. Frontline risk assessors may be constructing and using the concept of risk in line with values, beliefs and expectations which they consider to be both appropriate and legitimate. What they are and how assessors use them in their day to day practice is crucial to understanding how risk assessment instruments are received and used by staff when they are introduced into agencies.

The problem with measurement

The development of a number of risk assessment instruments has been concerned with the measurement of risk, and hence its more accurate prediction. Risk is defined as an attribute of individual offenders, and it is presumed that risk can be measured by applying the correct measurement to those offenders. This is the substance of actuarial risk assessment instruments which seek to measure the presence or absence of pre-specified risk attributes of offenders upon which an overall predictive score is based (for example Copas et al 1994, 1996). However, these instruments have been criticised for their static approach to risk (Fletcher 1995, Sutton and Davies 1996), and that they fail to adequately deal with changes in risk status over time or the process of becoming more or less risky (Kemshall 1997). The pursuit of accurate measurement can confuse what is being assessed with the instruments for its measurement, focusing increasing attention on refining the techniques of measurement at the expense of understanding the nature of risk. As Cicourel (1964) expresses it, measurement pertains to the properties of objects but not to the objects themselves. For example, it is possible to measure the length or width of something but not what it is. In order to facilitate measurement, the object, or in this case the concept, has to be translated into properties amenable to measurement.

The limits of measurement

The key issue is how are these properties arrived at? It is tempting to speculate that they are the product of the methodologies employed to measure them, and that the properties specified are limited by the measurement techniques available. The development of actuarial risk assessment instruments has been limited by a dependence upon those properties most amenable to statistical methods. This has resulted in an over-emphasis upon historical indicators such as previous convictions or demographic factors such as age and gender. Whilst these factors do have predictive utility across groups of offenders (Copas et al 1994, 1996; Farrington and Tarling 1985) they can be erroneously transferred to individual offenders and invested with a predictive utility which they do not have (Kemshall 1996). This point is well recognised by Copas et al (1994) who state that:

> It is important to remember that the predictor does not produce an individual prediction but represents the proportion of the sample who reoffended... (p. 32),

and by the Home Office Probation Circular which accompanied the distribution of the Offender Group Reconviction Score into area services (PC 63/1996). In this document OGRS was recognised as:

> ...no more than an aid to the judgement of probation officers in preparing PSRs...it cannot be a substitute for that judgement (Para. 6.7),

and that transferability of group characteristics to individuals can be problematic (para. 6.5). The statistical focus upon the static attributes of offenders also prevents OGRS from assessing: '...the likely nature or seriousness of possible further offences.' (Para. 6.6). The scale cannot distinguish between the risk of reconviction and the risk of future harm, and in this sense the scale is limited by its static and retrospective nature. Whilst risk probabilities are addressed, risk impacts are not.

The measurement techniques of actuarial risk assessment also present other difficulties, particularly in its use as an evaluative tool for probation practice. Actuarial measures of recidivism are prone to methodological difficulties, not least that they do not necessarily accurately predict the rate of recidivism (Hood and Sparks 1970, Lloyd et al 1994, Mair 1990, Vennard 1996). Mayhew and Aye Naung (1992) in the British Crime Survey state that: '...for every 100 offences committed only two result in a criminal conviction.' (p.5). Variations in detection rates, police recording processes, and cautioning practices all undermine the connection between further offending and reconviction rates upon which risk of reoffending predictors are so dependent. In addition, aggregate information does not reveal what may be significant differences between individual offenders, practitioners and teams (Vennard 1996).

Measurement of offender risk is dependent upon identifying and weighting the attributes of offenders which have a known association with reoffending. Actuarial risk measures have been dependent upon those static attributes most easily analysed by the retrospective methods and 'experience tables' of Burgess' initial technique. These attributes have been recently criticised as having a limited although useful applicability to the prediction of offender risk. In particular, Lloyd et al (1994) in reviewing risk of recidivism predictors for the Home Office stated that lists of indicators tended to obscure the fact: '...that many of the variables associated with reconviction are intercorrelated.' (p.33). In their opinion calculating the risk of reconviction requires a 'multi-variant analysis', appropriate weighting of relevant variables and a recognition that the variables used may need to change over time as circumstances do. In the insurance industry this leads to the revision of actuarial tables and the adjustment of premiums.

The lack of social or contextual variables has also been viewed as a limitation of actuarial risk prediction (Lloyd et al 1994, Association of Chief Officers of Probation 1995, National Information Probation Research Exchange 1995). This raises the important issue of exactly which attributes are to be included and why, and more importantly how they are to be measured. The inclusion of situational factors such as 'marital status, accommodation, drug/alcohol misuse, relationships' in addition to historical and demographic ones is advocated (Lloyd et al 1994). A number of techniques have been developed to incorporate these 'dynamic' indicators into risk assessment. The most notable are the 'Client Management Classification' (CMC) system in Texas (Harris 1994), and the 'Level of Service Inventory' (LSI) proposed by Andrews and Bonta (1995).

Harris' CMC utilises behavioural and situational factors in addition to the traditional actuarial predictors, and was developed in response to the earlier Wisconsin tool (National Institute of Corrections 1981) in an effort to increase its efficacy. The CMC involves:

> ...a semi-structured interview, differentiates five offender profiles, prescribes detailed supervision guidelines for each profile, and embodies a case planning procedure (Harris 1994, p.154).

The purpose of the CMC is to predict levels of risk in order to match offenders to supervision strategies, and in so doing adopts the 'risk-responsivity principle' of Andrews et al (1990, Andrews and Bonta 1994, 1995, Andrews 1995). Through in-depth interviewing the CMC aims toestablish an inventory of social variables, behavioural traits, and situational factors likely to precipitate re-offending.

The incorporation of 'dynamic' risk factors into risk assessment instruments is represented in other models, for example the Level of Service Inventory - Revised in Canada (LSI-R) (Andrews and Bonta 1994, 1995) and the Needs Assessment Scale in this country (Aubrey and Hough 1997). The LSI-R includes those 'criminogenic factors' which meta-analysis research has most closely associated with recidivism (Andrews 1995). Through structured interviewing following 54 pre-specified questions grouped under 10 issues areas assessors can make a comprehensive assessment of the risk of recidivism. The LSI-R is advocated as a mechanism for ensuring consistency of assessment, appropriate matching of resources to presenting criminogenic needs, assessment of risk in individual cases, and evaluation of probation performance upon subsequent reconviction rates.

Hough's Needs Assessment Scale has similar objectives and has been developed utilising similar techniques. The impetus for the development of such a scale came in part from a dual objective to improve the allocation of supervision resources and to evaluate the impact of such resources upon the offending behaviour of offenders. The inconsistency and potential wastefulness of resource allocation was noted by Burnett's research:

> A more systematic assessment of offending-related needs will enhance the accuracy and status of probation assessments, will foster optimum use of in-house and partnership specialists, and would facilitate integrated evaluation of the effectiveness of community supervision (Burnett 1996, p.69).

Aubrey and Hough (1997) advocate a needs assessment scale to facilitate a more systematic approach by structuring the assessment of need, the 'diagnosis of need', and 'diagnosing risk of reoffending' (p.4).

All these risk of recidivism instruments have common characteristics. They seek to increase the efficiency and effectiveness of resource allocation by structuring the assessment judgements of staff in order to more accurately classify offenders for levels and types of intervention. In addition, they seek to provide a tool for the retrospective evaluation of probation input upon reoffending rates (Aubrey and Hough 1997, p.2-3; Sutton and Davies 1996). These models also represent a widening of the 'risk attributes' to behavioural, situational and contextual factors, but despite this a number of issues still remain.

It is still necessary to break offender risk down into a number of properties which can be measured and weighed. The criminogenic needs based instruments are based upon those needs which can be easily identified by the techniques of meta-analysis. Whilst much championed as an evaluative technique (Andrews 1995, McGuire 1997), it has also received criticism similar to that levelled at probability assessment. Copas (1995) has suggested that whilst useful as a 'descriptive mode', its use in drawing inferences from the totality of the data is limited (p.12). However, it is exactly this which has generated risk predictors and 'criminogenic needs'. In addition, the complex outcome measures evaluated have been simplistically categorised for ease of comparative analysis (Copas 1995, Mair 1997), and that both the selection of studies and the statistical methods chosen are subjective (Losel 1995, McIvor 1997).

> Despite efforts to be systematic and objective, meta-analyses contain more or less subjective categorisations and decisions on the choice of methods. Although these can be tested, we are still basically confronted with the same problems of measurement that we find in primary studies (Losel 1995, p. 81).

In addition, each instrument presents differing properties: the CMC contains 45 questions relating to 4 issues areas and provides 5 offender profiles; the LSIR has 54 questions and covers 10 issues areas; and the Needs Scale has 12 questions relating to 12 issues areas . The key question is whether the risk of recidivism is more accurately measured by more exhaustive lists of properties, or whether what is actually being measured is the technical refinement of the instruments themselves? Whilst the creators of each instrument make claims for accuracy and validity (Harris 1994, p. 156 for example), meta-analysis by Gendreau, Coggin and Little (1995) of 133 scales suggests that LSI-R has the most predictive utility. An alternative view is that only those properties which the instruments have in common have any predictive value, and these instruments could be usefully streamlined.

Normative definitions and frontline perceptions

The selection of the properties and their use by frontline assessors can also be problematic. Aubrey and Hough partially acknowledge this in their discussion of need where they distinguish for example between basic needs and emotional needs (p.3). Offenders' needs are defined solely in relation to 'probation work as currently organised' and in terms of the types of problems they give rise to if left unresolved, that is: '...offenders' problems reflect needs only if their resolution *reduces the risk of re-offending...*'(p.3). This is in effect a normative definition of need and implicitly of the precursors of recidivism risk which Aubrey and Hough acknowledge may be at odds with the needs perceived by assessors:

> Some of the tensions in probation work stem directly form the application of this narrow criterion. Should a probation officer try to address an offender's poverty, for example, or poor housing, if these are unrelated to the probationer's offending or other anti-social behaviour? (1997, p.3).

In this work, the risk of recidivism is defined by reference to problems generated by unresolved needs. These needs are in turn defined and legitimated by the concerns and key objectives of the agency, in this case probation. Such needs and the risk they identify can also be constrained by the resources available to deal with them. As Aubrey and Hough express it: 'If there's no solution, there's no problem.' (p.4). Such a statement highlights the function of such instruments in both rationing and rationalising the allocation of resources.

Perceptions of criminogenic need and their associated risk levels can also vary. Assessors can both perceive and weigh needs differentially (Aubrey and Hough 1997), demonstrating the gap between the normative definitions of experts and the perceptions of assessors. Such a gap can be mirrored between agency personnel and offenders, whose perceptions and expressions of their needs, problems and risks may also differ (Bradshaw 1972, Kemshall 1984, G. Smith 1980). Aubrey and Hough (1997) experience these issues in addressing both the measurement of need and the dimensions of need. For example:

> A related issue is the extent to which needs assessment scales should try to chart the intensity of need. The difficulty of finding any objective way of differentiating between levels of high, medium and low need convinces us that the attempt should not even be made. This research indicates that the best option would be to use a simple binary classification system, in which officers have to decide whether or not a need should be addressed in the course of supervision. This ties the scoring system to decisions which actually have to be made, instead of imposing a veneer of objectivity on a judgement which is inevitably subjective (p.27).

As for the dimensions of need, they recognise that practice would be bound to gravitate towards those needs/problems which get measured, ignoring others, and that there is (as yet) no sound empirical knowledge base for the selectivity of items (p.28). What can be measured is what is prioritised. The parallels with offender risk measurement are clear. Risky behaviour is characterised primarily in terms of those attributes most easily accessed and measured.

Legitimate offender risk

Defining and categorising criminogenic need as a mechanism for assessing the risk of recidivism is prone to the same difficulties as the assessment of risk per se. Policy makers and service managers still have the problem of deciding what is risk and how it should be assessed. Subsequent chapters will address how both managers and staff have bridged the gap between policy expectations and use on the ground. Definitions of risk and the attendant tools of identification and assessment are not neutral but reflect the ascendancy of central government's interests in penal policy. This has resulted in a narrow, normative definition of risk which may not necessarily be reflected in use by either managers or frontline risk assessors.

In this context, the development of risk instruments is not an autonomous research enterprise, but should be understood as a consequence of the pre-occupations of the new penology. In the USA the development of risk assessment instruments has most often been funded by the National Institute of Corrections, and in England by the Home Office in order to resolve the practical implications of policy decisions (for example the development of the Offender Group Reconviction Score and Parole Predictors, Copas et al 1994, Copas et al 1996). Home Office policy has increasingly sought to define what offender risk is and how this should concern the work of the Probation Service (for example HMIP 1995, Home Office 1997), and through such statements has sought to legitimate a particular understanding of offender risk and the primary mechanisms for assessing it.

Risk and the economic rationality of penal policy

Garland (1997) has suggested that these statements can be located within a reconfigured field of crime control which has strategically impacted upon the character of both criminal justice and probation. Traditionally penal concerns could be located within a context of welfarism and a discourse of social engineering within which rehabilitative language and ethics had a key place. He argues that this has been supplanted by the 'economic rationality' of the new penology (Feeley and Simon 1992, 1994). This economic rationality is expressed in new modes of thinking and speaking about crime control:

> One sees manifestations of this new way of thinking in the new language of crime control and criminal justice (a language of risk, rationality, choice, the supply of criminal opportunities, market share, customers, etc.), ...The solution to crime is no longer thought to lie in social engineering and solidarity but in situational engineering and the economical management of dangers and risks (Garland 1997, p.4).

He rightly contends that this has resulted in a massive shift from rehabilitation to risk, from reformation to community risk management. Rehabilitation is subsumed to concerns of public protection and is: '...represented as an instrument of risk-management, inculcating self-controls, reducing danger, enhancing the security of the public.' (Garland 1997, p.6). If it does not work it can quickly be replaced by enforcement and control. Risk has become the central discourse of the new penology, dominating all criminal justice activities and providing a context within which definitions and classifications of offender risk gain both currency and legitimacy.

Finally, the location of offender risk within a specific discourse of penality inadvertently diminishes the role that social interaction and social context play in the production of particular risk concerns (Douglas and Wildavsky 1983, Douglas 1992, Green 1997). It is through such interactions and within particular contexts that risk is defined, understood and managed. This theme is further pursued in the next chapter through a broader consideration of the social construction of risk concerns, and by locating the current understanding of offender risk within a particular historical and policy context. Part two considers the specific social construction of risk within probation practice in detail using data from the study, and the extent to which the risk of the new penality is understood and mediated by practitioners and managers.

3. Social Theories of Risk: Implications for the Probation Service

Social theories of risk argue that definitions and assessments of risk are both negotiated and indeterminate (Adams 1995, Reddy 1996, Royal Society 1992). Assessments are intrinsically uncertain (Brearley 1982, Schon 1987, 1991), concerned as they are with the calculation of potential future events which may or may not happen and the impossibility of exhausting all eventualities and all potential sources of information. This understanding of risk as an assessment of uncertainties rather than a calculation of probabilities implies a different approach to risk decision making and its organisational management. This chapter will consider the implications of social theories of risk for risk assessment and risk management in probation.

Social theories of risk: a brief overview

Such theories predicate risk as a dynamic concept rooted in the dialectical relationship between assessors' meanings and practices; and the organisational context of their work. Such a view does not view risk as solely the product of individual cognitions and individualised decision making (Krimsky and Golding 1992, Singleton and Hoyden 1994), but rather as '...the product of an interplay between individuals, the actions of other individuals, their communities and social environments...' (Rhodes 1997, p.210). Social theories of risk attempt to understand risk decision making as an interaction of individual and social factors (Rhodes 1997), and attach importance to the meanings social actors give to the concept risk.

Situated rationality and social theories of risk

Rhodes (1997) distinguishes between two types of social theories: 'situated rationality theories', and 'social action theories'. Situated rationality theories emphasise that risk decisions occur within a context, and that as they are situation dependent differing, and at times competing, views of risk can be held. Risk decisions are not merely the product of the 'individual rationality' (Rhodes 1997) of the assessor which can be readily corrected if appearing irrational to experts, and differing rationalities can exist (Bloor 1995). Risk assessors may balance and weigh risks against other risks (Adams 1995), prioritising risks 'at odds' with expert opinion (Rhodes 1997) but in ways which make sense for them. This theoretical position proposes that risk decisions are made as informed and meaningful choices from a range of options, and that rationalities of choice can be plural, changing across situations and individuals. However, risk decisions are still conceptualised as individual choices. In this view, improving the efficacy of risk decisions in line with expert opinion would be achieved through greater understanding of why people make informed choices to behave riskily or choose the risk decisions they do. This information could be used to determine the risk priorities of risk decision makers and the perceived losses and gains to them of acting as they do. Risk-reward equations could then be altered, either by external influence such as removing potential rewards, or by assisting decision makers to re-frame such equations for themselves for example in motivational interviewing (Miller and Rollnick 1991).

Social action theories extend this conceptualisation of risk to understand risk as a product of '...social dynamics of particular relationships or situations.' (Rhodes 1997, p. 216). This view conceptualises risk as a negotiated concept situated in the interaction between social actors. In addition to viewing risk as a product of social interaction, it also views risk as context specific and bounded by group norms and values (Douglas 1986). Risk decisions are not mere individual choice (whether well informed or not), but reflect such group factors.

In considering intravenous drug use and HIV, Rhodes (1997) argues that social theories of risk help to explain why health promotion campaigns exhorting individuals to make 'healthy choices' fail. Such campaigns assume risk decisions are individual rational choices and are systematically calculated by those involved. An interactive approach recognises that choices are often negotiated and subject to severe constraints such as power and opportunity (Bloor 1995), and made (il)legitimate and (un)acceptable by social norms. In this context, calculations are either limited or ignored. In addition, the routinisation and group acceptability of risks impacts upon systematic calculations; risky behaviours and decisions become habitual and no longer subject to formal review (Bloor 1995). This may be exacerbated if over time harm has not resulted and benefits are perceived to still outweigh risks (Rhodes 1997). Even in the face of increasing statistical risk, perceptions of increased safety and acceptability can be held. This is not necessarily the result of individual irrationality, but rather is a condition of choice in specific social situations.

Risk and rationality

Integral to social theories of risk is the notion that scientific rationality can no longer guarantee certainty. Whilst the rationality of Western science has held sway as a dominant discourse for understanding and engaging with the world, this is now in dispute (Beck 1992, Green 1997). Scientific rationality can be characterised by its concerns with classification, order, measurement and calculability (Foucault 1977, Green 1997, Weber 1949).

However, the rational consensus established by Western science has been undermined by the 'Risk Society' (Beck 1992) in which the products of science are seen as not necessarily beneficial but as increasingly threatening and hazardous. Science is no longer viewed as the mender of ills but as their source, for example toxic waste, food contamination and nuclear discharge. The role of scientific rationality in assessing and managing risk is questionable given its increasing role in producing risks.

Risk and trust

Coupled with this is a growing distrust of 'the expert'. In a situation in which competing expert views are expressed how is the public to choose which view is correct? Freudenberg (1993) has argued that this is more often a question of trust than the accuracy of the information provided. In situations of low trust, for example in large corporations or government bodies, individuals will perceive risks as higher and as less acceptable. Diminished trust is a result of a perceived breach in social obligations and the fallibility of those charged with risk management (Freudenberg 1993). Analysis of these perceptions and the role of trust may be more empirically rewarding in understanding calculations of risk than the study of individual risk perceptions (Economic and Social Science Research Council 1993).

Trust also raises the central issue of credibility. Wynne (1982) in a detailed analysis of the Windscale Nuclear Inquiry examined how some definitions and understandings of risk gain credibility whilst some do not, and how this in effect functions to give some participants in the debate more power and credibility than others. At Windscale those without the 'proper talk' literally did not gain access to the debate. In the nuclear industry credibility stemmed from a conceptualisation of risk based in scientific rationality, calculations of cost-benefit, and an almost unassailable view that nuclear power presented high benefits for tolerably low risks in an era of scarce resources. In the post-Chernobyl era this credibility has been seriously undermined, trust has diminished and the nuclear industry is perceived as highly fallible if left to its own devices (Beck 1992, p.177-178).

Beyond individual irrationalities to the social organisation of risk

The work of Mary Douglas (1972, 1973, 1986, 1992) has refocused attention away from individual risk perception to how societal structures and organisational forms influence the perceptions of individuals and the saliency of certain risks over others. Douglas advocated a typology for the cultural location of risk perceptions (1973) using the concepts of 'grid' and 'group'. 'Grid' refers to the coherence and strength of the cultural system to which the individual belongs and from which classification and meaning are derived. 'Group' refers to the degree of control an individual can exercise over social action within the system. In essence, attitudes to risk are governed (in part) by the subtle interaction of group cohesion and individual power.

Douglas' 'Grid-Group' typology

Douglas' typology has been applied to studies of risk decision making in particular settings with varying degrees of success (Bellaby 1987, 1990 on pottery workers, Bellaby 1990a on road accidents, Douglas on the labour market 1992a, Douglas and Calvez 1990 on AIDS, Rayner 1986 on radiation hazards). Douglas' approach has been criticised for analysing risk as an abstract cultural concept, and for a cultural determinism in which culture is reified and posed as an over-arching explanatory concept of all risk perceptions (Hammond 1993). The cultural relativism implicit in Douglas' position is also problematic to some commentators (Gross and Rayner 1985). If rationality is undermined and risks are culturally bound, then how can different positions on risk be reconciled? However, Douglas' position is not quite so naive. For Douglas discussions of risk are intrinsically bound up with discussions of blame and accountability. Risk is not only used to hold persons accountable, it is also a mechanism for the allocation of blame, diminishment of credibility and the with-holding of trust. Child protection risks are a case in point (Parton et al 1997) in which blame and trust are as a much at issue as risk itself. This was exemplified by media and public responses to the activities of social workers in Cleveland (Butler Schloss 1988). Blame and trust render 'problems of risk perception [as] essentially political' characterising 'public debates about risk [as] debates about politics.' (Douglas 1992, p.79). Essentially the views expressed about risk are indicative of the values and beliefs about social order, societal hierarchies of authority and control, and of what should constitute a just society held by risk assessors. Risk debates are at heart debates about what should constitute the nature of contemporary society. Fundamentally such debates are concerned with power and how particular forms of authority (and therefore risks) gain legitimacy and predominance.

Douglas has importantly added the dimensions of group norms and power in understanding both social interaction and individual social action on risk, in addition to politicising the risk debate. Essentially all positions on risk are biased and political, deployed to reinforce or resist patterns of authority; and to re-assert boundaries against threats, thereby reinforcing power relations (Douglas 1992, chapters 1-4). This study is no exception in which comments on risk are also implicitly comments on mechanisms for maintaining social order, and in which the views of the research participants not only reveal their group norms but also their level of perceived power and trust in other views of risk.

Bellaby (1990, 1990a) in his work on risks in a pottery factory and on road accident risks noted that power was an important dynamic, and extended Douglas' rather static grid/group conceptualisation through its use. He initially characterised the factory as complacent over the health and safety risks facing workers, within an organisational form of hierarchical order and authority based upon strong group (that is high control over the social system), and strong grid (that is high coherence of group norms) existing within the managerial group. However, Bellaby noted that within this setting, a relatively senior safety officer who had previously held a union post, championed health and safety risks in an effort to influence his senior colleagues. He collected data on these risks which were disseminated to both workforce and managers, and an adversarial stance from the union was 'headed off' by management instituting a joint consultative group.

Bellaby concludes that:

> ...top management's attempt to neutralise the perceived threat from the union contributed to a process by which the firm was itself shifting from institutionalised complacency to risk aversion (Bellaby 1990a, p.475).

An entrepreneurial take over by an outsider of this family firm further altered the organisational culture to one of risk taking, and demonstrated how 'internal conflict and managerial succession' (Bellaby 1990a, p.476) could be prime movers in organisational change and subsequently in attitudes to risk. Importantly individuals may change their cultural view, classically in this example by changing roles, or by changes in one's life course (for example young risk taking drivers eventually become older risk averse ones, Bellaby 1990a). Recognising that power relations can change over time, and that individuals can change their cultural allegiances either by occupying different role positions or through life changes is an important added dimension to Douglas' grid/group analysis.

Rayner (1986) in analysing the management of radiation hazards in hospitals noted that in complex social organisations a person's position in the social system could impact upon their risk. Experiences within such social milieux influence a person's 'acceptability of certain distributions of liabilities and benefits' and indeed:

> ...that their recognition of a hazard, and their assessment of its probability and seriousness, will be strongly influenced by organizational factors (Rayner 1986, p.574. Reproduced with the permission of Sage Publications).

Risk, diversity and 'noise'

Rayner's study found diverse viewpoints on risk within the single institution of the hospital related to the various occupational categories existing in the setting. Different views of risk were held by participants at differing points of the institution, and differing levels of trust and confidence in the institution's risk management processes were expressed by each occupational group. Rayner identified plural rationalities within one institution based upon organisational experience, but more importantly that such differences could co-exist and need not necessarily attract 'noise'. In Rayner's study a key mechanism for avoiding noise was worker's confidence in the risk management process of the institution. This was usually achieved by enhancing the trust and participation of the workforce in the process and in their greater integration into the institution per se. Central to this is involvement in the due process of decision making, and that such decision making is seen as credible, open and fair. In the absence of such due process, Rayner contended that trust in the competency of others to manage risk is undermined and individuals prefer to resort to their own knowledge and competency to control risk. The lack of due process is also more likely to lead differing positions into adversarial conflict and of course increased 'noise'.

The immediate implications of such approaches to risk are that plural rationalities can exist, and that the views of risk assessors may be seriously at odds with the knowledge base of experts, policy makers and managers resulting in high levels of 'noise'. Within the Probation Service a significant source of difference and 'noise' is the existence of differing group norms and varying levels of individual and group power to control social action in the workplace. This may be expressed as differences between grades, as team solidarities against external threats, conflicts between different settings (e.g. hostels and the field), practitioner and management disputes over service objectives, and service responses to external directives. Discussions of risk quickly become vehicles for debates about norms and values.

Ham and Hill (1993) in a study of the policy implementation process in the welfare state noted that even those members of staff ready to comply with new policies filtered policy and procedures through their own beliefs and value judgements. Where consensus is lacking and there are no mechanisms for articulating and resolving difference, there may be a considerable gap between the stated expectations of managers and the practices of front-line workers. This is most often expressed in terms of 'street level bureaucracy' (Lipsky 1980) where workers administer procedures as they see fit, or in terms of 'occupational survival' (Satyamurti 1981) where workers function in order to protect their interests or to limit negative impacts such as stress. For example, Maupin (1993) found that the provision of juvenile after-care was driven by street level bureaucracy and that the managerially imposed classification system did not control the decision making of parole officers.

Without consensus, risks will be interpreted and dealt with variously against competing desirable outcomes. As Douglas and Wildavsky express it:

If the selection of risk is a matter of social organisation, the management of risk is an organisational problem (Douglas and Wildavsky 1983, p. 198).

Within this theoretical perspective risk practice cannot be understood as the product of a prescribed set of activities governed solely by the rules and norms of agency procedures. Rather practice is defined as a negotiated activity between workers, offenders, managers and agency context. This understanding of risk as a social construct can help to explain how differing views of offender risk can be held within the agency, and why risk assessors interpret and apply risk assessment instruments differentially (Glaser 1973), or choose to act contrary to risk information. Such actions are not mere irrationalities of choice or necessarily deliberate violations of procedure. Rather they can be constituted as alternative views of risk which may *seem as* legitimate and acceptable to the risk assessor as the views of risk articulated by policy makers and indeed experts.

Differing constructions of risk in the Probation Service

A comparison of one of the earliest Service documents on risk, the National Association of Probation Officers pamphlet on risk (NAPO 1977), to more recent Home Office and HMIP statements for example not only illustrates differing perspectives on risk in the Probation Service, but also the construction of offender risk as the major site of probation work in the intervening twenty year period. This is not merely a matter of a growing preoccupation with risk in criminal justice, but is rather the emergence of risk as the major classificatory principle or rational for organising both penal policy and probation work (Kemshall et al 1997). Within the NAPO document, risk is constituted primarily in terms of child abuse, or risks to the public and agency credibility incurred by mental hospital discharge or parole release cases which have resulted in 'adverse criticism' (NAPO 1977, p.1). In essence, risk is characterised as an exceptional concern (p1), rather than as the mainstream task, presenting risk decisions as a matter of casework dilemmas in high risk cases. By the mid 1990s, risk had become 'core business' (Kemshall 1995), with documents such as 'Crime, Justice and Protecting the Public' (Home Office 1990a), the Criminal Justice Act 1991, National Standards (Home Office 1995), 'Strengthening Punishment in the Community: A Consultation Document' (Home Office 1995a), the Three Year Plan (1992), and the Thematic Report on dangerous offenders (HMIP 1995) all asserting risk as the key service task. For example:

In every case an assessment of risk posed by the offender shall be made (Her Majesty's Inspectorate of Probation 1995, p.18. Crown copyright is reproduced with the permission of the Controller of Her Majesty's Stationery Office).

Whilst simplistically this can be viewed as the replacement of the language of 'client need' with the language of 'offender risk' (Kemshall et al 1997), it is also indicative of rather more wide-ranging changes. Principally, the move from an individualised officer -based approach to exceptional risks, to an increasingly corporate and managed approach to risk work. This is particularly exemplified by the strategic and externally driven risk-based penalty of the new penology (Feeley and Simon 1992) which is requiring an organisational (rather than an individual) response to risk classifications, resource allocation, and risk management tactics, (hence the proliferation of central and local 'guidance').

In addition to the increased policy framing in terms of risk, this twenty year period has also seen a significant change in the relationship between the Service and its clients (now constituted as offenders), and between the Service and the Home Office. This is characterised principally by changes in role, tasks and responsibilities of the Service, a change in the nature of its fundamental relationship with offenders well documented by McWilliams as progressively more coercive and socially distant (McWilliams 1987, 1992, 1992a), and a relationship with the Home Office which has become increasingly policy driven and managed (McWilliams 1990). This period has also seen an increased accountability for risk (Kemshall et al 1997) and the attendant blame allocation (Douglas 1992), resulting in an increase in what the NAPO paper called 'agency self-protection' (p. 8). This has radically transformed risk from the domain of case based 'ethical dilemmas' (pp. 8-9) and 'professional judgement' (p.12) of the NAPO paper to the organisational risk avoidance of the Inspectorate's guidance (HMIP 1997), and local risk procedures to enhance 'defensibility' in the light of public scrutiny. A full historical overview of this period is not presented here, (the historical precursors of a risk based Service are discussed in more detail in the next chapter). Rather, the focus in the rest of this chapter is upon the comparison of key risk statements in order to illustrate the broader themes of risk construction, risk conflict and 'noise management'.

Constructing risk in Probation Practice: From casework dilemmas to organisational risk avoidance

The National Association of Probation Officers' pamphlet: 'Risk: An Analysis of the Problem of Risk in Social Work Practice' (NAPO 1977) represents a specifically frontline worker perspective on risk in contrast to either a management or central policy maker view. A contrast between this document's conceptualisation of risk with the framing of risk concerns by the Home Office made from the late 1980s onwards illustrates the differing risk rationalities at work, and the progressive conceptualisation of risk away from the individual sphere of professional social casework to an organisationally managed approach to risk regulation. This transition is most easily discerned in the move from professional judgement to procedural accountability, and from professional autonomy to agency self-protection (NAPO 1977).

Risk and social casework

The NAPO statement clearly placed risk concerns within the principles of social casework prevalent in probation practice in the 1970s (McWilliams 1987). In the light of the Colwell inquiry (Secretary of State 1974), and subsequent public disquiet over child death tragedies, it is perhaps not surprising that the statement prioritises child protection risks as a major concern for workers, along with parole risks and those attached to the early discharge of mental health patients. Whilst risk reduction is accepted as a legitimate task (particularly in respect of the above areas of work), it is viewed as a task which should be pursued in a manner compatible with other current casework principles. Whilst it is noted that this may not always be compatible with growing public expectations to reduce risk through surveillance and control, the 'traditional approach to the offender' is prioritised (p.5). The statement strives to formulate a compromise between a growing emphasis upon risk reduction and the 'other aims which inform social work' (p.5).

In this statement NAPO contend that the emphasis upon risk reduction, public expectations, and the spectre of blame have combined to produce both a practitioner and agency concern with self-protection at the expense of 'working alongside clients in an attempt to alleviate the risk itself' (p.6). This self-protective approach, referred to as 'overkill', is contrasted to a casework based rehabilitative focus on 'the individual potential for growth and change' (p.8). This risk-rehabilitation dichotomy presaged the later value debates in services upon the introduction of risk policies (Kemshall 1997a, 1997c), and provides documentary evidence of a value clash between workers and policy makers on offender risk. The Probation Officer is characterised as the offender's champion against the condemnation of the public, cast at one point as the community's 'conscience keeper' (p.11); and offenders (or 'clients' as they are labelled) are viewed as the victims of social causal factors. This necessarily raises tensions for officers in reconciling their obligations to the 'community' and the pursuit of beneficial relationships with clients (a tension much expressed in subsequent risk discussions (Kemshall this volume, 1997a, 1997c).

Whilst the NAPO document accepts that officers fulfil their obligation to the community through their statutory responsibilities, the social distance of the community from the realities of clients' lives is seen as problematic. In this scenario, it is seen as incumbent upon officers to combat the indifference and blamism of the community, and to pursue a non-judgmental relationship with clients. This approach necessarily characterises the officer-client relationship as basically co-operative, and carries within it implicit theories of crime causation and human agency. The contrast to later compulsory risk reduction strategies is marked:

> An approach which relied principally on the attempt to impose control would be inherently negative and unacceptable to the Service because it would tend to focus on dangers rather than opportunities for growth...(NAPO 1977, p.12).

This quote well captures a central value dispute in the acceptability of risk work, but also highlights a major reconceptualisation of the offender, service tasks and officer roles and responsibilities which was to come in the subsequent twenty year period (Home Office 1997, HMIP 1997).

Acceptance and tolerance of risk

The NAPO statement also raises an implicit concern with the Service's risk bearing capacity, i.e. how much risk the Service can run, and how many failures the Service can stand? The NAPO statement sees the combination of increased public expectation, media scrutiny, and central policy demands as particularly potent in forcing a gap between internal Service views of role and task and those imposed from outside. In this scenario risk failures can be very costly, and disputes between Service and Home Office, and senior managers and workers, are predicted as senior or central personnel seek to regulate practice in order to avoid blame. The statement highlights the danger that over preoccupation with self-protection and blame avoidance will result in over-proceduralisation of a work task which is inherently uncertain, and the use of the hierarchical structure to implement procedures evolved at chief officer level in order to diminish the professional autonomy and judgements of staff. It is also noted that this can redistribute the risk load away from the policy centre to local services through the use of 'guidance', and from senior managers to frontline workers through procedures (NAPO 1977, p. 16-19).

Importantly the NAPO statement notes that risk preoccupations will also be dependent upon a person's position in the hierarchy and their membership of an organisational sub-set. This can result in differing risk rationalities across grades, with a practitioner perception that 'direct contact with individual clients is more real and unique', and a resistance to procedures on the grounds that they 'de-inviduate and depersonalise' clients (p.16). Such views can quickly become expressed as a conflict between those who control the work and those who 'actually' do it. An adversarial position epitomised by both Home Office and Inspectorate approaches to Probation risk practice some twenty years later (Home Office 1997, HMIP 1997).

NAPO conclude by proposing their own risk policy in which support for officers rather than blame is emphasised, and in which resources for risk are prioritised. Again this has all the hallmarks of later debates (for example Home Office Special Conferences 1998). However, the ethical considerations of NAPO's policy position and the concern for an evidenced based approach to registration and pro-active deregistration have been rather eclipsed in the meantime by attention to the technical refinement of assessment instruments (for example Home Office 1997).

From risk to dangerousness

By 1988 the 'administrative intervention' of the Home Office noted by the NAPO paper to support the work of officers and to provide 'protective guidelines' (p.19) had resulted in a Home Office letter to Chief Probation Officers on the registration of Potentially Dangerous Offenders (Home Office 1988). This followed a number of area reviews of work with dangerous offenders by the Inspectorate during the 1980s and cases which had attracted 'adverse criticism'. Whilst placing the risk load for the identification and registration of such offenders with local services, little practical guidance on how to accomplish this task was forthcoming from the Home Office. As Shaw's subsequent study revealed this resulted in a range of registration policies and practices across area services, although interestingly, the social work ethos prioritised by the NAPO statement was not in evidence. Rather, control, public protection, and staff safety were prioritised (Shaw 1991). In approximately a ten year period the 'prediction' of the NAPO statement, particularly in respect of protective and defensive approaches to risk, had come to fruition.

Shaw's study identified the inconsistent development of risk and dangerous policies in area services, with only one third of services having a policy in place. Categorisations of offenders as dangerous relied upon variable procedures and techniques:

> Not all categories most likely to include offenders whose previous behaviour suggested they might be dangerous in the future were included. ...some policies referred only to the protection of staff, or only to people released from prison, or only the mentally disordered (Shaw 1996, p.157).

Whilst risk was becoming increasingly prioritised the techniques for its reliable identification were embryonic. Risk was either framed as an health and safety issue (for example violence to staff), over identified with the mentally disordered despite evidence to the contrary (Ryan 1996), or with those considered to be self-evidently risky (for example parolees), again despite evidence on the nature of parole risks (Brown 1996). Shaw also found that differing management processes to ensure adequate supervision of dangerous offenders were adopted, including senior managers with functional responsibility, case conferencing to decide registration, or specific administrative procedures (Shaw 1996). Developments stemmed either from HMIP 'advice' or from specific serious incidents which had occurred within the area service (Shaw 1996, Wedge 1987). In considering registration, Shaw (1991) found murder and arson as the most commonly registered offences, although the most recent offence was not always that which prompted registration. Interestingly, Shaw found less registration of sex offenders than the Inspectorate some five years later, a discrepancy Shaw attributes to an increased concern with child abuse and attention to mechanisms to respond to it in the meantime (Shaw 1996). Parton et al (1997) would view this as an example of how particular activities are legitimated as dangerous over time, and how procedures can in themselves 'discover' a phenomenon.

Inspectorate and local area activities on dangerous offenders were paralleled by increased central policy attention to risk and dangerousness. The penal policy objectives of reducing 'risk to the public', minimising 'risk of serious harm' and ensuring 'public protection' enshrined in the White Paper: 'Crime, Justice and Protecting the Public' (Home Office 1990a) were given legislative force in the Criminal Justice Act 1991 (Wasik and Taylor 1991). In effect, section 1 (2) b offered a simple offence based classificatory system for the identification of potentially dangerous offenders, and section 2 (2) b gave public protection and harm prevention statutory force. Whilst clearly establishing a statutory obligation for the Probation Service, subsequently reiterated by National Standards (Home Office 1995), the implementation issues of risk assessment and management were devolved to local service managers to resolve. As Brown (1996) argues this enables government:

> ...to circumvent major problems that arise in attempting to predict exactly which individuals will pose a significant danger in the future and, *ipso facto*, in which cases special protective measures can reasonably be justified... (p.33).

This devolution of responsibility for operationalising the complex concepts of risk and dangerousness to local service managers enables central policy makers to:

> ...withdraw from what otherwise would be a very complex and uncertain exercise (Brown 1996, p.33).

This displaces the risk load onto area managers who have to reinterpret the 'lay' definitions of risk and dangerousness contained in penal policy to staff, literally providing workable definitions, predictors and assessment tools, techniques to ensure reliable predictions of both probability and impact, and procedures to enable staff to apply such techniques to specific offenders within time and place (Kemshall 1997c). In addition to the technical difficulties this raises (Kemshall 1997c), differences in risk perspective, value and legitimacy are also raised. Shaw (1991) notes in his study that the concerns with 'dangerousness' of senior local managers and of the Home Office are not necessarily shared by officers, and that whilst senior agency managers respond to external expectations, frontline staff may not:

> The precise purpose of these (Home Office) Circulars as instruments of public protection is not always accepted by field staff, since some of the assumptions are seen as unsubstantiated or as having little scientific validity. Discussions with practitioners engaged in the supervision of dangerous offenders disclose that the principal purpose of these Circulars is seen as the protection of government departments and the avoidance of embarrassment to ministers when disasters occur, as well as engendering a feeling in the public that supervision in the community is punishment rather than treatment (Shaw 1996, p.161).

Central 'guidance' and Probation Service responses

By the time of the Inspectorate's Thematic Report on Dangerous Offenders in 1995 there were already differing perceptions of risk both within and across differing areas, and differing perceptions of legitimacy in the task (Kemshall 1995a). Shaw's quote is also an example of worker lack of trust (and possible participation) in the management processes being created for risk work. As Rayner (1986) contended, this can result in conflict and doubt about the competency of others to deal with the issue. This was sharply raised by the Inspectorate's Thematic report on the supervision of dangerous offenders (HMIP 1995) which reported on various shortcomings in the supervision practices of officers. For example:

> ...staff too often fail either to record or respond to indicators of potential dangerousness in the offenders they supervise (Her Majesty's Inspectorate of Probation 1995, p.15. Crown copyright is reproduced with the permission of the Controller of Her Majesty's Stationery Office).

and:

> ...national standards must be complied with. Level of contact with offenders and enforcement of orders and licences indicate this is not currently happening in a significant number of cases, even where offenders are formally assessed as posing a risk to the public (Her Majesty's Inspectorate of Probation 1995, p.15. Crown copyright is reproduced with the permission of the Controller of Her Majesty's Stationery Office).

Managers did not fair much better:

> ...the identification of potentially dangerous offenders is a corporate responsibility but too often managers at all levels are insufficiently involved (Her Majesty's Inspectorate of Probation 1995, p.15. Reproduced with the permission of the Controller of Her Majesty's Stationery Office).

Combined with various Probation Circulars comprising instructions to local services (for example: PC 96/1994, PC 41/1995), and the subsequent draft guidance issued at the Public Protection Conference in March 1996, (HMIP 1996) this gave the view that the service could not be trusted to act competently on risk if left to its own devices. The cumulative effect of all this 'guidance' was an emphasis upon organisational self-protection and risk avoidance, and the displacement of the risk load and blame away from those formulating central policy.

The Probation Service, through the Association of Chief Probation Officers (ACOP 1994), attempted to respond to the growing imperative to assess and manage risk. The document illustrates the vulnerability of the Service in attempting to present a collective view of risk in the face of considerable differences 'on the ground.' This initial response was confused and unsystematic, although it marked the first explicit statement on risk on behalf of the service. The document correctly recognised that since the implementation of the Criminal Justice Act 1991 and the imposition of National Standards for Supervision in the Community (Home Office 1992a), a 'more active recognition of responsibilities for assessing risk to the public and its subsequent management' was required (ACOP 1994, p.1). This statement also acknowledged that risk had been externally defined and its effective management externally demanded. Whilst the document warned that the Service had a 'limited ability to protect the public' (p.1), its duty to the potential victims of risky offenders was stated.

The statement defined risk primarily in terms of the possibility of physical violence, sexual abuse, and dangerousness stemming from mental ill health; and victims as children, the public and staff. These definitions reflected the legislative concerns of the Criminal Justice Act 1991 in respect of violent and sexual offenders, and the overall concern to protect the public from further offending (Home Office 1992, 1992a, 1995, 1995a). In this sense the Association of Chief Officers of Probation statement readily accepted the normative perception of risk held by central policy makers, and the policy objectives of the new penology to pursue a bifurcated approach to penal policy in which those deemed to pose a risk to public safety require increased surveillance and control (Christie 1993, Cohen 1994, Feeley and Simon 1992, 1994). The dual concerns of dangerousness and recidivism of central policy makers was also implicitly re-stated and conflated, fuelling a conceptual confusion which has been frequently repeated (Kemshall 1996, Kemshall 1997, 1997a, Home Office 1997, HMIP 1997).

In addition, the statement focused on management systems and procedures, and in this respect initiated a higher management Service discussion on how to implement and regulate risk assessment and management policies. The over-riding concern with organisational protection and avoidance of adverse criticism forecast by the NAPO statement is exemplified by this Chief Officer response. However, it is important to recognise that this represented a Chief Officer response to an external demand, and was not necessarily indicative of the views of other grades of staff. Only that from Warwickshire acknowledged that the perceptions and values of individual risk assessors may be influential in the risk assessment process. The ethical and moral debate was largely neglected in the pursuit of systems to manage decisions safely.

Confusion and lack of clarity stemmed in large part from the highly individualised response of local services to the risk issue, resulting in varying policies and approaches. This ranged from organisational responses which were complacent (no policy or register in place) (Kemshall 1997b), to those which were risk-averse and attempting to control and avoid all risks through elaborate policies and procedures. During this period Home Office statements became increasingly risk averse. For example in discussing the service's public protection role the Inspectorate notes factors which have contributed to raising the importance of the issue and places the following at the top of the list:

> ...an increased public sensitivity to and concern about personal safety in response to rising levels of recorded crime and arguably, to the coverage given by the media to crimes of violence (Her Majesty's Inspectorate of Probation 1996, p.2).

In addition, the complacency of area services is itself viewed as problematic:

> ...an awareness within Government that it (Probation) must be seen to be acting to protect the public. Failures by public sector organisations to treat

or manage some dangerous offenders effectively have enhanced this awareness (Her Majesty's Inspectorate of Probation 1996, p.2).

The Home Office's risk aversion response to complacency resulted in a series of 'ought' statements. For example, Her Majesty's Inspectorate of Probations draft guidance comprised a series of 'do' and 'don't' statements and outlined responsibilities for officers and managers including Chief Officers (HMIP 1996). This was subsequently followed up by PC 63/1996 on the adoption of the Offender Group Reconviction Scale for the calculation of risk probabilities, and re-issued guidance from both the Home Office and the Inspectorate in 1997 (Home Office 1997, HMIP 1997). Whilst originally conceptualised as a rare case work phenomenon pertinent to a small number of clients, by the time of the Home Office and the Inspectorate's guidance risk had become the key classificatory mechanism for organising all probation work. The NAPO statement was concerned to see the client as an individual and to reconcile the needs of the offender with the expectations of the community. The Home Office statement is concerned with group categorisation for resource allocation and work control (Home Office 1997), and the Inspectorate with risk avoidance and meeting public expectations of protection.

Risk conflicts

These differing responses to risk can be understood as a clash of prevailing cultures between the Home Office and area services, and between managers and staff. Leiss and Chociolko (1994) argue that such clashes are not merely about differing perspectives on risk. They are also debates in which individuals and institutions attempt to avoid accepting responsibility for risk (usually by off-loading it upon others), and that within this process one side may under-estimate risks and the other exaggerate them. They also note that such disputes deflect attention away from the inadequacies of either party in assessing and managing risk (Leiss and Chociolko 1994, p. 58). In the uncertain world of risk this is a useful tactic. Attention can be drawn to the shortcomings of others rather than to the inexpertness of one's own position.

In such clashes the concepts of: power, blame, trust, credibility and acceptability are crucial. Risk priorities are power statements, and reveal not only boundaries of social order but where the power to legitimate risk concerns lies (for example reconciling risk concerns to traditional casework ones is not (HMIP 1995, HMIP 1997). In this case, the power is clearly with the Home Office to define and legitimate risk concerns through official communications with area services. These are often mirrored rather than challenged, for example in the Association of Chief Officers of Probation statement (ACOP 1994) or in individual service documents (for example Inner London Probation Service 1995). However, the exercise of power, especially when combined with exclusion, can be resented, hence the comment of Shaw's probation officer respondent.

Power can also be used to allocate risk responsibilities and hence blame in the face of things going wrong. This is particularly problematic if individuals or institutions perceive that the risks are not a matter of their choice (for example externally driven by politicians), or that they are responsible for risks which they cannot manage (Leiss and Chociolko 1994). If this is exacerbated by the imposition of processes for assessing and managing risk, then individuals may lose confidence in those controlling such decision making processes. Such lack of trust undermines both the credibility and acceptability of both risk priorities and the processes proposed for risk regulation. This can be expressed as 'deviancy' from the proposals or as conflict. In this situation risk management in organisations (and indeed between them) increasingly becomes an issue of 'noise' management rather than management for effective risk outcomes.

Probation Service noise management

At present three responses to 'noise' management can be discerned:

- Exercising greater power to enforce compliance.

- Attributing blame.

- Re-socialising through training.

In practice, these strategies are often linked, for example the Home Office Risk Management Pack, (Home Office 1997), which contains statements on service compliance with pre-specified outcomes (see Part One); statements on blame/responsibility for risk (see Part Four); and training material (see Part Three). This approach has often been mirrored at local service level, with great attention to compliance statements, i.e. policy and procedure statements; combined with measures to censure non-compliance (for example discipline or appraisal procedures) and to allocate blame; and compulsory training programmes increasingly based upon the Home Office endorsed materials. Such processes may only serve to distance workers from the institution rather than achieve greater integration (Douglas 1992, Rayner 1986) because they signal lack of trust in the competency and discretion of workers. In addition, they can replace 'due process' and participation by workers in the organisation's decision making on risk management. Compliance is then mistaken for ownership, and without vigorous reinforcement it can fall. Hence procedural compliance declines in the long term as shown by numerous 'disaster' inquiries (Cullen 1990, Hidden 1989, Health and Safety Executive 1988).

Reconciling risk differences

Rayner argued that difference was not of itself problematic, rather it is the organisational mechanisms chosen for managing difference which can be (Rayner 1986). Using Douglas' grid/group typology (Douglas 1992) in his hospital study he demonstrates how ineffective and conflictual a bureaucratic approach to risk management can be with workers who are individualist in their approach to risk and who are used to operating in an individualist culture. This individualist culture is particularly evident in the NAPO statement. For example, individualists doubt that 'routine procedures offer real protection' whilst bureaucrats are 'outraged by individual flouting of safety rules...' (Rayner 1986, p.586). Individualists prefer to trust themselves, whilst bureaucrats believe that competency can only be assured by rule following. Individualists are prone to risk-take whilst bureaucrats deny the possibility that risks will occur *if rules are followed.* This is a position adopted by many current risk policies and is played out in discussions between the Service and Home Office, and senior managers and workers.

However, outright conflict need not occur. Rayner found in his study that if the representatives of each group could respect each other 'their interaction need not be adversarial. It is when trust breaks down that the rival positions clearly crystallise' (Rayner 1986, p.588). Trust and respect are highly dependent upon access to, visibility and fairness of decision making processes, and the means by which consensus is achieved. Organisational management of risk requires identification of such differing rationalities of risk and adoption of risk management strategies well matched to the positions expressed. Some services (exceptions rather than the rule), have attempted this by the use of working parties to develop risk policies and procedures in order to incorporate differing perceptions of risk and to provide greater access to decision making (for example Hampshire 1995). Maynard-Moody et al (1990) following a comparative study of policy implementation and the impact of professional discretion in two states in America argued that:

> ...delegating authority and including the perspectives of street level workers in programmatic decisions is a realistic alternative to managerial control when the objective is to reduce the dangers of discretion (pp.844-845).

Gill MacKenzie, Chief Probation Officer of Gloucestershire Probation Service, drew attention to the organisational context of risk implementation in her address to the 1996 Public Protection Conference. In contrast to the 'enforcement' statements of Inspectorate personnel (Lawrie 1996, G. Smith 1996) in which officer compliance was conceptualised as an issue of exercising the appropriate amount of management power, MacKenzie focused upon the organisational requirements for getting risk right. She argued that a:

> ...coherent, developmental strategy on public protection is comprised of four independent components:
> (a) the circle of knowledge, expertise and research.
> (b) adequate resourcing.
> (c) vigorous ethical debate.
> (d) active engagement with the outside world.

Implicitly this approach recognised the varying perspectives on risk which exist, not least between probation and other agencies, and probation and the 'outside world'. MacKenzie acknowledged that risk practice takes place within a 'cultural web' and that excessive bureaucratisation of structures did not necessarily guarantee successful implementation.

Risk aversion, trust and blame

Finally it is in the fraught area of implementation that managers and the organisations which they serve display their attitudes towards risk. With a few exceptions, the present message is clear. Risk is 'core business' (Kemshall 1995, Home Office 1997, MacKenzie 1996), but it is also viewed as threatening, a task to be done well at all costs, and a task upon which service credibility will be harshly judged. The Inspectorate for example described it as a 'critical task' (HMIP 1997, p.1).

In this risk averse climate organisational messages are characterised by compliance, risk avoidance, and safety. Decision making is heavily proceduralised and workers are urged not to make errors by staying within the rules:

> There is a widespread fear of being blamed for the wrong decision and this can often result in no decision or doing nothing. It is always best to make a decision which is defensible and justifiable. The responsibility to protect the public is both a corporate one and an individual one, which means that the senior managers have a duty to ensure that the policies and procedures are effectively implemented and reviewed regularly and each member of staff has a duty to follow the procedures laid down in this document... (Burstein and Walters, Middlesex Probation Service 1996, p. 4).

Hierarchy and power can be too readily used to both enforce compliance and to allocate responsibility and therefore ultimate blame. Roles and responsibilities within Probation's hierarchical structure have literally been allocated (and along with them levels of blame) by the Inspectorate's guidance (HMIP 1997). Interestingly the burden of responsibility and blame appears to increase the closer one gets to the 'coal face', as evidenced by the task lists for officers in the draft and completed Inspectorate guidance (HMIP 1996, 1997), and in many local area documents (e.g. West Midlands 1997). Whilst it may be unintentional, one result of such approaches can be that organisational failings quickly become redefined as individual errors. In cases of negative outcome, differing perspectives on risk between workers and managers become discussions of who is to blame, and implicitly discussions of which construction of risk is deemed to be the most legitimate.

In the implementation of risk, attention needs to be paid to differing perspectives on risk, and perhaps more importantly to how they are accommodated. Disputes about risk are often disputes about trust and responsibility (Beck 1992, Leiss and Chociloko 1994), most especially about lack of trust and the unfair displacement of responsibility for risk decisions. A key question for Probation managers and central penal policy makers is the extent to which they have and deserve the trust of frontline risk assessors, and the extent to which responsibility is accepted or displaced.   In turn, workers' answers to these questions will crucially determine their response to the organisation's demands.

4. The Changing Nature of Probation: The Origins of Risk

The Cri... (Wasik and Taylor 1991) and the demands of Natior... he Office 1995) have placed the assessment and mana... at the centre of the Probation Service's work. In ... concept of seriousness, the Act, through section 2 (... ms and protective sentencing within a legislative f... tection and harm reduction were key principles of ... fically understood as the 'serious harm' of sexual or \... 1 (2) b, Wasik and Taylor 1991, p. 19). The earl... lisle 1988) and the subsequent early release arrange... irrored the risk and harm reduction principles and p... oncern of parole decision making.

The subseq... ef Officers of Probation position paper: 'Guidance ... of Risk and Public Protection. Position Statement ... Probation Inspectorate's thematic inspection: 'Dealing ... le: The Probation Service and Public Protection' (... the service's response to these legal and policy exp... ..text, it would be reasonable to assume that the serv... dramatic changes in its role and task during the 1990s, with ... of emphasis from direct work with offenders in need of rehabilitatic ... to the management of offender risk at point of sentence, during community supervision and parole.

Whilst there have been significant legal and policy statements in the 1990s which have impacted upon the objectives of the Probation Service, the history of changes in the service are inextricably linked to wider changes in the history of penal policy (Hudson 1993, 1996). The history of the service this century is in large part the history of a service re-establishing its raison d'être in line with shifts in penal policy (McWilliams 1987,1992, 1992a). The central argument of this chapter is that there have indeed been significant shifts in service policy and practice, culminating in the prioritisation of risk; but that these shifts were occurring well before the 1991 Criminal Justice Act. This chapter will outline the changing nature of the service task and highlight the particular factors which paved the way for risk. An in-depth historical analysis of twentieth century penal policy is not offered, this is excellently done elsewhere (see for example Hudson 1996). Rather attention is focused upon service activities, and in particular the changing role and nature of assessment as an exemplar of the changing nature of the service's raison d'être.

The journey is from the moral assessment of the police court missionary, through to the diagnostic assessments of treatability of the scientific caseworker, to the predictive calculations of risk by case managers. Whilst numerous histories of the Service already exist (Haxby 1978, McWilliams 1981, 1983, 1985, 1986, 1987, 1992, 1992a, and D. Smith 1996), the focus of historical analysis has more often been upon the transition from judicial to executive accountability (McWilliams 1992, 1992a, D. Smith 1996); the rapid expansion of alternatives to custody (Mair 1996); or the development of the management grade and the impact of administrative structures upon the Service (Adam et al 1980, Haxby 1978, Waters 1980). The focus in this brief overview will be the origins of predictive, routinised assessment by professional experts and the use of risk as a strategic tool in the management of offenders, practice, and resources.

The historical context: from divine grace to diagnosis

McWilliams' initial quartet of historical essays provides a useful starting point for charting the changing nature of offender assessment. McWilliams (1983, 1985) has identified the early era of probation as clearly rooted in the religious idealism of the police court missionaries. Such missionaries were concerned with the identification of those offenders deserving of leniency and amenable to salvation and moral reform. The penal context for their activities was an increasing desire to eliminate sentencing disparities (Cox 1877, McWilliams 1983), but to also allow magistrates to impose more lenient sentences where circumstances justified such an approach. As McWilliams expresses it, the role of the missionaries in providing such justifications was welcomed. The social context for the work of the missionaries was the high volume of offences of drunkenness and prostitution, and the desire of the religious temperance movement to resolve a growing social problem through the reformation of individuals. McWilliams argues that this, coupled with a vociferous advocacy of more humane approaches to offenders (1983), and a recognition of the extent of social deprivation in Victorian England, led to a desire for both leniency and moral reform in the sentencing of offenders.

In time the missionaries were required to conduct pre-sentence inquiries in order to structure and justify the allocation of mercy by sentencers. This resulted in a role of 'special pleading' and assessments of moral worthiness which continued to tinge social inquiry reports right up until recent times (Gelsthorpe et al 1992, Jarvis 1980, Raynor 1980, Raynor et al 1994). Following successful 'special pleading', offenders were placed under the supervision of individual missionaries in order for the offender's salvation to be completed.

In this era, assessment was moralistic in nature and its purpose was to identify those deserving of 'another chance' and earnest in their desire to reform. The intention was also underwritten by more practical and financial considerations of reducing strain and costs on courts and prisons alike (McWilliams 1983). Assessments were individually undertaken and individually presented by the missionary in court, based upon a personal view of moral character expressed in plain language (McWilliams 1986). In essence the missionary had a personal relationship with the magistrates and exemplified individual moral authority rather than the later expert knowledge of the agency worker.

In his quartet of essays McWilliams documents the demise of the missionary ideal and the eclipsing of the police court missionary by the 'scientific social worker'. In brief, a number of strands can be discerned in his historical analysis. Firstly, the replacement of the religious conception of the offender as the '...'sinner' susceptible to grace through moral reform;...' (McWilliams 1986, p.241), to the status of a person in need of treatment and cure. McWilliams (1983, 1985) suggests that this was possible because the missionaries increasingly identified 'stumbling blocks' to change and barriers to salvation, either in the social and personal circumstances of the offender or within his/her character. This deterministic understanding of the offender resulted in a diagnostic approach to offenders and the identification of behaviour and attitudes requiring modification through treatment. The increased volume and routinisation of pre-sentence assessments required by the 1907 Probation of Offenders Act also played a part:

> ...as the notion of routine assessment for probation gained ground attention...moved from the soul and its potential for grace, to the mind and behaviour and the potential for modification thereof. This latter form of

thinking brings with it...notions of predictive assessment, and in this way we may see the ground being prepared for the seeds of diagnostic thought to take root (McWilliams, 1985, p.260. Reproduced with the permission of Blackwell Publishers Ltd., Oxford).

This turned the moral assessments of special pleading into the diagnosis of problems. Assessment became the mechanism for establishing treatability. The credibility and expertness of such diagnoses was established through formalised training and the use of scientifically based forms of knowledge. Intervention, or more correctly treatment, was predicated upon an:

> ...accurate diagnosis based upon an objective, factual appraisal of the offender, his circumstances and his likely response to the repertoire of treatment (McWilliams 1985, p.260. Reproduced with the permission of Blackwell Publishers Ltd., Oxford).

Assessment was now an expert rather than a personal view, with the assessor representing a profession and expert body of knowledge in the court arena. In this mode the offender was presented as the repository of psycho-social problems in need of expert casework treatment in order to alleviate them. Whilst in practice missionary zeal and the diagnostic ideal co-existed for many years, McWilliams (1986) has convincingly documented the change in character of language, purpose, and ontological and epistemological grounding of social inquiry reports over the intervening decades.

However, as an assessment process McWilliams has argued that the diagnostic methodology was flawed, and as such was bound to be eclipsed (McWilliams 1986). He argues that the accurate, objective and factual information gathering process upon which both diagnosis and subsequent treatment is based is not a value free exercise, but is crucially dependent upon theoretical frameworks and moral imperatives. In particular, the gap between diagnosis and treatment is resolved through decisions of what ought to be done. McWilliams contends that it is this stage of the process which produces moral disputes over treatments and their relative efficacy. The moral and value framing of diagnosis resulted in the imposition of meaning, not least upon the offender who became a 'recipient of expert treatment rather than being a prime agent in his own rehabilitation' (Weston 1973, p.11). The probation officer was no longer the vehicle of salvation but could be the coercer of offenders to enforced treatment (Hunt 1964). Not only did this change the nature of assessment, but it also changed the nature of the relationship between the officer and the offender. The latter became a recipient of an expert professional service, often unwanted although consented to, with varying degrees of motivation to treatment depending upon the unpalatableness of the alternatives. Eventually this approach became known as 'sentencing to treatment' (Raynor 1980).

In this era of diagnosis and treatment the seeds were sown for both the coercion of offenders in the community and for their increased objectification. As will be explored later these two ingredients are also characteristics of practice under risk assessment and risk management. The era also saw the prioritising of the officer's view over both those of offenders and sentencers through the notion of the expert (McWilliams 1986). This created the role of professional advisor to the courts and weakened the shared goal of moral reform once held in common with sentencers (McWilliams 1981). In addition to creating distance from the magistracy, this role presented the officer as the only repository of knowledge about the offender essential to effective sentencing. As well as aiding effective sentencing, pre-sentence assessments could also aid supposedly rational and objective allocations of service interventions. This prepared the ground for the more managed approach to assessment and resource allocation which was to take hold from the late 1980s onwards (McWilliams 1992a).

An historical overview of the officer's role in pre-sentence inquiries illustrates that classification of offenders is a long established principle, as is the officer's expert role in accomplishing it. The nature and mode of classification has changed during the service's history, reflecting wider changes in the service's purpose and task. Whilst officers no longer classify offenders according to treatment needs, classification for risk is required. The diagnostic era established pre-sentence assessment and the court report as the main mechanism for such classifications, and the notion that the professional expertise of the officer was a sound basis for predictive assessments. It also established the principle that assessments could be future oriented, particularly in terms of the impact of future behaviours should they remain untreated. The ground work for the expert, future oriented risk predictions of pre-sentence reports was laid. The role of the officer was also reconstituted from offender's friend and saviour to the provider of (on occasion compulsory) treatment (McWilliams 1981,1985, 1986). The acceptability of coercion and the objectification of the offender as the site of treatment contributed to a social distancing of offenders. This has assisted in the legitimation of social regulation of offenders through increasingly controlling and exclusory mechanisms such as risk management (Christie 1993, Hudson 1996).

The diagnostic era promised the increased efficacy of treatment and effectiveness of sentencing. However, McWilliams (1986) notes that it failed in these twin objectives. Quoting Davies (1974) he points out that this approach has not decreased crime levels or lessened sentencing disparities. This coupled with negative research findings on the impact of treatment (Martinson 1974) led to the demise of the scientific diagnostic ideal.

The modern Probation Service: from rehabilitation to justice

The demise of the treatment model post Martinson (1974) is well documented (Bean 1976, Folkard et al 1976, Gaylin 1978, Hudson 1987, Thorpe et al 1980), and will not be extensively reviewed here. In the age of post rehabilitation the Probation Service found itself in a contradictory position. The number of pre-sentence social inquiries continued to grow but the number of probation orders resulting from such inquiries fell (Raynor 1980). Whilst some research demonstrated a degree of 'fit' between recommendations and sentencing outcomes (Thorpe and Pease 1976), the impact of the services' interventions and of pre-sentence predictions of treatability upon recidivism were low (Folkard et al 1976, Raynor 1980). Sentencing to treatment was not only discredited as ineffective (Martinson 1974) but was also shown to be potentially discriminatory (Bean 1976). In addition, the service experienced staff growth and the development of a managerial grade with attendant administrative structures (Haxby 1978, Mair 1996, McWilliams 1992a).

This placed the service in a vulnerable position, with a 123% increase in financial resources between 1983 and 1992, a 23% increase in staffing, coupled with a reduction in the average criminal caseload of officers from 27.5 to 20.8 (Mair 1996, p.25). The service was placed in a position of needing a justification for growth, for its court role and for probation supervision. In this climate probation commentators such as Bottoms and McWilliams (1979) argued for a 'non-treatment' paradigm of problem negotiation with offenders, and others for an increased focus upon sentencing as 'justice' rather than treatment (Hood 1971, Raynor 1980, Tutt and Giller 1984). Both approaches were important. The non-treatment paradigm for its emphasis upon humanist values, worker-offender collaboration of problem definition, the provision of appropriate help, and the rejection of 'manipulative coercion' (Bottoms and McWilliams 1979). The justice approach for its rejection of treatment's net-widening, the commitment to diversion and the systemic attempt to influence sentencers.

The doubt and uncertainty of the 1980s (Raynor et al 1994), resulted in a pragmatic response based upon the pursuit of the least intrusive sanction (Thorpe et al 1980, Tutt and Giller 1984). Responding to need, particularly in respect of juveniles was deemed to have net-widened (Harris and Webb 1987, Thorpe et al 1980), hence minimal intervention was advocated. Tariff position, and if possible 'down tariffing' was to outweigh welfare concerns. Whilst the place and content of pre-sentence assessments in the justice model was hotly debated (Bottoms and Stelman 1988, Raynor 1980, Tutt and Giller 1984), there was general consensus that the tariff position of the offender was central. Debate tended to focus around the degree of individualisation which was both appropriate and allowable within a justice approach (Raynor 1980). Raynor (1980) argued that sentences could be individualised on the basis of aggravating or mitigating circumstances, and that pre-sentence assessments should quite properly be concerned with issues of blameworthiness, intent and culpability. The justice approach, including this accommodation of individualisation, foregrounded sentencing commensurate with the offence, and formed the precursor of the later 'just deserts' approach.

The justice model gained legislative expression in the Criminal Justice Act 1982 (D. Smith 1996), particularly in respect of juveniles, and was vigorously implemented by some local services (for example see Kemshall's review of juvenile justice in Warwickshire, 1986). The act also strengthened community supervision for both adults and juveniles through the use of additional conditions in an effort to gain credibility for declining probation orders in the face of the rising popularity of community service with sentencers. This introduced the notion of supervision as restriction and control (Raynor 1985) rather than as vehicle for treatment, and was a precursor of the later policy statement of punishment in the community (Home Office 1988a).

Smith (1996) amongst others (Cavadino and Dignan 1992, Hudson 1993, 1996) has identified this period of penal policy as a crystallising of the bifurcation or twin-track approach to sentencing first identified by Bottoms a few years earlier (1977). Whilst not explicitly framed in terms of Bottoms' dangerousness, penal policy was increasingly concerned with distinguishing the serious from the non-serious offender, and in particular those who would recidivate. It is no coincidence that this is the era in which the Probation Service discovered offence focused work and the issue of recidivism.

Pre-sentence assessments in this period changed focus from identification for treatability to an identification of whether the sentencing criteria of the 1982 Act, particularly in respect of the imposition of custody on young offenders, were met (Burney 1985, D. Smith 1996). In effect, assessment was targeted at classifying offenders according to seriousness and distinguishing between those offenders deserving of custody and those whose offending could reasonably be contained in the community. This represents quite a different assessment function than the 'special pleading' of the police court missionaries. Whilst the latter is an expression of an individual officer's attempt to reclaim the soul of the individual offender, the former represents a strategic effort on behalf of the agency to reclaim a group of offenders (in this case juveniles) from custody. Pre-sentence assessments (SIRs) were no longer a moral plea or a diagnostic instrument, but became strategic documents in a systems management approach to sentencing (Blagg and Smith 1989, Tutt and Giller 1984). This strategic reframing of the objectives of pre-sentence assessment was not always as coherently played out by practitioners who in practice oscillated unpredictably between 'treatment' and 'non-treatment' ideologies (Hardiker 1977), and led to a questioning of whether there was any 'sense' and indeed place for 'old style' social inquiry reports in the justice model (Raynor 1980).

However, a number of principles for probation policy and practice in pre-sentence assessment, and for the relationship of the service to both sentencers and offenders were established. The first was the principle of bifurcation combined with a growing preoccupation to reduce future recidivism rates in the face of spiralling crime rates and costs (Bottoms 1977, Hudson 1993). The 1982 Act framed this as a dichotomy between serious and non-serious offending. In less than ten years the 1991 Criminal Justice Act provided a clearer division between offences against the person and the risk of serious harm on the one hand, and property offences on the other (Wasik and Taylor 1991). The ineffectiveness of correction through treatment also turned attention away from offenders per se to their offending, and the pursuit of correction through offence focused practice (Denman 1982, Priestley 1977).

Subtly the agenda became the prevention of recidivism through correctional strategies (for example intensive group work programmes), rather than the rehabilitation of individual offenders. Within juvenile justice in particular this was coupled with a managed approach to the offender group as a whole, with inter-agency diversion schemes and strategic policies to influence the juvenile courts towards the least intrusive sentencing options (Thorpe et al 1980). The service's relationship to the court was no longer one of individual advice to the bench, but of an agency seeking to strategically implement policy in the court arena. McWilliams refers to this as the era of 'educating the magistrates' (1992a). Where policy goals were misunderstood or unshared the service's relationship with local sentencers could often be difficult (Kemshall 1986). The mutually shared moral goals of the police court missionary era had passed.

The strategic and managed approach to juvenile offenders took somewhat longer to transfer to work with adults (Blagg and Smith 1989). However, the principles of bifurcation, and a strategic and managed approach to penal policy had already impacted upon the work of the Probation Service. As Feeley and Simon (1992, 1994) were later to point out, these are the key principles of the new penology and justice policy based upon risk management. By the early 1980s assessment was already fulfilling an agency and policy function linked to bifurcation and resource allocation.

The managed Probation Service: from justice to effectiveness

The Statement of National Objectives and Priorities (SNOP) (Home Office, 1984) marked a watershed in the history of the Probation Service and gave impetus to the above trends (Mair 1996). The document altered the relationship of the Home Office to individual services, initiating a period within which the Home Office has asserted a management role over the activities of the service. In the years following SNOP the service found itself increasingly under executive control and distanced from its judicial roots (McWilliams 1987, 1992a). Expectations, as expressed in terms of priorities and objectives, were signalled to the service, and a new era of greater accountability began. Three strands in this 'managed' approach can be discerned: financial management, information management and professional management (Smith 1996).

Financial management initiatives in the Probation Service reflected wider concerns to control public sector spending (Flynn 1993), and the work of the probation service was scrutinised by the Audit Commission in 1989 (Audit Commission 1989). Prior to this, the service had been subject to the government's Financial Management Initiative (Humphrey 1991), and the search for a manageable finance management information system (RMIS). This was accompanied by the development at both local and national levels of key performance indicators resulting in a statement from the Inspectorate on performance objectives in 1988 (HMIP 1988). Cash limits were subsequently introduced to control the expenditure of local service committees resulting in urgent activity in area services to manage internal resources more effectively (for example West Midlands 1993). With the passage of time the impact of financial constraint has harshened, leading to cuts in both staffing and service delivery.

Shrinking resources focused attention on mechanisms for allocating service delivery, and in effect rationing and prioritising service resources in a rational and systematic way. SNOP began this process by according lower priority to 'after-care' and through-care in particular (Smith 1996) and targetting those 'at risk' of custody. Probation Orders were to be offered as credible alternatives to custody, and the wholesale adoption of the risk of custody score (Bale 1987, 1990) assisted officers in the systematic targetting of those 'at risk'. Whilst the framing of risk in SNOP was those 'at risk' of custody, it did reveal the:

> Home Office's intent that the Probation Service's primary task should be to help reduce the prison population by providing persuasive 'alternatives' (Smith, 1996, p.15).

As such, it is an important national statement on the use of risk to allocate resources.

These initiatives to control resources were accompanied by an increasing attention to information management. Resource management itself generated information needs, not least to know more accurately the relationship between inputs and outputs in order to better inform judgements of economy, efficiency and effectiveness (Humphrey et al 1992). PROBIS (Probation Information System), and more recently CRAMS (Case Review and Management System) are examples of national computerised systems to collect and manipulate information across the 54 service areas. Information has been sought to evaluate 'value for money' and to justify the distribution of resources. Comparisons can be made between the impact on reconviction rates of various disposals (Lloyd et al 1994), cost per disposal and reconviction outcome (Mair 1996), and presumably in due course league tables of individual areas' performance (Bewley 1996). Whilst initial information systems were based upon crude input-output ratios (Humphrey 1991, Humphrey et al 1992, Kemshall 1993, 1993a), there has been a growing recognition that outcomes require as much if not more attention (Vennard 1996). Questions of impact, particularly upon reconviction rates has focused attention on effectiveness and risk. This has been paralleled by attention upon the merits of various disposals including community supervision (Lloyd et al 1994).

Following the demise of the rehabilitative ideal, the discrediting of the treatment model of intervention (Bottoms and Preston 1980, Home Office 1977) and the 'nothing works' pronouncement of Martinson (1974, Folkard et al 1976), the Service was required to reposition itself. McWilliams argues that this was achieved largely by answering:

> ...the pragmatic need to relieve the pressure on custodial institutions by dealing with a greater proportion of offenders than hitherto via community-based disposals (McWilliams 1987, p.105 Reproduced with the permission of Blackwell Publishers Ltd., Oxford).

The Service was repositioned as an 'alternative to custody', and instruments such as the 'Risk of Custody Scale' (Bale 1987, 1990) were developed to enable consistent and effective targetting of social inquiry reports. The score represents one of the earliest examples of a nationally implemented tool to manage practice towards policy driven objectives. In McWilliams' view the era of pragmatism also saw the rise of policy as the main mechanism for specifying service tasks and functions. This changed the relationship of the service to sentencers, to the Home Office and to the workforce. Practice was no longer conceptualised as a matter of individual professional judgement, but as an activity to be actively managed towards pre-specified policy ends. This period saw a continued increase in the management grade and the strengthening of line management as advocated by the Morrison report (Home Office and Scottish Home Department 1962), and the Management Structure Review (Joint Negotiation Committee 1980, Haxby 1978, McWilliams 1987, 1992a, Waters 1980); increased management preoccupations with local policy formulation in line with national statements (McWilliams 1992, 1992a); and attention to objective setting and resource management (Humphrey et al 1993, Lewis 1991).

Implications for practice have been great. Professional autonomy and discretion have largely been removed (May 1991), with an increased policy framework to guide practice and systems such as supervision and appraisal to regulate it. The shift from a largely individualised social work agency to a centrally driven agency of criminal justice is almost complete (Nellis 1995). In addition to increased control of policy and practice the purpose and character of practice itself has also changed.

As the service has altered its raison d'être in response to policy demands the practice task has also altered. In the 1980s the primary task was the provision of alternatives to custody through the increased use of 'credible' probation orders, day centres and community service (Mair 1996, McWilliams 1992a, Smith 1996), and increased provision for discharged prisoners under parole. As McWilliams expresses it, this was a rather debased raison d'être for the service, and one which the custodial figures suggest has neither been vigorously accepted or achieved. The cost advantages of community disposals alone have not been enough to justify the existence of the service, hence the pursuit of effective as well as realistic alternatives to custody. By the late 1980s effectiveness had been discovered (McIvor 1990, Raynor 1988, Roberts 1989), with Mid-Glamorgan in particular championing 'Straight Thinking on Probation' (STOP) (Raynor 1988, Raynor and Vanstone 1992, 1994). Effectiveness became the new watch word of the service spawning 'what works' conferences (McGuire 1995), projects (for example Bush 1995, Chapman 1995) and evaluation of effectiveness based probation interventions (Raynor and Vanstone 1994, Raynor et al 1994). By 1994 Raynor and Vanstone were recasting the 'non-treatment' paradigm as one of 'reasoning and rehabilitation' (Raynor and Vanstone 1994, Ross and Fabiano 1988) in which conditional help and crime reduction played a legitimate part along with a respect for persons. However, these persons also included victims and help was defined as help 'consistent with a commitment to the reduction of harm', and legitimate probation tasks were recast as those 'relevant to criminogenic needs, and potentially effective in meeting them' (p.402). The correctional perspective was clear but softened by an emphasis upon the enhancement of 'choice and empowerment both for offenders trying to find alternatives to crime and for communities oppressed by victimisation' (p.402). The essential humanism of the 'non-treatment paradigm' was still claimed although somewhat strained in reality.

The pursuit of effective practice has its roots in what McWilliams has described as the pragmatic era of the Probation Service (McWilliams 1987). It has proved to be an important addition to the service's pragmatic response as it provides the possibility of making a worthwhile contribution to both the criminal justice system and the lives of offenders. It has also facilitated the rediscovery of the rehabilitative ideal via a focus upon the cognitions of offenders and attention to thinking skills (Ross and Fabiano 1988). Effectiveness has also resulted in a growing preoccupation with 'empirically informed practice' (Raynor et al 1994) and evaluation of outcomes particularly in terms of reconviction rates. This broadened the service's understanding of evaluation from the ratio between inputs and outputs to a clearer focus on outcome measures (Everitt and Hardiker 1996, Vennard 1996). In addition, Raynor et al (1994) offered a broader understanding of effectiveness as more than a focus upon those problematic behaviours resulting in reconviction to include work with social problems. Effectiveness could be about both tackling the risk of recidivism and addressing the needs of offenders, a key selling point for officers long positioned as the offender's champion and 'friend'.

Raynor et al (1994) have also warned against the darker aspects of effectiveness; in particular the possibility of producing mechanistic practice and reducing practitioners to mere technicians. Effective practice is dependent upon strategies for targetting appropriate programmes at offenders, integrity of programme delivery (Hollin 1995), empirically proven methods and practices, and techniques for evaluation. This in itself requires a more managed approach to practice, and as resources have diminished the programme approach to offenders has increased (for example Devon, Hereford and Worcester, South East London). Individualised service delivery between officer and offender is increasingly a thing of the past. Whilst activities which reduce negligent practice, discrimination and unjustified intervention into the lives of others are to be welcomed, the managed approach also has its demerits.

Christie (1993) has noted the power of an increasingly commercialised and managed criminal justice system to objectify offenders, and one might also argue to objectify the workforce. Managers are the interpreters of national policy, practitioners are the instruments of its implementation and offenders are the 'units' to be managed through a process of contact with the agency. McWilliams expressed the impact on the service thus:

An organisational machine was created in which the individual offenders which it processed became units in a framework of policy, and of which no single probation officer could be the representation: the *service* came to define the officers within it, and provided their *raison d'etre* (McWilliams 1987, p.105. Reproduced with the permission of Blackwell Publishers Ltd., Oxford).

By the late 1980s assessment was serving a number of requirements. Most notably the expression of service policy towards the management of its client group. This transformed pre-sentence assessment from an individualised documentary assessment of treatability to a strategic document aimed at influencing sentencers towards desirable outcomes. Framing assessment in this way linked it explicitly to policy expectations, to issues of targetting and resource management, and to classification and management of offenders by status, offence type and group membership. Initially status was determined by 'risk of custody', with those at higher risk receiving more intensive and restrictive alternatives to custody. The bifurcation of serious and non-serious in the 1982 Act's criteria for custody prioritised offence type and tariff position in the classification of offenders for service delivery. In addition, the systemic and group management of juvenile offenders during this decade laid the foundation for the subsequent management of offenders by category.

By 1988 and the Home Office's publication of 'Punishment, Custody and the Community' (Home Office 1988a) in which the service was encouraged to take a similar approach to adult offenders, assessment (in principle at least) was already geared to the identification of seriousness, to matching levels of restriction to levels of seriousness, and to focusing upon offending. Important concepts for risk assessment and risk management were thus introduced. Principally that pre-sentence assessment (and in due course other assessments) should be geared to the identification and classification of offenders based upon a bifurcatory system and the subsequent management of offenders by category and status. This is supported by the notion of matching and targetting interventions and resources, along with the increased acceptance of restriction and control as elements of community supervision (Raynor 1985). Offending and offence type rather than the offender became the focus of attention, creating social distance and weakening individualisation (Christie 1993), coupled with a growing future orientation in both assessments and sentencing. The focus shifted from the alleviation of personal and social distress to the control of future offending behaviour and the reduction of recidivism. In essence minimisation and avoidance of future risks. The era of problem solving and social skills for offenders ushered in by Priestley (1977) is a precursor of many later strategies of risk management for offenders, including the ultimate goal of teaching self-risk management to risky offenders (Bush 1995).

The contemporary Probation Service: risk and public protection

This management of offenders by category has increased in the intervening period. Punishment in the community explicitly marked the transformation of the service '...from a social work agency to a criminal justice agency with a social work base' (Faulkner 1989, p.4), concerned primarily with the management of offenders in the community. The subsequent White Paper (Home Office 1990a) and the 1991 Criminal Justice Act continued the theme of bifurcation, the prioritisation of tariff position expressed as 'just deserts', controlism and restriction under the label punishment, and offence seriousness as the cornerstone of sentencing. Bifurcation and offence type were explicitly linked in the Act's divide between property offences and those of a sexual or violent nature for which non-commensurate and preventative sentencing could be justified. The uneasy response of the Probation Service to the explicit priorities of the Act is well documented (Nellis 1995, D, Smith 1996) and does not require restating here. In brief, the service had been invited 'centre stage' (Faulkner 1989) of a new and managed criminal justice system, but found the role and tasks which went with this somewhat unpalatable.

The Criminal Justice Act established the principle that severity should match seriousness, and this impacted upon pre-sentence assessments. Raynor's earlier principle of blameworthiness, and individualisation within aggravating or mitigating circumstances was adopted (Raynor 1980), capitalising upon the best practice principles of the justice style reports of the late 1980s (Raynor et al 1994). Whilst the subsequent 'u-turn' of the 1993 Act weakened the constraints upon custodial sentencing (Nellis 1995), key principles for a risk penalty were established. Preoccupation with future harmful behaviours was given legal validity in section 2 (2) b, and public protection and harm reduction were prioritised as penal policy objectives. Harm was defined in line with the bifurcatory process as physical or sexual harm (section 1 (2) b) and the offender was recast as the perpetrator of risks to others. Carlisle (1988) and the subsequent early release arrangements adopted similar principles. This was paralleled by increasing attention to the rights of victims (Victims Charter, Home Office 1990).

In due course National Standards (Home Office 1995), particularly on the preparation of Pre-Sentence reports, focused assessments on the offender's risk of recidivism and risk of harm status rather than upon the offender's risk of custody status. How this was to be achieved other than through the 'report writer's professional judgement of the risk of reoffending and the risk of harm to the public which the offender...now poses.' (Home Office 1995, p.11) was not clear. However, it was recognised that such 'risk estimates' should not be '...confined to cases of violent or sexual offences where there is a risk of serious harm to the community.' (Home Office 1995, p.11). This signalled the desirability of assessing risk in all cases and not just in those which obviously threaten public safety. However, the categorisation of risk in section 1 (2) b of the act was pervasive. Whilst National Standards acknowledged that a risk estimate had two dimensions: 'the nature and seriousness of possible further offences, and the likelihood of their occurring' (Home Office 1995, p.11), the distinction between the risk of recidivism and the risk of harm lacked clarity and force. The failure to distinguish between the nature, content and mechanisms for the prediction of recidivism and the prediction of dangerousness has permeated many subsequent policy and practice responses since (Kemshall 1996, Kemshall 1997).

Risk and the economic rationality of criminal justice

Recidivism dominated the post 1991 Act policy agenda (Nellis 1995). In this climate effectiveness was set against a 'prison works' philosophy and tougher community penalties (Howard 1993). Whilst actively championed by key figures such as Raynor (Raynor and Vanstone 1992, 1994a, Raynor et al 1994), Roberts (1989) and McGuire (McGuire and Priestley 1985) and finding growing acceptance amongst practitioners (Knott 1995), effectiveness did not become the sole raison d'être of the service. Effectiveness has been subsumed to the risk agenda, in which effective interventions are the vehicles for risk management but are not in themselves the sole purpose and function of the service. Whilst advocated as a means of achieving rehabilitation (Ross et al 1988, 1989), the effectiveness agenda is clearly rooted in the 'correctional curriculum' (Blagg and Smith 1989) and targeted at minimising the risk of recidivism. As such it is an instrument of risk-management aimed at reducing harm and protecting potential victims (Garland 1997). If subsequently ineffective it can quickly be replaced by community surveillance nets (Hebenton and Thomas 1996) or the ultimate control of incarceration.

Pitts (1992), in reviewing the re-emergence of an effectiveness agenda argues that the 'something works' doctrine gives legitimacy to 'government's attempts to rationalise expenditure.' (p. 133). He argues that the 'something works' approach has been hi-jacked to the late 1980s governmental objective of forming a 'rational cost-effective justice system...' based upon a '...'scientific' managerial style pioneered in Westminster...' (p. 135). The correctional approach of juvenile justice and its systems management style provided a commonality of language and objectives between the service and sentencers which government commended for its 'common sense' (Patten 1991). This 'common sense' frame displaced the previously existing humanitarian one for the service (Nellis 1995, Rutherford 1993), and provided a supposedly uncontentious and unifying frame for policy objectives in which consensus could be achieved by appeals to 'common sense' and reasonableness (Pitts 1992). Drawing upon the work of King (1991), Pitts argues that the foregrounding of 'common sense' as the dominant policy perspective is achieved through the use of legal discourse to resolve what would otherwise be the competing claims of social science 'experts'. Diversity and complexity of competing knowledge claims (Rorty 1989) are resolved by selecting only those which support the legal framing of the issue. This has been the case with effectiveness which, not withstanding its 'something works' efficacy, has well supported a penality of individual responsibility for crime, 'just deserts', and bifurcation.

Risk penality following the 1991 Act also marked the formalisation of a differing approach to social regulation which itself undermined the effectiveness agenda. Garland (1997) has argued that the dominant rationality of crime control pre the late 1980s was a social one in which the social regulation of offenders was achieved through their reintegration and normalisation. The problem of crime was constituted as a social welfare one located at the level of individuals and families in need of help and support. Such problems could be alleviated by welfarism and social engineering delivered through the expertise of the professional. However, crime is no longer constituted as a problem of individual deviants or families but as a problem of opportunities for criminality and distribution of crime risks within the population as a whole and how they should be managed

(Reichman 1986). In this form of social regulation effective practice becomes only one component in the strategic management of crime opportunities (O'Malley 1992, Reichman 1986). Other components such as 'zero tolerance', restriction of opportunities, incarceration and surveillance nets also have their place.

This change in social regulation and crime control has been accompanied by what Nellis (1995) has termed 'benevolent corporatism'. In essence, the characteristics of this corporatism are increased centralised state power and managerialism as techniques by which the centre controls the periphery. Policy is centralised and administrative decision making is preferred over professional. 'Commonsense' and populism inform policy rather than expert opinion (Garland 1997). Nellis (1995) and other commentators (Pratt 1989, Pitts 1992, Rutherford 1993) have argued that this corporate benevolence or 'expedient managerialism' is the mechanism by which the new economic rationality of penality is legitimised and delivered.

Within the managerial mode of corporate benevolence, correctional technology has played its part in supporting the development of an economic and pragmatic response to justice issues. However, in order to gain legitimacy for 'corrections' and for the policy that some offenders at least could be both punished and corrected in the community (Home Office 1990a), the delivery of such corrective programmes by the Probation Service had to be evaluated. Evaluation and effectiveness have formed a striking partnership, coupled with a proceduralisation and routinisation of service interventions in order to investigate and validate worker activities (Roberts et al 1996). The competent technician has replaced the diagnostic expert, and the knowledge base of the profession has been redrawn and functionalised towards the provision of objective, scientific and effective interventions (Coleman 1989, Davies et al 1989). Technical rationality has superseded professionalism as the legitimation for worker activities (Pitts 1992). This development in penal policy and probation work has been paralleled in child care policy and the subsequent responses of those working in statutory child protection (Parton et al 1997).

Technical rationality (Habermas 1968, 1976) has also contributed to the largely uncontentious, depoliticised presentation of risk management in criminal justice, in which risk management is presented as a problem of appropriate techniques rather than as a moral enterprise within potentially conflicting knowledge claims. This is exemplified by the Association of Chief Officers' statement on risk (ACOP 1994) which devoted remarkably little space to discussion of the moral imperatives or understandings of offenders and crime implicit in the risk based penality other than to sound a cautionary note about the service's (in)ability to prevent risk (p.1). After locating the task within the legislative and policy context of the 1991 Act and the 1995 national standards, the document focuses upon issues of implementation and exemplars of 'best practice' guidance. Similarly the Inspectorate's thematic report (HMIP 1995) presented the issue of implementing the risk penality as one of practice regulation and increased managerial vigilance. By the time of the Inspectorate's 'Public Protection' conference in March 1996 and the draft Inspectorate guidance (HMIP 1996), the reduction of risk to a matter of correct management and practice technique was set. The title 'public protection' set the tone, and along with key documents such as the thematic report, national standards 1995, a further victims charter (Home Office 1996), a new three year plan for the Service (Home Office 1996a), and the publication of: 'Protecting the Public-The Government's Strategy on Crime in England and Wales' (Home Office 1996b), clearly signalled the new raison d'être to the service.

The impact upon local service assessment procedures and practices has been marked. Area services have developed local policies and procedures to standardise the practices of workers and middle managers and this has been supported by a central concern to improve and standardise the technique of risk assessment. This was exemplified by the development of the statistically based Offender Group Reconviction Scale launched by Probation Circular 63/1996, and the investigation of other assessment instruments aimed at standardising and regulating the professional judgements of staff in line with desired expectations (for example the LSI-R Andrews and Bonta 1995). This was coupled with a Home Office recognition that highly structured assessment procedures could assist with the allocation of diminishing resources upon more rational and objective criteria than the personal professional judgement of officers (Burnett 1996).

If resources are to be allocated on a bifurcatory principle of high risk and low risk then it is essential that risk is reliably and consistently identified in every case. In addition to performing a function of reliable and consistent identification of risk, assessment must also perform a 'triage' function, establishing levels and grades of risk at initial screening. How to develop and implement a method of triage which will be appropriately undertaken by staff in all cases and stand the test of public scrutiny in the light of 'something going wrong' has tasked probation and Home Office personnel alike (Kemshall 1996b).

This problem has in part been addressed by the de-professionalisation of decision making and the rise of case management. Pitts (1992) argues that this has reduced assessment to a technical task rather than a professional problem, and distinguishes between the two thus:

> A professional has a hand in defining the problem and determining the response that will be made to that problem. A technician, by contrast, applies techniques devised by somebody else to problems defined by somebody else. Professionals and technicians must both develop skills and techniques but professionals carry an additional responsibility to exert judgement and discernment (Pitts 1992, p.143. Reproduced with the permission of Blackwell Publishers Ltd., Oxford).

A technical approach routinises assessment towards pre-specified ends (for example 'triage'), and is essentially uncontested and more accountable practice. This is exemplified in local areas by detailed practice guidance for risk assessment accompanied by lists of criteria of what to look for in order to categorise offenders as 'high', 'medium' or 'low' risk (for example Inner London Probation Service 1995). Following this categorisation, decision making for case management is often highly prescribed and represented by flow charts of managerially preferred outcomes. Practitioner indecision and doubt about categorisation are dealt with by exhortations to consult the line manager, and decisions are often quality assured by panels of senior managers (Middlesex 1996).

Techniques for standardising assessment also assist with the standardisation of interventions and the programme approach to the supervision of categories of offenders, often replacing individual supervision as the main mode of intervention (for example South East London Probation Service). Within this style of service delivery individual supervision is replaced by case management, into either internal agency based services or brokering into external services.

Risk assessment and risk management are integral to the current economic rationality of penal policy. The impact upon the service has been wide ranging, particularly upon the role and function of assessment. Risk assessment has to fulfil two functions: the enhancement of public protection and the rational allocation of diminishing criminal justice resources. The pursuit of both objectives has resulted in greater regulation of the content and nature of assessment and the assertion of agency control over professional judgement. This has been accompanied by an increase in prescriptive programmes of intervention based upon the 'Something Works' approach, and the allocation of service delivery to offenders based upon their risk status.

Risk in probation policy and practice can be understood as a further pragmatic adaptation to the most recent of penal policy concerns. However, there is a danger in conceptualising the service as a totally reactive body to the whims of changing penal policy, and that risk penality is an essentially post 1991 penal construct. This is to over-simplify matters. Whilst the history of the service should not be understood as an inexorable journey towards risk, the origins of risk in both policy and practice can be identified in earlier service activities. Predominate amongst these is the bifurcatory principle of sentencing, a systems approach to the management of offenders, offence focused practice and the increased objectification of offenders, the rise of a 'correctional curriculum', and the use of assessment to categorise offenders for types of service delivery and level of resource. These changes had already begun to reconceptualise the service as an agency of a wider criminal justice system concerned with the reduction of recidivism, and not as an agency solely concerned with the treatment, help or rehabilitation of individual offenders. By the 1980s the role of the service had been redefined in terms of crime management, setting the scene for a future role in risk management some ten years later.

Part Two: Risk Differences

The following chapters present the data on risk in Probation practice, and present the 'meanings of risk' of probation staff as an antidote to the naive realism of many current risk assessment methods. The data illustrates the interpretive process of assessment, and that even checklists or prescriptive tools require a degree of interpretation (White 1998), and therefore the gap which necessarily exists between assessment methods and their use in the field. The focus is upon the 'sense making' practices of assessors and the knowledge and value base upon which such practices are contingent. Data analysis is rooted in the analytical induction technique of 'Grounded Theory' of theory generation, and chapter eight explores an explanatory model for explaining decision making on risk in probation practice.

Demonstrating the underpinning processes through which probation risk assessors understand their professional world is however not without some difficulties, not least that the researcher's analysis is itself little more than another contingent sense making practice (Silverman 1993, White 1998). Whilst the position stated by Hammersley (1992) that research cannot entirely reproduce reality is accepted, and indeed that competing knowledge claims can exist, the inevitability of 'anarchic relativism' (White 1998) is rejected. Claims to validity were reviewed in chapter one, and those principles hold here. In addition, it is possible to deconstruct and establish the *grounds* to knowledge claims both of researchers and workers, and to evaluate both the nature of these grounds and the action choices they result in. Chapter seven reviews a mechanism for enabling assessors and their supervisors to examine the basis of knowledge claims on risk and a tool to promote self-reflexivity on the process of decision making. The impact of competing knowledge claims on risk on policy and practice in probation, and in particular how conflicting risk discourses may be reconciled is further pursued in part three of the book.

5. Vignettes on Risk: Values and Knowledge in Risk Assessment

This first stage of the research was designed to gather data on the values, beliefs and knowledge which staff (including managers) used in their risk assessment and risk management decisions. The Concise Oxford Dictionary (1995) defines values as: 'one's principles or standards; one's judgment of what is valuable or important in life'. In respect of probation practice, Nellis (1995) defines values as: ' deeply held beliefs about what it is right to do or be' (p.350). Compton and Gallaway (1994) describe professional values as those beliefs which a professsion holds about people and about appropriate ways of dealing with them. In essence, beliefs can be subsumed under values, and the latter can be understood as an expression of those beliefs which inform practice (and management) decisions. Vickers (1978) has expressed this as the 'assumptive values' which professionals draw upon in order to carry out their work. Whilst commentators have often struggled to clearly identify social work or probation values (Nellis 1993, 1995), there is little dispute that probation work is essentially a moral enterprise (Spencer and Ward 1994, 1997), and that values are crucial to the daily life of practice.

Whilst risk itself may objectively be construed as a neutral concept, the subjective belief that a loss, unwanted damage or negative outcome may result is not. As Brearley expresses it:

> Any discussion of risk rests on assumptions about values. The concepts of loss, danger, costs, gains, etc., are all value based in that they rest on beliefs about certain factors or possibilities being good or bad, positive or negative, useful or not useful (Brearley 1982, p.52).

Judgements of both risk and safety are often as dependent upon perceptions of acceptability as upon empirical evidence (Douglas 1986), and in the world of professional practice with risk may '...be reflected in current, or usual practice, or in [their] ideas about good practice' (Brearley 1982, p.51). Such expressions of acceptability are also expressions of value.

Values

Whilst difficult to precisely define within social and probation practice, values can be understood as the beliefs informing strategic choice of actions, and are therefore discernible through such action choices (Brearley 1982, Finch and Mason 1993). However, actions do not necessarily fully reflect expressed values. We do not always do what we either believe or intend. For example, actions can be constrained by inequitable opportunities of choice, limited and unequal power, structural or systems constraints on action, and lack of commitment or motivation. In addition to identifying the values informing practice it is also neccesary to identify the constraints upon their deployment by social actors in the field.

Such constraints can be derived from the policy and agency context within which workers are required to act on risk in situations in which they risk blame. This is particularly so in those complex and uncertain situations in which 'what is correct' may only be known after the event with 'hindsight bias'. For Brearley this professional risk is exacerbated in those situations where guidelines for action are 'generalised, vague, unexplicit and discretionary' (Brearley 1982, p.51).

In these situations, workers must assess and weigh a number of factors, not least the probability of various outcomes, their impact and cost to various individuals, the desirability or otherwise of these outcomes, and the acceptability or otherwise of the risks identified. This involves identifying the range of possible outcomes, calculating their probability, and the seriousness (or cost) of the various outcomes. As Brearley (1982) expresses it: 'decisions are likely to be influenced by a combination of what is known about probability with values held.' (p.53). In risk decision making, values, probability calculations and knowledge play an integral part.

Brearley argued that assessments were the 'messy' products of the interaction of professional value systems and the knowledge base used to frame the assessment problem (Brearley 1982). In this framing he importantly distinguished between objective risk, and the subjective perceptions brought to the estimation of risk by the assessor. This distinction has been the site of much subsequent research (Royal Society 1992), and is recognised as the source of uncertainty in risk decision making.

The difficulty in identifying accurately the range of possible outcomes and the probability of any one of them occuring gives rise to these 'feelings of uncertainty' (Brearley 1982, p.13), and how individuals subjectively respond to risk is in part an expression of how this uncertainty has been resolved. Many tactics can be used (consciously and unconsciously) for such resolution, and this stage of the research was interested in the role of values in 'decision making under uncertainty'.

Responding to uncertainty has been seen as one of the key elements of professional work, with workers responding to: '...novel, indeed apparently unique, situations' (Jones and Joss 1995, p.20). This requires the exercise of both judgment and discretion, a key characteristic of professional activity (Schon 1983). Indeed Walker (1992) has argued that the ability to exercise judgement is a key prerequisite of the competent professional. This stage of the research attempted to establish the basis of such judgments on risk in comtemporary probation practice.

Knowledge

Knowledge can be defined as 'theoretical or practical understanding', but also as knowing 'gained from experience' (Concise Oxford Dictionary 1995). Whilst it can be argued that a knowlege base is essential for any work activity, it has long been argued that professional activity is underpinned by a particular type of knowledge, and that this is not necessarily entirely based in technical/rational knowledge, but can be displayed through action, reflection and experience (Schon 1983). Walker (1992) has argued for three types of knowledge underpinning professional practice: content knowledge defined as the systematic theories informing practice, bodies of procedures and professional information; cognitive processes, literally problem solving techniques; and finally the practical knowledge of the profession as displayed in activities 'on the ground' and often tacitly acquired and used. In the acquisition of such tacit practical knowledge Jones and Joss (1995) make an important distinction between 'learning by experience' and 'learning from experience'. They define learning by experience as learning by doing on a trial and error basis, 'with very little building of models of practice' (p.22). In contrast, learning from experience can mean learning from the collective experience of the profession as well as from one's own practice, and should include reflection, testing and refinement of models of practice.

Technical and reflective knowledge

Such differing approaches to the acquisition and use of professional knowledge can helpfully assist in distinguishing differing types of professional activity. For example, Jones and Joss (1995) associate learning by experience with the didactic, apprenticeship model of craft based professions in which 'know-how' is valued above the application of theory. This is contrasted to technical-expert professionalism, and reflective professional activity. The former is characterised as professionalism based upon technical expertise rooted in the knowledge and use of formal theories, with cognitive processes deemed to be objective and the application of expertise as 'value-free'. Knowledge is derived from empiricist research, and its application is viewed as a matter of appropriate technique and the use of rule-governed procedures. This type of professionalism is particularly exemplified by a functional approach to problem solving and the consistent use of pre-specified competences. Process skills are valued less than rule acquisition, and training is often experienced as both knowledge and rule acquistion, along with socialisation into agency expectations and procedures. In the world of management this approach to professionalism is epitomised by 'management by objectives' and a managerialist concern with outcomes above process, and non-consensual decision making characterised by prescriptive rule governed operations.

The reflective practitioner on the other hand is characterised as a professional engaged in determining the best course of action from a range of options in an uncertain world. Interactions are characterised by their uniqueness, in which the ability to assess a range of probable outcomes and to determine the desirability of competing outcomes is essential. In these situations, what has worked in the past may not neccesarily work in the future, and knowledge (past and current) may be incomplete. Theoretical knowledge is refined through its use, hence there may be a gap between the formal espoused theories of the profession and those 'theories-in-use' as deployed by practitioners in the field (Schon 1983). This can result in uncertainty in the field, and workers resolve this uncertainty through theories in action and the deployment of tacit, practical knowledge to make sense of new situations. In turn, this can re-shape both formal and tacit knowledge, and add to the rules of practice in the field. This stage of the research was concerned with the characteristics of professional activity on risk, and the types of knowledge deployed by risk assessors in their daily practice.

Data collection

Data was collected using Finch and Mason's (1993) vignette technique. Whilst Finch and Mason used their vignettes in a survey format across a large sample, in this study they were employed in an interview format to elicit open ended participant comment. Participants were given the vignettes to work through at their own pace and control of the tape recorder. Six vignettes were purposely chosen from the local area case load to represent a range of common cases and work situations, resulting in an interview of about an hour. This stage took place in late 1994 and early 1995, largely predating local area policy on risk, and to some extent official prenouncements on risk such as the Inspectorate's Thematic Report (HMIP 1995). Presentation of case material to respondents attempted to avoid any implicit or explicit definition of risk or acceptable course of action. Following an initial pilot and minor amendment they were applied across the sample as a whole. The vignettes are reproduced in appendix one, and in the text as required.

The purpose of the vignettes was not to collect quantitative data on the range of respondents' respsonses to the case scenarios. Rather it aimed to collect in-depth data on values, beliefs, and knowledge used by staff in their risk decisions. However, in initially approaching the data, the variability of responses even within individual teams was striking, especially as cases developed in terms of complexity over time. The key question is why do risk assessors make differing decisions based upon the same information? This required detailed attention to the *accounts for their actions* given by respondents, and this is the subject of the rest of the chapter.

Analysis of the data

The process of analytic induction based upon Grounded Theory techniques (Glaser and Strauss 1967, Strauss and Corbin 1990) has been extensively presented in chapter one. The vignette data was open coded using in vivo' codes, derived from participants' own language and meanings to create anintial taxonomy of respondents' accounts of their decisions (Coffey and Atkinson 1996). This produced 124 codes which were then grouped under categories of similarity. For example, those factors most associated with risk were:

- Unpredictability of the offender's character (literally do not know what he/she will do next).

- Motivation of the offender to crime, for example malicious and instrumental.

- Age (young offender as more risky).

- Level of maturity (immature as more risky).

- Gender (women as less risky than men and more likely to be 'at risk').

- Previous convictions.

- Harm to others is likely. This was viewed as primarily risk to staff or to other known victims such as children or previous victims. Potential harm to the public was much less employed. In respect of the sex offender vignette the notion of 'grooming' was used.

It was also possible to analyse the data for knowledge and use of actuarial predictors such as: age, gender, previous convictions; and use of clinical predictors such as personal and social circumstances, motivation and attitude.

In this way it was possible to establish the knowledge; theoretical, practical, and experiential, used to identify risky offenders and how it was strategically deployed in practice. For example:

- Under what circumstances and conditions was information categorisied as indicative of 'risk' and under what conditions was it not?

- What knowledge was drawn upon to make these categorisations and what factors facilitated or inhibited its use?

- What are the rationalities of risk held by workers and managers, and how are these negotiated and deployed in the workplace?

The process was repeated to investigate the values used by the respondents in their accounts of the vignette decision making. The key categories were:

- Trust, that is wishing to display trust in the offender.

- 'Giving the benefit of the doubt', that is presuming that the activities of the offender are legitimate or genuine.

- Fairness, that is wishing to operate in a fair and anti-discriminatory manner towards offenders.

- Ethical considerations, for example about breaches of confidentiality or inappropriate labelling.

- Conceptions about appropriate role and tasks, for example not wishing to act as a 'police officer'.

This provided an overview of the 'assumptive values' (Vickers 1978) used by respondents in their work. As will be demonstrated these values can be characterised as rehabilitative and client orientated on the one hand, and public protection and risk orientated on the other.

The data collected was extensive and highly detailed, and cannot be reproduced in its entirety here. Rather, the data will be presented under the following key themes:

- The construction of offender risk: knowledge, cues and information.

- The type(s) of knowledge used in constructing offender risk.

- The role of values in constructing offender risk.

- The nature of the interaction between knowledge and values in the construction of offender risk in probation practice.

Constructing offender risk: knowledge, cues and information

Analysis of the accounts of staff revealed the factors which they use in defining both the presence of risk and its extent and nature. These can be understood as the cues or case based information which respondents focus upon and treat as important for the process of case assessment. These included the actuarial predictors of age, gender and previous convictions, for example:

> PO 16: ...plus taking into account his age and his present attitude to the offences.

> PO 19: ...because he is such a young offender and I don't know if he has a long record at all...

but also more clinically based cues such as: unpredictability, motivation, maturity, response to supervision, likelihood to harm others, and who the potential victim might be (known and easily identifiable victims were prioritised over risk to the public), for example:

> PO 19: It would depend ...on how he is responding to the probation element of the combination order. If he responds favourably to that the likelihood is that I would follow the initial option...It would depend on if he was keeping the probation appointments...

> PO 19: Clearly it has not brought about a change in attitude as he has still committed offences...

> PO 23: Nothing has changed, he is still offending, he is up for another serious offence...exactly the same, he is not ready to acknowledge his actions and I think the courts will inevitably give him custody.

> PO 25: The man is on a contract of accomodation, there are fears that he may be trying to make contact with the family. That is enough for a warrant.

In case reasoning, both types of indicators were often combined:

> PO 24: He is very immature, he is a 17 year old youth, I would hope that there is potential for him to learn and change and develop which is why it is important for him to have a community sentence which tackles all thoserisks. If he goes into custody his behaviour would be reinforced by similar offenders.

Clinical indicators could be strategically deployed to reinforce intervention choices as above, or for example:

PO 24: Looking at the information I have I would want to know more about the kind of approach he has made to the family home, did he actually enter the property, was he seen in the neighbourhood or what. He has broken the curfew again and he has been warned and secondly it has proved that he is not responding to the treatment requirement of the order so in effect it is not working. Apply for a warrant immediately.

Whilst some factors were more often used in determining the presence of risk, these factors were not uniformly applied by all participants in respect of all the cases, and could be applied differently to differing case scenarios by the same respondent. These differences cannot be attributed to differences in terms of age, gender or length of service/experience in post of the individual respondent. Rather they are more readily explained by considering them as expressions of Rhodes' 'situated rationalities' (1997) bounded by social context and social dynamics. For example, actuarially based indicators were most often used in respect of the young male offender and the sex offender, and clinically based indicators more often in the other vignettes. This suggests that a degree of practice wisdom or knowledge had been accumulated in respect of the actuarial recidivism predictors derived from expert risk rationality. However, they are not necessarily consistently applied to all offenders and to all situations. Knowledge of the relevant indicators does not necessarily result in their technical application.

A key issue in the deployment of risk indicators by staff is the existence of constraints upon their choice of action, and other considerations to be weighed against the risk cues. This is not necessarily a matter of officers lacking the relevant 'expertise', as officers were capable of recognising the relevant risk of recidivism indicators but of deciding differing courses of action as the reasons and responses to case scenario five demonstrated.

Case vignette five:

Paul is a white 17 year old youth. The probation officer is currently preparing a pre-sentence report on Paul for offences of: take without the owners consent and take and drive away, driving whilst disqualified, and driving with no insurance. During interview Paul displays little remorse for his offending, does not seem to recognise the possible danger to others, and is unconvincing about not driving again. However, the offence seriousness score could just place Paul in the top area of the community sentence band.
(The full vignette is reproduced in appendix one).

The major cues for risk identified in case scenario five by respondents were: age, immaturity, previous convictions, attitude to present sentence, presence or absence of motivation to stop offending. However, decisions on courses of action were not based solely upon this information. Other considerations played a part, such as the legal power and authority of the officer to intervene and report the matter to the police; the ethics of doing so in a situation where the evidence of continued offending may not be clear cut; and the desirability of taking such a course of action and whether this was commensurate with the probation officer's role. The following quote illustrates one of these alternative considerations:

> PO 6: I don't know where you stand legally in terms of having somebody observe him driving a car, when we are talking about the breach in terms of him not complying with community service.

These considerations can be conceptualised as constraining factors either upon the assessment of risk or upon subsequent decision making, and can outweigh the importance of actuarial predictors even when they are known and recognised. In effect PO 6 is weighing up the appropriateness of courses of action in a situation of uncertainty, although risk had been identified. In this situation actions are not governed by rules or the application of technical knowledge, rather officers are concerned with the 'correctness' of their actions and their future impact, particularly upon the offender. This is more indicative of reflective knowledge in action than of the proceduralised application of techincal knowledge. 'Correctness' is decided by recourse to values, especially in situations where the fit between the presenting problem and formal theories of explanation is lacking. This also raises the key issue of what types of knowledge are used by respondents in their risk practice, and this is addressed in the next section.

The types of knowledge(s) used in constructing offender risk

Respondents drew upon the technical knowledge of actuarial indicators, but in terms of factors to be considered rather than as statistical factors in a probability calculation. A statistical risk rationality was not in evidence, rather respondents approached risk as a situational and individualised phenomenon:

PO 24: My immediate reaction is that he has probably breached his parole licence and that there is risk present. I think I would probably want to act reasonably quickly. He blames his parents for his prison sentence and given that he has learning difficulties, his ability to change is quite limited.

And actively sought such information where it was absent:

PO 24: ...it is something I would want to investigate further so I would certainly want to know more about the background to the actual fire, whose life was endangered and I would want to know what the family's views were about his release from prison, whether it be to their home or anywhere else.

Risk was not viewed as a static phenomenon, but rather as dynamic and subject to a number of 'it depends', these were situational and individual in nature:

PO 23: I think it very much depends, I would want to know a lot more about where the police are getting their information from, is it concrete proof, suspicions that she is continuing are very vague. I would want to know a lot more information before I parted with mine, because the relationship I have with Joan is confidential and yes I have information that she, at one stage, some months previously did have a [Invalidity] book in her house, but I don't think that is enough to accuse her of something without a lot more information.

PO 27: I would want to know whether Michael is still working, he may not be working and would therefore be entitled to DSS.

PO 13: ...it would depend on what he was saying...It would very much depend on whether I felt there was a risk to his family.

PO13: Again I would have to be looking at the nature of his previous offences of burglary and theft. Were they against the elderly? Were the elderly involved? If they were then I may then take action...what I would do though is certainly discuss the matter with him and find out more about it and perhaps be looking for an ulterior motive in working with the elderly...I probably wouldn't take any action at this stage but discuss it with him and investigate it further with him.

PO 5: It depends on his background, on his kind of previous, on what he has actually said to me and about what actually happened, what these offences are about.

In these fluid situations of risk, professional knowledge is neccesarily incomplete, tacit and practical. In the absence of important knowledge of the situation, respondents seek further information (PO 13), literally 'wait and see (PO 5)', seek advice from colleagues or managers for example:

> PO 5: I think I would have to speak to my senior and say this is the situation what do I do because I have great difficulty with that...Some advice really because I don't think any of these options are right...

Or explore more than one avenue and practically resolve dilemmas:

> PO 5: I couldn't not do anything about it, couldn't not take any action because I think it has got to be raised but I don't know whether I would tell them, I don't think I would do either of those things. I think the most likely would be to try and do it together.

Probation Officer 5 epitomises the process of reflective reasoning in situations of dilemma and incomplete knowledge demonstrated by respondents in the vignettes. In addition to the deployment of differing types of knowledges (further discussed in the next chapter), respondents also resolved difficult decisions by recourse to professional values. The next section examines the role of values in decision making on risk.

The role of values in constructing offender risk

Values have a key role in the framing of assessment problems, and importantly in how actions are chosen for the resolutions of such problems (Brearley 1982, Schon 1983, Strachan and Tallant 1997), particularly in situations requiring discretion and judgement. The responses to case vignette three provide an interesting illustration of the impact of values on risk decision making.

Case vignette three:

Joan is a white 33 year old woman currently on probation for one year for offences of theft and DSS fraud. She is a single parent with 3 children under the age of 10. She has recently lost a part-time job and the extra income this provided. She is waiting for the Department of Social Security

*to process her benefit claims. During a home visit the officer notices an
Invalidity Claim book made out to someone else.
(The full vignette is reproduced in appendix one)*

In decision making on this case principles of 'trust', 'genuiness',
'fairness' and ethical considerations of appropriate action were central.
These can be considered as components of a broader value position of
'respect for persons' in social work (Brearley 1982), and as enshrined in the
rehabilitative ethic of traditional probation casework (McWilliams 1985,
1986), in which the process of interaction with the 'client' is prioritised.
This relationship is viewed as essentially collaborative and consensual
(Jones and Joss 1995), and as essential to positive outcomes in the longer
term (Payne 1997). This is expressed in the respondents' reasons for
decision choices:

> PO 4: Like I said before, I wouldn't want to pursue it like that anyway. I
> think I would just have a general chat about the dangers of doing something
> like that. I'd accept her statement, ...I also think that I'd have probably got
> to know her sufficiently to assess whether or not she was having me on. So
> yes I would accept her statement.

PO 4 places the decision choice firmly within a value frame within
which 'trust', that is wishing to display trust in the offender; and 'giving the
benefit of the doubt', that is presuming that the activities of the offender are
legitimate or genuine, are central. Trust is also seen as integral to the
establishment of a constructive relationship and the impact of supervision.

> PO16: I think it might be helpful to the relationship between the officer and
> Joan to actually be seen to be accepting what she says. I think there is
> something within supervision about taking responsibility for their behaviour
> and I would see this as part of the officer and the client accepting that she
> has responsibility for her behaviour.

Encouraging clients to take responsibility via supervision was set
against a more overtly 'policing' or controlling role, for example in the case
of the DSS fraud:

> PO 22: ...if we can encourage our clients to take responsibility for their own
> actions, in this case to be honest, it is more constructive in the long run than
> us acting as informants.

These factors were often coupled with officer and manager deliberations about the 'genuiness' of the offender per se, for example:

> PSA 1: I think from past experiences and involvement with people you have a gut feeling if you like. Some people who are ...very nice, welcome you to their home and put a good front on, underneath they are very devious...Other ladies that I have met have genuinely been in trouble, they have done the fraud, they don't know how they have got in the situation and they are so remorseful that yes, we do trust them but people like the one I described previously you just can't trust them...Its how they come over to you, I don't know, I think I have a knack of sussing them out very quickly...

Other factors were: fairness, that is wishing to operate in a fair and anti-discriminatory manner towards offenders. For example:

> PO 23: ...He would need a lot of suport in terms of being able to cope back in the community and doing a good piece of work, so he would need a lot of strengthening on that. The other issues that would have to be tackled is how he feels as a Black offender that he is not getting fair treatment by an organisation.

> PO3: ...if he is a Black offender in ...a predominantly white organisation then he is falling into the stereotypes: 'Oh we know he's a burglar and a Black man, that's how they earn their money, so yes he's in danger...I don't want to fall into the telling on his behalf I would much rather that we do it together.

> SPO 3: ...because you have the added hazard of feelings of rejection in a Black person with all the statistics of Black people going to prison more than White people and that sort of stuff. You've got the added sensitivity really within his society and his feelings about it.

Ethical considerations, for example about breaches of confidentiality or inappropriate labelling were also important. For example:

> PO 21: I would withold the information until I had done my own checks.

> SPO 5: I think that I would argue that breach is not appropriate. I am not really clear whether they have given him proper warnings about attending regularly...

Conceptions about appropriate role and tasks were also important contraints upon decision making, for example epitomised by the following:

> PO 4: I wouldn't see it as my job to inform the police of this but I would like the police to confirm their suspicions of what Joan is doing and what Joan tells me may still be legitimate.

> SPO 1: I think I would be reluctant to share the information at a case conference so I suspect I would withhold it at that stage. Police may well have their suspicions but its their job to prove that not mine... I would want to know a bit more about the police's position, what their suspicions are and I suspect that I would communicate it softly to the client, but I think I may not immediately leap in at a case conference to talk about having seen it (the Invalidity book) because I have got no proof that it is anything other than what she says it is.

The appropriateness of role and tasks was particularly pertinent in respect of the vignette of the offender defrauding the DSS, where the appropriateness of disclosure was a key issue for most respondents:

> PO 4: I'd warn Michael that he is risking being breached but I wouldn't do anything about the social security. I don't think its my job to do that. I think it is my job to warn Michael of the risks he is undertaking but I don't see my job as getting involved with the social security.

As SPO 4 expressed it:

> We have always made moral decisions and disguised them as professional ones...and that...information is used to confirm already chosen courses of action.

In addition, respondents who prioritised the process of client interaction also prioritised the offender as the main focus of attention and responsibility:

> PO 4: Also I think it shows a bit of solidarity with John, that you understand his concern and that you are prepared to do it with him, not expect him to do it on his own.

> PO 4: Obviously you would have explained to John that it would have put him in danger and at risk of being accused if anything did happen and then it was found out.

Constraints upon choices of action

Decisions were also constrained by respondents' perceptions of their power to act, that is whether legally empowered or obliged to act in certain situations. This was exemplified in case scenario five quoted above, and also in case scenario two.

Case vignette two:

John is 18 years old. He is currently subject to a one year Probation order for offences of burglary and theft. He reports regularly and is co-operative in supervision. The probation officer supervising the case learns from another probationer that John has started to do voluntary work with the elderly.
(The full vignette is reproduced as appendix one)

In this case, respondents identified a number of 'it depends', in particular the nature of John's previous convictions as well as the intention and genuiness of his present actions:

SPO 6: Clearly the offence of burglary and theft whilst serious might not have been against an elderly person, it might have been a house which was empty...

PO 21: I think voluntary work is different to employment. Because in employment the employer asks you to fill out an application form and I think in voluntary work it is more of a reference...and you don't have to tell them what you are not asked.

PO 26: I think I should discuss with him why he is doing the work, what sort of work it is, what are the risks involved for him and for them.

PO 24: One of the things I would be reinforcing is that I would be prepared to speak on his behalf to give additional information, if I felt it was somebody who could be fairly trustworthy in that kind of situation, had the right motives and wanted to work very hard to get their life back...

These 'it depends' appeared to require high levels of discretion for the resolution of the situation, especially in a situation where there were no clear rules governing worker activities. One senior probation officer clearly recognised the imponderables in the situation:

SPO 3: ...it depends on the voluntary work he is doing. If it takes them into their homes they should have the right to know that he might be tempted and it would have a terrible effect on the elderly who would be trusting him...I think it would not be good for the voluntary organisation to be using an offender with a record without knowingly doing it, they could look very silly if something went wrong.

When asked if the Probation Service had a policy on disclosure of offending history in such situations SPO 3 answered:

SPO 3: I don't know.

This position was reiterated by Assistant Chief Officers in the sample, and it was noted by a Senior Probation Officer (off the tape) that lack of service policy could result in 'fudgy decision making' as officers used their discretion as they saw fit. Perceptions of power and obligation to act are central to the exercise of discretion, and raise key issues about roles and responsibilities, not least how they are perceived and enacted.

Conflicting values in the construction of offender risk

Nowhere do values come into sharper focus than in the exercise of roles and responsibilities. Brearley (1982) distinguishes between three types of responsibility which have applicability here: moral obligation, legal liability, and organisational accountability (p.51). Responsibilities and therefore accountability in each of these areas can conflict, for example officers can feel a moral obligation towards the offenders with whom they have a professional relationship, whilst their organisational obligations might be to implement agency procedures to 'cover the agency' and to avoid legal liability for their employers. Different responsibilities may prioritise differing actions, not all of which will be conducive with the value base of practitioners. This gap is likely to be heightened when organisations introduce new tasks and responsibilities, and alter the main role of its professional workforce. The statutory and policy expectations of public protection and risk reduction now placed upon the Probation Service is an illustration of how shifts in role and responsibilities can result in value disputes.

Victims, public protection and control

Statements prioritising responsibility towards the offender are not entirely new (McWiliams 1992a), nor are statements eschewing a policing or controlling role. However, responses to offender risk cannot be understood as a mere recasting of the traditional 'care-control' debate. The shift in role and task is more fundamental, from the foregrounding of the individual offender to the identification and regulation of groups of offenders to enhance public protection (Feeley and Simon 1992). It is the latter, and its exemplification in protecting individual victims which is now the primary objective of professional activity (Kemshall 1995). Control is not an end in itself but a mechanism to ensure risk reduction and public protection (Garland 1997). Some respondents recognised this function, for example:

> ASW 3: At the present time I would not recommend parole...mainly because of the offence of arson which took place in the family home. The officer could have applied for Jason to go to a hostel but I wouldn't recommend that because of the offence and with the amount of people whose lives could be at risk...

> ASW 2: I would initiate breach. He is obviously not responding to the trust and the order that was given to him. I feel that is why I would go along with the breach before he got into anything worse or endangered somebody.

Also that levels of control and mechanisms of intervention should be commensurate with the risks presented, although how this matching was to take place was not always clear cut:

> PO 13: I would rewarn or recall him, again it would depend upon his attitude, and whether there was a risk to the family...so is he visiting and making telephone calls, are they threatening, or is that Jason wants to get back into the family? Are the family threatened by this? Do they feel at risk? It would certainly depend upon that, if I felt there was any risk to the family then I may recall him, but that would depend really on circumstances and meeting with the family and assessing the risk.

Other respondents recognised the growing priority of victims, especially in situations where they were considered to be particularly vulnerable. This was illustrated by the case scenario on the sex offender and the perceived risk to children:

PO 3: We have a responsibility to the victims in all of the offences which the offenders come to us on probation orders or whatever and we have a responsibility in child protection terms to his daughter.

PO 2: Where and what was he doing, he shouldn't be around children and if he was with the partner or was anywhere near the daughter, if it was that then I would be talking about breach...

PO 2: ...there is a danger to the family, to the girl.

PO 20: I would recommend against parole. For safety reasons I am not giving him the benefit of the doubt...Jason is a danger, he's obviously got a strong grudge against his parents coupled with learning difficulties and his refusal to accept blame and wanting to get even with them, and I think at the moment it is the best solution.

Whilst risk and protection issues were most often referred to in situations in which victims were both individualised and easily recognisable, risk to the public did figure in the reasoning of some respondents, for example in the case of the reckless driver:

PO 24: I think he has always presented as a high risk offender and he has now displayed the fact that he has not only reoffended but has reoffended more seriously, reckless driving is a very serious charge and usually carries a custodial sentence.

However, in priortising victims and public protection the type of risk is important, with risks potentially resulting in physical or sexual harms prioritised above property crime and recidivism per se:

PO 20: Well its dishonesty. He is committing an offence, but may be there is not so much risk to the public, I don't know.

PO 4: I don't think its my job to do that. I think it is my job to warn Michael of the risks he is undertaking...I'd warn him that he is going to be breached (for non-attendance), but I don't see my job as getting involved with the social security.

PO 2: Its just typical, signing on and working. I think I would have to warn him that he is committing an offence, which I always do, and advise him to cease claiming...I don't think I would check that. Not sure if I would inform the DSS.

This is in sharp contrast to the perceived risk of the sex offender and the actions proposed to deal with it:

> PO 2: I would apply for a warrant. Because I don't know where he is and I would be thinking he could be doing anything, with anyone, anywhere, so I would apply for a warrant immediately.

Public protection concerns could also lead to a recasting of the 'client' and to a change in the characteristics of the supervisory relationship as respondents adopted 'protective' responsibilities:

> PO 3: I would be saying to Joan very clearly that in the light of the offences that she is on probation for she needs to be extremely careful about her handling of other people's DSS books...The risks for me are about not sharing and collusion and I am supervising a woman who, at the end of the day, is defrauding people of money...It is important to try and keep a relationship with your client because you can find out a lot of information and discuss it with them and sort of look at their offending behaviour, but I wouldn't keep that like a priest and parishioner relationship, there is no way that I would be colluding with her to commit an offence.

> PO 3: At the end of the day I think my stuff comes from a victim perspective. If I didn't believe in an individual's ability to change then I wouldn't be in the job, so I believe in rehabilitation very strongly, and I also believe that we, as probation officers, as well as our clients are all potential vicitms. So I think it's a game that you have to play. I'm not sitting down and holding this guy's hands whilst he's driving around town and not turning up for the punishment that he has been given...

Probation Officer 3 expresses a potential conflict between responsibility to the client and to victims, describing the management of the potential conflict as a 'game you have to play'. However, the conflict is ultimately resolved through prioritisation of the 'victim perspective'. Within this perspective, the exercise of control to reduce risk effectively is experienced as non-problematic, for example:

> PO 3: Its about the not engaging as well. Its about how we see enforcement action. I have got the highest breach rate in the team and I find I do use enforcement action in it's totality quite a lot because it is not just about breaching an order and getting it revoked, it can also be a warning and sometimes its like I need someone with a bigger stick to give the warning to

the client...If the man was in prison and he ran away they would send people out to look for him, just because he is on a community sentence doesn't necessarily mean that he should get away with it.

Some respondents also recognised that this role change and reconceptualisation of the work was relatively new:

PO 24: I think that a number of years ago some people would have said it would have been invading somebody's private situation too much to be investigative about it, it would be negative, showing that you don't trust the client, you are actually looking for fault with them and expecting them to reoffend...That is very much like a police role and I think sometimes because of our understanding of people and their situations we have to strike a balance...

Risk to workers: blame and censure

In addition, respondents identified risks and responsibilities towards themselves, and therefore the necessity of implementing agency expectations or procedures:

PO 3: The risks are that he will do the 'my probation officer knew' bit, that the client has told me and I would record it, what I have said to them, that I do report on a regular basis on people who have been done for DSS fraud and I tell them upfront that it is an offence and all the rest of it and I record it.

PO 3: If it comes to the worst and she does commit an offence...its 'my probation officer knew I had the book, I told my probation officer' and then its going to be serious that's why I'm talking about recording it. I may bring it to my senior's attention just to say that it's around. I can't prove it, can't do anything, I'm not out there to do the police investigation but I have tackled it with the client. To cover my own back at the end of the day.

PO 23: Because at a later date clients have often said when they are caught, 'I told my probation officer', so in my documentation it is clearly set out that I have told the client what his responsibilities are and what the consequences of his actions are...clearly I have warned him and I am not colluding with him.

The avoidance of blame and agency censure, along with adopting a clear non-collusory stance with their 'clients' is important for these respondents in their supervisory relationships. These considerations can outweigh concerns with the needs of the offender, the preservation of the supervisory relationship, or rehabilitative casework aims. Awareness of public protection responsibilities, agency expecations on this issue, and perception of self-risk 'if things go wrong' are reflected in the decision choices of respondents especially in those case situations where risk of physical or sexual harm is viewed as 'clear cut', and victims are easily identified. Decision choices are made, especially in situations of conflicting responsibilities (see PO 3 above), by adopting courses of action which fit with an existing value frame, for example Probation Officer 3's 'victim perspective', or which will avoid later censure and blame.

Value frames in action

However, value frames do not operate in a 'neat and tidy' fashion. Whilst it is possible to identify expressions of a rehabilitative/client primacy value base, and a public protection/victim safety one from the data, their operation in practice is often fluid, dynamic and interactive as well as conflictual. Respondents drew on both value frames to determine both assessment problems and their resolution:

> PO 2: for me it is about making sure that he is telling them everything that needs to be told, and then after doing that it would be about support.

> PO 6: ...so I'd want to, within the context of the licence, use that restriction to actually give him some proper support but also protect his family as well.

> SPO 1: ...because its about giving the client the benefit of the doubt...If she has offered to do that she's offered me an explanation which could be quite reasonable. I'm not there to police in that way, I would just need to hear what she had to say if she's offering me the opportunity of confirming that then I would do that. Clearly she has to be aware that any kind of suspicions of mine, given the nature of her offence, are real because that's the offence she has been convicted of and there might be a possibility that she would in fact resort to that sort of offence again. I would need to confirm that she wasn't offending again.

That offender primacy and rehabilitative values are strongly influential in risk assessments should not be surprising. The service has a long history of indiviudalised assessment of the offender and of interventions rooted in the one to one relationship. However conceptualised, the offender has long been the site of the work (McWilliams 1992a). Victims and the public are relatively new discoveries (Home Office 1990), and whilst the differing priorities accorded to offender, public and victims may have been changing within Home Office statements (see for example the Three Year Plan, Home Office 1992), this has not necessarily translated to either local management or practice level. Visible, personalised victims or vulnerable groups such as children are more easily conceptualised as being 'at risk' than the nebulous concept of the 'public'. Literally being required to protect everyone is more difficult than protecting a known victim, and can easily be over-ridden by the more visible and pressing concerns of the individual offender in front of the officer.

This offender - public dichotomy is well summed up by the following comment of an officer on one of their own cases in which the difficulty is well revealed:

PO 25: ...he (the prisoner talking about his parole recommendation), actually did verbalise this: 'you are supposed to be helping me, you are supposed to be on my side, you are supposed to be getting me out'; now...I'm really intrigued by how, with all my knowldege of this case and the fact that I have very regular contact with the victim, his ex-wife, I'm still pulled back into this (sympathy for the offender). Its such a powerful thing that we have, this inability to hold the balance between the public and the offender, and the fact that we still see ourselves as the offender's representative.

Interviewer: Why do you think thats so?

PO 25: Two things come immediately to mind. One is, I think very few of us come into this seeing it as a broad universal thing about serving society and wanting to make society a better place. I think most of us come into this much more for helping the offender right, ...and I think we only grow ...as the years go by into a strong sense that my role is much more one about a broader criminal justice system and protection of the public as well as attempting to rehabilitate and not stigmatise the offender.

Implicitly the comment recognises that the probation service has a strategic role to play within a wider criminal justice system and that rehabilitative concerns now have to be balanced against public protection ones. Interestingly Probation Officer 25 recognises that within the day to day reality of practice this can quickly be forgotten. Payne's interactive triad of worker, client and agency within which 'social work gets done'

(Payne 1997) is exemplified by Probation Officer 25's perceptive comment about her/his own practice.

The comment also represents the rehabilitation - risk dichotomy perceived by respondents in the vignettes. The conflict between rehabilitative aims and public protection ones should not be surprising. Whether by reclaiming sinners through religious zeal or by treatment, the service has a strong and lengthy rehabilitative ethic (McWilliams 1985, 1986, 1987,1989, 1992a). Whilst the 'new penology' of the 1990s has prioritised the risk management of offenders (Feeley and Simon 1992), the policies of this new penology have to be implemented within the context of existing practices and the value base of the community practitioners (Schon 1983, Vickers 1978). This community of practitioners can also include managers as the following indicates:

SPO 1: (on whether to inform the DSS of a fraudulent claim): ...I feel very uncomfortable about informing the DSS. The middle ground for me is to make it clear to a client and hope that nothing happens as a result of that.

Interviewer: Whats the uncomfortableness about?

SPO 1: Because I know he is committing an offence and I know its illegal but its a system that doesn't pay them enough and I can't blame anybody for trying to get more out of the system because I think the system is unjust, so I go through the motions.

Probation managers are largely promoted from within the organisation and will necessarily share some of the assumptive values of the community of practitioners. This can be problematic if managers assume that they have an expertise on risk which they do not have, or that their policy formulation and implementation will be immune from more traditional values. Whilst risk may be the explicit subject of policy and practice discussions, values and service priorities are often the implicit subject of such discussions and disputes. Consensus, even at managerial level, should not be presumed. At senior management level these disputes can be revealed in discussions about the allocation of resources:

Interviewer: Do resources follow risk?

ACPO 3: I don't think they do.

Interviewer: Why?

ACPO 3: One of the factors is that some of the provision we currently have was set up at a time when resources were more available than they are now and at one level you could say that we are stuck with them or we have them and reducing the input shifts the usefulness of the provision...The other factor is that there may well be differing views about where resources should go overall.

Interviewer: So there aren't always common assumptions about resource and risk?

ACPO 3: Resource and risk and everything else!

Strategic reasoning on risk

This lack of consensus on risk also reminds us that a range of assumptive values can exist in organisations and that 'practice ideologies' rarely exist in a pure form (Hardiker 1977). Respondents expressed more rehabilitative and offender primacy views in some vignettes rather than others, and cannot easily be classified as entirely risk or rehabilitative oriented. The sex offender vignette resulted in the most consensus, both about the nature of the risk and subsequent interventions. Whilst one might speculate that agency registers and procedures has made this area of work largely uncontentious, this was mentioned in a very few cases as a (negative) incentive to do things. Rather the key characteristics of respondents' accounts in this case were: easily identified victim, child victim as especially vulnerable, acceptance that victims' rights and needs outweigh those of offenders, and that protection outweighs rehabilitation. However, this case is not typical of the vignette responses which display more uncertainty and less consensus. Sex offender work has been characterised by the foregrounding of the victim, clear conceptualisation of the offender as the perpetrator of risks, and a concern with protection issues (McEwan and Sullivan 1996). This has not been the case with other areas of probation work, and has resulted in both policy and practice difficulties when a change in focus has been required (for example in throughcare work with victims, Johnston 1997).

That respondents can display contrasting value bases in their case based reasoning is not necessarily indicative of confused thinking, but may be indicative of strategic reasoning to achieve desirable ends. For example, Probation Officer 3 stated that:'my stuff comes from a victim perspective...'

in discussing the case of the reckless driver, and yet later in the vignette offered the following reasoning on a Pre-Sentence Report proposal to the court:

> PO 3: ...the court is saying custody is inevitable so part of the job is to argue if possible for consideration to take into account Paul's age and all the rest of it, and to influence the judge to err more leniently...I would be very up front about that. I would also be stating that Paul was on a Probation Order for a very short period of time.

This illustrates the type of strategic reasoning and strategic decision making officers engage in depending upon the purpose of the risk assessment, who it is for, and what they view 'the job is'.

The interaction of knowledge and values in the construction of offender risk

Decision making on risk is located within a complex interaction of the knowledge base and value system. The extent and content of knowledge can vary in any assessment situation, and is mediated by the value system of the risk assessor. These values are not the individual beliefs of each assessor, but have a commonality within the community of practitioners, and function as an 'appreciative system' (Vickers 1978) through which respondents make sense of the practice situation and decide upon professionally acceptable goals and standards of action. In essence, staff resolve the 'indeterminate zone' of messy assessment problems through the use of assumptive values. Assessment problems are framed through this value system and resolved according to its primary principles. For example:

> SPO 1: On the information given here if I had seen the (Invalidity) book I would have raised it with the client straight away as to whether she was in fact eligible for that benefit and what it was doing there and would have listened to what she had to say first of all, before doing anything else, ...because there could be a good reason and I think the client has got a right to be able to explain it. I feel it would be dishonourable to leap to the worst possible conclusion. I might like, in fact, to leap to that conclusion but I think she should be given a chance to explain herself and depending on what information she comes up with would inform what I did next...its giving the client the benefit of the doubt I suppose.

Risk assessments can be understood as a product of an interaction between knowledge of risk from case based cues and information, the assesor's value base, and concerns about impact, blame and censure as the following piece of reasoning shows:

> PO 3: At this stage I would certainly need more details about the offence and what work Jason has been doing since imprisonment and of course the family's attitudes, whether or not they want him back in the house...looking at his reasons for committing the arson and criminal damage and whether or not those were still around for him or whether or not they had been resolved. Working with the family, I would be worried if there were any young children in the family, etc., and working with them to sort of bring them together...Hopefully there would have been some sort of condition to the parole licence, I see from the scenario that he is returning home frequently so obviously there should have been some conditions so that could be dealt with...so that would have been an important aspect of the parole licence. To keep him in check really and to monitor and control, which is part of parole at the end of the day...I wouldn't like to wake up to a fire in my house in that situation, so he is a danger to his family and danger to himself.

In this piece of reasoning on decision choices the officer is actively seeking certain risk cues exemplified by the statement: '...I would need more details about...' followed by a wide ranging list focused largely upon situational factors. Potential victims can be clearly identified: '..I would be worried if there were any young children in the family...' combined with protective values. Role responsibilities are clearly stated, for example the expected conditions and purpose of a parole licence, and the concluding line expresses fear of impact and censure should the worst happen: '...I wouldn't like to wake up to a fire in my house in that situation, so he is danger to his family and danger to himself.' The vividness of the impact of the risk should it occur, and that the risk assessor can imagine it impacting upon them also contributes to the easy identification of risk (Combs and Slovic 1979, Tversky and Kahneman 1973, 1974).

Risk assessments as the product of knowledge-value interaction

This example raises the important question of how knowledge of risk expressed as cues and information, and values interact to produce risk assessments? By examining which of the risk cues were present when, to what extent, and with what values, and with what decision outcomes,

(NUDIST facilitates such searches and provides numerical as well as textual information), it was possible to make some intial hypotheses:

- Low level of risk cues combined with a high level rehabilitative/client primacy values produces a low risk assessment and minimal intrusion intervention strategies.

- Low level of risk cues combined with a low level of rehabilitative/client primacy values produces a low risk assessment and minimal intrusion intervention strategies.

- High level of risk cues combined with a low level of rehabilitative/client primacy values produces a high risk assessment and high intrusion intervention strategies.

- High level of risk cues combined with a high level of public protection values produces a high risk assessment and high intrusion intervention strategies.

This indicates that risk assessments are the product of an interaction between level of risk cues and level of rehabilitative/client primacy values and level of public protection values.

However, when reapplied to the data, negative cases led to further refinement of the hypotheses. Rehabilitative values can be overridden by the presence of other factors, for example respondents' perception of blame or censure should something go wrong, fear of physical risk to self, or fear of managerial sanction if certain tasks were not done. These factors can be conceptualised as incentive factors, literally providing a (usually negative) incentive to staff to do something.

Respondents construct and use the phenomenon 'offender risk' along a continuum of 'no risk to high risk' dependent upon the presence or absence of certain risk cues. These cues can be diminished or outweighed by rehabilitative values such as 'giving the benefit of the doubt', demonstrating 'trust', or accepting the 'genuiness' of the offender. Risk cues can be given added importance if combined with incentive cues like blame or self risk, and these can outweigh rehabilitative values, for example in the sex offender vignette where officers referred to agency policy or sanctions if certain things were not done:

PO 24: I would be discussing with my manager about the appropriateness of instigating breach proceedings...

SPO 6: Apply for a warrant immediately. We have lost him so we need to be seen that we are acting decisively, to apply for a warrant.

In these situations, public protection concerns and the fear of blame could over-ride initial perceptions of low risk, for example Probation Officer 4 in deciding action on the sex offender:

PO 4: Warn him in terms of breaching the hostel curfew and explain that I wouldn't breach him, it depends why he has broken it...

And then:

PO 4: I am veering towards breach proceedings...it would depend but I would certainly be leaning towards breach proceedings.

And finally:

PO 4: I'm very reluctant to breach people but this is about as far as I go...I gave him a last chance last time, there is a danger to the family, to the girl.

Values, both rehabilitative and protective functioned as 'intervening conditions' (Strauss and Corbin 1990) in the assessment of risk and in subsequent action choices, but to differing degrees. In the uncertain and indeterminate zone of risk assessment, values are crucial to framing the problem and its resolution. This is especially so in situations where calculating the probability of possible outcomes is subject to numerous variables and 'it depends', and where the desirability of possible outcomes is itself open to conflict and debate.

Operational knowledge and situated practical reasoning

Investigations into medical clinical assessments have established uncertainty as central to the medical assessment encounter (Adamson 1997). A similar concept has already been posed for social work assessments (Brearley 1982, Schon 1983). Uncertainty is associated with 'incomplete theoretical understanding' (Adamson 1997, p.135), and incomplete understanding of why and how particular outcomes are achieved. Such uncertainty can be hidden by routinising practice and reducing dilmmas of problem framing and solution to bureaucratic procedures (for example checklists). However, in the absence of such techniques to remove uncertainty, practitioners resolve the 'indeterminate zone' of assessment through the application of their own normative ideals. In effect, our risk assessors (including managers) both state what the 'problem' ought to be and how it should be resolved. In this sense, knowledge about risk is rarely 'just applied' but is mediated by other concerns of value, strategic intent, and avoidance of blame or self risk. The application of knowledge in a case and how the problem is subsequently framed and resolved is a negotiation across a number of factors within Payne's (1997) triad of worker, client and agency expectation. Hardiker (1977) conceptualised officer ideologies as 'operational philosophies' because 'workers rarely carried out an ideology in pure form in practice' (p.152), and a similar conclusion can be drawn about the practice application of risk knowledge.

In addition, offender risk assessors are also drawing upon assumptive values known and operationalised from within the community of practitioners. Whilst in terms of 'ideal types' it is possible to identify a set of values which prioritise rehabilitative work aims and clients' rights and needs; and a set of values which prioritise public protection and the rights and safety of victims/public, again these do not operate in a 'pure form'. It is possible to identify some respondents as more oriented towards one set of assumptive values than another from the presence or absence of such values in their accounts, however this is too simplistic as respondents do not operate such value sets consistently across the vignettes. Key features for the operation of the public protection value set are: easily identifiable victims, vulnerable victims such as children, offence type as self-evidently risky (e.g. sex offending), and acceptance of the offender as a perpetrator of risks on others rather than as the person 'at risk'. Without these key features the assessment process is more likely to involve both sets of values (for example PO 3 in case 5), with respondents balancing the risks presented against the rights and needs of offenders, and 'weighing up' action on risk against what they perceive to be professionally desirable case outcomes. For example:

(Case two: after finding out that an offender on probation for theft and burglary has obtained voluntary work with the elderly, respondents were asked what they would do next.)

SPO 1: I find this one harder to be clear about. He is a Black offender and it depends upon the nature of the organisation that he is working for. Working on the assumption that it is basically a white organisation that does affect my thinking about what I would do. I'm struggling with why I would want to tell them at this stage. Again it comes back, for me, as to the nature of his offence, whether that was anything to do with the elderly in their homes, particularly the elderly...if I could think of something else to do I would do it. I wouldn't be happy about telling the organisation without his permission. I think I would go for getting the client to do it and then checking but I'm not entirely clear about that, I feel a little hesitant about that and the thing that makes me hesitant is he is a Black offender and he doesn't expect to be treated fairly by the organisation and I think I would have to listen to that. So if I could think of something else to do, but I can't, but if I could I would look for that choice. I suspect I would have to go for instructing him to do it, time limited and then checking with the organisation, but again I'm not sure.

The defintion and assessment of risk is rooted in this practical reasoning of risk assessors in which many factors play a part. Risk decision making is a 'situated activity', that is located in a particular social setting and embedded in the sense making practices that risk assessors use to navigate the indeterminate nature of their assessments, and subject to many 'it depends'. Risk is constructed from this practical reasoning, and is not a product of the mere application of knowledge or 'risk cues'. Whilst the advocates of technical instruments (including managers and central policy makers) presume that risk is both self-evident and uncontested, and knowable through the correct application of technical assessment instruments, the vignette data suggests otherwise. Risk is not self-evident but is arrived at through a complex process of reasoning. What constitutes a risk and who is at risk is defined through this reasoning and can vary even when the same information and case work options are provided. This is not necessarily because risk cues are unknown, but because they are mediated by other factors in the assessment process. What may be at issue in risk assessment is not what officers do not know and how this should be corrected, but rather the nature of the assessment process itself. The vignettes demonstrate that the real world of practice assessment is as much a process of value framing and acting out the normative ideals of practice as it is about knowledge application.

Reasoning and practice values

The reasoning of respondents' demonstrated the presence of two sets of practice values or 'appreciative systems' as Vickers dubbed it (Vickers 1978) to guide both practice goals and acceptable professional conduct. The present position on risk practice in probation is an example of a traditional 'appreciative system' of offender rehabilitation being superceded by a public protection one. This is not to say that in reality they may not co-exist, indeed we see respondents use both in their vignette reasonings, but it is clear that the differing appreciative systems can result in differing categorisations of offenders and differing case management strategies. These categorisations and subsequent interventions may not always coincide with those considered to be desirable by senior agency managers or central penal policy makers.

Technical risk assessment instruments appear to resolve the issue of desirable practice because they carry a managerial expectation of practice, and avoid contentious disputes over appreciative systems by obscuring value choices behind checklists and weighting systems. The choices and weightings become self-evident, i.e. generated by the 'objective' application of the instrument itself, thereby reducing the reasoning of workers and the scope for moral debate. This eptitomises the homeostatic approach to risk management which seeks to replace reasoning and judgment with the application of rules, procedures and technical instruments.

However, the reasoning of SPO 1 above is not exceptional, and demonstrates that respondents actually adopted a collibrationist approach to risk assessment and its management. That is approaching the practice situation of risk as an essentially uncertain exercise in which risk can come in many forms, change over time, have differing consequences for different people, and needs to be balanced against competing concerns. The reasonings quoted above illustrate the 'trade-offs' and balancing endemic to this approach. In collibrationist risk assessment, issues of failure arise not because of mis-calculations per se, but because of a mis-fit between the 'trade-offs' made by frontline risk assessors and those which (usually with hindsight) managers think are desirable. This mis-fit will be particularly acute in situations where competing value frames and appreciative systems are in operation. The vignette data suggests that this is the current state of probation practice on risk.

Conclusions and implications for policy and practice

The chapter has reviewed the reasoning accounts given by respondents in their assessment of risk across a range of cases. The data illustrates that real value dilemmas exist for all staff engaged in risk work, and that risk assessments contain the potential for contradiction and dispute, particularly in situations of low knowledge and uncertain probability. What constitutes a risk and how it is to be identified is variable, and this level of difference is not neccesarily easily resolved by recourse to increased knowledge or probability assessment methods. Whilst increased knowledge, including of probability, may increase worker awareness of the range of possible outcomes and their probability, this alone does not resolve the more difficult issue of how the (un)desirability and (un)acceptability of the likely outcomes is to be interpreted and weighed. In essence this is a question about whether the risk is acceptable or requires attention, and at what level of intrusion.

The vignette data demonstrates that there is a lack of consensus about the acceptability of certain risks and how they should be dealt with, and of what constitutes a tolerable risk outcome and what does not. This is resolved on the ground as a matter of value by both practitioners and managers, and at present illustrates an organisation which is collectively unsure of its value base. This is particularly problematic in the area of risk, as it will result in varying assessments of risk based upon the same information, and therefore variable risk management responses. Such discrepancies may well appear indefensible with hindsight in the light of negative outcomes, and attract blame and censure for individual members of staff who may however believe that they have acted 'in good faith'. In resolving such discrepancies, value debates are essential, as is greater articulation and consensus about what the desirable outcomes on risk practice actually are, for whom and in what circumstances.

Collibrationist aproaches to risk management emphasise open debate and participation in deciding acceptable outcomes. In this approach the focus of attention is not upon the setting of prespecified outcomes for every eventuality (a near impossibility in probation practice), but upon the processes, organisational as well as individual, by which decisions are taken. In effect, the emphasis is upon 'structuring the way that decisions are taken' (Royal Society 1992, p.166), and quality assurrance systems for learning from and improving decision making at all levels of the organisation. Central to this approach is moral debate and open discussion of the necessary uncertainties of practice, and a degree of tension between conflicting positions. In marked contrast to the homeostatic approach, collibrationism places emphasis upon processes rather than procedures, and in probation practice this would require more attention to value discussions, mechanisms for achieving consensus on desirable outcomes, training on knowledge and decision making skills rather than on procedures, quality assurrance mechanisms including staff supervision, and practice guidance which pays attention to the process of reasoning rather than the mere imposition of rule-governed procedures.

Finally, reasoning and judgement cannot be eradicated, especially in assessment situations of great uncertainty and numerous 'it depends'. In this situation it is essential to understand the knowledge base as well as the value base underpinning such judgements. Whilst this has been partially discussed in this chapter, the following chapter explores in more detail the nature of current practice knowledge or 'wisdom' on risk.

6. Risk and Practice Wisdom: The State of the Art

The application of knowledge to the practice of social work and probation has long been a thorny issue (Carew 1979, Payne 1997, Sheppard 1995), not least what constitutes such knowledge, how it should be taught and subsequently used by the profession (Sheldon 1978). Indeed, the claim to professional status has itself been seen as highly dependent upon the establishment of a credible knowledge base (Nellis 1993, Sheldon 1978). In this context professional knowledge has been defined as 'theoretical orientation' (Jones and Joss 1995), in other words a:

> set of systematic underpinning theories in the knowledge base, their degree of sophistication and, importantly, the values attached to them. Again these vary between and within professional groups. Similarly, there is variation in the methods of application of knowledge, and in particular whether or not there is an implicit or explicit practice theory which governs this process. Practice theory allows the integration of theory with practice and puts an emphasis upon the professional values of practice. (Jones and Joss, 1995, p.21).

As has been demonstrated in the previous chapter, a consistent value base for risk practice is not present in the organisation currently, and informal rules of practice and values held by staff can conflict with formally stated and externally promoted practice expectations. This can result in knowledge being variably applied as differing pragmatic and sometimes tacit practice theories are used. This raises the important issue of the types of knowledges used by probation staff in their risk work, and the current 'state of the art' in risk knowledge.

Data collection and analysis

Data was collected through in-depth interviews and observation of practice and management encounters. The interviews took place in late 1995 early 1996 and paralleled the publication of Her Majesty's Inspectorate Thematic report on Dangerousness (HMIP 1995) and the circulation of local service area draft guidance on risk.

The interview schedule is reproduced as appendix two, and 120 hours of observation across the teams was carried out and contemporaneous notes were kept. In-depth qualitative interviews have an established history in exploring both beliefs and knowledge about risk, particularly in health care (Cornwell 1984, Blaxter 1983), however a number of limitations were encountered in their use.

The accounts given of their practice by respondents were produced in the particular arena of an interview with a researcher, and as such are prone to some extent to the 'public account' syndrome noted by Cornwell (1984) in which respondents seek to provide a 'professional account'. The observation of practice and the earlier vignettes provide some check against which such public accounts can be evaluated. In addition, interviews do not fully reflect the social or interactive nature of work in the field (this was partially imitated by the vignettes), or the extent to which individual views of risk can be a product of such social contexts. For example, Probation Officer 14 pointed out that most decisions in the team were actually made in consultation with others in a process of 'checking out', and observation subsequently bore out that this was very much the pattern of working in this team. Decisions are also made over time, and again whilst the vignettes attempted to incorporate this processual nature of decisions in the field, interviews necessarily impose an artificially static view.

The vignette data also illustrated the contested nature of risk, and whilst interviewing can again illicit individual views and how they may differ, it cannot necessarily illustrate how such meanings are negotiated between individuals or groups. Kitzinger (1994) has demonstrated how focus groups can explore how individuals negotiate such meanings in practice. Whilst this would have been a useful technique in this research, particularly to explore how risk was negotiated across grades, the method was discounted because of issues of confidentiality and the restrictions on open discussion which would be encountered by putting workers and managers together in a situation of unequal power and possible evaluation of comments made.

Analysis was carried out using the previously described Grounded Theory technique. The NUDIST computer software programme facilitated textual searches, and qualitative and quantitative data retrieval. The material is extensive and is presented under a series of key themes, followed by a broader discussion on implications for probation policy and practice.

Defining and using risk in Probation Practice: The current state of practice wisdom

An important distinction between technical/rational knowledge and reflective/critical knowledge in professional practice has already been made. Bines (1992) has described technical/rational knowledge as research based empirical knowledge, but that application in the field does not necessarily represent this. Rather, Bines argues that practice is dependent upon Schon's 'knowledge in action' (Schon 1983), knowledge which is more often tacit and grounded in activities. This can be supported by personal knowledge (Carper 1978) and intuitive knowledge (Benner and Tanner 1987), therefore an investigation of empirical knowledge alone is unlikely to reflect the extent of the knowledge base used by probation practitioners in the field.

This stage of the research was concerned with the knowledge of risk held by participants, how consistent and shared this was particularly across grades of staff, and the content of this knowledge. In particular, the extent to which the self-reported subjective experiences of respondents drew upon the technical/rational discourse of expert statistical risk and involved probability calculations and estimates of impact; or the extent to which other discourses of risk were deployed and what constitutes them. This is not simply to pose an expert discourse versus 'lay accounts', but rather to provide an exploration of the knowledge base used by respondents in order to present themselves as competent risk assessors in their everyday activities on risk. In constructing themselves as competent risk assessors the tacit, practical knowledge of their professional world may be as important as the rational/technical knowledge of experts. The crucial issue is the content of this knowledge and how it is applied.

Definitions of risk used by staff

Risk was defined as predominantly risk to staff (usually of assault, 46%), or of reoffending (41%). Risk as dangerousness to others comprised only 21% in sharp contrast to the Home Office guidance and the Probation Inspectorate's thematic report (Her Majesty's Inspectorate of Probation 1995, 1997, Home Office 1997). Interestingly no Assistant Chief Officer mentioned risk of reoffending, and 2 of the 6 mentioned risk to the public. Again in sharp contrast to Home Office National Standards (Home Office 1995) and key objectives for the Probation Service (Home Office 1992). The hostel workers most often mentioned risk to staff and risk to the public reflecting the ever present concerns of their particular setting. Managers were more likely to use the probability aspect of risk in their definition than staff (they were the majority of the 31% of the sample who mentioned this). Other words used were 'chance', 'possibility', 'unpredictability', and 'likelihood'. Managers have the clearest (this is not to say the most adequate) definition of risk, with frontline officers deploying the greater variety of definition. The divergence of definition across grade was striking and has implications for communicating and implementing policy, and for subsequently training the workforce. Definitions were often a combination of all the above components such as:

> ASW 1: It covers all sorts of levels. We've got risky residents, we've got a sex offender who is a risk to the public, so there's risks to the public, there's risk within the hostel and there is risk towards staff.

> SPO 7: It depends on what you are trying to measure in terms of risk, if you're talking about the risk of reoffending then anybody is a risk, it is a matter of degree I suppose. There is a risk of anybody reoffending. In terms of dangerousness, again it is what you're trying to measure. If you are trying to measure reoffending, that can be different from trying to measure dangerousness per se.

This lack of clarity was mirrored at more senior management level, for example an Assistant Chief Officer Probation on defining the term risk.

> ACPO 3: Its a broad term and can mean different things in different contexts. There is risk to the public by violent offenders or by other serious offenders being free in the community whether that's under supervision or not. I would say that the element of risk is slightly reduced if they are under supervision. There is the more general risk to the public by our knowledge of the volume of that group of people and the nature of behaviour that they can indulge in whether that be assault physical or sexual on children or elderly people, whether it is in generating public displeasure for example racist behaviour...I suppose there are other risks, for example of narrowing those male offenders who have difficulties in relating to women and in any situation which produces evidence of violence and nasty assault and that can lead on to children being a risk or so, but not always.

Definitions of risk are variable, covering a range of offenders and potential situations. Violent and sexual assault are viewed as self-evidently risky offences, however this is not without difficulty as SPO 4's comments on measuring the different properties of the risk of reoffending and dangerousness illustrate:

> SPO 4: It depends on what you are trying to measure really. The risk of reoffending is not necessarily the same as the risk of harm should that offender reoffend. Its very complex...I think it is very difficult to identify groups but I think sex offenders is the one that springs to mind probably because of the attitudes that they carry around with them about women and that could put women staff in a vulnerable position.

In particular the gap between officer and manager definitions of risk was viewed as problematic:

> ACPO 3: I think interpretation of the term is likely to differ depending on where you are coming from in an organisation. If you are an officer with a responsibility for doing it you may include in your definition risk to yourself as well as risk to others and to protect the offender as well. Management may well take a much more administrative approach. We need to have a more explicit recognition of what the term can mean and the range of definitions that are possible.

This manager recognised that responding appropriately to differences of definition was crucial, and more importantly that such differences could be valid:

> ACPO 3: The range of difference of definition and interpretation needs to be made explicit and an acknowledgement of where people are sitting could change views and approaches and that those differences are valid and should not be used offensively.

This lack of explicitness on both definitions of risk and how different they might be is also reflected in a lack of clear organisational priorities on risk:

> ACPO 3: I'm not sure whether it [the Service] has a priority, a defined list of risk priority, I'm not sure. I think there are certain assumptions that we would be fairly agreed about, some groups of people being a risk or being at risk, and maybe we need to test those assumptions a bit more explicitly but I

still think there would be some agreement and there may be some additions that some of us haven't thought of.

This comment reflects a larger issue about the introduction of a crucial policy on the assumption of consensus about key terms, objectives and priorities. This can lead to substantial problems in the implementation process where such assumptions are unfounded. The repercussions can be far reaching, including an increased 'polarisation' of views (Reder et al 1993) in which existing views become entrenched and mistrust of other perspectives grows. If not resolved, this can lead to 'incompatible emphases' in the work with workers prioritising differing objectives and outcomes to managers. This is not a matter of intent or malice on the part of either workers or managers, but is a result of a hardening in an existing pattern of communication (Reder et al 1993). Differences are mirrored and accentuated, particularly as staff seek those with similar views and both avoid interaction with and dispute the legitimacy of different views.

How do staff know who or what is risky

This ranged from comments that it was or could potentially be everyone (46% of respondents):

> SPO 1: There is a potential for risk in everybody...it is very complicated...(it) runs through all sorts of things so I think there is a risk element in almost everything we do because the potential for things, not having control over things, not being able to control outcomes, is potentially a risky situation and some of it is good risk and some of it is bad risk...it's for me to separate the two. I tend to think about risk as unpredictability.

> PO 4: Everyone is a risk. Everybody has the potential to behave in an anti-social way, certainly offenders because of their previous record.

In addition to the potential for unpredictable behaviour, or risk as unpredictability per se, staff identified sex offenders (33%) and violent offenders (31%) as risky:

> PO 14: Sex offenders - because you have to assess a certain amount of risk and think about victims; also violent offenders.

These categorisations reflected very clearly the statutory concerns of the Criminal Justice Act 1991, and Home Office instructions to services on the registration of violent and sexual offenders as 'Potentially Dangerous' (Home Office 1988). The perceived vulnerability of victims, particularly children was also influential:

> PO 5: Most people - different types of risk are taken more seriously than others. Child protection is taken much more seriously, very seriously. Violence as well. Crimes against property are less of a risk.

This officer well expressed the prioritisation of risks implicit in both agency and Home Office statements (for example HMIP 1995, 1997, Home Office 1992a, 1995). However, only a third of respondents prioritised risky offenders in this way, and only 23% saw risk in terms of risk to children. In effect, staff are attempting to grapple with the moveable feast of risk and how to grade or prioritise potential activities where context and comparison are highly significant:

> PO 7: ...virtually all of the people on the ...caseload will be 'risky'. Virtually everybody that Probation deals with will have offended so they will be at a high risk of reoffending. Murderers...sex offenders, kidnappers, people with mental illness. Its a bit like saying, if you live in Lincolnshire, which is a flat county, what is hilly? The Welsh hills are hilly. But if you live in the Himalayas then Mount Everest is hilly. It rather depends on where you are living. I think we live in the Himalayas.

Senior managers also noted the moveable and contextual nature of risk:

> ACPO 3: Probably most clients at some level or another, everybody presents some level of risk, but some clearly much less than others, but anyone who is likely to reoffend presents a risk and then it depends what the nature of that reoffending would be, how seriously you would regard that risk.

The issue of defining and grading risk is reiterated by another officer:

> PO 31: Initially we are looking at the clients themselves...all clients are at risk of doing again what they have once done but that isn't to say that we would necessarily consider the majority of them being very high risk, so you are looking for a definition of what is risky, what is acceptable risk and what isn't. If you are looking at Pre-Sentence Reports...most of the reports I write will be at relatively low risk of reoffending...The notion of danger

bit...someone is enough of a risk to be imprisoned...his offending is so minor that it doesn't deserve that...but it is a minimal risk as far as its irritating but it is not pleasant to be at the receiving end.

Distinguishing between levels of risk is noted by senior managers as a difficult issue, not necessarily easily resolvable by using offence classification as a risk index:

ACPO 3: I think it is important to separate out reoffending that is, in a sense, a nuisance, an irritant, but doesn't place anybody else at risk, and risk of damage or harm to themselves, and reoffending that does, and it is quite difficult sometimes to sort out which is which, because some burglaries upset people tremendously whereas the same set of events in a different household would have a very different impact...

ACPO 2: ...it is not categories of offence, its about attitude to offending and their awareness of other people, its about motivation and understanding that, I suppose I expect people to be doing assessments of motivation and their understanding of themselves.

Initially staff view everyone as potentially risky, but within this distinctions and gradings are sought. This is predominantly around estimates of impact, for example distinguishing between offending which is a 'nuisance' and offending which results in 'harm'. However, this is not seen as a simplistic exercise. Beyond the recognition of violent and sexual offending as risky in terms of harm, as per the Criminal Justice Act 1991, there is a subtle recognition of the contextual and situational nature of risk, expressed for example by ACPO 2 in the reference to assessments of motivation and self-understanding.

Expert, actuarial knowledge is in limited use, and is not immediately applied in establishing either potential to commit acts of harm or gradations of harm. Establishing the potential for the risk of reoffending is not presented as an issue in itself, rather it is the potential nature and impact of that offending which is seen as the assessment problem. As PO 31 expresses it, workers are 'looking for a definition of what is risky, what is acceptable risk and what isn't'. Whilst for PO 31 this is linked to notions of 'danger' rather than 'minor' offending, it is recognised as a potentially contentious and difficult issue by the senior managers, not least because views on 'acceptable risk' may vary. For ACPO 2 this is most easily resolved not by using offence type as a risk classification, but by carrying out a clinical assessment of motivation and understanding.

The use of credible risk indicators is often advocated as a mechanism for resolving differing views of risk, including differing priorities. Part of the interview schedule addressed the extent to which the indicators advocated by research were known and used by all staff including managers.

Risk indicators used by staff

Fifty nine % of respondents used past offending history as a risk indicator, including 52% who used previous history of violence. This was supported by alcohol (26%), drugs (23%) and previous sex offending (21%). Patterns, history, and past behaviour were emphasised, for example in answering how they knew who or what was risky:

> PO 1: Its patterns really, to see if there has been an offence against an officer or social worker...I suppose just to analyse what was going on in their offending history and that forms a backdrop...

Whilst this officer defines risk as primarily risk to staff, there is a recognition of the importance of past behaviour and criminal record in assessing risk. This officer is using the key indicator of past behaviour as an assessment tool, demonstrating awareness of a prime actuarial indicator and some formal knowledge of the risk of recidivism. However, this knowledge is mediated by its *practical application,* for example probation officer 1 continues:

> PO 1: ...and that forms a backdrop until you meet the person and ask them questions, that's only a backdrop its not the person...

In addition, the relationship the officer had with the offender was seen as an effective assessment tool often combined with formal indicators, and in particular the 'gut reactions' or judgements which officers can make as a result:

> PO 5: ...previous history, convictions is quite useful, interviews with the client, ...I suppose with some of it you do get feelings about people and you do get to know people. You build a relationship and you use that to determine how much a risk you think they are...

> SPO 6: Gut reaction...previous offending history.

ASW 3: Pre-cons, frequency of offending, seeing if the offender is on the Probation Service register of risky clients. You can see or spot someone and think this person is going to be trouble. Its a gut feeling.

SPO 4: Known history...and something about the manner and attitude they present. Knowledge of offender characteristics and their attitudes towards offending, how they perceive the victim. Some of this has come from knowledge gained by working with sexual and violent offenders.

In this comment SPO 4 draws attention to the formal knowledge of actuarial predictors by reference to 'known history' and 'offender characteristics', but also to clinical factors such as 'attitudes towards offending' and perception of victims. This combined knowledge is accrued through experience with no reference to formal training, the 'knowledge' is gained through the work.

Static actuarial factors are readily combined with dynamic situational factors as in the following example:

SPO 7: In terms of reoffending you look for patterns of behaviour...you have to look for certain factors and be able to spot the likelihood of them recurring. Just what they are will depend on the individual case, upbringing, parenting, schooling, education...will be important in one case and not in another. In terms of dangerousness, you need to look at what triggers the behaviour...and try to isolate that...it is not always easy to do...look for some signs that repeat themselves and look for that pattern repeating itself.

Knowledge from research (although rarely stated as such) was combined with individualised knowledge of the offender and his/her particular circumstances in order to capture the full complexity of risk:

PO 22: For some offenders it is situational...for others the problem is a bit deeper...it may be there are more fundamental issues that need to be addressed...they represent a higher risk. Also young males, 'twockers', this is where the confusion about risk comes in where the likelihood of reoffending is weighted off in terms of the potential consequences of reoffending. Other factors, ...your own conversations with offenders, previous information...knowledge of some of the research based on a group of offenders to which they belong...patterns of offending...I feel much safer in my assessments with risk the longer I've been working with somebody.

Officers placed a high degree of trust in their experience:

PO 13: I'd be making an assessment and that would be happening through experience, through various things I have in my head, I would sit down and write an assessment and I think I would have a fairly accurate picture about assessing the risk.

Senior managers also noted that experience could be a useful tool in risk assessment:

ACPO 2: I think they do it by a variety of methods because no doubt most of my seniors do it down to sheer experience, they know what they think causes them concern and I think I have a group of seniors who are wise enough to tell me...and I actually don't worry too much about what they don't tell me because they are generally sensible...and I think you do that when you go into a job, you assess people you are supervising as to whether you think their judgements are within the frame of reference that you are comfortable with and I think my seniors, by and large, are.

Implicitly this is also a comment on how risk assessments are quality assured, by the exercise of individual judgement on the acceptability of the 'frame of reference' of the assessor. Whilst this can reduce anxiety, it may also contribute to the reinforcement of views which subsequently turn out to be misinformed or biased. In effect, views remain unchallenged and a 'closed professional sub-set' can develop in which critical reflection is largely absent (Reder et al 1993). If this occurs at management level then it may be mirrored by workers who seek to carry out assessments in line with their managers 'frame of reference'. This may inadvertently reproduce a closed professional system with a narrow focus and lack of critical inquiry. The relationship between the social worker and the supervising Team Manager in the Jasmine Beckford child death case epitomises exactly this mirroring of a closed professional system (London Borough of Brent 1985, Reder et al 1993, p.73).

Alternatively the 'frames of reference' of managers and workers can become competing professional systems leading to a polarisation of views and disputes over values, roles, tasks, and what constitutes legitimate activity (Reder et al 1993). Policy implementation can literally become management of 'schism' in these circumstances in which the judgement of workers is both constantly monitored and corrected.

However, judgements were recognised by senior managers as integral to the process of risk assessment:

ACPO 6: ...the officer makes a judgement...it is a matter of taking people through a helpful mechanism but its people's judgements that actually count.

The 'unknowns' also present significant assessment difficulties, especially where the easily recognisable risk indicators are missing. This can be most difficult where staff are required to grade and prioritise risk:

PO 7: ...there is definitely a gradation and it is by people's actions that they ...get themselves to a point of being more at risk. The continued abuse of drugs and alcohol. You go on pre-cons...your response to a person ...we do a sort of gut-analysis on that person...you tend to feel that the relationship you have will protect. That is slightly dangerous in that the relationship you have with them does not mean as much to them as it does to you. We haven't been properly trained on the use of the risk assessment grid. We apply rules of thumb about careers in terms of reoffending: if they started at six and they have moved through seventeen, eighteen...and are still reoffending...it's likely they are going to go through to twenty four. It is the ones that are outside those fairly easy perimeters. If they are twenty seven...and roaming around with shot guns and robbing jewellers and going to Crown Court...there is a fair risk that that is the job they do, they've served their apprenticeship and they are likely to do it for the rest of their lives.

This problem is acknowledged by an Assistant Chief Probation Officer:

ACPO 2: I do not think officers are as systematic as I would like...with the middle range. They always want to believe that people aren't going to reoffend...so they don't ask the question that would tell them that somebody is going to reoffend. That would undermine what they are doing with that person and they don't want that undermined...they want to believe that they are having some impact...there are the ones they are not having an impact on who are going to present a risk.

This can result in the professional and personal values of the officer impeding the risk assessment process, for example:

PO 25: I worked with an offender doing a parole assessment. He was most put out and said: 'you're supposed to be helping me.' Very few of us come into this job seeing it as a broad universal thing about serving society and trying to make society a better place. I think most of us come into this much more about helping the offender...as the years have gone by (I realise) my role is much more about a broader criminal justice system and protection of the public as well as attempting to rehabilitate and not stigmatise the offender.

The need for 'objectivity' and less identification with the client was noted by a team manager:

SPO 4: A good risk assessment looks very closely at the details of effects, one that then does some work looking at underlying attitudes, a set of standards and perceptions about themselves and the potential victims and society at large, people's readiness to accept responsibility for their behaviour, if you can pull together information and treat it objectively, rather than simply taking the client's side of things and trying to see them in the best light, rather look at the evidence that is around. I think we need to move more in the direction of thinking more objectively at the range of information rather than siding with the offender.

This tension of values and cultural expectation in risk work and the variability of practice was not lost on senior managers, as one Assistant Chief Probation Officer expressed it when asked how officers were doing risk assessments:

ACPO 2: I think some are doing it better than others. Some of the culture of the service is unhelpful in that I think some officers have always given more attention to risks of reoffending and there have always been some staff who have actually not tried to face up to what the offenders might be doing when they are not with them, that it produces some very uncomfortable answers and some of the whole shift that is part of the criminal justice act and everything else has been about whittling away at that denial of what is really happening out there and I think it was part of bad practice historically. I wouldn't claim that everyone is where we would like them to be but I think they are moving in the right direction.

This Assistant Chief Probation Officer captures the cultural and value shift necessary for risk work, with the final sentence acknowledging the difficulty in practically achieving it. The quote is also a statement about what constitutes for managers an acceptable value base and frame of reference for risk work.

The role of 'gut instinct' in risk assessment

In resolving the difficulties inherent in offender risk assessment some staff resorted to seeking external validation for their 'gut instincts'. Comments on how they knew who or what was risky were prefaced by all staff with references to 'gut reaction' and 'life experience'. Officers viewed this as a testing out or matching up process:

> PO 14: ...you match up your information with the knowledge you have or the theories that you have been trained in and your instincts and see if they match up.

> PO 16: It may sound a bit vague but there is a body of knowledge and experience that you build up unconsciously I suppose doing the job which you get a gut feeling about, but beyond that we are working to specific theoretical models...sometimes it is just a gut feeling.

However, unlike Sheppard's championing of critical evaluation in the use of induction and practice wisdom (1995), officers did not display a critical evaluation of such assessments. Whilst relying on their past experiences to inform current assessments, officers did not have the mechanisms to monitor the outcomes of these past assessments. For example, when asked if they had kept a check on cases to see how risk assessments came out, a typical response was:

> PO 13: No I haven't.

Lack of formally recording risk assessments adds to this problem of evaluating practice:

> PO 28: I have not done any risk assessments, not per se, each new case is automatically assessed by myself when I read through the paperwork and I get an impression of what the guy is like and it is done, and risk assessment is done automatically in my mind, but it is not put in the file, it is not recognised in the file in a written form.

Hunches and gut reactions may have a role in alerting staff to the possibility of risky outcomes, however, mechanisms to reduce false positives and false negatives and avoid discriminatory practices are also required.

The following officer was exceptional in recognising the tentative and provisional nature of risk assessments:

> PO 22: Take your time, don't rush to make a judgement, spend as much time as you can interviewing a person...collecting information and forming opinions...gather information from all available sources, try to make sense of it...see if anything emerges in a pattern which you can make sense of and be tentative about...judgements you make and then talk about them.

This is a practitioner description of Sheppard's (1995) analytic induction method of practice wisdom. However, PO 22 was the exception rather than the rule. This raises the issue of what currently constitutes practice wisdom and how staff use it to present themselves as competent risk assessors. In the examples given here (typical of the sample as a whole), Sheppard's retroductive search for meaning via a critical mode of inquiry is not self-evident. Rather, the mode of inquiry appears to reflect Reder et al's restrictive practice of the closed professional system in which information is matched to existing beliefs (1993).

Components of a 'good' risk assessment

Defensible and acceptable decisions on risk will be highly dependent upon the quality of risk assessments, and how these subsequently 'stand up' when subjected to hindsight bias in the event of negative outcomes. However, this also depends upon both staff and managers being able to identify the components of a 'good' risk assessment, in effect the standards of a quality risk assessment, and to the extent to which these components are shared within and across grades. The term 'good' risk assessment was deliberately left unspecified in the interviewing to reduce researcher bias. Rather, the question was framed in terms of teaching others a best practice expectation, and what this would involve.

Half the Assistant Chief Probation Officers (3 out of 6) stressed analysis of information, and a third particular 'triggers'. Half the senior probation officers stressed reading all the information (4 out of 8) and consideration of previous offending, with a quarter concerned with identification of triggers to offending (2 out of 8). Whilst extremely small numbers, what is of significance is the difference between this management view and those of frontline officers working with offender risk in a large probation service. Of note in the officer responses is the sheer range of components mentioned, with few mentioning anything like a full range of actuarial factors, and most responses falling into the category:

ASW 2: Feeling your way around.

Combined with face-to-face work with the client, and placing the offender in a 'broader context'. Only one officer spoke explicitly of estimating the impact of risks:

PO 31: If it's a high cost risk then you should put a great deal more effort into getting the information you need than if it was a low cost.

Statistical, group information and research based knowledge was only mentioned explicitly in one instance in the context of being clear upon what evidence a risk assessment was based:

PO 29: If you are passing an opinion you should state on what basis it's formed whether it is just information from the client that may be verified or whether it's statistics about a particular type of offence or if you are quoting research on a particular offending group...if is an opinion based upon your experience then you should say that. I think if we are honest about where the stuff is coming from we are less likely to get ourselves into a mess.

This approach to risk assessment could be described as reliance on clinical assessment techniques and clinical factors, with some reference to past offences and patterns of behaviour:

PO 5: ...look at people in a broader sense...so whilst you have to start from offending behaviour...we have to spiral out...things that are significant for people in terms of offending...looking at their situation as a whole...family and friends, their state of mind, how they view themselves, their self-confidence...presence (or otherwise) of ambitions...you know from when you are talking to them whether they are making connections (as to why) they are in trouble.

PO 11: I really don't know. I rely on myself, my bank of experience.

Some officers referred to a range of factors, but also noted the limited and 'inexact' nature of the task:

PO 24:   ...we can't make scientifically exact statements about whether somebody is high, low or medium risk, but what you can say is...there are certain risk factors about that individual or their circumstances that means they may offend in a particular way...and what the Service may have to offer that might have an impact.

Only one officer mentioned matching the client against formal risk indicators:

PO 16:   ...have a clear framework of risk indicators but be flexible in terms of the way you work and the way you fit an individual to the framework. Its about social work skills, listening, creating an environment in which they are able to disclose indicators of risk, but they are able to participate in a proper dialogue.

In defining the components of a 'good' risk assessment, managers are predominantly concerned with the collection and analysis of information, particularly about 'triggers.' Officers were less explicit, literally 'feeling' their way to a risk assessment through the process of face to face work in which the offender is placed within a 'broader context'. Whilst patterns are mentioned, there is also a concern with 'the person', for example:

PO 30:   ...look at the person and get your impressions and the vibes, look at previous convictions and the history and draw threads out.

'Impressions', 'cues', and 'vibes' are combined with formal knowledge of previous convictions and behaviour. A wide range of situational factors such as homelessness, employment, substance abuse, family background were referred to, along with motivation, attitude to offending and to victims, and particular circumstances or 'stress situations' which led to offending. No respondent advocated 'best practice' on risk as a statistically based aggregate of probability, rather situational and individualised assessments were stressed. Competency in risk assessment was defined predominantly in terms of personal assessment skills, 'seeing the person', 'locating people in the broader sense', or using social work skills to facilitate disclosure. Even when a formal risk framework was advocated, 'flexibility' in how individuals are fitted to it was seen as essential (PO 16).

Managers and Probation Officers views of risk management

Managers understand risk management as almost entirely a matter of policy statements and procedures, for example:

> ACPO 3: Policies, ...if implemented properly...would diminish the risk of known offenders and known families where there are children. I don't know that that diminishes the risk to the general populous but there is always the unknown. (In managing risk)...the policy is set down - there is a regular review of the cases that are on each listing and each team. SPOs have to demonstrate that they have looked at them regularly, signed them and then sent them to their ACPOs at different time intervals.

> ACPO 3: People (are to be made) aware of the policies that exist, what they contain and how to implement them and also the training issues as well as helping people. I...have systems in place to monitor how seniors carry out their responsibilities..

> ACPO 6: ...The bit I wouldn't want to underestimate is the procedural system of getting information and not just going by how things appear to be, how people feel about things. To do that you have to put systems into place and to actually hold staff to ensure that information is forthcoming...

Senior Probation Officers (i.e. middle managers) saw themselves as responsible for the practices of their team members, particularly for the implementation and adherence to procedures:

> SPO 6: ...we have to ensure that the policies...are adhered to...that people interpret them in a very positive way...

> SPO 7: We have a responsibility to the Service to make sure policies are carried out and people are doing their job and we have a responsibility to staff to make sure they are adequately supervised.

However, this is not viewed as without difficulty:

> SPO 1: ...only at my request would senior (i.e. higher) management provide clarity. It is not something done as a matter of course, ensuring that my level is clear about the interpretation of policy. The assumption is that the SPO will know what it's about.

The clarity and support of higher managers is also doubted when 'things go wrong':

SPO 6: When things go wrong it's a sort of umbrella reaction. Those on the coal face have very small umbrellas and those at the top very large umbrellas so when the 'shit hits the fan' and it comes down it's the small umbrellas that get soaked. Its my impression that there's more blame lower down.

This contrasts with the 'enquiry' and 'learning' approach stressed by the Assistant Chief Probation Officers:

ACPO 2: It is very much a process of inquiry.

ACPO 3: ...we have to make an inquiry as to what happened and identify where responsibility should lie - to apportion blame and to learn.

ACPO 4: ...an investigation is a learning process for me.

ACPO 5: When things go wrong it is difficult to try and focus on learning rather than people getting very up tight about being blamed...You've actually got to have some sense about you being responsible and I think we are under a lot of pressure to prove that we are doing things right and correct...You learn best if you think you are doing a bad job...it's one of the paradoxes isn't it?

Probation Officers perceived critical differences in how risk was seen at differing levels of the organisation:

PO 1: I think we are all at risk, obviously in a different way though. My manager might experience risk in a different way to me through reading the case files, thinking I'm taking risks that I shouldn't be taking...so unless you come together you can't see how risk is assessed differently. I still think the responsibility lies with management, we've all got personal responsibility but the oversight and co-ordination lies with management.

However, managers were seen as distant from risks encountered by officers:

PO 1: ...the higher up you go the less you have to deal with people, like the Chief Probation Officer, he's the one implementing policies and arguing with the Home Office, deputies basically just don't see higher risk and its easy to forget. Say an Assistant Chief Probation Officer has been in post for five or ten years, the financial climate has changed considerably, more people are unemployed and homeless, so unless they are hearing that how is that going to affect the policies they make, they also change from being a Probation Officer to being a money manager, an accountant, a personnel officer or whatever, and their rules are very compromised and I think there are considerable differences between main grades and people in management...

Managers were seen to exercise their responsibilities harshly and inflexibly and that this affected their ability to understand the risks facing officers:

PO 1: All risk is relative really, if you are at risk then that's quite considerable but the problem is the hierarchy...I think macho policies in the service impact on the individual at risk in that if its about resources...its quite easy at Assistant Chief Probation Officer level to say 'this is how it is'...I just question if the people in management were probation officers. Compared with friends that work in industry, it seems our management is a lot more hardline...

Officers perceived the agency as blame oriented when 'things went wrong':

PO 14: Oh God all hell would break loose. If things go wrong its a case of checking files and making sure all files are up to date and checked, its a case of a flap and everyone saying 'have you reported this, have you recorded that' its not just covering one's back, its making sure that procedures have been followed. If procedures have been followed then its okay...Its a first reaction because the communities are out to apportion blame, because something has happened its somebody's fault.

Agency credibility is seen as a major preoccupation of managers:

PO 14: Its about getting the agency a bad name, about what officers are doing, are they operating in a certain way so that things don't blow up basically.

Officers doubted the level of support they would receive:

PO 4: ...well ultimately the buck stops with you and I feel very much that you're on your own...I don't feel I would hear the patter of tiny feet behind me to support me if something went wrong.

Managers were not always seen as appropriately fulfilling their responsibilities:

PO 4: I think managers should make quite clear what is expected. The policies we've got now in terms of risk, I think it is up to managers to make officers aware of those policies and not just let officers find out, they should be aware of them, they should be supportive of them. To do with children at risk, that actually was a long drawn out process, it took ages to write that policy and that was done with the union members and practitioners and I thought in the end that was quite a good way of doing it so I was quite impressed with the way they did that in the end. They made a hash of it to start with. I think also for the managers to take some responsibility with their officers.

This consensual and participatory manner of developing policies was viewed as more constructive than the 'hardline' management described earlier:

PO 1: I would be looking for consensus from other people, I wouldn't be on my own, I think that's when you're at greatest risk when you are isolated and do things off your own bat, probably consultation is the way forward really, so my style if I were the Assistant Chief Probation Officer...would be to look at what's common for people and take that as a consensus and check it out and offer other stimulus. It would have to be what we see as the risks we would be prepared to take, because you can't take them on your own, you need support if you are going to do it.

Officers viewed risk management as an issue of managing individual risks within their caseload, often perceived as risks to themselves, and that this was largely not understood by managers. Lack of clarity, minimal support and the spectre of blame were key issues for officers, although some feared blame and lack of support more than others, usually dependent upon personal experience of managers' previous responses. Procedures were viewed by officers as a mechanism for protecting the agency or allocating blame in the event of 'something going wrong'. They were not viewed as aids to risk assessment or risk management.

The contrasting views of senior managers, middle managers and officers hasimplications for policy formulation and implementation. These differences must also be placed within an organisational context in which management is perceived as distant, out of touch and unsympathetic to the concerns of officers. In this situation blame and fear of censure appear to be the driving forces in carrying out the work, and not necessarily consensus on key objectives or outcomes.

The implications for the Probation Service

The practice wisdom of probation officers can be characterised as dependent upon past professional experience with some reference to the past offending behaviour as a key risk indicator. Officers in particular responded to the unpredictability of risk by divining patterns from the past through the process of supervision, however this was not a process of aggregating risks by actuarial techniques, but rather was a process of resolving the unpredictability of the *individual offender* by recourse to information on social and personal circumstances and context.

> PO 24: I think we are breaking it down into internal and external factors that might influence risk and how they have...we've got to acquire information to see whether they represent a risk, e.g. external factors like homelessness then the potential to reoffend is much higher, environmental pressures. Internal factors e.g. their own level of insight into their behaviour, the degree to which they show any kind of remorse. The influence of drugs and alcohol, also looking at the resources we have...which might reduce or assist those needs...In all situations people may be at risk of reoffending but its knowing in what way...you can help to try and combat that.

Interestingly the officer redefines risk indicators as needs, and frames interventions in terms of needs reduction rather than risk management. The social and personal needs amenable to case work intervention are prioritised, and this description of a 'good risk assessment' is just one of many examples of reframing knowledge of risk through a value frame of rehabilitation and need.

Existing knowledge

The collective description of risk assessments illustrates that a body of knowledge to 'map' a full range of risk indicators does exist, however very few officers were able to draw upon this full range in a systematic way as lamented by Assistant Chief Probation Officer 2. Indeed, Officers presented as highly dependent upon the eclectic collection of information, not least from the offender, often seeking external validation for gut instincts on risk. Grading risk, and distinguishing between the risk of reoffending and the risk of dangerous behaviour was particularly problematic. Risk was used as a variable concept, both within the frontline worker grade and across grades Managers were particularly concerned with the outcomes of risk assessment and correct adherence to procedures. Workers were more concerned with the process of their work and responding flexibly to the range of risks and other problems presented to them.

The data indicates that workers negotiate the reality of risk from the information collected, but also from the process of supervision (that is interaction) with the offender. Previous knowledge and experience interacts significantly with new information as workers literally make sense of the problem, for example:

> PO 14: ...you match up your information with the knowledge you have or the theories that you have been trained in and your instincts and see if they match up.

The 'indeterminacy of assessment' is resolved by application of past experience to produce a 'sense of risk'. This 'sense of risk' is not necessarily congruent with those held by experts or managers, particularly in the 'middle range' of the caseload where issues of both probability and impact are more difficult to calculate. Particularly in this area of the caseload, although not exclusively so, the discourse on risk used by officers is a professionalised discourse of individualised judgement and past experience.

Only one Probation Officer epitomised Sheppard's practice wisdom by acknowledging the provisionality and 'testability' of risk assessments, and the critical seeking of meaning and hypotheses least likely to be wrong. Other workers regarded provisionality as a major anxiety producing feature, and potentially past experience is resolving anxiety rather than fulfilling Sheppard's role of: '...critical awareness distinguish(ing) mere experience from its intelligent use' (p.285).

Lack of consensus

In addition, there is little consensus about the term risk and how it should be assessed, particularly across grades of staff. The manager-frontline staff divide is quite marked. Managers' attention is focused upon correct and blame free outcomes, whilst workers are focused upon the individualised assessment of the offender before them. Managers espouse the certainty of 'information analysis' and 'trigger identification' in best practice; workers refer to 'feeling their way around'. These two statements illustrate the gap between management expectation and practitioner reality.

How best is this gap to be jumped? At first sight, it may appear to be an issue of replacing the 'rule of thumb' of frontline risk assessors with the procedural expectations of managers. However, a number of problems remain. Firstly, assessors seek a congruence and therefore acceptability of the procedural expectations with their own work practices and belief systems. For example:

Interviewer: Would formal risk indicators be useful?

PO25: ...as a starting point for your thoughts these checklists can be very useful although I know what we'd do as soon as we got one, we'd say oh they're trying to make us think in a mechanistic way, we don't want that, we want our professional judgement.

Interviewer: Would such indicators be helpful?

PO 2: I'm not sure if I'd use them to be honest, I'd mmm...Its so spontaneous, the assessment is mmm..because its an everyday part of our job and each individual circumstance is so different, no, I'm not sure if that would, mmm... It might help first year officers and less experienced officers. I'm not sure it would help more experienced officers to be honest. Students something like that.

Procedures are re-interpreted or circumvented, a process well documented by Ham and Hill (1993, Ham 1981, Hill 1993), as workers seek to operate comfortably or without stress, for example Satyamurti's 'occupational survival' (Satyamurti 1981) or according to their own occupational philosophies (Hardiker 1977). In addition, organisational constraints and existing work *and managerial* practices can inhibit change. History, culture and existing organisational forms can literally inhibit or reshape new practices. For example, the Probation Service spent much of the 1980s assessing the offender's risk of custody and proposing community alternatives to sentencers. This traditionally characterised the offender as the person 'at risk', with some limited attention to the risk of reoffending, and resulted in reports concentrating on community options and the strategic influencing of sentencing away from custody.

The Criminal Justice Act 1991 shifted the assessment emphasis to both the offender's potential to present a risk of reoffending and a risk of serious harm to the public. The offender was recast as a perpetrator of risks to others, with sentencers requiring a credible and 'objectified' assessment of this risk in order to inform their sentencing, particularly under section 2 (2) (b) of the Act. This shift of assessment focus has taken place within traditional styles of report writing and existing professional views of the task. Despite the added impetus of National Standards (Home Office 1992a), and in the absence of clear risk assessment tools for report writers changes in report writing have been slow, with subsequent criticism of their usefulness and quality by sentencers (Raynor et al 1995).

Improving judgements

If procedures do not necessarily guarantee the right outcomes (Starbuck and Milliken 1988) or indeed compliance towards managerially desired outcomes; is there any alternative way of improving judgements? For example, can more effective 'practice wisdom' on risk assessment be taught, and how could practitioners be assisted to tolerate higher levels of provisionality in the quest for hypotheses least likely to be wrong? The latter will be particularly difficult to achieve in situations where managers expect to identify and predict the full range of risks, and where unknown and uncalculated risks are not easily tolerated. Coupled with the spectre of blame and censure, this undermines any assessment technique based upon such provisionality and uncertainty.

However, the contextual and variable nature of risk (Douglas 1986) may be better served by an assessment tool which is open to change and which can capture the dynamic nature of risk (Brearley 1982). Munro (1996) in respect of child protection assessments has attempted to encapsulate this notion within the concept of the competent practitioner as someone who can change their mind in the light of new information. She argues that the revision of judgement is the key to the avoidance of error. Misjudgements, whether due to value framing or the limited knowledge available on the day can be challenged by further information and evidence to the contrary. The issue for Munro is the reluctance of social workers to refine their judgements and to admit that their decisions may be wrong.

In the uncertain world of child protection risks, Munro acknowledges that 'correct predictions' cannot be guaranteed but that there is an important distinction 'between good and bad mistakes' (Munro 1996, p.794). The key for social workers is how to distinguish: 'Which errors of judgement are due to our limited knowledge and which to inadequate investigation and woolly thinking?' (p.794). In effect, the distinction between informed reasoning and mere 'gut reaction'. Munro argues that:

> Analysis of the many public inquiries into child abuse tragedies reveals that inquiries understand the distinction between reasonable misjudgements and errors that deserve to be censured. However closer study of these reports shows how resistant social workers are to changing their minds and how powerful an influence this has on the conduct of a case. This reluctance to abandon beliefs should not be seen as a particular fault of social workers but as a general weakness of intuitive reasoning (Munro 1996, p.794. Reproduced with the permission of Oxford University Press and the British Association of Social Workers).

In effect, some mistakes are 'forgivable' and some are not:

> ...while mistakes due to our limited knowledge are unavoidable, the errors arising from the biases inherent in intuitive reasoning can be reduced by social workers' adopting a more critical approach to their judgements (Munro 1996, p.794. Reproduced with the permission of Oxford University Press and the British Association of Social Workers).

Whilst 'gut reactions' may often inevitably be the starting point, they cannot substitute for informed reasoning based upon an evaluation of the evidence. Such initial reactions should be seen as highly tentative and provisional requiring rigorous investigation. Judgements based upon such rigour and 'reasonableness' are at the heart of the 'defensible decision' (Carson 1996, Kemshall 1996b), that is decisions which are viewed as defensible and correct based upon the knowledge known at the time despite subsequent negative outcomes. Inquiries are well able to distinguish between such avoidable and unavoidable mistakes (Munro 1996). However, there are significant barriers to the operation of such critical and rigorous judgements.

Bias and persistence with value beliefs in the face of new information is a well documented trait, not just of social or probation workers (Nisbett and Ross 1980). The psychometric tradition of risk research has explored the various 'defects' in intuitive reasoning about risk, not least that information is sought and processed according to our beliefs (Kahnemann et al 1982); that we seek and use information which confirms our existing views (Kahnemann et al 1982,); and that conflicting evidence is easily discounted or ignored (Reder et al 1993). Munro (1996), from her critical examination of inquiry reports, argues that the 'social worker's appraisal of a family strongly influences the quality of investigations and assessments' (p.801). Value framing is integral to the application of knowledge in problem framing and resolution.

Reder et al (1993) in their analysis of inquiry reports identified four themes leading to errors in assessment:

(1) The failure to see the bigger picture in which discrete pieces of information remain unconnected.

(2) Persistence with belief systems despite evidence to the contrary.

(3) Failure to consider alternative explanations and courses of action.

(4) Focus on results and tasks rather than the full investigation of complex situations and relationships.
(Reder et al 1993. pp.83-94).

In this situation, existing opinions and previous experience are pervasive, resulting in 'unreal optimism' (Dingwall et al 1983, Parton 1986) and a lack of 'rational', critical discussion in which opinions can be 'tested'. (Munro 1996, p.801-802). The key issue is how can a climate for critical testing of views be created, and how can workers be taught both 'the errors of their ways' and how to improve the judgements which necessarily have to be made. Quite rightly, Munro argues that: 'Senior management needs to ensure that time for thinking and supervision is valued and protected from competing demands' (1996, p.805). However, the development of a critical attitude to decision making requires more than this. The next chapter considers how workers can be facilitated to explore the basis of their own decision making and the 'systemic flaws' of their intuitive reasoning.

7. Developing Critical Awareness of Decision Making

Assessment is central to social work and probation practice. Not only does it frame problems, it defines their solutions. As Reder et al, in a work on the assessment of child protection risks, express it: 'The aim of assessment is to guide action' (1993). This involves collecting and weighing up information in order to determine the most appropriate course of action. They state that assessment is an:

> ...ongoing process and at each step new information needs to be evaluated and given meaning. In this way, a picture emerges of the possible origins of the problems and how they might be resolved or contained. Assessment is thus both an activity in itself and a process of understanding. Without it, workers are left to react to events and intervene in an unplanned way. (Reder et al 1993, p.83. Reproduced with the permission of Routledge).

Assessments literally determine interventions, and as such are integral to subsequent risk management strategies. Inadequate assessments are likely to result in inadequate or misdirected risk management strategies as numerous child protection inquiries show (Reder et al 1993). Effective risk management is highly dependent upon the matching of interventions to the hazards identified. However, this identification and matching are prone to numerous flaws.

Assessment flaws

As Reder et al convincingly demonstrate, without a clear framework for assessment within which systematic exploration of the meaning of events and behaviours can be made the process is open to serious error (Reder et al 1993). In addition to the pervasiveness of value beliefs, there are serious constraints upon the processing of information by workers and the subsequent application of knowledge. Cognitive psychology has a long history of documenting such errors in intuitive reasoning, most notably the use and application of 'knowledge structures' and 'judgmental heuristics' (Nisbett and Ross 1980, Reason 1990). Knowledge structures are used to identify, label and categorise the world, providing a 'short-hand', routinised way of dealing with the multitude of data presented to us in our daily lives. Whilst they make our social lives manageable, they are only an approximation of reality and can remain 'fixed' in the light of new information and evidence (Kahneman and Tversky 1973, Nisbett and Ross 1980).

Heuristics

Judgmental heuristics, or cognitive strategies are the 'rules of thumb' routinely deployed by individual's in carrying out inferential tasks (Nisbett and Ross 1980). The two most influential heuristics are: representativeness and availability (Kahneman and Tversky 1973). Representativeness is crucial to the correct categorisation of objects and data. Such categorisation is dependent upon judgements of similarity and representativeness between objects and ascribing categories upon the basis of such similarity.

However, in situations where the similarity of features is ill-defined, then it is argued that statistical calculations are necessary in order to make accurate categorisations. However, practitioners are often ignorant of the available statistical information or unwilling to use it, particularly ignoring base rates as a baseline against which to evaluate their clinical assessments (Kahneman and Tversky 1973, Gottfredson and Gottfredson 1993, Pollock, McBain and Webster 1989, Webster, Dickens and Addario 1985). Practitioners prefer to give weight to case based information (Carroll 1977, Kahneman and Tversky 1973, Nisbett et al 1976, Shah 1978), with the individual case carrying more weight than statistical base rates.

This is compounded by the availability heuristic with which workers estimate frequency and probability from data which is most available and vivid in their memory (Tversky and Kahneman 1973, 1974). This can lead to both over and under-estimation of a behaviour or event. Availability can also impact upon assessments of causality, resulting in the imputation of causal connections between factors in a case where none in fact exists, a phenomenon labelled 'creeping determinism' by Fischoff (1975). This is exacerbated by the tendency of practitioners to record and account for case based information in terms of a narrative of past behaviours and events. In the production of a coherent narrative causal connections and correlations are imputed literally to make sense of what they see and of a vast array of information (Einhorn 1986). This sense making is also highly dependent upon the theoretical views of the assessor, their biases, previous practice experiences, and values and beliefs (Kemshall 1993b, Kemshall 1996).

In sense making, practitioners draw conclusions or inferences from the evidence presented in case situations. Wason and Johnson-Laird (1972) found high error rates in such deductive reasoning due to the process of 'similarity-matching' rather than the application of logic, and that information is more often used to confirm rather than deny generalisations. In effect, 'short cuts' to reasoning are taken to avoid what Bruner et al (1956) called 'cognitive strain', that is reasoning against the normal habits or experiences of the thinker. To avoid costly and potentially stressful thinking, people resort to the 'criterion of verisimilitude' (Reason 1990, p.40).

> That is, they tended to prefer cues that had proved useful in the past, and thus had the 'look of truth' about them, regardless of their present utility (Reason 1990, p.40).

In this case, staff were extremely trusting of cues which past experience suggested had utility for predicting the likelihood of future offending. In the practice reality of competing tasks and quickly made assessments it is perhaps not surprising that staff routinise assessment and resort to short cuts which seem to stand them in good stead. Reason (1990) refers to this as 'persistence- forecasting', that is forecasting on the basis of past experience of regularities rather than logically calculated probabilities. It is literally the application of 'pre-packaged solutions to recurring problems.' (Reason 1990, p.41). Whilst it can lead to error, in situations of limited resources and limited tools it can provide a reasonably credible and resource lean way of solving assessment problems (Bruner et al 1956). However, problems arise because it is:

> ...likely to lead to an excessive reliance on what appear to be familiar cues and to an over-ready application of well-tried problem solutions (Reason 1990, p.41).

It compounds existing modes of thinking and prevents the exploration ofpotentially more productive pathways. Within probation practice it is likely to compound existing work patterns, beliefs and knowledge structures.

The application of knowledge structures and judgmental heuristics to decision making on risk is not a matter of worker negligence or malicious practice, rather it is a recognition that all decisions are made within what Russo and Shoemaker (1992) call 'decision frames'. These frames are cognitive mechanisms for simplifying and accessing highly complex situations. Such simplifications can inadvertently build error and bias into decisions. As Strachan and Tallant express it:

> ...frames have enormous power and the way in which people initially frame a problem directly results in their final decision (Strachan and Tallant 1997, p.17).

The two preceding chapters have illustrated how staff currently working with risk in probation are framing both assessment problems and their resolutions. In their application of knowledge to assessment problems, staff demonstrated the use of tacit knowledge structures predominantly rooted in previous case experience of offenders, and the use of judgemental heuristics in 'matching' case information to tacit theories and past knowledge of offenders.

However, as previously argued, decision making cannot be understood as a totally individualised activity, but rather as an activity which takes place between social actors in a social context (Payne 1997, Rhodes 1997). Reder et al (1993) noted the contextual nature of such decisions by drawing attention to a number of key issues rooted in the social systems of teams, agencies and inter-agency relationships. Assessment decisions were seriously constrained by a number of factors including: 'closed professional system', 'polarisation', 'hierarchy', and 'role confusion' (Reder et al 1993, pp 71-76).

The closed professional system can operate on all levels including the individual worker, and refers to the operation of a 'closed' value and knowledge system in which conflicting information is discounted or ignored. Importantly, such systems depend upon a degree of shared knowledge and values, and in subsequent interactions workers can reinforce both the shared nature of such knowledge structures and values, and the exclusion of those which do not fit. Berger and Luckmann (1967) have argued that such 'typifications' for understanding the world are shared and routinised through social processes and the use of language, and thereby gain a facticity and legitimacy beyond the activities of individual social actors. In this situation, the cognitions of individual workers are not only severely constrained but may appear to them to be both reasonable and legitimate.

This can be reinforced by work practices and the social system within which workers practice. For example, in Team One information on difficult, 'risky' and 'notorious' cases was shared, although the informal system of sharing outweighed the time given to formal review in team meetings. In effect officers approached each other for discussion within an office lay-out which facilitated high levels of informal contact, particularly in a communal seating area. The office was geographically distant from the area it served, and for health and safety reasons home visiting had diminished. This reinforced the operation of a closed professional boundary. Case advice was primarily provided by colleagues sought out by the individual officer, and the manager was often excluded from such discussions and indeed subsequent decisions. In effect, Team One operated as a closed professional system in which a consensus of team views on particular issues and cases was informally maintained, and confirmation of existing views was eagerly sought.

Such a system operates against the key principles of Sheppard's practice wisdom, that is: an interactive process between data collection and theorising; constant hypothesis testing and reformulation; refinement in the light of negative evidence; and the development of hypotheses least likely to be wrong. (Sheppard 1995). Team Three operated a more open system within which views were more critically evaluated. The hostel setting of this team prevented the operation of a strict boundary between staff and residents, and indeed the hostel and local community. In addition, case reviews were highly formalised in weekly team meetings during which all staff contributed their views on each resident. During a discussion of one offender the Senior Probation Officer highlighted the progress and change of attitude of the offender evidencing this by reference to his contribution in the hostel garden. A debate quickly ensued between the key worker (the Probation Officer) and the Senior, with the former reminding the Senior of the nature of the original offences and how little actual progress on offence focused work had been made. The Senior finished the discussion by acknowledging the critical contribution of the officer in refocusing attention:

SPO 3: ...if we're not careful we'll be in a catch 22. I know how I feel about the garden, I have that weakness in me and I must be careful.

In this situation both work practices and the culture of management facilitated an open professional system in which the staff group strove to develop a coherent view of the case. This approach translated into risk management strategies which were agreed and reviewed as a group, an essential process as their effective implementation often depended upon collective rather than individual responses.

Closed systems, especially between differing agencies, or where they operate as a distinct sub-set of a wider system can produce polarisation (Reder et al 1993). This is evidenced by the perceptions of service management held by some respondents, and worker perceptions of blame attribution. It was also raised by officers in respect of risk assessments for use by courts, and whether sentencers and Probation Services would agree on risk. In particular the impact of more explicitly stating risks to sentencers was a cause for concern as officers distrusted what use sentencers would make of this and that it was likely to lead to less community sentences. During observations of report writing and informal discussions a small group of officers did discuss the selective presentation of information in Pre-Sentence reports for this reason.

Polarisation between parts of the agency, for example hostels and the field, were also exaggerated by the operation of status and power. Notions of hierarchical status can outweigh more collaborative approaches to risk assessment and risk management (Reder et al 1993). This can present itself as field officers discounting the information and views given by hostel assistant wardens about the behaviour of residents, or in hostel personnel distrusting the referral information provided by field staff. Hierarchy can however be subsumed to more co-operative styles of working, for example in the hostel team where assistant wardens were actively incorporated into the review process.

Tension between agencies, and between parts of the agency can also be the result of role confusion, that is unproductive overlap or ambiguity of roles between workers (Reder et al 1993). However, workers can also experience role confusion as the raison d'être of their agency changes. This can be exacerbated if their professional sub-set becomes isolated and de-legitimised. In these situations, practitioners may engage in defensive practice and operate under a professional dissonance in which professional dilemmas or fallibilities are denied. The fallback position in such situations is the routinised use of one's own taken for granted biases, assumptions and values. This is the intuitive reasoning or 'gut reactions' which Munro (1996) has argued is so problematic for social workers.

Facilitating critical awareness of decisions

Decision making can be understood as the use of formal or informal judgement to resolve a question or issue. Literally to make up one's mind about a course of action or a potential outcome (Concise Oxford Dictionary 1995). The cognitive approach to decision making has characterised decision making as a matter of individual cognitions or thought processes for which normative standards could be prescribed and any deviations could be understood as a matter of human frailty or irrationality (Reason 1990). However, the work of Kahneman and Tversky in particular (1973) demonstrated that decision makers did not necessarily employ logical principles in their decision making or utilise statistically based expectations of utility in deciding the 'best' outcome. Normative theories expect that decision makers will have the full range of information about possible outcomes which in reality is rarely so (Reason 1990). In addition, decisions often interact and impinge upon one another, literally having 'knock on effects' and involve or affect others beyond the individual. Decisions, particularly in social work, are made under conditions of uncertainty in circumstances of imprecise knowledge (Brearley 1982).

Perceptions of optimal outcome can also vary due to differing subjective values, resulting in contextually bound decisions and a more limited notion of rationality (Rhodes 1997). Decisions then become context specific and thereby disputable rather than error prone. Such disputes tend to revolve around the desirability of subsequent outcomes and error becomes a mechanism for the attribution of blame. Disputes over risk (such as Windscale, Wynne 1982) draw attention to the interactive and negotiated nature of risk in which concepts of power and legitimacy are central to understanding how strategic choices on risk are actually made (Bloor 1995a, Douglas 1986, Rhodes 1997).

Decision 'errors' can therefore be understood as individual, collective and systemic. Such errors are more likely to be cumulative rather than one major error leading to the great catastrophe (Cullen 1990, Reason 1990). Major disasters and subsequent inquiry reports such as the Clapham rail crash, Piper Alpha, Zeebrugge Ferry, and the Challenger Shuttle disasters illustrate latent decision failures within the system rather than individual errors by frontline workers (Hidden 1989, Cullen 1990, Sheen 1987, Starbuck and Milliken 1988). These errors are literally 'accidents waiting to happen' prior to the individual decision errors of frontline staff, and have their origin in the planning, design and implementation of risk assessment, monitoring and management procedures (Clarke 1995, Reason 1990).

Whilst the full implications of latent errors cannot be discussed here (for a full review see Reason 1990), the concept provides an important reminder of the organisational and structural limits upon individual decision making which do exist, and to avoid Perrow's 'attribution error' of blaming people at the expense of ignoring situational factors (Perrow 1984). It is therefore essential that a critical approach to decision making at both the individual and organisational level can be developed. This chapter explores one method for facilitating greater practitioner awareness of decision making through the systematic application of critical path analysis (Lynch 1976). The method could also be adopted by supervisors to both quality assure and facilitate improved decision making, and by senior managers for tracing the paths of 'serious incidents'. In addition to facilitating practitioners to hold 'critical conversations' with their own work (Schon 1987), and in identifying heuristics and judgmental errors in their decision making, the method can also highlight organisational and systemic constraints in decision making. The method can also be used prospectively to rehearse probable decision outcomes prior to action.

The use of critical path analysis to enhance practitioner decision making

Critical path analysis (CPA) is a method well used in the evaluation of nursing clinical judgements (Minghella and Benson 1995, Orme and Maggs 1993, Sims 1976), and has its roots in the evaluation of engineering processes (Battersby 1964). In effect, the method enables practitioners to trace the critical factors involved in their decision making, and to identify the variables which have resulted in particular decision outcomes, hence the notion of criticality, and the use of the term path. The technique accepts that practitioners are presented with choices as cases progress, and that there are differing decision pathways probable in any one case. The importance for the practitioner is to reflect upon this process of decision making, and to identify both the decision choices which can be made, and the decision outcomes or consequences they are likely to result in.

Critical path analysis has also been used to encourage a more reflective approach to decision making and clinical risk assessments by practitioners (Minghella and Benson 1995). This is crucial to risk decision making as such decisions are characterised by high levels of uncertainty (Brearley

1982) where more than one possible outcome can occur and where the penalties for 'getting a decision wrong' can be severe.

The tracing of decision paths is also helpful in making explicit the knowledge and value frames which practitioners necessarily bring to their decision making. Critical path analysis can engage practitioners in a reflective investigation of the 'tacit processes' they are using in their practice with risk, and assist them in evaluating the efficacy of the decisions made upon these processes when the method is used retrospectively and decision outcomes are known.

Paths can also be used as an investigative tool after accidents or serious incidents. Hendry and Lewis (1990) demonstrated the use of path analysis in understanding the Zeebrugge disaster, in particular how situational factors interacted with and exacerbated the consequences of individual decisions, (for example that the captain did not know the bow doors were open, that there were few other ships on hand to assist them, and that the rescue plan was out of date); and how errors were compounded by subsequent decisions (for example to have a divided deck and to turn into a choppy sea). This can raise issues of systemic faults for which managers are primarily responsible (Clarke 1995). This is illustrated by the findings of the Herald's subsequent inquiry. In summing up the disaster Mr Justice Sheen allocated the primary responsibility to corporate management rather than to the activities of any one individual. He characterised management of the company as 'sloppy':

> All concerned in management, from the members of the Board of Directors down to the junior superintendents, were guilty of fault in that all must be regarded as sharing responsibility for the failure of management. From top to bottom the body corporate was infected with the disease of sloppiness...The failure on the part of the shore management to give proper and clear directions was a contributory cause of the disaster (Sheen 1987, p.14). (Crown copyright is reproduced with the permission of the Controller of Her Majesty's Stationery Office).

This inquiry report well illustrates the cumulative and collective nature of decision making and that error faults are rarely totally individual. Corporate rather than individual responsibility for decisions was stressed, and whilst blame was attributed it is collective rather than individual. This is supported by numerous other inquiries, for example: Piper Alpha (Cullen 1990), Clapham (Hidden 1989), Kings Cross (Fennell 1988). Management therefore has a responsibility to both understand all the potential sources of decision errors, and to support frontline workers in avoiding them. This requires a learning approach to how decisions are actually made, including the role managers and the systems they implement play in individual frontline decision making, rather than the attribution of individual blame in moments of hindsight bias. The emphasis is shifted from corrective approaches after incidents have occurred to a proactive focus upon the quality of decision making and the organisational structures (including supervision and quality assurance mechanisms) used to promote effective decision making. Critical path analysis can play an important role in both understanding and improving decisions.

Practical application of critical path analysis

The method was used in workshops in the research area in late 1996 and early 1997, and in other Probation Service areas as a training tool. It was originally used to provide a checking mechanism on the data collected during the vignette and interviewing stage of the research. In effect checking the impact of knowledge structures, value base and situational factors upon risk assessment by tracing decision paths). This quickly developed into workshops aimed at facilitating and improving practitioner decision making. A review of the aims, objectives and content of the workshops is briefly presented in this chapter prior to a discussion of the use of critical path analysis in supervision, quality assurance and organisational risk management.

Aims of the workshop

In addition to collecting further data, the primary aim of the workshops was to assist practitioners in guided reflection of their decision making. Boyd and Fales (1983) have defined reflection as:

> The process of internally examining and exploring an issue of concern, triggered by an experience, which creates and clarifies meaning in terms of self, and which results in a changed conceptual perspective.

In particular, practitioners should be encouraged to reflect upon those uncomfortable situations in which existing knowledge:

...was not sufficient to explain what was happening in that unique situation. The focus of learning is upon critical analysis of these unique practice situations (Murphy and Atkins 1994, p.13).

Through reflection the practice knowledge base is extended, and this knowledge may include:

...aesthetic, personal, moral, as well as empirical knowledge...Reflection therefore has the potential to address the problems of practice in a way that the application of technical rational approaches does not (Murphy and Atkins 1994, p.13).

Critical path analysis offers a structured approach to Schon's reflection-on-action (1983), allowing practitioners a precious opportunity to reflect on action and its consequences after the event.

Objectives of the workshop

(1) To provide participants with an increased understanding of how they are assessing risk, particularly how they are assessing the key components of risk: probability and impact.

(2) To provide participants with increased knowledge and understanding of the common errors in estimating probability and impact.

(3) To provide participants with increased knowledge and understanding of the most common faults and errors in risk assessment.

(4) To provide participants with knowledge and understanding of the cognitive biases, heuristics, and values which have an impact upon their risk assessment decisions and which can lead to error.

(5) To provide participants with an understanding of the situational and organisational factors which impinge upon their decision making.

(6) To provide participants with a technique (i.e. CPA) for reviewing and evaluating their own decision making in risk assessment.

(7) To provide participants with an opportunity to relate CPA to their case decisions, or other risk assessments (for example court reports).

(8) To provide participants with an opportunity to identify future learning needs and action plans in respect of their own decision making on risk, (and/or the decision making of their supervisees).

(A further exploration of CPA in risk decision making is provided in Kemshall 1998. The training exercises used in this chapter are reproduced from Kemshall 1998 with the kind permission of Social Work Education).

Process

Participants brought recent or current cases to the workshops and the techniques of critical path analysis were demonstrated by the researcher using the Zeebrugge example and then case examples from offender work. In addition, participants were introduced to the concepts of values and heuristics in decision making and how these can impact upon their own practice, and the situational and organisational factors which can also impinge upon their decision making in the field (Reder et al 1993).

The aim of the workshop was not to censure current practice, but to enhance it. Participants were treated as adult learners and their viewpoints valued, with the emphasis upon self-discovery through the exercises. It was acknowledged that participants were themselves taking a risk in exposing their practice, and that there was no obligation on participants to disclose material beyond what was comfortable. Naturally there will have been occasions when participants experienced decisions 'going wrong' and perhaps personal and professional consequences. These issues required sensitive handling. Some participants may have felt that their decision making had been unsupported by managers, or that their decision making had been seriously constrained by managerial failures. Whilst it was important to validate individual experiences in order to facilitate learning, it was imperative in the implementation of the method to avoid blame allocation or an adversarial approach to manager-practitioner relationships.

Content

Session One Participants were invited to reflect upon a recent risk assessment and to account for how they calculated both probability and outcome. This exercise demonstrated that such calculations were most often carried out in the absence of all the relevant information (Prins 1995), and informed by heuristics, such as 'vividness' of the event or incident leading to an overestimation of risk (Kahneman et al 1982). The absence of, or difficulties in using probabilistic information on offender risk was also revealed. This provided important confirmatory data on the findings of stages one and two of the research.

In training terms, the session was used to increase the understanding of participants on how they usually carry out risk assessments. In particular the session aimed to increase participants' ability to recognise their individual dependence upon heuristics and tacit knowledge structures in preference to empirical actuarial indicators; and an increased awareness of the situational and organisational factors which impinge upon their decision making.

Session Two The aim of this session was to enable participants to increase their understanding of the impact of heuristics, bias and values upon their risk decision making. The specific objective was to ensure that by the end of the session participants could identify the most common heuristics and biases and review which of these were present within their own decision making. In addition, participants should gain an increased understanding of the role of values and framing in the assessment process, and the values which they most often utilise to resolve decisions of uncertainty. Participants should be able to evaluate the balance between heuristics, values and risk indicators in their risk decisions, and the extent to which their decision outcomes and the subsequent efficacy of their decisions are affected by the relationship between these components.

Values, whilst difficult to define in social and probation work (Payne 1997), are viewed as an acceptable and desirable feature of practitioner decision making (CCETSW 1996). They are often viewed as integral to our awareness of and relationship to others, to the avoidance of discrimination and oppressive acts, and to the empowerment of service users (Kemshall and Pritchard 1997).

However, there can be severe difficulties for practitioners in translating these to settings in which statutory responsibilities and a duty of care to both service users and to non-service users such as the public or victims is required. Values can conflict, and previous patterns of working can be challenged. To avoid 'cognitive strain' (Bruner et al 1956), decisions may become routinised with workers resorting to familiar and trusted cues to resolve their practice dilemmas. Routinised and closed thinking patterns can result in avoidable error.

In essence, the session should enable practitioners to distinguish between errors which are 'unavoidable' and those which arise from 'the biases inherent in intuitive reasoning' (Munro 1996, p.794), and to correct such errors through the systematic analysis of the basis upon which their decisions choices are made. It should also enable participants to acknowledge the value choices which are implicit in every case based decision, and whether those currently being used are ethically desirable and result in desirable and defensible outcomes. This was achieved by using exercise one below:

Exercise one

Exercise on: Heuristics, values and indicators

Identify in your last risk assessment the heuristics, values and risk indicators you used.

Heuristics	Values	Risk indicators

With hindsight bias how might your risk assessment change between the use of heuristics, values and indicators?

If the values and heuristics outweigh the indicators column, what do you think this probably results in?

How could you change the "weighting"?

In addition, to identifying the interaction between heuristics, values and indicators of risk in any risk decision, the exercise can also enable practitioners to explore the value frame of their decision making in a relatively unthreatening manner. Practitioners may experience dissonance, not only between what they wish to do and what they actually do, but between the activities they wish to carry out and those seen as managerially desirable. James (1994) has suggested that such dissonance stems from workers (including managers) acting 'inauthentically', that is not 'in accordance with their own values and their agreed professional standards.' (James 1994, p. 200). The exercise can assist participants in establishing whether their individual value base is commensurate with that seen as desirable by agency management, and the extent to which they may be experiencing both dissonance and inauthenticity. This can result in distress and low morale, but also a flight into activities and decisions which workers experience as comfortable and reassuring and avoidance of those which challenge deeply held views or well entrenched work patterns. This can have severe implications for practice on risk, for example increased polarisation between workers and management, role confusion, and compromise over responsibilities. These are systemic rather than individual sources of error, and require attention at the corporate as well as team and individual level.

Session Three The aim of this session was to improve the risk decision making of practitioners to ensure that such decisions are 'defensible' in the light of 'hindsight bias' (Carson 1996, Kemshall 1996b, 1997b). A defensible decision is one which can demonstrate that reasonable steps have been taken within an acceptable value frame, and that the assessment was rooted in a sound knowledge base and utilised the most credible risk indicators available based upon the information available to the practitioner. Critical path analysis can enable practitioners to evaluate the defensibility of their decisions.

The clarity and acceptability of the value frame is essential in risk decisions (Carson 1996). For example, if the risk policy of the agency is set within a well established principle of normalisation and the service user is located in a situation of diminishing supervision and increasing independence, and an adverse event subsequently occurs, then the risk taking of the agency and worker may still be viewed as acceptable. However, if the risk policy is framed within an expressed commitment to public protection, as is the current case in probation work, then the above decision making may not be viewed as acceptable. This highlights how the value frame of risk decisions must be commensurate with the expressed values of the agency, and increasingly with those of funders and the public in order to be defensible. Values are not the sole prerogative of social workers or probation officers. It is essential therefore that values are clearly articulated and located within a context of agency and statutory responsibility. Where they are not, workers themselves run the risk of making decisions which are later censured as 'undesirable' or which result in harm to service users or members of the public.

By the end of the session participants should be able to identify the key characteristics of a defensible decision, and be able to apply critical path analysis to their cases and have practised the technique on a number of their risk decisions. In addition, participants should be able to identify those values which result in indefensible decisions or actions which are harmful to end users. The exercise is reproduced below, and requires brief, anonymised information on the case, the drawing of a decision path, and then attention to the questions outlined.

Exercise two

Exercise on: Effective and ineffective risk decisions

Whilst the full outcome(s) of your risk decisions may not yet be known, you are asked to consider two risk decisions which have 'made an impression' on you in the last few months. You are asked to consider:

(1) One decision with which you are satisfied and which you think is (or will be) effective.

(2) One decision with which you are dissatisfied and which you think is (or will be) ineffective.

Effective means: based on evidence and indicators, likely to be reliable, assists in decisions on intervention plans, is 'defensible.'

Review each of these decisions by drawing a CPA (like the Case of John) and identify:

(1) The components which you think are contributing to effective and satisfactory decision-making.

(2) The components which aren't.

(3) Action to improve your decision-making.

The path analyses made the value frame used by practitioners explicit to them, and also encouraged them to weigh the desirability of the various decision options and outcomes before them. In effect, some decisions have differing results and impacts, not least for service users. Critical decision paths have the power to demonstrate this to practitioners. This is illustrated by the following case study used extensively in both the research study and the training:

John is a black, 18 year old. He is currently the subject of a one year probation order for offences of burglary and theft. He reports regularly and is co-operative in supervision. The probation officer supervising the case learns that John has started to do voluntary work with older persons.

What is the level of risk in this case and what action should the officer take?

Responses to the case study fell into two basic types represented in figure one, resulting in differing assessments of the risk level and differing proposals for intervention.

The contrasting paths illustrated the power of initial value frames on the final decision. More importantly, John experienced different responses from officers on the basis of their value frames rather than upon the information of the case. Each of these responses carry potentially radically different outcomes for John. If he is assessed as high risk for example, there is the possibility of disclosure of his offences to the voluntary organisation and the possible loss of this working experience. If he is assessed as low risk there is a possibility that further offences may occur, members of the public are placed at risk and John himself is left in a vulnerable position. Path analysis can make the delicate job of weighing the rights of individuals against potential harms to others explicit, and facilitate risk assessors in rehearsing the possible outcomes of their decisions from the point of view of all involved in the case. It is essential that the dilemma of balancing rights, risks and responsibilities to others beyond the service user is foregrounded in every decision, otherwise there is a temptation for decision makers to operate in ways which are professionally comfortable or least damaging to the worker (Kemshall and Pritchard 1997).

Figure 7.1 Decision path in case of John

In addition, to illustrating value frames, the paths drawn by participants also illustrated the importance of situational and organisational factors on making risk decisions. For example, one path in particular demonstrated how an inadequate transfer of a case due to sick leave affected the appropriate communication of information, and that this was subsequently compounded by lack of supervision of the worker and a period of inactivity on the case due to annual leave. Risk escalated during the absence of the 'pivotal worker' (Reder et al 1993) and a serious incident occurred prior to the completion of a risk assessment. The worker perceived the subsequent internal inquiry as an attempt to allocate the blame to her/him in circumstances which s/he felt were not only beyond her/his control but in part due to management inefficiency.

The close of the session was used to develop a consensus on the components of decision making which contribute to defensible decisions by collecting feedback and data from the path analyses under the following headings:

Components contributing to effective and defensible risk decisions

Participants viewed defensible decisions as enhanced by the adoption of an increased investigative and questioning stance by practitioners, a responsive approach to new information and situations, and a more provisional approach to risk assessment. In essence adopting an assessment process informed by Sheppard's 'retroductive analysis' (1995). In addition, practitioners looked for organisational support, for example over information flow, and the resolution of key systemic issues such as flaws in inter-agency work and increased co-ordination of risk management responses.

Components which do not contribute to effective and defensible decision making

Assessment processes over-dependent upon value biases and heuristics were seen as most likely to contribute to ineffective decision making, combined with collusive practices and the avoidance of appropriate responsibilities. The most often identified systemic problem was the inheritance of inappropriate decisions made elsewhere.

Recommendations for improving risk decisions

In addition to self-monitoring for the impact of value and bias, inquisitorial practice and the checking of assessments against the views of others were seen as important quality assurance mechanisms.

Session four The aim of this session was to equip participants with the ability and confidence to apply critical path analysis to their future practice decisions on risk, either retrospectively to evaluate decisions over time, or prospectively to evaluate the efficacy of various proposed decision choices. The latter can enable a more structured analysis of the future consequences of decision choices, and in effect assist practitioners in deciding the most appropriate risk decision path. This could be extremely useful in those highly complex situations where there are competing risks and more than one person is potentially at risk. In these situations practitioners have to weigh up the varying costs and benefits to all those concerned in the case (including themselves) of differing responses to the risks identified. In addition, some practitioners have responsibility for other members of staff involved in risk decisions, and critical path analysis is likely to be a useful tool in supervision for encouraging reflection upon assessment and intervention decisions.

Session five Consideration must also be given to the impact of critical path training on decision making over the longer term. Participants were asked to formulate an action plan requiring a specific focus on the transferability of the training input to the practice arena. In particular participants were asked to identify how they would integrate the use of CPA into their assessment practice, for example in their initial assessments and/or during reviews. Participants were also asked to identify how they might use CPA not only to quality assure their decisions, but also rehearse likely outcomes prior to implementing risk management strategies. In addition, participants were asked to review how they might use CPA individually and in teams to identify the situational factors affecting their decision making, and the organisational issues which need attention in order to facilitate more effective risk decision making.

These action plans can be followed up in a 3-6 month period via the local training section through a short questionnaire to participants on the outcomes of their plans (although in this case this was not part of the research project). Modification to the training input can take place as required by this more practice related feedback. The situational factors and organisational issues impacting upon risk decision making raised by participants should also be noted and feedback into the agency's senior management group through training section.

Evaluation

Participant feedback was taken against specific questions, and an overview indicates that participants found the workshop useful in identifying values, heuristics, and situational factors which impact upon their decision making. Importantly, participants could envisage the prospective use of critical path analysis in order to evaluate possible decision outcomes prior to making them and recommended increased attention to this in future workshops. Participants also advocated the use of path analysis in evaluating serious incidents and in evaluating risk decisions more generally.

Enhancing supervision and improving quality assurance

Supervisors are highly dependent upon the written record and the self-report of workers when assessing the adequacy of risk assessments. This can have severe limitations. Records are only as adequate as those who make them, and are prone to both filtering and interpretation. Nor are records necessarily representative of the thoughts or activities of workers (for example PO 28 who did risk assessments in his/her head but committed nothing to record). Records will also implicitly contain the judgmental heuristics instrumental in completing risk assessments, and reading cannot guarantee to uncover them. Self-report is also prone to the manipulation of presentation. In an atmosphere of heightened blame and accountability workers will naturally wish to present themselves as competent. Alternatively workers with 'stuck' and anxiety provoking cases may present as defensive and inactive. In these circumstances it is imperative that supervisors can engage in a meaningful and critical way with the decision making of their staff.

In a study of the supervision of child protection work Rushton and Nathan (1996) advocate an 'inquisitorial' approach to the supervision of staff in order to establish the quality of risk assessments, combined with an 'empathic-containing' function, that is enabling workers to appropriately contain their feelings. In focus groups experienced supervisors gave examples of how they quality assured assessments. This included reviewing sources of information, the evidence upon which assessments were made, and more importantly facilitating worker evaluation of the information gathered:

> The supervisors saw their task as encouraging staff to distance themselves from the information and to sift and evaluate it carefully in order to reach a sensible judgement about what action should follow (Rushton and Nathan 1996, p.366).

Judgements of worker competence were based upon: '...their capacity to validate their initial hypotheses, and to judge from the evidence the level of risk presented.' (Rushton and Nathan 1996, p.366). However, carrying out the techniques of clarification and confrontation seen as essential to such judgements of competence was not without its problems (Rushton and Nathan 1996). Supervisors could be overwhelmed by the anxieties, distress and feelings of workers, or find it difficult to '...confront staff who might be vague, evasive or defensively aggressive' (p.372). In this situation (although not exclusively so), a method which can facilitate an inquisitorial approach without alienating workers is essential.

Critical path analysis, as well as providing information for supervisors in their quality assurance task, also provides practitioners with an opportunity for guided reflection enabling practitioners to reflect upon and learn from their decision experiences in a structured and supported way (Johns 1994). Through workers drawing the path in supervision, supervisors can 'tune into' the decision making of their supervisees, but just as importantly so can workers. The process can then be supported by asking the supervisee the following questions:

- What factors, values and knowledge influenced your decisions and actions in this case?

- What have been the consequences of your decisions and actions?

- Could you have dealt with this case differently and with more desirable consequences?

- What other choices did you have? Why didn't you take them?

- How have you made sense of this experience and what might you do differently in the future?

(Adapted from Johns 1994)

Workers are facilitated to reflect upon the knowledge they have applied to the case and the full range of factors which have impinged upon their decision making, but also to consider the efficacy of their decisions, and to consider and rehearse alternative courses of action.

Critical path analysis could also have a broader role within the evaluation of risk decision making on offenders. Everitt and Hardiker (1996) argue that the more prevalent form of evaluation, the 'rational-technical', is limited by its focus upon the ratio of inputs to outputs. In essence, this type of evaluation can tell you that practice has taken place and at what cost, it cannot tell you the *value* of the practice in terms of its impact and effectiveness. They argue that this requires a more critical process for 'making judgements about the value of practice' (p.9), and a greater concern with the conditions that contribute to 'good' practice taking place. Critical path analysis can enable practitioners and their supervisors to identify the conditions for both 'good' and 'poor' practice, and contribute to the dissemination and replication of practices which are making a difference. In respect of offender risk assessment, critical path analysis could be used to identify the conditions under which the most effective risk decisions are made, and this could be replicated in practice guidance to staff. Negative conditions could be regularly monitored for by supervisors, in peer reviews, or through gatekeeping processes. These negative conditions should then receive managerial attention to reduce them.

Organisational management of risk

Evaluating risk assessment and risk management strategies is a key issue for senior managers. Currently it is easier to evaluate decisions retrospectively with hindsight, usually in the light of something 'going wrong'. In these circumstances the identification of how false negatives have occurred is a major preoccupation of inquiries, usually resulting in the attribution of blame and corrective actions. However, learning from mistakes in these circumstances can be a costly business, not least in terms of agency credibility and public trust. The reduction of error and promoting defensible decision making is more likely to preserve both, and requires managers to consider the quality of decision making *before* mistakes occur. Critical path analysis can assist with the development of quality assurance systems, monitoring, and the development of a more critical and prospective form of evaluating risk decisions.

Potentially critical path analysis could contribute to managerial inspections of risk assessment and risk management. Managers must be concerned with the efficacy of risk assessments as well as with how many of them have been completed. Practitioners need to be able to learn from 'mistakes' and to enhance defensible decision making. The characteristics of effective practice are too often hidden at the level of the individual practitioner. In the area of risk assessment it is essential that practitioners can access this information as well as general statistical information on the ratio of inputs to outputs. Managers and practitioners need to be informed about the rates of true positives as against false, and true negatives as against false ones. The crucial question is whether assessments of risk are more often right than wrong, and how many risk assessments with negative outcomes are defensible in the light of 'hindsight bias'? These questions should lead service managers into the area of quality decision making and how to evaluate it, in addition to concerns with input and output measures.

8. Risk Decision Making in the Field: An Explanatory Model

The data in this study illustrates frontline risk assessors and their managers striving to understand and manage an ambiguous and uncertain concept:

> PO 6: I think it's quite ambiguous really, it's quite subjective and it's caused me quite a bit of anxiety as to when you discuss with colleagues as to what perceptions about risk mean...I would very much like to have a definition or definitional criteria that would firm up some of the things I'm already doing.

Knowing what risk 'really is', is seen as the key to resolving anxiety provoking uncertainty, as long as this is in line with existing practices, and implicitly, values and beliefs about acceptable professional practice. Risk assessments in probation practice can be characterised as decisions to resolve uncertainty by the use of tacit, practical based knowledge and professional assumptive values made within the particular social and organisational setting of probation work. Such a characterisation draws upon a range of theoretical positions to explain risk perception, such as those on heuristics and cognitive reasoning (Reason 1990); situated practical reasoning (Garfinkel 1967) and plural rationalities of risk (Rayner 1986, Rhodes 1997); social constructivist theories (Berger and Luckmann 1967); and social and cultural theories of risk (Douglas 1992, Krimsky and Golding 1992). The challenge is how these differing theoretical conceptualisations of risk can be combined to provide a conceptual model with sufficient depth to capture the complexity of risk decision making in the field.

Psychometric versus social and cultural explanations

Traditionally theories of risk perception, assessment and management havebeen characterised by two distinct positions: the psychometric using the discipline of cognitive psychology and decision theory, and social/cultural theories of risk based within sociological and anthropological concerns (Douglas 1992, Rayner 1992).

The psychometric tradition proposes a notion of 'Homo Prudens', the 'zero-risk man' epitomising 'prudence, rationality and responsibility', (Adams 1995, p.16), and that risks can and will be rationally calculated if only the 'lay public' has the same information as the expert. Research within this paradigm is concerned with how risk information is received and processed, and most particularly with error, bias and how irrational decisions are made with a view to developing corrective approaches to assessment and management (Slovic et al 1980). The main outputs of this work have been on the distinction between the risk assessment judgements of experts and 'lay people' (Fischoff et al 1983, Slovic et al 1980), the impact of cognitive heuristics on judgement (Reason 1990), and the attempt to statistically produce an inventory of factors pertinent to risk assessments (Slovic 1992).

Limitations of this approach to fully explain attitudes to risk and risk decision making are now widely recognised (Adams 1995, Jasanoff 1993, Rayner 1992), in particular a refutation of homo prudens (Adams 1995) and of the individual as the primary or sole unit of analysis (Rayner 1992). People are not necessarily risk averse, risks can lead to rewards and risky behaviours can be actively sought (for example many risky sports are based upon active risk seeking for the 'thrill'). Risk is not unidimensional, it 'comes in many forms' (Adams 1995, p. 19), occurring within a social context and subject to a number of interactive factors. The difficulty is not necessarily with conceptualising risk in this way, it is more usually with measuring it. Complex interactions do not readily lend themselves to quantitative investigation. The psychometric tradition has predominantly concentrated on those factors most amenable to scientific, quantitative measurement.

More recently Slovic (1992) has noted the importance of moving from the individual as the sole unit of analysis to social and cultural factors. Slovic noted the inherently subjective nature of risk assessment, and that this subjectivity is influenced by: 'a wide array of psychological, social, institutional, and cultural factors' (Slovic 1992, pp.119-120).

Whilst this approach endeavours to collapse the subjective-objective dichotomy, and to take seriously the views of assessors, the unit of analysis is not entirely transformed to the social or cultural, or to the interaction between individuals and social context. The methodology remains questionnaires to individuals and the research concerns remain the 'cognitive models, assumptions, and inference methods that comprise lay people's "intuitive toxicological theories"' (Slovic 1992, p.147).

Social theories of risk, of which the principle example is cultural theory (Douglas 1966, 1972, 1992), move from an individualist paradigm to a contextual and social one (Krimsky 1992). The major contribution of cultural theory has been to refute the realist ontology of risk (Wynne 1989a) and to emphasise that risk is 'inevitably subject to social processes' (Thompson and Wildavsky 1982, p. 148), and that 'Risk is always a social product' (Thompson and Wildavsky 1982, p. 160). In addition, social and cultural theories (in particular the latter) have provided a theoretical understanding of how risks are selected for concern and how these concerns are legitimated (Douglas 1966, 1992). In essence risks are chosen for concern because of their usefulness to the social system. Risks are intrinsically bound up with belief systems resulting in plural rationalities (Rayner 1986) and competing conceptualisations of risk where such belief systems are at odds (Krimsky 1992, Thompson 1980). Cultural theory offers an explanation for how social structure, social groupings and risk concerns interact with cultural theory arguing: '...that risks are defined, perceived, and managed according to principles that are inherent in particular forms of social organisation' (Rayner 1992, p. 84). Most notable for explaining this interaction is Douglas' grid/group framework (discussed in chapter 3), with its emphasis upon membership of distinct group types and affiliation to particular cosmologies which maintain social order (Douglas 1966, 1992, Rayner 1992).

Social constuctivism has similar concerns to cultural theory and treats risk as a socially constructed concept determined by social processes. Risk disputes are understood as disputes of value and belief (Wynne 1982a) as social actors and social groups struggle to impose their own meaning on events (Rayner 1986). Both positions have been criticised for cultural relativism (Hammond 1993), however, Rayner (1992) disputes this by contending that knowledge can be known and shared by groups (for example Berger and Luckmann's 'typifications' (1967)), and can have transferability across groups although the process of communication can be hindered by resistance:

> ...we should start by asking what is at stake for those involved in developing a cross-cultural consensus, and how flexible is the knowledge process to enable it to accept or resist the change? (Rayner 1992, p.100 Reproduced

from S. Krimsky and D. Golding (eds): Social theories of Risk, (1992), Praeger Publishers with the kind permission of Greenwood Publishing Group)

A charge of static cultural determinism has also been levelled at these theoretical approaches. In essence individuals appear to be ascribed to an unchanging cultural perspective or 'worldview' (Bellaby 1990a). Rayner (1992) disputes such determinism by suggesting that cultural theory is not predictive of individual actions, rather:

> It is a social theory that views social organisation as presenting patterns of opportunities and constraints for what can be said in a particular social context (Rayner 1992, p.107. Reproduced from S. Krimsky and D. Golding (eds): Social theories of Risk, (1992), Praeger Publishers with the kind permission of Greenwood Publishing Group).

Whilst context will limit the possibilities of arguments 'that can be used with credibility' (Rayner 1992, p. 108), individuals can belong to and move between contexts changing their 'talk' accordingly. Social organisation is viewed as a constraint but social actors are not viewed as entirely passive.

However, as Krimsky (1992) expresses it this leaves one unresolved issue in considering the individualist and contextualist paradigms of risk theorising. That is, which comes first: the individual and cognitions, or the context and the social? Most recent empirical and theoretical approaches suggest that this is a sterile dichotomy (Marris et al 1995), and that a dialectical approach is likely to offer greater empirical and theoretical rewards (Douglas and Wildavsky 1982, 1983, Jasanoff 1993). Jasanoff has argued that the two theoretical traditions can themselves be understood as competing risk cultures (Jasanoff 1993), and that greater interaction between them would add greater depth and understanding by adding layers of 'cognitive complexity to the original, simple comparison of risk probabilities' (p.128).

This complexity can be gained by considering three key factors: 'scale', 'interactivity', and 'contingency' (Jasanoff 1993). Scale is presented as a concern with the 'distributive' components of space, time and cross-cultural boundaries; interactivity with the interaction between 'nature and society in the production of risks'; and contingency with the 'contextually delimited character of virtually all knowledge about risk.' (p.125). Jasanoff demonstrates how some traditional approaches to risk artificially manipulate features of scale, for example by applying statistical models to small samples and then averaging to larger populations, or using computer simulations to model future predictions of global situations such as climate change. In criminal justice the Offender Group Reconviction Score is a case in point.

Alternatively, large scale studies can ignore important local factors. For example, Wynne (1989) demonstrated that radiation experts underestimated the impact of Chernobyl radiation in Lancashire because they had not taken the acidity of local soil into account. In the case of siting probation hostels, local communities may exaggerate the level of risk according to experts, but experts mis-calculate the impact of involuntary risks carrying no perceived benefit to the recipient of those risks.

In a brief review of technological disasters Jasanoff illustrates the fallibility of a dichotomy between nature and society, actions and institutions. For example in the Bhopal disaster (Shrivastava 1987) a technology developed within and for America was transported to a country with a different understanding and experience of technology. This technology was integrated into the lives of its workers and users in terms of their own 'cultural necessities and presuppositions' (Jasanoff 1993). Operation of the plant was mediated by local practices and cultural experiences, for example workers monitored for leaks by using their sense of smell and disregarded the alarm system which constantly mal-functioned. Ultimately this personally based alarm system proved inadequate (Jasanoff 1993). Other instances of worker mediation of officially prescribed practice exist, for example Wynne on the Abbeystead methane explosion (1988) and Cullen (1990) on Piper Alpha.

Finally risk assessment is mediated by the contingent nature of knowledge of risk. As Jasanoff expresses it:

> What we claim to know about risk, how we acquire more information, and how we interpret the facts in our possession are all contingent on contextual factors, ranging from individual or organisational experience to national and political culture (Jasanoff 1993, p. 127).

For example, in Probation practice what Probation Officers have traditionally perceived and known as risk has been contingent upon the political framing of law and order and penal policy concerns prevailing at the time. As this has shifted so have risk concerns, and the facts and knowledge which staff are meant to have and to take seriously. This knowledge is:

...produced to serve different functions and under different constraints across political and cultural functions (Jasanoff 1993, p. 127).

The conceptualisation of risks is both directed and constrained by such forces, but at an individual level risk assessors are not merely the passive recipients of risk information (Jasanoff 1993). Rather, individuals seek to make their engagement with risk a meaningful personal experience through a process which involves a number of variables such as group norms, beliefs, values, trust, past experience, and power to control or influence events. Jasanoff concludes by arguing that this contingent nature of risk places emphasis upon the perceiver's prior experience, context and capacity to learn and adapt to new risks. It also stresses the credibility of the information source and how trust, empowerment and participation in the risk decision making process are achieved. Her conclusion is for an essentially collibrationist approach to risk in which interaction and negotiation are emphasised above didactic communication to passive receivers.

Developing a dialectical and 'layered' approach to risk theorising

This research has drawn upon components of both traditions to explore risk in probation practice, but importantly has attempted to locate the individual risk assessor within the wider organisational and national policy context. Occasionally this has presented conceptual tensions, for example critical path analysis whilst presented here as a reflective tool for individual performance within an organisational context, has its roots within a psychometric and corrective tradition (Flanagan 1954). Situated rationality theory is a powerful tool for explaining plural rationalities within an organisational setting, but can be severely limited in its capacity to generate theory of broader applicability (Bloor 1995a). Social theory clearly focuses attention on the social construction of risk and how certain risks gain currency and saliency and has a key role in examining policy formulation but may not totally explain how strategic choices are made in particular situations. Cultural theory clearly links risky behaviour to social institutions and affiliations to distinct world-views or cosmologies, but can appear static (Bellaby 1990a) and empirically unwieldy in the field (Gross and Rayner 1985, Rayner 1992). What is required is an approach which can integrate the key components of each into a conceptual framework.

In developing a theoretical understanding of 'HIV-Related Risk Behaviour' Bloor (1995a) importantly distinguishes between theories which have predictive utility and those which have 'heuristic merits', that is the ability to describe and explain activities and events. The latter can have practical utility in assisting future action and policy development, in Bloor's case health education and promotion campaigns. In providing a theoretical approach to compensate for the deficiencies of psycho-social models, situated rationality theories and cultural theory, Bloor emphasises that any theory must be able to respond to the oppositions of habituation/ routinisation of activities versus calculation, constraint versus volition, and situated activities versus shared world views or 'relevances', and the temporal and processual nature of decision making (Bloor 1995, p.26).

Whilst Bloor's work is significant in paying attention to habituated action and the tacit 'taken-for-granted meanings' in influencing cognition (Garfinkel 1967, Schutz 1970), and also the constraints upon what actions can be performed in the immediate situations of choice, the connection to social norms (as opposed to group norms) and the role of power in negotiating rationalities of risk remains underdeveloped. The emphasis remains upon 'local strategic relationships as well as orientations brought to the situation' (Bloor 1995a, p.28).

Theoretically any framework must be able to relate such individual orientations and local strategic relationships to issues of power, structure, and the social and cultural formations of risk. Such a framework must be able to encompass the following concepts: individual agency, constraint, opportunity, contingency, context, power, and the cultural and social saliency of risks, and bridge the gap between the individual and social units of analysis. In this framework risk assessors are characterised as active, they take decisions, make choices, and exercise volition. However, individual agency can be limited by constraints, these can be social norms and expectations (Douglas 1966, 1992), or interactivity with others in particular settings and locals (Garfinkel 1967). Literally Rayner's 'patterns of opportunities and constraints for what can be said in a particular social context' (Rayner 1992, p.107).

Volition is bounded by what can be known and what can be expressed in any social situation. This raises the contingent nature of both knowledge and action dependent upon specific conditions, and the contextual nature of risk decision making. However, this does not necessarily raise the spectre of individual or contextual relativism, as in the production of their situated reasonings on risk social actors both use and reproduce social meanings intrinsic to the achievement of social order (Giddens 1979). This order can however be in dispute (Rayner 1986, 1992). Giddens has argued that in presenting their accounts of the world social actors are doing more than merely stating meanings, they are also pursuing 'practical motives and interests' (Giddens 1995, p.243). Accounts can reveal vested interest and conflict as well as mutuality. As Giddens expresses it:

> ...every relation of meaning is also a relation of power-a matter of what makes some 'accounts' *count* (Giddens 1995, p.244).

Power inevitably raises issues of structure (Giddens 1995), and the 'duality' of agency and structure, or 'structuration' as Giddens dubbed it (1979, p.69, 1984), and the interactive nature of individual action with the rules and resources intrinsic to social structures. That is:

> By the duality of structure I mean that the structural properties of social systems are both the medium and the outcome of the practices that constitute those systems (Giddens 1979, p.69).

Structure is conceptualised by Giddens as both 'enabling and constraining' (Giddens 1979, p.69), essentially a resource for social action, but it can also be mediated, reproduced and changed by the activities of actors. Giddens rejects the notion of the social actor as a 'cultural dope', rather social actors are very knowledgeable about the operation of their society (p. 69), and in their everyday activities they can have a reciprocal impact upon the properties of social structures.

However, an important distinction is made by Giddens between the practical knowledge of actors that literally informs how they 'know what to do', and the discursive knowledge or discourse which frames what social actors are 'able to talk about' (Giddens 1979, p.73). The latter leads us to issues of legitimacy and saliency, in effect how some discourses and the accounts they facilitate come to count. This focuses attention on the social and cultural functions of risk, for example the legitimation of certain types of social order and authority, the re-emphasis of moral orders and cultural values, and the attribution of blame and delineation of 'outsiders' (Douglas 1966, 1992, Kemshall et al 1997, Sparks 1992), and vested interest and power in the prioritising of risk discourses (Rayner 1992). Certain conceptions of risk are prioritised and legitimated, in this case negative impact and high danger based upon a normative presumption for safety concerned with 'preventing the worst and protection from harm' (Kemshall et al 1997, p.223). This social functioning of risk comes full circle and impacts upon the social activities of social actors and the organisations they operate in, both facilitating and constraining talk and activities on risk, but also providing the medium for interpretation, dispute, and mediation of the risk discourse itself. The overall framework is presented as Figure 8.1:

Figure 8.1 The Reciprocal Relationship Between Individual Agency and Discourse

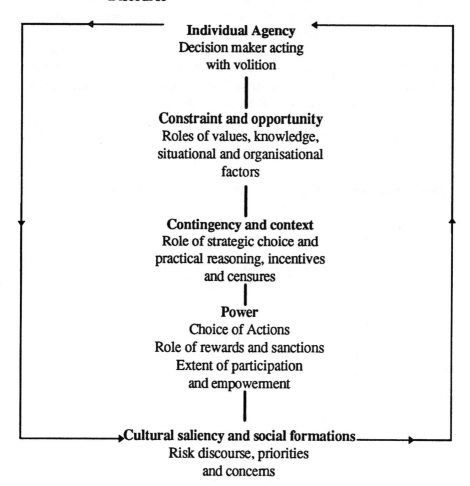

Individual Agency
Decision maker acting
with volition

Constraint and opportunity
Roles of values, knowledge,
situational and organisational
factors

Contingency and context
Role of strategic choice and
practical reasoning, incentives
and censures

Power
Choice of Actions
Role of rewards and sanctions
Extent of participation
and empowerment

Cultural saliency and social formations
Risk discourse, priorities
and concerns

This conceptual framework will now be applied to the specific activity of doing risk in probation practice.

The application of a dialectical and 'layered' approach to risk in Probation Practice

The empirical data has presented risk assessments in probation practice as a product of the interaction between knowledge and values in the particular organisational setting of probation work. Assessments, whilst located at the individual level of decision making are not viewed as the outcome of individual choice, but as the outcome of 'negotiated actions' (Rhodes 1997). Whilst probation staff were making risk decisions based upon how they perceived the risk, their perceptions were both organisationally and socially constructed (Kemshall 1997c, Rhodes 1997).

Strauss and Corbin (1990) have argued that 'explanatory conditions' of Grounded Theory must not be 'restricted only to those that seem to have immediate bearing on the phenomenon under study' (p.256). Macroscopic as well as microscopic concerns must be considered and their impact upon action and interaction. In effect, to consider various levels of analysis and the 'interactive nature of events.' (Strauss and Corbin 1990, p.159). The application of this to the present research is represented in Figure 8.2:

Figure 8.2 Decision making in Probation Practice

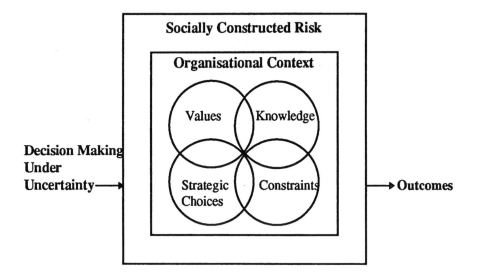

Risk assessments are posed as decisions made under conditions of uncertainty (Brearley 1982), taken by individuals within an organisational context and within a process of interaction between worker, agency and client (Payne 1997). The organisation is placed within a broader penal policy context which in turn is located within broader societal constructions of risk concerns. Uncertainty in decision making is resolved through the interaction of professional value systems and knowledge bases which assessors bring to their decision making, and these can be variably applied due to conditions of constraint and incentives such as legal opportunities to act, blame and censure, and the desirability of achieving particular strategic ends such as lenient sentencing or preservation of supervisory relationships. Risk assessors engage in strategic reasoning to resolve the indeterminate nature of risk in which weighing a number of 'it depends' and 'trading off' various outcomes is completed by recourse to the normative ideals of practice.

This strategic reasoning takes place within a specific organisational setting and policy context which is generating new expectations and conditions for practice, and challenges to existing values and normative practice ideals. This is most often expressed as value disputes and challenges to the practice knowledge base of staff. Two competing value bases can be discerned, reflecting both organisational and policy change and the growing predominance of central policy makers' construction of offender risk, along with the increasing saliency of certain categories of crime risks in the wider society. A risk discourse is superseding the traditional needs and rehabilitative one (Garland 1997, Kemshall et al 1997), impinging upon organisational priorities and practice activities.

In this bounded sense, Probation risk assessors are construed as intentional actors, engaging in activities which are habituated, that is based upon tacit knowledge, reflexive that is able to reflect upon and provide accounts for their actions, and able to engage in calculated activities which can be moderated through the process of reflexivity and the impact of situational constraints and structural properties (Giddens 1979, Schutz 1970). The process of decision making, or negotiating actions on risk comprises the key components of individual agency, constraint and opportunity, contingency and context, power, and cultural/social saliency outlined above. Their application to this study will now be explored. Despite the linear presentation in the text, the model is conceptualised as interactive and non-hierarchical.

Individual agency

Probation risk assessors bring their tacit understanding of the social world, their individual and shared tacit knowledge and value systems, past experiences and self-conception to their experience of risk and assessment of risk. They are intentional actors acting with volition, and actively seek to make their experience of risk meaningful to them by recourse to their available stock of knowledge and values. Within probation practice at the present time this available stock of knowledge and values is predominantly the tacit accumulated case based practice wisdom of practitioners and the traditional value base of client need and rehabilitation. Practice wisdom functions as 'practical consciousness' informing assessors of how to do the risk task (Giddens 1979), that is, Schutz's 'routinised activities' (Schutz 1970) or Garfinkel's 'commonsense knowledge' (Garfinkel 1967). It is this knowledge which staff have most recourse to in order to resolve their uncertainty and make meaningful their risk encounters. However it is this practical consciousness which is challenged and delegitimated by formal policy statements on risk, formal assessment methods and central government expectations.

Discursive consciousness or discursive knowledge is concerned with 'what actors are able to 'talk about' and in what manner or guise they are able to talk about it' (Giddens 1979, p.73). In probation practice this is particularly problematic, as the discursive knowledge of central policy makers and frontline workers appear to be at odds, with the latter considered to be lacking in the 'proper talk' by policy makers (Wynne 1982a).

Discursive knowledge can be particularly significant to calculated rather than habituated actions, that is actions which have been taken following the deliberation of differing options and possible outcomes. This is most often the case in new, non-routinised situations. Schutz (1970) understood this realm as 'topical relevance' (pp.111-122) as distinct from the domain of interpretative schema used for routinised decision making. In essence, it is discursive knowledge or topical relevances which determine 'whether or not a situation becomes problematic for an individual.'(Bloor 1995a, p.27). Situations may be self-selected as problematic by individuals or imposed by 'the actions and utterances of the individual's significant others' (Bloor 1995a). Schutz (1970) expressed this as the difference between 'intrinsic relevances' and those 'imposed' (p.114), the latter are not chosen by us and our only option in responding to them is to transform them into our intrinsic relevances. Schutz contends that whilst this remains unachieved we do not consider them to be connected to our interests. In these situations, because relevances remain imposed they 'remain unclarified and rather incomprehensible' (Schutz 1970, p.114).

In probation practice the differences in discursive knowledge means that differing situations are selected as problematic, and on occasion the imposed 'topical relevances' of central policy makers and local managers are resisted by frontline risk assessors. Risk assessors seek to operate with a degree of congruence between their taken for granted intepretative schema and topical relevances whether intrinsic or imposed. Where this congruence can not be achieved risk assessors experience contradiction and uncertainty, even dissonance and distress as they lack the repertoire of options to act as they would wish. This is most clearly evidenced in debates about values and practitioner resistance to activities which they perceive to be 'inauthentic' (James 1994).

Constraint and opportunity

Topical relevances and mutual, taken for granted knowledge can be understood as both constraint and opportunity. In probation practice the assumptive values of the profession, practice wisdom, practical knowledge and situational/organisational factors can all be posed as components of both constraints upon action and opportunities to deploy routinised social actions. Action in uncertain assessment situations is facilitated by the interaction of professional values and knowledge systems, but action is also stymied in situations where 'cues' do not fit the existing knowledge base, or the actions required by role and responsibility are not commensurate with preferred value systems.

Action is also constrained and facilitated by incentives such as the avoidance of blame and censure, managerial expectations, legal requirements to act, and fear of professional or physical risks to self; or constraints such as resources, and lack of legal authority to act. Organisational and situational factors such as information flow, work organisation, professional networks, polarisation, hierarchy and culture also play their part. Action choices are not only informed and reasoned, but are also bounded and limited.

Contingency and context

Constraints and opportunities necessarily lead to the contingent and contextual nature of action on risk, and the conditions under which certain types of strategic reasoning will be deployed and why. In Probation practice this is exemplified by contrasts between field and hostel staff in assessing and responding to risk, officers displaying differing value bases dependent upon the nature of the case based information or the outcomes prioritised as desirable, differing perceptions of risk dependent upon grade, and the significance of numerous 'it depends' in decision making.

Power

Competing views of risk dependent upon context and the contingent nature of knowledge available to assessors raises the issue of power. Power is defined in the Foucaultian sense as strategically deployed in relationships rather than as a commodity owned by individuals or groups (Bloor 1995a, Cousins and Hussein 1984, Foucault 1970, 1980). In this sense, relationships within Probation practice express relationships of meaning and how such meanings are prioritised for concern. In Giddens terms: how accounts come to count. (Giddens 1995), and how rationalities of risk are negotiated (Rayner 1992). At the individual decision maker level this is expressed as the power to act in line with values and beliefs, or 'authentically' as James (1994) expresses it, and the extent to which decision makers can influence or control events, even 'act otherwise' (Giddens 1979).

The differences of view between frontline staff and managers on risk management in this study illustrate both the use and *perception of use* of power in relationships between managers and workers about risk and indeed other issues. Workers perceived practice as increasingly constrained and management as managing by dictate rather than consensus. Officers viewed themselves as largely excluded from the development of policy and procedures on risk. This had explicitly prioritised managerial views of risk, but also signalled quite clearly the likely outcome of negotiating risk concerns with managers. In cases of negative outcomes most workers believed that agency priorities and views would predominate, and that managers would seek to 'cover their backs' and protect agency credibility at the cost of individual workers.

At a broader level power also raises issues of participation and empowerment in organisational decision making. These local strategic relationships between senior managers and frontline workers can be characterised as predominantly low participation and low empowerment (although differences in the extent of this may vary at team level, for example in the hostel team). The lack of consensus on risk definitions, risk criteria, features of best practice, and differing perceptions of risk management at all grades is particularly illustrative of the worker-manager divide and the lack of inclusion in organisational life. This can result in 'noise management' through prescriptive procedures and vigorous compulsory training programmes. Local relationships of power also reflect relationships of power between the Probation Service and the Home Office, and current social and cultural formations of risk concerns. These have been expressed predominantly through legislation, policy statements, Home Office circulars, and guidance, expressing central policy expectations with which Services are expected to concur.

Social and cultural formations of risk

Crime risks are an important indication of the risks which have acquired cultural and social saliency (Sparks 1992). In this case reflecting a normative imperative for safety from hazards and dangers presented by 'opponents' and 'intransigients' resulting in proactive strategies for the identification and regulation of offender groups classed as risky. Douglas (1992) has argued that risk is not a neutral term but serves a particular purpose in the society within which it is deployed. In this case the provision of 'self-validating legitimacy to established law and order' (Douglas 1992, p.29). The traditional penal practices of the state, normalisation and rehabilitation, are being replaced by the risk concerns of the new penology (Feeley and Simon 1992, 1994, Garland 1990, Kemshall 1997c). This is the context within which actions on risk are negotiated and accomplished.

The major issue in probation practice and policy at the present time is the extent of congruence between the views and activities of individual assessors and the policy expectations of the new penology, in effect the degree of 'fit' between official discourse and action in the field. At present this is variable as individuals deploy other discourses, and the legitimacy and acceptability of official definitions and concerns with risk are disputed on the ground. Such disputes and resistance can be tacit, for example in recasting risk concerns into the language of need, implicitly by choosing courses of action 'at odds' with managerial expectation but in line with professional values, or explicitly by prioritising client need and rehabilitative objectives over risk concerns.

Official discourse on risk is also interpreted and mediated by local policy managers (Kemshall 1997c), and the existing practices and concerns of the agency. In this process trust and credibility play a crucial role in the effective communication of risk concerns and the acceptance of their legitimacy (Rayner 1992). Whilst Rayner's work is primarily focused upon public acceptance of technological risks, his key points have relevance here. In essence can those defining and regulating the risks be trusted, is the system of liability and accountability for risks equitable, and to what extent has consent for risk concerns and subsequent actions been achieved? (Rayner 1992 p.95, Rayner and Cantor 1987). Answers, particularly negative answers, are crucial to the acceptability of risks. Within probation practice on risk the views of officers on managerial responses to risk strongly suggests that trust, liability and credibility are real issues in accepting responsibility for the risk task. This is also mirrored at the wider institutional level between services and the Home Office (Kemshall 1996b).

Wynne (1982a, 1992) has argued that issues of trust arise in risk debates because risk and its presentation is inextricably bound up with how particular forms of social relations are legitimated and maintained. Risk rationalities, and the knowledge which underpins them, are shaped within these social relations. Whilst Wynne's work is focused upon institutional settings rather than the broader concerns of cultural theory, his work is central to understanding how differing rationalities can collide and the role of trust in such disputes (Wynne 1982a, 1987, 1988, 1989, 1989, 1992). He argues that all definitions and approaches to risk are dependent upon 'a priori framing' based upon implicit assumptions about the social world, the behaviour of social actors and the circumstances under which 'a particular kind of risk is thought to arise.' Such a priori framing is present within scientific, expert and official discourses on risk as well as those of the 'lay' pubic. (Wynne 1992). In this sense all knowledge of risk is conditional and at the:

> ...heart of all risk perceptions and risk conflicts [is] not the issue of technical magnitude, but rather trust in institutions (Wynne 1992, pp.277-278. Reproduced from S. Krimsky and D. Golding (eds): Social theories of Risk, (1992), Praeger Publishers with the kind permission of Greenwood Publishing Group).

Expert, official and policy languages of risk provide their own definitions of risk, but also their own legitimation for what can be included or excluded as rational and pertinent to the risk debate. Other languages and knowledges are thereby discounted, for example in the Windscale inquiry (Windscale 1982a). The 'tacit social model' of experts is imposed and becomes 'prescriptive', requiring social behaviour to validate both the implicit a priori assumptions and knowledge base advocated. This imposition results in the 'denigration' of alternative positions and a threat to those whose social identity is delegitimated by the undermining of their world view (Wynne 1992). In effect, those who do not comply with official views are dismissed as incompetent or irrational. Those who champion expert and official views of risk are in danger of underestimating the anxiety and threat caused by lack of consent and lack of trust, and the escalation of resistance which can result as they seek to make their view work.

Wynne's work has predominantly been in the area of public perception and resistance to technological risks such as nuclear energy (1982a, 1986, 1987, 1988, 1989). However, his work can usefully be applied to the institutional management of risks, in this case the collision of official and practitioner views of risk, and the collision of two distinct knowledge bases for offender risk assessment. Official views of risk can be seriously at odds with how practitioners perceive risk to 'really' be on the ground or how interactions with offenders 'really' take place. Official guidance for example contains implicit assumptions about the nature of the social world, organisational life, and practice with offenders and can be experienced by workers (and of course managers) as not related to the realities of practice life. This results in dismissal of the guidance as practically unsound and leaves workers feeling misunderstood and undervalued.

From data based on a number of inquiries of technological risks Wynne demonstrates that such formal models of risk management systems are often ideal types lacking any existence in the real world of operation (1987, 1988, 1989, 1992). The 'fit' between such models and the real world is more often expressed by experts and policy makers as an issue of compliance and enforcement than of the limits of the models themselves. What is frequently overlooked is that experts/officials and workers define 'different' but 'actual risk systems'. (Wynne 1992, p.286). Where these remain at odds then acceptability and compliance remains a key issue.

The conceptual model of risk in probation practice, including the role of trust and worker mediation of practice is represented in Figure 8.3.

Implications of the conceptual framework for risk in Probation Practice

The resolution of risk rationality disputes is not a matter of deciding who is right or who is wrong. In Wynne's terms all knowledge is conditional and the object of analysis is to make this conditionality explicit (Wynne 1992). Each group in any risk debate can always say it knows best. However, the explicit articulation of assumptions can form the basis of 'critical engagement' across positions, and assist in a more consensual and integrated approach to risk management (Wynne 1992). In Wynne's view, the local knowledge of farmers combined with expert views could have been more productive in estimating radiation risks in Lancashire post-Chernobyl (Wynne 1989a, 1992). Jasanoff (1993) has also highlighted the productive combination of local, informal 'lay' knowledge with formal technical knowledge.

Figure 8.3 Trust, Credibility and Mediation

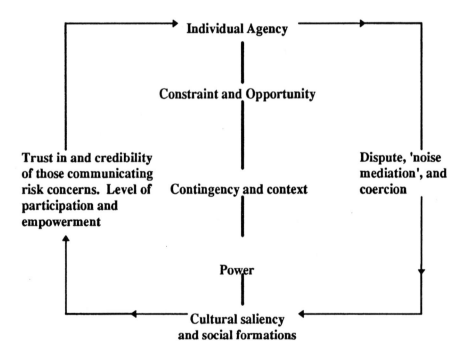

Critical engagement can also make explicit the grounds upon which knowledge systems are based, and provide a system for evaluating the claims to authority and legitimacy proffered. Whilst this does not necessarily lead to the 'truth of the matter' it does make explicit the grounds upon which claims to 'rightness' are made (Mannheim 1982, Wynne 1992). This requires a degree of reflexivity on the part of experts, officials and workers to consider the basis of their contrary positions, and the likely impact upon policy formulation and implementation. This process can illuminate why risk policy models transfer so inadequately to the 'real' world and the inherent threats to social identity contained within them. There is also the potential that those holding alternative positions can learn that expert views 'can provide reliable and robust knowledge, within conditions that need to be identified...' (Wynne 1992, p.292. Reproduced from S. Krimsky and D. Golding (eds): Social theories of Risk, (1992), Praeger Publishers with the kind permission of Greenwood Publishing Group).

This mutual learning and reflexivity is at the heart of Wynne's 'social learning' approach:

It creates a basis for negotiation of mutually authoritative knowledge across paradigms rather than merely intensifying the brittle circles of (attempted) self-reassurance within existing paradigms (Wynne 1992, p.292. Reproduced from S. Krimsky and D. Golding (eds): Social theories of Risk, (1992), Praeger Publishers with the kind permission of Greenwood Publishing Group).

However, this has real policy implications somewhat contrary to experiences of current organisational life in Probation. The growth of managerialism has distanced both local and central policy makers from frontline staff and from a consensual style of working. Procedures and guidance are easier to engage in than critical reflection and negotiation. Frames of reference have become polarised and to some extent institutionalised, and there is high investment in maintaining existing patterns of communication and existing organisational structures. In essence, it is difficult to act differently beyond existing boundaries. However, it is important that institutional structures and decision making cultures are questioned.

Integrated knowledge systems and negotiation are key characteristics of the collibrationist approach to risk management. This style of risk management requires a different organisational form, what Thompson (1991, Wynne 1992) has called 'clumsy institutions':

> They trade narrow, and in the end self-defeating, efficiency for greaterresilience and much richer learning capability by embracing multiple rationalities (Wynne 1992, p.293. Reproduced from S. Krimsky and D Golding (eds): Social theories of Risk, (1992), Praeger Publishers with the kind permission of Greenwood Publishing Group).

In essence, this is Schon and Argyris' (1978, 1996) learning organisation, with emphasis upon individual and organisational learning and attention to the type and quality of social relations which constitute it. This organisational form complements the reflexive and learning practitioner, and has the potential to value and integrate a number of positions. As such it may provide a practical mechanism for resolving the current gap between official discourses on risk and practice on the ground. The alternative is the organisational enforcement of the nuclear industry which demands high discipline, collective commitment, and operation within a domain of absolute certainty. However, as Wynne suggests, this attitude itself creates threats for the nuclear industry as the:

> ...intense and disciplined collective commitment that requires the eradication of doubt, and hence the denial of uncertainties, conditions, and qualification. This is a Catch 22 situation for nuclear power because these necessary properties are precisely those that encourage arrogance and manifest self-delusion, hence understandable...oppression and fear (Wynne, 1992, p.294. Reproduced from S. Krimsky and D. Golding (eds): Social theories of Risk, (1992), Praeger Publishers with the kind permission of Greenwood Publishing Group).

What is at stake is more than risk. It is the nature of social organisations and institutional life, the level of trust and commitment we can have in one another. These are fundamental questions about how we want to do the 'risk business'.

Part Three: Reconciling Risk Differences: Optimum Risk Management Systems

The following chapters explore the various organisational responses to risk management, and their effectiveness in controlling and facilitating the risk decisions of frontline workers. A key issue is the degree of prescription and proceduralisation required to deliver effective risk decisions. In effect, can risk follow rules, or do rules merely obscure the inherent uncertainty of risk decisions and the contingent nature of 'on the ground' decision processes? The current 'anticipationist' approach to risk management exemplified by the precautionary principle is explored in chapter nine, and contrasted to other more resilient and collibrationist approaches. The role of blame in reducing implementation deficit, and the problem of literally insuring against every future eventuality of risk are seen as particularly problematic for the implementation of Probation risk policies.

The possibility of developing a credible 'insurance system' for offender risk is further explored in chapter ten. The minimum standards required of both policies and decision making in order to achieve 'defensible decisions' are reviewed. Chapter eleven concludes by considering the wider implications of an increased actuarially risk based approach to social regulation, and the implications for the Probation Service of adopting a key role in the 'risk society'.

9. Approaches to Risk Management

Experts and policy makers in the realm of risk have long advocated a prescriptive, rule-bound approach to the management of risk in organisations. This approach assumes that expertise can only reside in scientific and technical discourse, and lay expertise is denigrated (Grinyer 1995, Wynne 1982a, 1988, 1989a). Risk is viewed by policy makers as a uni-dimensional phenomenon rather than as a multi-dimensional one embedded in particular contexts and social processes (Grinyer 1995). As Wynne (1988, 1989a, 1992) and Grinyer (1995) express it, this is symptomatic of a 'naiveté' on the part of both policy makers and managers. Indeed the latter can be described as non-experts:

> Managers and policy makers...are themselves experts in neither the technical sphere nor the social or working environments which are the settings of application. They are, however, frequently the purchasers of the technical expertise which forms the basis of policies on risk and safety, although it is usually the workers who face [or work with] the risk (Grinyer 1995, p.31).

This can lead to significant mis-matches between the risk management systems advocated by policy makers and managers to regulate the risk decision making of staff in their organisations. The complexity of the systems within which risk decisions take place is frequently underestimated by experts, policy makers and managers alike (Perrow 1984). Experts, in posing effective risk management systems, do so in terms of 'ideal types', making assumptions about human behaviour such as 'homoprudens', and the nature of social life in institutional settings (Wynne 1987, 1988). Risk management is characterised as controlled, subject to vigorous monitoring and inspection, and well prescribed and well followed rules covering every eventuality. However, by reviewing technological accidents Wynne (1988) illustrates how the:

...operating rules of technologies are an ad hoc brew of informal modes of accommodating imprecise general principles to particular circumstances of implementation. These practical rules are more complex, ambiguous and very different from the neat, rule-bound image of technology projected in public (Wynne 1988, p.149. Reproduced with the permission of Sage Publications).

By taking data from Windscale (Wynne 1982), the Challenger Shuttle inquiry (Report of the Presidential Commission on the Space Shuttle 1986), and the Manchester airport disaster (Wynne 1988), Wynne illustrates how risk management systems are rarely operated according to the publicly stated rules but rather according to a '...different, more ambiguous set of rules...' (p.152).

In the case of the Boeing 737 at Manchester the engine had shown signs of failure previously, but staff interpreted this as a non-fatal risk in line with previous experience, indeed it was viewed as a 'relatively common problem' (indeed the alarm system had no credibility due to the number of false alarms), and the failure could be compensated for by implementing routine procedures. This was weighed against the disruption that a full engine check would cause, and the knock on effect of checking all planes with similar problems (Wynne 1988). In effect, potential risks can be normalised and formal procedures for their identification and regulation can be circumvented by informal processes. This circumvention is often essential to getting the job done, for example meeting targets or maintaining production, and can be interpreted by both managers and workers as a higher priority than risk management (Clarke 1995). This is often a matter of what is organisationally rewarded, for example production rather than safety during the July 1988 oil rig fire at Piper Alpha (Cullen 1990).

This highlights the important factor of context. General principles and rules have to be carried out within local contexts. Whilst consistency and universality are highly prized, particularly by central policy makers, the impact of local needs and circumstances should not be underestimated. As Wynne (1988) expresses it, the skill lies in practically reconciling universality and consistency with context and local. Universality versus context debates can be very common between central policy makers and local managers (Ham and Hill 1993).

Risk management procedures can be adapted in part rather than in whole, for example in order to make certain procedures work in that particular context or simply to 'get the job done' (Clarke 1995, Shrivastava

1987, Wynne 1988), or to respond to particular pressures in the system. In the Abbeystead methane explosion (Lancaster, May 1984), the fault was caused by informal work practices which had allowed a large void to build up in the tunnel to facilitate extra drainage. The drainage was seen locally as desirable because of complaints by local anglers about muddy water and poor fishing. This unofficial practice only came to light in the subsequent inquiry (Wynne 1988). This and other inquiries illustrates how the impact of 'local practical norms' upon risk management systems and how this is usually underestimated by experts and policy makers (Wynne 1987, 1988). Whilst public accountability creates a pressure to:

> ...standardise design and operating rules, so as to present a clear, intelligible account to third parties... (Wynne 1988, p.156. Reproduced with the permission of Sage Publications).

In practice this results in a naive and simplistic notion of risk management in organisational settings and an underestimation of the contingent nature of risk control.

The failure of simplistic risk models is not restricted to technological risks. Grinyer (1995) in reviewing HIV risks and public health campaigns notes how competing cultures and agendas of risk management undermine the simplistic notion that campaigns will result in awareness, and awareness in changes of behaviour. For Grinyer, such a view of policy underestimates:

> ...the way the structuration of an organisation informs the way in which a text is interpreted, and feeds back into the organisation to reproduce the organisation in a circular process (Grinyer 1995, p.33).

In a study of occupational HIV risks in two health authorities Grinyer examines how managers and workers have differing conceptualisations of risk and of the efficacy of health authority risk management policies. The interpretation and efficacy of the policy was crucially dependent upon the work conditions under which it was used, and the trust and credibility workers placed in the communication process. For example, safety leaflets had been circulated in wage packets to save money, but as this system had been previously used to advertise products and health insurance it had fallen into disrepute. Worker reaction was epitomised by:

> Another leaflet in the wages packet - forget it, it'll just get thrown away (Grinyer 1995, p. 41).

As Grinyer expresses it:

> If information designed to reassure is received from a source which has
> already had its credibility damaged, or which the recepients of the
> information believe has a vested interest in cutting costs, any further attempt
> to inform, however accurate and well-intentioned, may be mistrusted and
> therefore rejected (Grinyer 1995, p.42).

This perception can also extend to management responses in the event
of incidents having occurred. Responses to staff who contracted
occupationally related HIV were seen as ineffective, for example AZT
treatment which can involve greater risks for the recipient, but which was
seen by workers as assisting the health authority in avoiding costly
litigation. Most staff subsequently refused such an option. Crucially,
existing relationships between managers and staff affected the trust and
response of workers to both risk policies and post-incident support (Grinyer
1995).

In Grinyer's study the failure to recognise the institutional setting of the
workplace as a complex social system undermined the effective
communication of official information on risk. Whilst Grinyer's study
concerns those workers 'at risk', the present study on probation practice
illustrates that similar issues apply to those settings in which workers are
not only 'at risk' but are required to assess risk to others. The importance of
such studies (including Rayner 1986, Wynne 1987, 1988), is in illustrating
the source and process of worker resistance to official policy statements and
risk procedures. Rather than locating such resistance at the level of
individual incompetence and intransigence, it is located at the organisational
level in the institutional inability to recognise and deal with a complex social
system and the multi-dimensional nature of risk, and in 'policy makers' wish
to monopolise the accredited account of risk, thereby reinforcing
'institutionalised bias' (Grinyer 1995, p.47). Such institutionalised bias is
reflected in the discourse which is prioritised as central to constituting
organisational life. Challenges to this discourse, including research findings
can be dismissed as irrelevant or irrational (Grinyer 1995). In the case of
academic reports which prioritise the social nature of risk, findings are
dismissed as academic complexities unhelpful to the commonsense reality of
risk utilised by managers and policy makers. However, as Grinyer
expresses it:

Official information is only one of a number of different routes through which a hazard is understood. Powerful social forces shape the way in which information is perceived and acted upon in a way which may be underestimated by those responsible for risk assessment and the compilation of official information. Connections may be made by the recipients in unexpected ways, and the resulting interpretations of official data may be substantially different from official predictions (Grinyer 1995, p.49).

This raises real issues for the formulation and implementation of risk policies in Probation and for the management of risk decisions made by both local managers and frontline workers.

Current approaches to risk management in Probation

In Probation the institutional bias is increasingly towards the discourse of expert technical risk rationality. However this research illustrates that there is a significant gap between the official position and that held by frontline workers and local managers. The communication of the official position on risk can be characterised as a predominantly 'decide-announce-defend' strategy of low consultation and participation (Wilkinson 1997) in which only the official view appears to count, and which is continually defended against the challenges and non-compliance of the workforce. This is a strategy which can have severe limits and costs for those organisations involved in the risk business.

Wilkinson (1997), in reviewing Shell's communication strategy with community groups over the disposal of the Brent Spar oil storage and loading buoy in the Atlantic (summer 1995), illustrates the ineffectiveness of the 'decide-announce-defend' form of communication. Whilst the disposal plan had expert endorsement, it was strongly resisted by Greenpeace and public outrage soon followed. Shell had significantly underestimated the value-laden nature of risk judgements, and in particular the role of imposed risks and distrust in amplifying resistance:

Trust is a critical factor in bridging the differences between our different 'world views'...A common starting point in our developing approach to wider engagement and communications has been to re-establish and continue to build trust-based relationships (Wilkinson 1997, p.940).

Shell quickly recognised that they had focused on the technical aspects of the problem and had:

> ...failed to incorporate the elements of risk perception and relevance - to 'win hearts and minds' (Wilkinson 1997, p.942).

Ignoring the values and perceptions of others cost Shell its original disposal plan despite initial approval from experts and government. Shell now had to be seen to meet more than minimum standards in terms of environmental risks and to achieve public acceptability for its risk management plans. To achieve this Shell embarked upon a radically different communication strategy. Firstly they sought suggestions, receiving over 400 including some from members of the public, and these were passed to the contractors in the tendering process (Wilkinson 1997). This was paralleled by a series of seminars with interested parties and greater attention was paid to:

> ...enabling different interest groups to raise their specific concerns and debate these in an open and constructive manner, building public confidence and trust through wider and more open dialogue, using feedback from our open communication initiatives to inform our decision-makers (Wilkinson 1997, p942).

This has formed the basis of an open communications and engagement approach to risk management decisions in Shell in which understanding and accommodating the views and values of others is emphasised rather than the tactic of ignoring them (Wilkinson 1997). Wilkinson expresses the key components as a move away from adversarial positions, listening and responding to the concerns of others, confronting the issues of concern rather than 'defending', avoiding an 'us' and 'them' climate, identifying and using commonalities, and engaging in dialogue and debate (Wilkinson 1997).
As Wilkinson expresses it:

> ...we are trying to build bridges, instead of barriers, and to engage rather than enrage (Wilkinson 1997, p.943).

This is a practical application of Wynne's critical engagement and social learning approach (Wynne 1992), and could have real benefits for the effective communication of risk policies from central government to the

Probation Service and between local managers and staff. Importantly, it could also be a useful tool in communicating risks and the possibility of their effective management to the public. This is quite different from a communication strategy of a central powerful group 'circulating for comment', or consulting on an ad hoc basis with certain 'official' vested interest groups, usually in response to criticism or resistance.

Managerial responses to risk management in Probation at present exemplify both the 'decide-announce-defend' communication strategy and a more open response. One example of the former was the large metropolitan area which circulated the risk policy to staff via pigeon holes, an institutional tactic for providing coverage of the issue without engagement. Non-compliance was then reduced to an issue of worker negligence or incompetence to be addressed through a combination of management enforcement and compulsory training. As time passed, interpretation of the policy by local divisional managers and staff became increasingly problematic leading to variations in both assessment and management practices. This was again characterised as a training issue, and a vigorous programme of centrally organised and centrally delivered training was instituted to socialise the workforce into the risk practices deemed appropriate by headquarters staff. This was viewed by frontline staff and local managers as 'too little too late' and an exercise in headquarters 'back covering' rather than as a genuine attempt to equip staff to do the job. The policy approach of headquarters was seen as protective of senior managers but difficult in practice for workers to implement in a situation of shrinking resources, conflicting priorities and lack of reliable assessment methods to credibly identify potential risks.

This is in contrast to the minority of services which had used a working party and consultative approach to the development of risk policies and a planned strategy of communication with staff prior to the implementation of the policy (Kemshall 1996b). Central policy makers have also adopted a predominantly 'decide - announce - defend' communication strategy with the Service, for example through the use of probation circulars, guidance, and conferences. This has often been mirrored at local level in how services have chosen to develop and communicate risk policies to staff.

The former communication strategy characterises organisations which are closed with low participation and low empowerment. Approaches to risk management policies in such organisations have been described as 'lifeboat' responses to risk (Hood et al 1992, Kemshall et al 1997), troubled by the inherent uncertainty of the task and attempting to cover all the angles.

In the absence of totally reliable predictive methods the primary organisational response is to substitute the prioritisation of actions or areas requiring attention for predictive tools (Kemshall et al 1997), or to devolve the choice of tool to local managers (Home Office 1997, HMIP 1997). Responses to risk errors (or to 'lifeboat failure') are usually characterised by hindsight bias (Carson 1996) and allocation of blame on staff in an effort to encourage staff to take more care in future (Hood et al 1992, Kemshall et al 1997), and a lack of emphasis upon a learning culture. In such organisations risk management strategies are prone to hindrance from resistance and debates about the legitimacy of risk priorities. Ultimately this can result in inefficiency in risk management strategies, policies which quickly fall into disrepute, and of course disasters.

'Lifeboat' approaches fail with the public as well as with staff. They result in a disaster-inquiry-disrepute cycle which undermines the long term credibility of the relevant organisation. Initiating open discussion after such events can be difficult as public confidence has already been lost and subsequent statements are interpreted by recipients in this context. The 'lifeboat' is notoriously difficult to re-float.

'Lifeboat' responses to risk are exemplars of anticipatory risk management systems based upon the 'precautionary principle' (Hood et al 1992, Hood and Jones 1996). The hallmark of such systems is an emphasis upon identifying potential risks in advance and implementing risk intervention strategies on a 'just in case' basis (Tait and Levidow 1992). Proof and false positives are weighed as less important than prevention, and high resources are put into identification and assessment procedures although the benefit in terms of the number of risks ultimately prevented can be low. This can be contrasted to the alternative 'resilience' approach (Collingridge 1996, Wildavsky 1988) which emphasises a 'wait and see' strategy characterised by greater flexibility, trial and error, learning, and decision making which keeps options open rather than closed.

Anticipationism can also adopt risk management strategies based upon the application of expertly validated technical tools to every potential risk situation. This is particularly the case in the management of engineering risks, however there have been criminal justice parallels for example the Offender Group Reconviction Score (Copas et al 1994) and the Level of Service Inventory - Revised (Andrews and Bonta 1995). In essence every situation is reduced to its probability calculations. However, in situations of mis-calculation or where the unexpected occurs the ability to adapt and respond to new dangers is limited. This has been described as the 'Titanic effect' (Hood et al 1992, Kemshall et al 1997). Compliance is valued above discretion, and the punishment for deviance or disaster is only a matter of degree.

Anticipationism is the prevalent approach to risk management systems in criminal justice and Probation at the present time (Kemshall 1997c), of both the 'lifeboat' and 'Titanic' types. The recent example of anticipationism is the development of registers and surveillance nets for sex offenders (Hebenton and Thomas 1996), an extreme example of a proactive 'just in case' response to potential risk. Her Majesty's Inspectorate of Probation's guidance on risk (HMIP 1997) is also anticipatory, focusing upon the proactive identification and prevention of risks. However, the 'ambiguity, variety, uncertainty and complexity of situations faced by Probation staff' is emphasised, and the subsequent guidance responds to this uncertainty by listing simple points of guidance to inform practice rather than providing risk assessment methods (HMIP 1997, p.3). How applicable and useful such advice is in the actual setting of Probation work is a moot point (Grinyer 1995, Wynne 1988). The more difficult issues which tax practitioners and local managers are left unresolved, referred to as: 'Dilemmas and Brick Walls' (HMIP 1997, p.14). The 'lifeboat' approach is epitomised by reference to best practice 'bullet points', for example:

> ...assessment, monitoring and surveillance to assess the likelihood of serious harm occurring, followed, in relevant cases, by action to forestall dangerous behaviour (HMIP 1997, p.23).

This is a clear attempt to 'cover all the angles', and places a significant responsibility upon supervising officers, particularly onerous in the absence of reliable assessment methods and effective risk management techniques.

At times the document implicitly recognises that a 'wait and see' approach to risk rather than anticipation is necessary. This is particularly the case with the 'dilemmas' identified in decision making, and case by case decision making is advocated in order to resolve these imponderables (HMIP 1997, p.15). The case studies which are meant to 'speak for themselves' also seem to imply that all embracing advice cannot be given, and the final reference to 'professional skill and judgement' (HMIP 1997 p.2). Ultimately responsibility (and of course blame) is implicity devolved to individual managers and assessors for decision making (HMIP 1997, p.2, p.15):

There are no 'answers' to these problems except that supervisors and their managers must explicitly decide, on a case by case basis, how to deal with them and record their decisions and the reasons for them (HMIP 1997, p15).

The use of quotation marks around 'answers' illustrates the inherent uncertainty of the risk task, and the struggle which central policy makers will inevitably have in proceduralising it away. Her Majesty's Inspectorate of Probation's guidance is itself an example of the limits of aniticipationism, in effect anticipationism only works in situations that are fairly 'clear cut'. In situations of more complexity requiring trade offs between rights, risks and potential protection the guidance devolves the resolution of difficult decision making to local supervisors and managers. However, the primary directive is that such decisions should ultimately prove to be defensible with hindsight bias. Whilst central policy makers may consider that they have constructed a reasonable 'lifeboat', frontline risk assessors and their managers may consider that it is a 'Titanic' waiting to happen.

The joint Home Office/Association of Chief Officers of Probation statement on the combined risk/needs scale also adopts an anticipatory stance in respect of both reoffending risks and risk to the public. However the uncertainty inherent to this task is noted:

Combined scales can help officers to assess the risk or likelihood that a person will commit an offence and the needs that should be addressed to reduce that risk. While they should trigger concerns about the risk of harm to others, which can be further assessed, they will not be enough in themselves to enable an accurate assessment of the danger that a person poses. Services implementing a combined scale will need to produce in tandem a policy and practice framework for identifying and handling dangerous offenders. This should dovetail into a structured scale (Home Office/Association of Chief Officers of Probation 1997, Part One, p.3).

Exactly how the parallel work on dangerousness is to be progressed or 'dovetailed' is not stated. The emphasis in both documents is upon systems to monitor and increase the accountability of decisions (Home Office 1997, HMIP 1997); including the development of early warning systems for identifying risk, (for example the Home Office review of needs/risk scales, Home Office 1997). Attention is also given to the creation of mechanisms which can be defended in the light of hindsight bias, that is: '...a 'defensible position' - one which would stand up to scrutiny if the handling of the case were to be investigated...' (HMIP 1997, p. 15); and the allocation of roles and responsibilities to various grades of staff. These are all characteristics of anticipationism and blamism (Hood and Jones 1996).

However, anticipationism has its limits. Whilst advocated as 'commonsense' by the policy makers who favour it, the over-reliance upon adequate forecasting can be resource intensive as every case and every eventuality has to be considered. Assessment and identification come to dominate the risk management process, on occasion being mistaken for effective risk control strategies (e.g. registers). In criminal justice, anticipationism can result in net-widening and an over emphasis upon preventative strategies (for example preventative sentencing) which can over-ride moral and ethical issues. The least harm and lowest possible risk principle which dominates the anticipationary mode is itself a matter of value and choice and governs the extent to which the precautionary principle will be applied. Risk taking is largely eschewed in criminal justice with public protection at almost all costs acting as the over-riding imperative of the precautionary principle (Home Office 1997, HMIP 1997). This precautionary principle can drive risk policies even in situations where the efficacy of risk management strategies remains empirically unproven (for example the use of registers, Bean 1997, Wyre 1997), or where such strategies merely displace the risk or at worst exacerbate it (Hood and Jones 1996, Megan's Law 1997).

The precautionary principle inhibits the trade off of risks which is inherent to risk decision making in complex situations (Adams 1995, Hood and Jones 1996, Shrader-Frechette 1991). What is 'of benefit' and 'least harmful' is assumed as non-contentious and self-evident by anticipationists, and yet lack of acceptability of these 'benefits' and 'harms' by those implementing the risk management system can result in system failure (Hood and Jones 1996). The role of trade-offs and cost-benefit calculations in the decision making of frontline risk assessors is usually underestimated.

Whilst anticipationism does not necessarily have to be characterised by low participation and low consultation, this is most usually the case, and is particularly evident in policy and organisational responses to offender risk. In this context Bell's participation gauge is useful (Bell 1979), and current levels of participation can largely be characterised as management making decisions without any prior discussion with employees, subsequently informing the workforce of these decisions and the reasons for them. On Bell's gauge this is a very slight improvement on zero participation. Low participation can be particularly disabling for workers when coupled with a risk management system dependent upon hindsight bias, blame and censure for its effective operation. Workers may view themselves as readily punished for failing to carry out policies which they may perceive as alienating, impractical and distanced from their everyday concerns.

A resilient approach to managing risk has been posed as a useful alternative to anticipationism (Collingridge 1980, 1983, 1992, 1996) in which learning from trial and error is suggested as a more effective technique for responding to the uncertainties of risk than attempts to develop anticipatory methods to respond to all eventualities. In this framework best practice would be developed from the effective resolution of risk problems rather than specified in advance and imposed. Whilst general principles and desirable outcomes may be negotiated and stated, routes to their achievement may be flexible, leaving greater options to frontline risk assessors. Such systems, whilst they can leave central policy makers nervous about the apparent lack of consistency and accountability, can provide greater responsiveness to risks at the frontline and ultimately greater effectiveness (Collingridge 1996, Hood and Jones 1996). The Chief Officer of the Durham Probation Service in an address to a local managers risk conference (McPhee, 1997), expressed this as the difference between 'sailing boat' systems which can tack, adapt and change, and 'oil tanker' systems which are one track, find it difficult to change course, and are difficult to stop. Whilst in practice few risk management systems are solely one or the other (Collingridge 1996, Hood and Jones 1996), it is a question of where the emphasis should be in order to facilitate the most effective responses to risk.

Alternative risk management systems and the Probation Service

Risk management can mean different things in different contexts, for example the risk management concerns of the nuclear industry are not the same as those of social services departments managing child protection risks (Adams 1995, Hood and Jones 1996). However a number of key characteristics can be discerned. In essence, they are systems designed to set and achieve desired goals, to gather and interpret information pertinent to risk concerns, and to influence the decision making of frontline assessors in line with desired goals and outcomes (Hood and Jones 1996). In practice this can encompass a range of tasks including the identification and assessment of risk, risk analysis and strategies for intervention, monitoring, review and evaluation (Hood and Jones 1996). Carson (1995) has expressed this as a 'system for implementing, controlling and learning from risk decisions' (p.26). In particular, the focus of attention should be the whole decision making process and the extent to which this is facilitated by policies and procedures:

> Employers and managers have a responsibility to develop risk taking policies and procedures to help staff to make high quality decisions which are readily justifiable when harm results, as it occasionally will (Carson 1995, p.26-27).

The key issue is which type of risk management system will lead to 'high quality' and 'justifiable' decisions in the Probation Service.

At present the anticipatory approach is predominating, however the limits of anticipationism identified in other risk settings apply to Probation (Hood and Jones 1996). In particular anticipationism can over-emphasise identification and assessment, leading to resource intensive screening of every eventuality of risk. Resources are deflected from interventions, or screening itself comes to be seen as the risk management intervention. Such screening can have low benefits in terms of risk minimisation for the costs involved, and the rate of both false positives and false negatives can be increased as screening expands (for example the recent cases of cervical cancer screening, The Times 1997). When coupled with a blamist approach to error, failing to screen is viewed as potentially risky for agency, managers and staff, resulting in a reluctance to target screening although local resources may dictate that this is a more reasonable long term option. As the definition of risk expands along with the potential pool of risky people and situations so does the task. When combined with shrinking resources this is particularly problematic and will result in distress, back covering at all levels, and ad hoc prioritising at the frontline for 'occupational survival' (Satyamurti 1981).

Anticipationism's precautionary principle presents ethical and moral issues as well as practical ones. The principle assumes that a norm of safety can be specified and achieved, and that there is consensus about what should and should not be tolerated. Tait and Levidow (1992) in discussing pollution risks have illustrated how safety levels are often unknown or empirically unproven but that public policy driven by a precautionary principle can demand actions and outcomes beyond what is known (Hood and Jones 1996). It is difficult to pull back from such positions once they are established, particularly in situations where empirical evidence remains low, no-one wants to take the risk. Within criminal justice the precautionary principle is now well established resulting in a number of practical measures (for example sex offender registers, and the hand gun ban following the murders at Dunblane), and legislative change (preventative sentencing, Crime Sentences Act 1997, Crime and Disorder Bill 1997), for which authoritative empirical evidence on their efficacy is still required.

Anticipationism is also less able to deal with complexity and the variety of outcomes which can potentially result (Wildavsky 1985, 1988). This is demonstrated when errors are all too well seen with hindsight although they were not anticipated at the time. The predictable is only predictable once it has occurred (Wildavsky 1988). Whilst anticipationism can have benefits in situations of high certainty, in situations of greater uncertainty and contingent knowledge and information the spectre of the 'Titanic' can loom. This is particularly exemplified by the proliferation of risk policies and methods which still leave a number of imponderables to be decided by assessor judgement in individual case situations (HMIP 1997), and frontline complaints that procedures do not match the complexities of practice in the field. In essence, frontline assessors may wish to operate in a more resilient manner but perceive themselves to be constrained by procedural anticipationism.

Anticipationism, quantification and specification of goals, outputs and outcomes are the hallmark of the homeostatic system of risk regulation (Hood and Jones 1996). This system has been reviewed in previous chapters (for example chapters 2 and 3), and is particularly limited in its neglect of risk systems as social systems and for its presumed normative consensus on risk concerns. In particular the presumption that normative rational decision making will predominate in organisations is fundamentally unsound (Grinyer 1995, Wynne 1988, 1989, 1989a). Hood (1976) has expressed this as 'implementation deficit':

> When there is a long linkage between the processes of goal-setting and the processes of implementation on the ground, and when goal-setting takes place through a top-down process (as typically arises in public risk management...), it produces the classic conditions for an 'implementation deficit'...dramatically illustrated by the case of the Chernobyl engineers who turned all the plants safety systems off and thereby triggered the world's worst nuclear accident (Hood 1996, p.213).

This can be accompanied by an 'atrophy of vigilance' (Freudenberg 1993) in which attention to risk drops during periods of normaly, and safety rather than threat is presumed (for example the degrading of safety systems at Piper Alpha, Cullen 1990). Degradation of vigilance is a key issue in situations where risks are routinised by procedures and workers are overloaded.

Dunsire (1990, 1992) has posed the alternative of collibrationist regulation. In contrast to the static homeostatic approach Dunsire posed a system in which the lack of consensus on goals is turned to advantage. The tension of opposing views, rather than being disruptive, literally keeps the system alert, flexible and responsive. The metaphor suggested by Dunsire was of the 'anglepoise desk lamp' (Dunsire 1978), stability is achieved (as in the lamp) through the balance of competing forces.

In reviewing the public policy implementation process Dunsire contends that there is a tendency to over implement and over regulate:

> Politicians show what they are made of by having new laws in their knapsacks. The urge to seize the reins, to take charge, and use legislative power to change things to how you want them, is strong. This corresponds to the first three modes of control...steering or regulating: setting a datum or norm, and then using power to correct deviations from it (Dunsire 1990, p.5).

Politicians are not alone in such actions, central policy makers and service managers often follow suit. Dunsire contends that this mode is however 'implementation-intensive and enforcement-expensive' (Dunsire 1990, p.5), and is not guaranteed to get results. Constant correction is required and there is always a disturbing time-lag between error occurrence, identification and correction. Such systems are especially costly in situations where there is low self-regulation as constant monitoring and correction are required, and the more resistance there is the higher the enforcement costs. This reliance on negative feedback to correct action, and exercised through top-down control, is a key characteristic of homeostatic systems.

Whilst this top-down control can be partially relaxed by encouraging self-regulation, as Dunsire states this is only a matter of degree and is more felt than real, 'the standards to be achieved, the limits to be observed are still set from above, or outside' (Dunsire 1990, p.6). Dunsire proposes a system of balance derived from ecological and cybernetic theories of equilibrium in which competing systems seek to maximise their own position within a positive feedback loop. His example is that of water regulation in the human body, which is not a homeostatic system returning to pre-set limits, but is the product of conflict between two hormones, vasopressin and renin, and the maximisation of their own positions through which the body can achieve high self-regulation in changing situations (Dunsire 1990, p.6). The homeostatic return to a pre-set norm would not avoid death from dehydration in situations of extreme heat for example. As Dunsire expresses it:

> This yoking of incompatibles, the mutual battle of opposing tendencies, or simply competition, is Nature's typical control mechanism. For a technical term, we can use *isostasy* : equilibrium brought about by equal pressures... (Dunsire 1990, p.8).

Dunsire illustrates the frequent use of isostasy in managing both government and organisations, for example the use of 'checks and balances' in the American political system, the English separation of powers, market economies, and bureaucratic organisations. The latter in particular are an important case in point to the present study. Such organisations have to accommodate high specialism of function and 'managerial hierarchical command' which Dunsire argues are intrinsically incompatible. Senior managers cannot tell frontline decision makers what to do on substantive matters because they do not know enough to do so. However, they do issue policy expectations and procedural goals to decision makers, 'often mutually incompatible', for example in Probation high accuracy of risk assessments and high throughput of work. Managers, particularly middle managers act as controllers 'with authority to monitor performance' across all the incompatible dimensions in which decision makers will have to make substantive decisions. This creates real dilemmas for frontline decision makers:

> The decision-maker must 'prioritise', but in the knowledge that an explanation may be required for not maximising all such goals at the same time (Dunsire 1990, p.9).

The 'reality' of organisational life for Dunsire is therefore essentially collibrationist:

The decision environment thus corresponds to isostasy, and control over specialised decision-makers in a bureaucracy is maintained by selective crackdown on one goal at a time, 'steering equilibrium' - without ever acknowledging that tightening up on one matter implies slackening off on another (Dunsire 1990, p.9).

This statement captures the reality of risk management in Probation at the present time. Individual decision makers are left to prioritise general, competing goals within their substantive areas of operation, and the extent to which this is controlled is reflected in the degree of 'steer' provided by managers, usually by the priorities they explicitly state and of course by what they fail to say. Problems arise in Probation risk management when collibrationist systems are treated as homeostatic ones, with an imposed view of risk which can be seriously at odds with how risk is perceived and experienced at the frontline. In effect, senior managers and external policy makers do not recognise how equilibrium is achieved within the organisation, and their actions constitute implicit and unintentional 'equilibrium steers', often resulting in unintended consequences and disequilibrium, for example Rayner's 'noise' (Rayner 1986), or James' 'inauthenticity' (James 1994).

The role of blame

Homeostatic approaches also reduce complex situations and uncertain reasoning to technical standards and specific functions, often through the technique of quantifying essentially qualitative judgements. Responsibility for effective risk decisions is devolved almost entirely to frontline risk assessors. When these judgements fail, homeostatic systems stressing anticipationism can quickly allocate blame away from central policy makers and organisational managers to individual risk assessors. Whilst liability may ultimately be corporate (Carson 1996, Wells 1996), blame is targeted at individual decision makers. Blame allocation may be championed as a mechanism for preventing recurrence although this is rarely achieved in reality (Horlick-Jones 1996). Its other major function is 'ritual damnation' (Horlick-Jones 1996), expressed by Jenkins in a Sunday Times article entitled: 'Its the doers wot get the blame':

Find someone to blame, cries the mob, and off runs Whitehall to offer up someone to blame (Jenkins, Sunday Times, 20 August, 1989).

However, Horlick-Jones (1996) has argued that the identification of individual 'doers' for blame is difficult, unjust, and inefficient. The decisions of individuals take place within the social systems of organisations and settings in which individuals rarely have total control over all their actions (Horlick-Jones 1996, Toft and Reynolds 1994, Turner 1978). This is particularly true of the collibrationist systems described by Dunsire (1990) although homeostatic systems operate *as if* individual decision making can be totally prescribed and controlled. Decision errors and the risks, accidents and disasters they lead to can be understood as: 'sociotechnical events in which social, administrative and managerial factors tend to play major roles' (Horlick-Jones 1996, p.62, Horlick-Jones et al 1993, Toft and Reynolds 1994, Turner 1978).

Turner (1978, 1994) has argued that errors 'incubate', and that errors resulting in disasters are cumulative, often amplified by the context and organisational setting in which they occur (for example Bhopal, Shrivastava 1987; Challenger, Presidential Committee 1986; Chernobyl, USSR State Committee 1986; Clapham, Hidden 1989; Kings Cross, Fennell 1988; Piper Alpha, Cullen 1990; Zeebrugge, Sheen 1987). 'Human error' appears self-evident only with hindsight (Wagenaar and Groenewold 1987). The complexity of the context and the lengthy causal chain of events:

> ...may not be clearly apparent to the individual who makes the mistake, leading them to being caught in what one might call a 'systemic net' of circumstances beyond their control (Horlick-Jones 1996, p.63).

This lack of clarity can also apply to senior managers and external policy makers whose primary response to errors and 'disasters' is to pursue the easier route of 'ritual damnation' rather than the more difficult task of identifying and resolving 'systemic nets'. However, because such nets remain unresolved errors recur, hence the inefficiency of blamism (Horlick-Jones 1996, Turner 1978), and over the long term the lowering of staff moral and loss of public confidence (Daily Record, November 12 1997).

Collibrationist understandings of risk systems are more able to bring organisational failures and 'systemic nets' to attention through increased attention to resilience, and the 'specification of process and qualitative debates over uncertainties' (Hood and Jones 1996, p.206). In particular, attention is diverted from a narrow functionalism in which the specifics of individual decision making are highly prescribed to organisational processes and how quality decisions can be facilitated by improved managerial and administrative procedures. The tensions between conflicting goals and lack of power to act otherwise at the frontline (Rasmussen 1990) can be openly examined and resolved, and 'equilibrium steers' can be explicit, negotiated and intended. The role of managers and external policy makers can be prioritised for attention as well as that of frontline workers. As Horlick-Jones expresses it: '...senior managers are often happy to accept the rewards of corporate success, while distancing themselves from failure' (Horlick-Jones 1996, p.64). Indeed, citing Jackall (1988) he contends that one of the conditions for corporate advancement 'is the ability to avoid blame by the development of networks and alliances' and the subtle avoidance of liability through the 'production of unwieldy formal operating procedures...which may be unworkable in practical situations' and thus set workers up to fail (Horlick-Jones 1996, p.65). The extent of such unworkable and unwieldy risk procedures in probation services at the present time should not be underestimated.

The reaction of senior managers and external policy makers to such a contention may resemble that made by the Chairman of P&O to the blame allocated by the Sheen report following the inquiry into the Herald of Free Enterprise sinking:

> Although there have been discussions and talk and accusations about sloppiness in the management...to suggest that they had a direct effect in that ferry capsizing in my view would be totally wrong...it gets a bit far-fetched that someone sitting on the shore should be hauled up for something not happening (Horlick-Jones 1996, p.64 citing Spooner 1992, p.104).

Drawing on the evidence of the Sheen inquiry (Sheen report 1987) and other inquiries (for example the Purley rail crash, Department of Transport 1990), Horlick-Jones presents a compelling case that the operational conditions imposed by managers on the decisions and actions of workers are not only inadequate but critical in subsequent disasters. The policy framing of senior managers and their exercise of power can operate as substantial limits and constraints upon the individual agency of workers. This strongly suggests that systems of risk management which take the substantive concerns of workers seriously are more likely to be successful. It also suggests that greater attention should be given to policy design and systems for its introduction and implementation. Where this does not occur, policy makers, both external and internal, are in danger of programming in 'latent failures' for which individual operators are ultimately blamed (Clarke 1995, Sagan 1993).

Within Probation latent failures can already be discerned. For example, risk assessment checklists which over-emphasise unreliable clinical factors, assessment techniques which encourage a static and non-interactional view of risk (Kemshall 1995, Prins 1995), the simplistic equating of dangerousness with offence type (Brown 1996, Kemshall 1997c), procedures which fail to prioritise levels of harm, risk management procedures which do not prioritise the allocation of resources, and systems of information flow which are in adequate to the risk management task (Sheppard 1996). This is not an exhaustive list, however they are the most often mentioned in training sessions and management workshops, and have been noted by both child protection (Reder et al 1993) and mental health inquiries (Sheppard 1996).

Collibrationism relies upon high participation and high engagement with the views of others, particularly contrary views and mechanisms for resolving such tensions which are seen to be open, just and fair. Resilience, as a feature of collibrationist systems, depends upon flexibility and a willingness to learn from mistakes and to tolerate some degree of error, especially in the initial stages. Both depend upon a no blame culture to risk management, requiring the disclosure of 'near misses' from workers and a management group receptive to constructive 'shop floor' criticism of operational procedures and goals. It is no surprise then that the 'hearts and minds' campaign of Shell to win the co-operation and approval of workforce and public to its risk management strategies exemplifies not only a collibrationist approach and resilience, but also no blame (Wilkinson 1997). This culture has resulted in increased safety on their oil tankers (Horlick-Jones 1996, Lloyds List 1994, Seatrade Review 1994). Such an approach recognises that organisational systems can foster good judgement and safety as well as error and disaster.

However, the efficacy of such systems are dependent upon the provision and receipt of feedback, willingness to act upon feedback, and mechanisms for empowerment and participation in organisational life. Open institutions rather than closed are therefore more likely to be more conducive to collibrationism, resilience and no blame. The challenge for Probation at present is how to achieve this in a climate where blame is endemic to social and political life (Douglas 1986, 1992, Johnston 1996). As Douglas expresses it we are now existing in a blaming system in which we are 'almost ready to treat every death as caused by someone's criminal negligence, every sickness a threatened prosecution' (Douglas 1992, p.15-16). In this blaming system retribution, deterrence and the allocation of responsibility are central (Johnston 1996).

Johnston (1996) advocates the initiatives pioneered in the aviation industry as a possible way forward. In particular collaborative efforts between workers, managers and in this case external regulators in the early identification and redress of frontline activities leading to risk (in the aviation industry the example was pilot alcohol abuse). The primary objective was the identification, removal, treatment and return to work of 'at risk' individuals, 'not to blame, label or punish them' (Johnston 1996, p.79). Identification was primarily through peers on the understanding that colleagues would be assisted back to work and not sanctioned.

This approach to individuals was supported by the identification and resolution of systemic and organisational factors. Pilots were encouraged to report cockpit design errors and systems failures again without sanction, coupled with independent quality assurance of crew performance through the use of flight record data. This was supported by sanction free reporting of 'near misses' from flight personnel. This information was fed back into the training and operational sides of the industry. Johnston contends that the 'immunity' and 'anonymity' of the system leads to greater collection of information and can therefore assist policy makers in addressing the 'whys' as well as the 'whats' (Johnston 1996, p.81). This is an important distinction between the examination of causes rather than the treatment of mere symptoms. Chappelow (1994) in a study of serious incidents in the Royal Air Force found that systems were at fault in about 90% of cases, and that the causes of risk were multiple and systemic.

Vested interest, retaliation, and sanctions must be set aside in order to facilitate prompt, accurate, and usable feedback systems. As Johnston expresses it:

> Those involved in such risk management activities normally accept that the overall integrity of system function is best assured by open lines of communication, combined with proactive structures and processes (Maurino et al 1995) (Johnston 1996, pp.82-83).

It also requires recognition from managers that risk is often systemic and not individual, and that managers themselves may contribute to latent failures (Clarke 1995). Vincent et al (1993) in a study of health care risks found that health care workers often inherit latent failures: faulty policies, poor communication, and poor management decisions. Whilst individuals are often blamed, a full analysis of the risk situation would reveal the systemic nature of risks, and that workers are often put into situations where failure or accidents are inevitable (Runciman et al 1993, Vincent et al 1993).

Closing the gap in Probation Service risk management policies

The effective implementation and use of risk management policies and procedures is highly dependent upon avoiding 'implementation deficit' (Hood 1976), 'ritual damnation' (Horlick-Jones 1996) and closing the gap between the institutional bias of managers and the perceptions of frontline workers (Grinyer 1995). Collibrationist systems incorporating resilience, openness, participation and Wynne's 'critical engagement' (Wynne 1988) have an increasing track record in achieving tangible outcomes in this area (Hood and Jones 1996, Horlick-Jones 1996, Johnston 1996, Wilkinson 1997). Greater attention will have to be given to negotiation and incorporating a range of views into the risk management process, in effect taking seriously Shell's 'hearts and minds' campaign (Wilkinson 1997). Communication and trust have been shown as integral to both the acceptance and implementation of risk procedures (Rayner 1992), along with managerial and administrative processes (Horlick-Jones 1996). This suggests that managers and central policy makers should pay rather more attention to what they are doing and rather less to the activities of frontline workers.

Policy makers and senior management attention should be focused upon the features of risk management systems most likely to result in desirable risk decisions on the ground. These features are not necessarily prescriptive procedural rules. As Wynne states there is often a considerable gap between 'the rules' and practice reality (Wynne 1988), and that the primary function of rules is in evaluating risk decisions in cases of 'disaster' which are usually only predictable in the light of hindsight bias (Hood and Jones 1996, Wynne 1988, 1989, 1989a). In essence, rules are more often for blame allocation and blame avoidance than for safety.

The first requirement must be for open and non-adversarial discussion about which decisions are desirable and why. In Wilkinson's terms, the removal of barriers (Wilkinson 1997). This places a vigorous 'hearts and minds' campaign at the centre of policy formulation and implementation rather than managerial enforcement against differing values and perspectives on risk. As part of this, senior managers and central policy makers may have to accept a degree of tension between differing views, and acknowledge this as a mechanism to sharpen debate and refine what is proposed rather than respond to it as threat, incompetence or resistance. Greater engagement with how the policy process actually works may pay real dividends in the long term, particularly in accepting that evolving practice can inform 'the rules', and that institutional learning should be prioritised above institutional bias. Such a process requires more participation and inclusion in organisational life at all levels and between centre and locals.

In addition, there is a greater need for tolerance of 'unsafety'. Whilst this will be notoriously difficult to achieve in the light of Home Office serious incident reporting, media coverage and public confidence, senior managers and central policy makers have to accept that certainty and zero risk can not be achieved, and that any risk management system has to tolerate error. How that error is ultimately treated is crucial to subsequent staff and public confidence in the organisation's risk management strategies. Increasing regulation (especially in stable door situations) does not necessarily lead to greater safety/lower risk, in fact the opposite can occur (for example Chernobyl, Wildavsky 1988). Such systems can lead to needless anticipation, squandering resources and increasing the rate of both false positives and false negatives bringing the system into disrepute both internally and externally. System overload occurs and minor errors lead to major disasters. More importantly resources are diverted from effective risk management (Wildavsky 1988) and increasing effectiveness where it really counts. As activities are routinised alertness falls, and just at the moment the system promises the greatest level of safety to its users the vigilance required to deliver it falls. Just as the costs of low risk are hidden, so are the trade offs necessary for effective risk decision making. Displacing risks in unintended ways or eroding the civil liberties of non-risky persons are cases in point.

The precautionary principle is ultimately self-defeating. It is impossible to insure against everything. The more you try the more you fail, and the more the system falls into disrepute. As Wildavsky expresses it, safety is relative, there is always a better position that could be achieved with more resources and the fullness of time (Wildavsky 1988). Once one danger is eradicated another can be found. Some situations are 'uninsurable', and caveats need to be more clearly stated and indeed accepted. The important question is 'how safe is safe enough' (Schwing and Albers 1980) and what can realistically be achieved and afforded in risk management systems, and therefore what level of error and absolution (rather than blame) needs to be accepted and implemented in risk management systems. The following chapter considers the practical implications of these broader considerations for policy makers, managers and workers.

10. The Precautionary Principle and Insurance Systems for Offender Risk

In her book: 'Risk and Misfortune', Green (1997) quotes an actuary to illustrate the uncertainty of applying actuarial tables to the assessment of individual risk. For insurance actuaries, it is possible for the customer to meet the 'good risk' profile of the actuarial table and then 'pop his clogs for no reason'. In the words of the actuary, it is possible to get actuarial statistics 'down to a fine art', but that this cannot eliminate uncertainty. At the end of the day 'you're dealing with uncertainties and no matter what you base it on, its basically an estimate' (Green 1997, p.164).

Green's actuary sums up the plight of current risk assessment; the difficulty in designing methods accurate enough to predict individual misfortune. In the world of offender risks this is particularly pertinent. Whilst statistically based methods for aggregating risks continue to develop, the Probation Service's credibility is judged on a case by case basis. Its the 'one which gets away' which results in individual blame and public censure. Whilst retrospectively such methodologies can be helpful in evaluating the effectiveness of targetting strategies on risk (Copas et al 1994, Wilkinson 1994), their efficacy in prospectively predicting individual offender risk cannot deliver 100% accuracy (Monahan 1981, 1993). Probation risk assessors have to face the actuary's problem, resulting in high anxiety and on occasion back covering. For Probation managers the problem is one of providing enough insurance without squandering resources, 'going broke', or running too many risks.

Central policy makers tend to be preoccupied with credibility, blame attribution (away from the centre), and political threat. All players are operating within a system characterised by the 'precautionary principle'. The key question is: how far do you take the precautionary principle and to what extent can reliable insurance systems for offender risk be created? This chapter will review some of the key issues in adopting particular risk instruments and their use in promoting a 'precautionary' or insurance approach to offender risk.

In 1978 Flynn wrote the following:

> Today, the American criminal justice system is buffeted by strong winds of public discontent and is in great turmoil concerning its purposes, objectives and methods (Flynn 1978, p.131).

These words could easily be transposed to the British scene some twenty years later. Flynn noted the growing 'hard line' of American corrections, reflected in the increasing use of mandatory sentences and the increased use of custody at the expense of non-custodial alternatives. The result:

> Tents, trailers, airport hangers and even old battleships are now being used to accommodate the fast-rising numbers of prisoners. Across the nation, inmates are reported to be crammed into every conceivable space and prison conditions are deteriorating fast (Flynn 1978, p.132).

Coupled with this Flynn noted a 'disenchantment with the rehabilitation model' and a move towards deterrence, public protection and a 'just deserts' punishment model. Whilst she rightly asserted that no criminal justice system operates entirely upon one principle, but rather fulfils a number of functions, she identified a shift towards an increasingly punitive approach. One result of such a shift is a burgeoning prison population and prison management problems exacerbated by prison building time lags. In this situation:

> ...the search is on for new techniques designed to reassess the use of corrections and detention institutions and to find ways to reduce the populations in a manner consistent with public safety (pp.133-134).

A similar pattern can be discerned in Britain, resulting in penal policy strategies to manage such growing populations in England and Wales (Home Office 1990a, 1996a, Home Office 1997) and more recently in Scotland (Scottish Social Work Inspectorate 1998). Such strategies have adopted the concept of risk, noted by Flynn as at the root of the emerging American justice system twenty years ago, as the core of its developing classificatory system.

Whilst Flynn optimistically argued that the primary purpose of such a system was the reduction of the prison population, and that the system should be based upon the principles of equity, justice, and the preservation of individual liberties, the practical reality is somewhat different. Rather than securing an active programme of decarceration, the risk principle has extended progressively into the community arena, for example through sex offender registers, extended periods of supervision for risky offenders (CJA 1991 section 44), the McLeish proposals in Scotland, and the extended incarceration of risky offenders provided by the Crime Sentences Act 1997 (Home Office 1997a).

Flynn's key principle was that risk classification should facilitate minimal contact and involvement with the criminal justice system of those classified as low risk (Flynn 1978, p.136). In turn, any system should be able to identify those who 'commit serious predatory crimes and violence' in order to treat them differentially from the rest. However, it is in credibly achieving and operating such a key differential that the major problems occur for Probation risk management systems.

Assessment methods: 'horses for courses'

Classification systems can have numerous functions, and this is particularly true of those used for risk. Some systems are aimed at 'diagnosing' offender problems and focusing interventions upon those factors most likely to result in the effective resocialization of offenders and the prevention of recidivism (Flynn 1978). Key examples of such systems are Aubrey and Hough's risk/needs model (1997), and Andrews and Bonta's Level of Service Inventory (1995). In essence these systems classify offenders for treatment interventions, are primarily concerned with recidivism rather than danger, and may not necessarily have any greater predictive utility than pure actuarial methods like the Offender Group Reconviction Score (Raynor 1997). However they do provide an internal mechanism for resource allocation, control of professional interventions, accountability and evaluation. They serve a rationing, administrative and management function in addition to their diagnostic one. It is usually these other functions which are resisted by workers (personal communication to author in training events, also Fletcher 1995), and a perception by frontline risk assessors that the predictive utility offered does not guarantee enough worker safety for the effort invested, particularly if this assessment is mis-construed by managers as an assessment of dangerousness.

In addition to the above function, and usually operating alongside it, is the use of a risk classificatory system in order to effectively manage offenders in the community. This is most often expressed as the identification of offenders for particular programmes aimed at resocialisation and change. This can range from the careful matching of offenders to effectiveness based cognitive behavioural programmes, to the management of offenders through their agency contact by increasingly resource lean group experiences such as induction groups, report centres, minimal contact groups etc. The individual professional discretion and autonomy of workers is eroded in this more managed approach as more consistent and effective interventions with offenders are pursued (Burnett 1996). Most classificatory systems of this type are designed to facilitate programme or individual evaluation of the impact upon future recidivism (for example LSI-R, or the Warwickshire Ace model, Roberts et al 1996,), and again this consideration has often clouded their initial implementation and acceptance by the workforce (Fullbrook 1998, Roberts et al 1996).

Ideally, such classificatory mechanisms should enable more rational and objective decisions to be made at point of sentence, during supervision and at parole (Flynn 1978). In particular, who should have minimal contact and intervention from the criminal justice system, and who should receive increased contact and restriction because they present a high risk 'in terms of recidivism and dangerousness' (Flynn 1978, p.137). However, the practical implementation of such a two-tier system is proving problematic.

Predicting recidivism is not necessarily the same as predicting dangerousness. It would be possible in the present system for an offender to score highly on the risk of recidivism but for this offending to have a low impact and low consequences in terms of harm to others. This difficult need to assess both probability and impact is particularly problematic in the world of risk, and presents difficulties in the construction of any prediction instrument and is routinely encountered by risk assessors. In answering who is a risk, an Assistant Chief Probation Officer in the sample summed up the dilemma thus:

> Probably most clients one level or another, everybody presents some level of risk, some clearly less than others. Anyone likely to reoffend, then it depends on what the nature of the reoffending might be, how seriously you would regard that risk. Most of our offenders, many don't accept the risk

they do present, so are very likely to reoffend. Some of the people we tend to get most worried about tend to present much less of a risk...unlikely to do it again. It is important to separate out reoffending that is a nuisance...but doesn't place anybody else at risk, or damage or harm to themselves or anybody else...and reoffending that does. This is difficult to distinguish. Some burglaries are very upsetting whereas the same set of events in a different household would have a very different impact. Burglaries on industrial premises I would not lose much sleep about (ACPO 2).

This raises the pertinent but more challenging issue of 'risk of what', 'with what consequences', and 'to whom' (Kemshall 1995). Actuarial methods cannot operate at this level of specificity and indeed are not designed to do so (Copas personal communication with the author). Their major contribution is in identifying the predisposition of certain offender groups to recidivism, and for retrospectively evaluating the Service's interventions in reducing future rates of recidivism. To compensate for the limitations inherent in the actuarial method when applied to the risk assessment of particular individuals a holistic approach combining the static indicators of actuarial methods with the dynamic indicators of the clinical mode has been advocated (Kemshall 1996, Limandri and Sheridan 1995). This has resulted in a plethora of 'structured interviewing methods' in America and Canada (CMC Harris 1994, LSI-R Andrews and Bonta 1995), and the exportation of the methodology across the Atlantic (for example the LSI-R). The English focus is now upon a combined risk/needs scale (Home Office 1997).

However, the key issue of identifying risk of harm is not necessarily resolved by these methods. Whilst the identification of areas for professional intervention and the introduction of more rational resource allocation techniques may be comforting to hard pressed managers and central policy makers, this does not resolve the difficult assessment problem facing Green's actuary, that is, 'the one that gets away'. In the case of offender risk, this is particularly problematic if the individual offender goes on to commit an act of great harm. Whilst current risk assessment instruments may predict recidivism reasonably well, managers and workers should not mistake this for the reliable prediction of dangerousness. This is partially acknowledged in the Home Office review of risk/needs assessment instruments which devotes 14 pages to the discussion of risk prediction tools and then inserts the following caveat:

Combined scales can help officers to assess the risk or likelihood that a person will commit an offence and the needs that should be addressed to reduce that risk. Whilst they should trigger concerns about risk of harm to others, which can be further assessed, they will not be enough in themselves to enable an accurate assessment of the danger a person poses. Services implementing a combined scale will need to produce in tandem a policy and practice framework for identifying and handling dangerous offenders. This should dovetail into a structured scale (Home Office/Association of Chief Officers of Probation 1997, Part One, p.3).

What this policy and practice framework should be, which methods should be adopted and how it should be integrated into assessments of recidivism is not pursued. Not surprisingly central policy makers have avoided engaging (and indeed advising) on the most tricky of assessment issues. Attention has subsequently been diverted into inter-agency risk management protocols and minimum standards for case management without the adequate resolution of the identification and assessment of dangerousness. (HMIP 1997, Home Office Special Conference Unit 1997, 1998)

In choosing risk assessment instruments services should remember that it is literally a matter of 'horses for courses', and the design and key objectives of any instrument should be well matched to the purposes it is acquired and deployed to meet. The following are suggested as key considerations in the selection of risk assessment instruments:

Balance the cost of acquisition and implementation against the proven predictive utility of the instrument

In some cases, such as LSI-R, the cost of acquisition and continued use is 'up front', however there are also hidden costs of staff training, implementation and management costs. These will be incurred regardless of the instrument. Cost-benefit calculations do need to be specifically made rather than the adoption of instruments which seem to solve a short term management problem (for example being seen to tackle risk), or instruments which have received particular 'championing', or largely unevaluated use in a few services (Home Office 1997). The proposed comparative study of various risk/needs instruments by the Home Office (1997) is timely in this regard as is the current independent study by Raynor (1997) of the comparative predictive utility of OGRS and LSI-R. Copas (personal communication with the author) has argued that beyond the major actuarial indicators, other indicators have a limited predictive utility although they may present areas for professional intervention. If risk assessment instruments reach a 'predictive plateau' then the question must be asked as to why other areas are explored and whether the resource cost has a worthwhile benefit. This leads to the second area of consideration, the expected use of any instrument, including its 'value-added' component.

Consider carefully the expected use of the instrument to the service

Greater clarity is required about the expected use of the chosen instrument: risk prediction, resource allocation, classifying for interventions, classifying out low risk offenders, programme matching, accountability or evaluation. It is possible that one instrument cannot perform all functions, and that certain functions such as predictability are undermined by the simultaneous pursuit of other objectives. This may be particularly true if these objectives remain unarticulated but nevertheless place requirements upon staff. Suspicions are raised, trust is diminished, and resistance to the instrument exacerbated (personal communication to the author in training sessions, also Rayner 1986, 1992).

The Oxford University/Warwickshire Assessment, Case-recording and Evaluation system (ACE) is one example of a systematic attempt to integrate a number of the above objectives into one model. In addition to providing an assessment and measurement tool, the model also structures the supervision interventions of staff, providing greater matching of effective interventions to the criminogenic needs presented by offenders. A natural consequence of this model is a perceived reduction in the autonomy and discretion of staff and an increasingly managed approach to practice:

> There was a degree of resentment levelled against the Supervision Practice Development Initiative which seems to reflect reactions to wider change. As a result of recent developments, including cuts in resources and an emphasis upon 'value for money', the service is now subject to more scrutiny and standardisation than in the past. Given concerns about the implications of such changes, it was not surprising that some officers were quick to interpret the form-filling as professionally threatening... (Roberts et al 1996, pp.62-63).

In addition, the initial pilot was dependent upon the systematic collection of information at varying stages of the supervision process. Such data collection can be resource intensive and viewed as an unnecessary intrusion into the reality of their practice lives by staff:

> Its been a mixed bag...it was too time-consuming and involved too much paper work (Respondent quoted in Roberts et al 1996, p.64).

As a result of the initial pilot, forms have been shortened and made more user-friendly. In translating the pilot into a long-term practice instrument, Fullbrook (1998) has argued that the involvement of practitioners and the focus on low prescription within an overall emphasis upon effectiveness led practice has paid dividends in terms of practitioner acceptability.

Again managers would have to consider the relative merits of resource costs in implementing this, or any other model, and the ultimate benefits in terms of practice changes resulting in reduced recidivism, and the extent to which the latter is proved over time.

Is the instrument task specific or can it operate on the continuum of assessment?

Assessment is a dynamic process and must take place in a range of settings and in respect of a range of tasks and offender types. It is important that any instrument can be applied across this range and can be adapted to tasks as variable as pre-sentence report writing, case planning, parole assessments, selection of community service placements, hostel referrals and group work to name a few. Some risk assessment tools are particularly geared to the assessment of the risk of recidivism in pre-sentence report writing (for example LSI-R and OGRS) in order that proposals should more effectively match presenting criminogenic needs, although the LSI-R does make more extensive claims to usefulness. At present there is no evidence for the efficacy of LSI-R when used at PSR stage although this is its most extensive application in services to date (Home Office 1997, part one, p.9).

To what extent does the instrument aid the selection of interventions and facilitate case management?

Whilst OGRS does not claim to facilitate the selection of interventions or case management, those instruments based upon structured interviewing methods do. This has resulted in increased attention to the so called 'dynamic' variables or 'needs areas' based upon personal and social factors pertinent to continued offending. The approach to interventions is in essence a deficit one through the identification of areas of deficit in the life of the offender and focused remedial action to tackle them. Whilst the efficacy of such variables in predicting recidivism more accurately than actuarial methods alone is largely unproven (Ditchfield 1997, Raynor 1997), and their collection and interpretation is resource intensive, they do provide a mechanism for structured interventions based upon proven 'what works' techniques (Andrews 1995, McGuire 1995). Their true worth may therefore lie in structuring professional activity towards effectiveness based programme goals and assisting in subsequent evaluation of probation interventions rather than in recidivism prediction per se. It is therefore important that managers are able to make this distinction, that staff are clear about the differing utility of each approach, and that actuarial methods are appropriately combined with dynamic ones.

Consider the contribution the instrument will make to assessments of dangerousness (if any), and how this may 'dovetail' into existing procedures for responding to dangerousness

The Offender Group Reconviction Score makes no claims to predict dangerousness (Copas personal communication to author), and whilst the structured interviewing methodologies claim to differentiate between levels of service intervention to offenders they cannot predict the likely impact of reoffending. Risk in the context of these instruments refers to the probability of reoffending occurring rather than to the degree of danger should it occur. Impact assessments, particularly of dangerousness are notoriously difficult to accurately perform (Lidz et al 1993, McNeil and Binder 1987, Monahan and Steadman 1994).

    The term 'dangerousness' has also proved extremely difficult to define and operationalise in practice (Brooks 1984, Kemshall 1996, Monahan 1981, Monahan and Steadman 1994). Monahan and Steadman (1994) helpfully suggest that dangerousness should be separated into three distinct parts, that is:

- The 'risk factors' used to predict violence,

- The type of violence and likely harm anticipated,

- The probability that the violent act will actually occur (p.2).

In addition, they argue that both harm and probability should be understood not as dichotomous variables but as points on a continuum, in other words as degrees of harm and extent of probability, and that this can fluctuate over time. This type of assessment requires extensive knowledge of both the actuarial factors and clinical cues associated with violent behaviour, and a structure to assist analysis of these variables and to aid decision making in this complex area. In the pursuit of recidivism predictors this has been overlooked. Whilst some risk assessment practice guidance attempts to helpfully distinguish between recidivism prediction and the assessment of dangerousness (for example Durham 1997), and many such documents encourage practitioners to assess 'risk of what' and 'levels of harm', the knowledge base to support such assessments is largely absent as is the formalised use of violence predictors (Kemshall 1997, Kemshall 1997b, Kemshall 1998a).

Brooks (1984) has suggested a useful framework for assessments of dangerousness and argues that they must contain the following seven components:

(1) the nature of the harm involved; (2) its magnitude; (3) its imminence; (4) its frequency; (5) the likelihood or unlikelihood that it will occur; (6) situational circumstances and conditions that affect the likelihood of harm occurring; (7)...balancing between the alleged harm on the one hand and the nature of society's interventions on the other (p.295).

This suggests that assessments of dangerousness require at least the following:

- A different knowledge base from that involved in the prediction of recidivism.

- Attention to different risk factors.

- Credible estimations of impact.

- Attention to specific situational factors as well as use of well researched actuarial indicators for the prediction of violence.

This suggests that overall risk assessment systems require at least a two-tier approach to the assessment of offenders, and a 'triage' system in which low harm cases can be assigned minimum intervention, and in which cases can be classified not only for *differing levels* of service but for *differing types* of service dependent upon the risk of recidivism or the risk of harm. (This will be given further attention later in the chapter)

Consider the extent to which the risk assessment instrument will contribute to 'defensible decisions' in the light of 'hindsight bias'

It is the nature of precautionary risk systems that they operate upon a 'what if' principle with high expectation that future risks can be both identified and avoided. In this context, because much is promised and expected, failures are costly in terms of blame and credibility. However, prevention has its limits, not least because we cannot know the future with certainty or the full range of possible outcomes from any behaviour, event or occurrence (Brearley 1982). Knowledge is more often gained through 'hindsight' after risks have occurred (Carson 1996), for example through inquiries (Parton 1986).

In these situations inquirers have the benefit of knowledge of the outcome and are prone to 'hindsight bias' when retrospectively judging the efficacy of the original risk assessment (Carson 1994, 1995, 1996). In law, courts may be concerned with the culpability of individual risk assessors, and the extent of negligence or recklessness involved.

In addition to risking 'legal repercussions' (Carson 1996), practitioners, managers and agencies also risk public shame, loss of credibility, disciplinary procedures and occasionally dismissal. It is therefore imperative that both agencies and their workers can demonstrate how decisions have been made, and that when initially taken they were credible and defensible. Carson argues that this is imperative in those situations where the range of possible outcomes is extensive, and where risks may be taken in the pursuit of the 'greater good' (Carson 1994). In social care, such decisions may involve a balance of rights, risks and responsibilities (Kemshall and Pritchard 1997) to a number of individuals in addition to the primary service user (for example victims in addition to offenders). It is therefore essential that risk assessors have an explicit framework for exploring and articulating the weighing and balancing which necessarily forms any risk assessment.

Brearley (1979, 1982, 1983) proposed a system for making risk decisions in social care more analytical, explicit, and balanced. In addition to proposing a holistic approach of specific and general predictors similar to the dynamic and static combination proposed for offender risk, he also argued that strengths should be weighed against weaknesses in any risk situation, and against the desirability of any possible outcome. In child protection for example Dalgleish (1991) has argued that the strengths of the family should be a consideration in any risk assessment. Brearley (1983) applied the checks and balances approach to risk assessment of older persons, and in offender risk a common argument is that the risks presented by a prisoner can best be addressed by early supervised release (Carson 1996, Kemshall 1997d).

In the event of a negative outcome how potential risks were balanced against attempts to achieve desirable outcomes will be heavily scrutinised. This necessarily focuses attention upon the process and quality of decision making, and in particular the quality of knowledge and information upon which assessors based their judgements. How this information was weighed and assessed is also crucial, and this is heavily influenced by the values of the risk assessor and the stated intentions of the agency (Carson 1996). For example in the case of Rikki Neave (a child death in which the practices of Cambridgeshire Social Services were indicted), the view of workers and managers that family unity should be preserved at almost all costs was offset against the presenting risks of abuse, ultimately outweighing their view of risk. In the light of hindsight bias such a value based judgement seemed seriously at odds with the stated child protection goals of the agency, and at odds with the presenting information on risk. In the absence of explicit systems for articulating values and attributing weights to risk factors, strengths and weaknesses, then complex issues are more often resolved by recourse to 'experience', cognitive heuristics, and choices most commensurate with the practitioner's value base. This can result in actions and outcomes later seen as undesirable by public, courts and agency.

Defensible decisions therefore must have at least the following characteristics:

(1) Be grounded in a sound knowledge base of offender risk, and use the most credible assessment methods. In situations where an holistic combination of actuarial and clinical methods can improve accuracy agencies should adopt this approach.

(2) Be grounded in an explicit system for data collection *and it's evaluation.* This should include an explicit statement based upon evaluative research for the weighting of particular risk factors above others (at present much of this necessary research is on-going).

(3) An explicit statement of value and desirable outcomes commensurate with the stated goals of the agency. For example if public protection is to be prioritised over confidentiality, or risk reduction above rehabilitative efforts then such value choices should be made clear in policy statements and reflected in the decision making of risk assessors.

(4) If (3) is well stated then managers are entitled to have an expectation that risk assessors will stay within agency policies and procedures. However, managers also have an obligation to provide clearly stated, well researched and evidenced based policies and procedures, including the administrative, management and resource systems to enable such procedures to be carried out.

(5) Be based upon sound information collection and exchange systems, including a presumption that information will be actively sought from, and exchanged with, relevant others.

(6) Decisions should be recorded. This can involve a record of the analysis undertaken of the situation, the assessors thought processes, and the weighing of competing factors and desirable outcomes as well as the fact that the decision was taken. This is particularly important if the risk assessor has to account for her/his decision in the light of hindsight bias some time later. In such situations it is imperative that the risk assessor can demonstrate that she/he acted 'reasonably'.

(7) Decisions should be quality assured. However, the emphasis needs to be upon systems to ensure that more decisions are 'right first time' rather than the corrective monitoring of decisions once made. If the latter course is adopted then it is possible to end in the resource intensive position of recent cervical smear testing in which 100% of tests were routinely rechecked due to previous high error rates (The Times 1997, October 21st, p.6). Alternatively management attention can be focused upon facilitating the efficacy of risk decisions through supervision, training, learning positively from 'mistakes', and implementing policies, procedures and risk management

systems most likely to facilitate effective risk decision making by frontline staff.

Any risk assessment instrument must be able to support these seven characteristics. Whilst OGRS and the LSI-R can claim both a grounding in an established knowledge base and substantial evaluation (Andrews 1982, Andrews and Bonta 1995, Copas et al 1996, Gendreau et al 1994, Raynor 1997), they do not provide a mechanism for weighing differing values or desirable outcomes. In essence these instruments (and others with similar characteristics), provide inventories of risk and therefore assist in consistent assessment practice. However, they do not necessarily assist officers in the analysis of complex situations and in choosing acceptable courses of action. This highlights the subtle distinction between risk assessment and risk analysis, that is, the difference between a probability calculation of risk on the one hand, and the systematic analysis of the presenting risk indicators, potential range of outcomes and their desirability, and the balance of risks, rights and responsibilities on the other.

However, the methods currently on offer do assist with information collection although this still remains dependent upon the 'integrity' with which they are used (Raynor 1997) and to some extent the self-disclosure of offenders. There is however a danger that completion of any checklist becomes an end in itself, prohibiting an investigative stance from workers and providing a false level of reassurance (Prins 1995). It is also possible that in the daily reality of busy practice checklists will come to replace the adequate recording of risk decisions. This is likely to have serious repercussions for assessor and agency in the event of negative outcomes and subsequent inquiries.

These risk instruments, particularly the LSI-R and to a less evaluated extent the Oxford/Warwickshire ACE model, also provide mechanisms to achieve more consistent practice and systems to account for and evaluate professional activity. For example, Roberts and Robinson (1997) found that the LSI-R improved the quality of pre-sentence reports in the Greater Manchester service. Raynor (1997) also suggests that the LSI-R could be used to evaluate the impact of programmes upon future rates of recidivism. Whilst these instruments offer the potential for increased consistency of practice and increased control of professional activity towards managerially desirable ends, they also raise significant quality assurance issues of their own. Raynor's study highlights a small but significant number of officers who implemented LSI-R incorrectly, avoided the task, or mis-applied it either intentionally or unintentionally. He suggests that:

This may well be an example of the kind of quality control issue that probation services and continuing training inputs need to address (Raynor 1997, p.16).

Again this raises the spectre of continually checking the assessments of the assessors, and leads to a consideration of how to achieve implementation integrity and staff acceptance of methods which reduce discretion and autonomy.

Consider the acceptability of the instrument to staff and the likelihood that it will be applied with 'integrity'

In any risk assessment and management system staff acceptability of policies and procedures are crucial (Grinyer 1995, Rayner 1992, Wynne 1992) to their effective implementation. Probation officer perceptions (real or otherwise) of reduced discretion and autonomy, of methods which run counter to long held professional values, or to theoretical conceptions of offending behaviour and its causes can hinder the successful implementation of risk assessment instruments (Raynor 1997). Whilst hardline managerialists may consider that this ought not to be a consideration, Dunsire (1990) has convincingly argued that senior managers are often distant from both the substantive and operational issues of frontline practice and therefore have a limited grasp of the implications of their policy statements. In such situations it is imperative that managers actively listen to the views of staff and not dismiss them as 'mere resistance'. In the introduction of risk assessment methods, senior managers will have to consider their 'hearts and minds' strategy in addition to the technical and administrative issues of implementation.

Senior managers (and indeed central policy makers) may also have to accept that the optimum use of any risk assessment instrument will degrade over time. Paper dependent systems and their underpinning administrative systems become less rigorous as they are used, and vigilance atrophies (Cullen 1990). The Wakefield risk assessment instrument (Clark et al 1993) is a case in point. Whilst a figure of 65% accuracy was achieved in the first instance this was not maintained over the longer term. A retrospective evaluative study of the efficacy of Her Majesty's Prison Wakefield's tool by Law (1993) demonstrated that whilst an accuracy level of 45% could be achieved for predicting prison behaviour, the assessment tool could not predict accurately the rate of recall based upon the pre-specified risk factors. The method was highly dependent upon the intensive collection of information on the behaviour of inmates through the use of observation and reporting by a number of personnel, with particular attention to highly contextualised risk variables. Whilst close institutional monitoring of prisoners' behaviours may have taken place during the course of the pilot, presumably both rigour and consistency degraded overtime. In such cases the risk accuracy subsequently achieved is literally not worth the resource input.

Senior managers will therefore need to consider a range of factors in the selection and use of risk assessment instruments. These will not merely concern predictive utility, but may also have to cover a range of 'value added' components and include issues of implementation and resource.

Common characteristics: antecedents, behaviours and conditions

Central policy makers, senior managers, and practitioners are all likely to make different demands upon any risk assessment tool. Any tool will be judged therefore not only on its predictive efficacy but also on its ability to:

- Enable the appropriate matching of offenders to disposals/ interventions.

- The appropriate allocation of resources to offenders, and in particular the appropriate allocation of offenders to intervention programmes.

- The safe use of community disposals with a minimum of false negatives.

- Minimisation of false positives and the appropriate allocation of scarce resources to high risk cases.

- Minimum intrusion in low risk cases.

- Increased accountability for professional activity and evaluation of interventions in the reduction of risk.

- Its contribution to 'defensible decisions'.

• Acceptability to practitioners, easy integration into current assessment procedures, and its ability to facilitate risk management strategies.

A review of current methods here and in America and Canada (see Kemshall 1996 for example) strongly suggests that the most useful risk of recidivism instruments will be rooted in a methodology which has a combined approach of static actuarial factors with attention to behavioural traits, environmental factors and stressors, personal characteristics and social variables (Kemshall 1996, p.19). Whilst the predictive accuracy of pure actuarial methods are not always outperformed (Ditchfield 1997, Raynor 1997), the contribution of combined methods to the issues raised above can provide a 'value added' component to policy makers, senior managers and practitioners.

The key components of any risk assessment instrument are therefore its ability to gather credible information on the following:

• Antecedents.

• Behaviours and

• Conditions.
(Kemshall 1996a, Kemshall 1997, 1997d)

However, it is the appropriate and accurate combination of actuarial and clinical factors which has traditionally proved problematic. In the area of recidivism predictors Lloyd et al (1994) have noted that the absence of social variables is problematic although the selection and appropriate weighting of such variables is itself difficult. This is exactly the area which the LSI-R, the Client Management Classification system (Harris 1994), and Aubrey and Hough's risk/needs scale have attempted to tackle. However, as Lloyd et al point out, 'many of the variables associated with reconviction are inter-correlated', and calculating the risk of reconviction requires a 'multi-variant analysis' and a recognition that some variables carry more weight than others (Lloyd et al 1994, p.33). Such variables and their inter-action can change over time, hence tools and their prediction scales require revision over time (just as the prediction tables of insurance actuaries do).

Senior managers are then left in some difficulty, how to choose a risk of recidivism instrument in a situation where no instrument can meet all the criteria discussed in this chapter, and where more than predictive utility is often required. There is also a paucity of comparative evaluative evidence upon which to base such judgements although this situation is changing (Raynor 1997). In the meantime it is suggested that managers consider at least the following:

- The full cost of adopting and implementing any instrument.

- The balance of predictive utility against the resources required to apply the instrument.

- The 'value added' component of the instrument.

- The 'defensibility' of the instrument in negative cases. This will be particularly important in the light of 'hindsight bias', inquiries, public scrutiny and media attention.

- Acceptability to practitioners and fit with existing assessment procedures. 'Bolted on' components are more costly to deliver, less acceptable, and more likely to degrade.

- The level of 'fit' with dangerousness procedures and how any system of 'triage' might operate.

- The potential for integrity to be maintained over time.

Finally, whilst the collection of information can be difficult (Sheppard 1996), the research presented in this volume has shown that the analysis of information and the ability to make an informed judgement on the level of risk based upon the most significant factors is more problematic. This is particularly pertinent in situations where there is uncertain or competing information, where desirable goals are unclear, and where workers are striving to balance differing rights, responsibilities and risks. It is therefore important that senior managers can encourage the use of an analytical framework for risk analysis in which such judgements can be made both explicit and defensible.

Brearley (1982) offered a clear conceptual framework for combining both general predictive hazards (actuarial predictors) and specific hazards (clinical predictors) and for balancing strengths and weaknesses. This was extended by Kemshall (1995) into a series of key questions to guide risk analysis and case planning:

- General predictive hazards.

- Specific hazards.

- Strengths in the situation, either of the person, of others, or of the environment.

- Level of risk likely.

- Risk of what?

- Risk to whom?

- Consequences of the risk, to whom?

- Costs of acting or not acting, to whom?

- Likely danger(s) should the behaviour or the event take place.

- Action required to minimise the hazards.

- Action required to enhance strengths.

- Consequences of no action, and to whom?

- Recommendation to include a case plan reflecting work proposed on hazards and strengths, including evidence for level of risk.

- Date for review.

(Kemshall 1995; Kemshall 1996a, p. 140)

The intention is not to produce yet another piece of paper, but to incorporate this as a *style of thinking* into the assessment process, in effect to facilitate Sheppard's critical analytical retroduction (M. Sheppard 1995), and to make a sharper connection between assessment, case planning and case management.

Harm and dangerousness: the potential for integrating the risk of recidivism and the risk of danger

The assessment of dangerousness

Walker (1996) has argued that debates about dangerousness are in essence debates about the extent to which the precautionary principle should be taken, in other words how much protection it is desirable to provide and the cost of this in terms of prevention and intrusion. This essentially moral and ethical debate is exacerbated by difficulties in achieving predictive accuracy in dangerousness assessments. The problems encountered in recidivism prediction are increased in dangerousness prediction. Statistical prediction is less accurate due to low base rates (Monahan 1981, Walker 1996), and whilst past violent behaviour is the best predictor of future violence, situational factors have also been significantly highlighted (Megargee 1976). However, as with recidivism prediction, such situational and contextual variables can be highly variable and personal to the individual offender, and difficult to systematically identify and weight for predictive power (Carson 1997). This makes the production of a reliable assessment tool notoriously difficult (for a literature review see Kemshall 1996, Kemshall 1997).

However, key indicators and a framework to assist assessment can be identified (Kemshall 1997, Scott 1977). Whilst dangerousness cannot simply be equated with physical violence but can also include psychological trauma (Butler Committee 1975), predictors for violent behaviour are available. Based upon a review of the most pertinent research (Kemshall 1996), they are:

- Actuarial factors:

  past violent behaviour as the best predictor of the future,

  age, (being young), and

  gender (being male).

- Situational factors:

  substance abuse, although only as an 'associated factor',

availability of weapons,

proximity to victims,

socio-economic status, and

the behavioural traits of the particular individual in question.
(Kemshall 1997b)

Substance abuse and mental illness are somewhat contentious as predictors. Substance abuse cannot be convincingly demonstrated as a causal factor (mostly due to the methodological limits in the studies concerned), but can be shown as an 'associated factor'. For example, Genders and Morrison's study of section 18 and section 20 woundings in the West Midlands found that 41% of the section 18s and 29% of the section 20s were 'pub-related, in that they occurred inside or within the vicinity of public houses' or similar venues. Whilst the exact relationship between any substance misuse and violence is not known, it is accepted as a disinhibiting factor and may result in social interactions in which violence is the norm (Genders and Morrison 1996).

Mental illness can again be understood as an associated rather than causal factor. Whilst particular conditions such as schizophrenia (Howlett 1997) are viewed as more significant, the Boyd Committee found that the failure to take medication was a much more significant indication of future violence than mental illness alone (Steering Committee 1994, Ryan 1996). Ryan (1996) reminds us that of the minority of mentally ill people who do commit homicide:

> males tend to kill adults who are known to them and females are most likely to kill their children. It is rare for homicides to occur at the hands of mentally ill people who are unknown to the victim (Ryan 1996, p.100).

This is in sharp contrast to the few cases which gain a high media and public profile, for example the homicides of Jonathan Zito (Sheppard 1996), and Georgina Robinson (Blom-Cooper et al 1995), and Ben Silcock's entry into the lion's den at London Zoo (Ryan 1996).

Monahan (1992) suggests that when other factors such as male gender, youth, substance misuse, and low socio-economic status are taken into account, then mental illness is of minimal use as violence predictor.

However, if combined with a previous history of violence and medication breakdown it is a significant alarm bell. In a more recent study, Mulvey (1994) agrees that the association between mental illness and violence is small when compared with other characteristics such as socioeconomic status and a history of violence. Whilst the identification of causal links is problematic, 'the combination of a serious illness and a substance abuse disorder probably significantly increases the risk of involvement in a violent act' (Mulvey 1994, p.664).

As with the prediction of recidivism, a key issue is the interaction of static actuarial factors with situational and context specific indicators. Actuarial methods are 'most effective where the base rate for recidivism is around 50% or above' (Towl and Crighton 1997, p.191). As base rates reduce so does the effectiveness of the method. This is problematic for predicting dangerousness as this necessarily involves behaviours for which the base rate is low. In Towl and Crighton's case: homicide and suicide. In addition, Pawson and Tilley (1994) have argued that the scientific approach does not transfer well to the investigation and assessment of social behaviours. In effect, such models presume a linear causality and high control of the factors involved. However, analysis of major disasters demonstrates the high role of contextual factors and the non-linear progression of many risk events (Reason 1990, Wynne 1992). Individual assessment of the predisposing hazards and situational triggers are therefore essential to the identification of dangerous behaviour. This is distinct from the prediction of risk probabilities for groups within the population (Towl and Crighton 1997).

Limandri and Sheridan (1995) have argued for an interactive approach stating that:

> predictions can be made more accurately when evaluators take into account such interactive factors as gender, marital state, concomitant use of disinhibiting agents, and availability of victims and weapons (Limandri and Sheridan 1995, p.10).

This emphasises both the interactional nature of key demographic factors and contextual factors, but also the social interaction between perpetrator and victim (Shaw 1996). In essence this can be characterised as an assessment of:

- Predisposing hazards.

- Offender motivation.

- Access and proximity to victims.

- Conditions and opportunities under which behaviours take place.

Whilst previous research has concentrated largely upon the identification of personality traits associated with violent behaviour, it is now recognised that combined attention to personality factors and situational cues is likely to be more fruitful in dangerousness assessment (Borum 1996, Howells and Hollin 1989, Litwack 1994, Megargee 1976, Menzies et al 1994, Mulvey and Lidz 1995, Novaco 1976). The key issue for the Probation Service is how to appropriately combine these factors in a structured assessment, particularly as actuarial methods alone are likely to prove unhelpful. An adaptation of Scott's (1977) model provides a useful starting point. This would involve an assessment of:

- The key demographic factors about the offender (for example age, gender, and the presence or absence of the main violence predictors).

- Attention to antecedents and past behaviour (for example past history of violence).

- Conditions, circumstances and situational triggers under which harmful behaviour has occurred in the past.

- Past and present motivations to harmful behaviours.

- Presence or absence of internal inhibitors and of pro or anti-social values.

- Present conditions, circumstances, triggers, (for example is the past repeating itself?).

- Availability and preparedness to use a weapon.

- Access and proximity to past or potential victims.

- The type of social interaction likely between offender and potential victim (for example is this a long standing violent relationship? Is this offender in a position of trust which has been violated in the past?).

(Megargee 1976, Monahan 1981, Monahan and Steadman 1994, Mulvey and Lidz 1984, Novaco 1978, 1994, Scott 1977)

Checklists are unlikely to assist with the complexity of such an assessment. In these situations service managers will need to encourage staff attention to the main violence predictors grounded in an adequate knowledge base, combined with the best of investigative clinical interviewing to establish motivations, intentions, and triggers. The latter has been particularly promoted by Weist's technique of 'getting the offender to walk the therapist through the crime' (Weist 1981) and is common to much offence analysis work. It is possible to contend that the issue for dangerousness assessment is not the development of an 'instrument', but the acquisition by staff of the relevant knowledge base and appropriate violence indicators, and the integration of best practice clinical offence analysis techniques to all assessment.

Central to such complex analysis is the assessment of escalation, and the ability to differentiate between differing levels of dangerous behaviour. Walker (1991, Shaw 1996) has provided a four point typology to enable practitioners and their agencies to operate with a greater degree of refinement. This typology usefully incorporates the notion of progression:

The individual who harms others only if sheer bad luck brings him/her into a situation of provocation or sexual temptation.

The individual who gets into such situations not by chance, but following inclinations.

Individuals who are constantly on the look-out for opportunities.

Individuals who do more, and who create opportunities.
(Reproduced from Shaw 1996, p.170)

Such a typology assists in identifying those who are a 'chance one off', those who have an initial predisposition, those who are actively grooming, and those for whom committing the dangerous act is their sole 'raison d'être'. This can aid judgements of repetition, escalation, and amenability to intervention.

Integrating recidivism and dangerousness assessments

Whilst risk assessment procedures, instruments, and procedures for identifying harm have proliferated, there have been few successful attempts to integrate assessments of the risk of recidivism and dangerousness assessments. (The NAPO pamphlet: 'Risk: An Analysis of the Problem of Risk in Social Work' represents an early example, NAPO 1977). This has led to management and worker confusion over the use of the term risk, what is actually being assessed and how, and presumptions that risk assessment instruments are more effective in assessing dangerousness than they actually are (Kemshall 1996). On occasion it has also resulted in copious risk assessment or 'public protection' documents for staff in which managers have attempted to capture every eventuality of risk (for example Inner London 1995, Warwickshire 1995). In the absence of an adequate knowledge base, training, and in some cases the absence of consultation, this has resulted in staff confusion, fear, and resentment (Kemshall 1998a).

Some area services, (for example Durham 1997, Hampshire 1995 (revised 1996, 1997), Middlesex 1996) have conceptually separated the assessment of recidivism and the assessment of harm, and have stressed differing assessment techniques and risk factors for each specific area. In essence, two-tier systems have developed, although to staff this may initially appear cumbersome and as 'double assessing'. The distinction between recidivism assessment and the matching of effectiveness interventions to offenders on the one hand; and the assessment of dangerousness, registration and intensive monitoring on the other is often neither well made in policies nor well understood by staff.

The Scottish Social Work Inspectorate has attempted to pursue a more integrated approach to the risk of recidivism and harm than has tended to be the case in England. Actuarially based predictors for recidivism combined with criminogenic needs analysis are used to predict the risk of reoffending, and this is then combined with a potential harm analysis to rate the 'overall risk of reoffending and harm level of concern'. This is done by plotting both the risk of recidivism and the likelihood of harm on an integrated matrix in order to indicate the 'overall level of risk the offender poses to the public' (Risk Assessment Framework, form RA1, Scottish Social Work Inspectorate 1998).

Figure 10.1

FRONT SHEET

ASSESSING OVERALL RISK OF REOFFENDING AND HARM
LEVEL OF CONCERN

Name [   ]   Reference Number [   ]

Date [   ]   Social Worker [   ]

Current Offence [   ]

Using the matrix -
From RA1 identify the *Risk of re-offending* and identify the appropriate *row* (low, medium or high) on the matrix below;
From RA3 identify the *Risk of harm* and identify the appropriate *column* (low, medium or high) on the matrix below;
Indicate the box on the matrix where the risk of re-offending row and the risk of harm column intersect.
The box indicates the overall level of risk the offender poses to the public.

RISK OF REOFFENDING			
LOW	medium	low	low
MEDIUM	high	medium	low
HIGH	high	medium	low
	HIGH	MEDIUM	LOW

RISK OF HARM ⟶

Comments
Comments, date and signature of line manager in those cases which are identified as high risk (shaded).
(Scottish Social Work Inspectorate, 1998)

Whilst this is currently the subject of a pilot to evaluate the ability of staff to consistently use the matrix, it represents a constructive attempt to integrate the probability of recidivism with impact issues of harm into an overall framework in which a unified risk level for offenders could be offered. In terms of facilitating the appropriate allocation of both resources and interventions such a classificatory schema has much to offer.

However, some difficulties with the matrix can be immediately discerned. It is possible to present a low risk of recidivism but the potential for great harm should an offence be repeated. Exactly the dilemma many practitioners face with life licences. On the matrix this would result in a 'medium' categorisation, and whilst given the evidence on the low rate of repeat homicides this may seem reasonable (Ryan 1996), in the context of the 'precautionary principle' this may not seem entirely defensible in the event of negative cases. Similarly, high recidivists may present enormous harm to their victims but because there is no previous history of physical harms the impact is assessed as low. This was exactly the scenario in the case of Compton in the West Midlands. In situations of repeat victimisation, for example of burglary, neither victims or public may share the matrix view of low or medium risk. The extent to which the matrix would be shared by sentencers is of course another issue.

The problem here is that such objectifications of risk appear to solve pressing managerial and practitioner issues, but crucially overlook the social construction of risk concerns and the varying perceptions of harm and danger which can exist not least amongst public and sentencers, and the extent to which the Probation Service's categorisations will have to be evidenced and defended against public scrutiny. However, this does represent a laudable attempt to integrate probability and impact concerns, and to make 'risk of what' the overall test of risk level and subsequent classification. It's long term efficacy in accurately predicting overall risk levels, particularly in diminishing both false negatives and false positives, is worthy of further evaluative research.

Risk, harm and resources: an optimum risk management system

The appropriate integration of risk and dangerousness assessments into current practice and the rational allocation of resources have become key issues for senior managers. In this context risk management needs to be understood as a process for facilitating and monitoring quality risk decisions by all staff at every stage of the process (Carson 1995). Figure 10.2 outlines the responsibilities of managers in appropriately managing all risk work:

Figure 10.2 Managing Risk Decisions

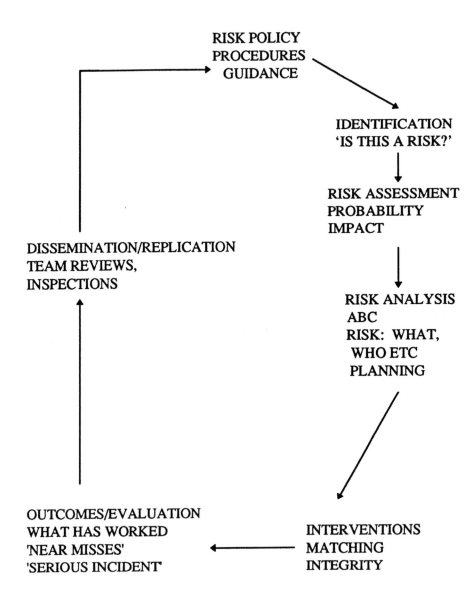

However, feedback from both the senior manager training, and the regional training the trainer events suggests that the managerial approach to managing the risk task has been largely piecemeal. This is likely to result in slow implementation, lack of consistency, and problems with sustaining the quality of risk work over the long term. In addition, the rush to train frontline risk assessors has often meant that the training needs of managers have been overlooked, and the management process is largely carried by personnel who have neither expertise on risk or a full appreciation of the implications of this major change in service work for the policy process.

Resources and risk

The requirement for the registration of dangerous offenders (Home Office Letter to Chief Probation Officers July 1988) and the identification of sexual and violent offenders as risky under section (1) (2) (b) of the Criminal Justice Act 1991 has already prioritised certain categories of offender as risky. Whilst categorisation based upon index offence is a reasonable and pragmatic response to a difficult issue, service managers will require techniques for ensuring that resources, professional time, and service intervention programmes are effectively targeted.

A model based upon more extensive assessments of risk of harm, assessment of offender motivation and the more careful targetting of effectiveness based work is proposed. This approach uses Andrews (1995) risk/responsivity principle to establish level of risk and to match programme interventions to the learning styles of offenders. This is combined with Miller and Rollnick's motivational interviewing (1991, Prochaska and DiClemente 1986) to establish those most 'amenable to resocialization' (Flynn 1978), and Walker's model of progressive dangerousness. Offenders can then be categorised not only for level of intervention but also for the type of intervention. This is represented in figure 10.3.

Offenders must be allocated correctly to box (2) in order to avoid wasting precious programme resources. It is also crucial that offenders who are not 'amenable to resocialization' and who require high levels of vigilance and control are appropriately allocated to box (1) for increased levels of monitoring, and not processed through programmes with little beneficial result. Officers may need to be encouraged to adopt a more explicit 'eternal vigilance' role (Prins 1988) in respect of box (1), and to devolve or refer to other agencies or to partnerships any presenting needs under boxes (3) and

(4) in order to prioritise risky offenders. In addition, offenders can be rapidly reallocated if their risk level and consequently their resource status changes. The grid could be used by managers to prioritise individual and team case loads, to enhance the allocation of professional time by officers, to carry out case reviews, and to prioritise the allocation of resources within area services.

Figure 10.3 Prioritising and Allocating Risk

BOX 1 High risk, Low motivation Low responsivity	BOX 2 High risk, High motivation, High responsivity
Surveillance and Control of 'Intransigents' or 'Career Criminals'. Extreme Dangerousness as Per Walker's Model. Those Who are Actively Grooming Victims.	Effectiveness Based Work Motivational Interviewing to Establish Propensity for Change Matching Programmes to Learning Styles and Personal/Social Circumstances of the Offender Pre-disposition to Dangerousness or Beginning to Groom.
BOX 3 Low risk, High motivation High responsivity	BOX 4 Low risk, Low motivation, Low responsivity
Monitor for Signs of Escalation Maintenance and Reinforcement Diversion Where Appropriate Some Predisposition to Dangerous Behaviour	Enforcement of National Standards Monitor for Signs of Escalation Walker's 'Chance One-Off'

Note: Motivation refers to an offender's attitude to changing their behaviour. Responsivity refers to an offender's ability to engage with structured cognitive-behavioural programmes.

The grid represents a model to allocate resources on the key principles already established within the numerous assessment and allocation models which actually exist (for example LSI-R, the Client Management Classification system, the Needs Scale). However the assessment process is dynamic and it is recognised that offenders may change their risk, responsivity and motivation status over time and that in effect re-allocation to differing types of intervention could then occur. Therefore it is important that the approach of 'eternal vigilance' (Prins 1988) is promoted amongst staff. The grid also attempts to incorporate the 'harm' principle, and attempts to integrate Walker's model of progressive dangerousness, key ingredients if staff are to accurately identify the likelihood of harm and appropriately plan for its management.

As well as rationalising intervention responses and resources to risk, and to responsivity and motivation levels, this approach also explicitly integrates the effectiveness and risk agendas. This would also allow managers to pursue a more integrated approach to risk, and to in effect manage offenders through their agency contact dependent upon their risk of recidivism or risk of harm status. This is represented by figure 10.4.

This system provides for the optimum allocation of resources, appropriate levels of supervision and differing types of intervention dependent upon the classification of the offender. Importantly, it also acknowledges Flynn's key principle of least intrusion possible and classifying out those who are low risk (Flynn 1978). The system also strives for a dynamic approach and a built in mechanism to both reassess and reclassify offenders.

Training

The risk management system above makes explicit links between risk, effectiveness based interventions, and the intensive surveillance of those deemed the most dangerous. The training implications of this risk management system are fully discussed in the training report prepared for the Home Office (Kemshall 1997a), and only the key points supported by an example of service implementation will be reiterated here.

The Home Office risk training materials (Kemshall 1997b) represent the first stage in essential training for all frontline risk assessors, supported by various other components such as child protection, mental health, sex offender training, working with violent offenders, etc., dependent upon the role and responsibilities of staff. It is recommended that these various components are provided as part of a coherent and developmental training strategy, for example as a 2-3 year programme on 'Risk and Public Protection'. In the longer term this could be integrated into qualifying training and first year officer training extending over the first 2-3 years in post.

Figure 10.4 Risk Assessment and Risk Management Process

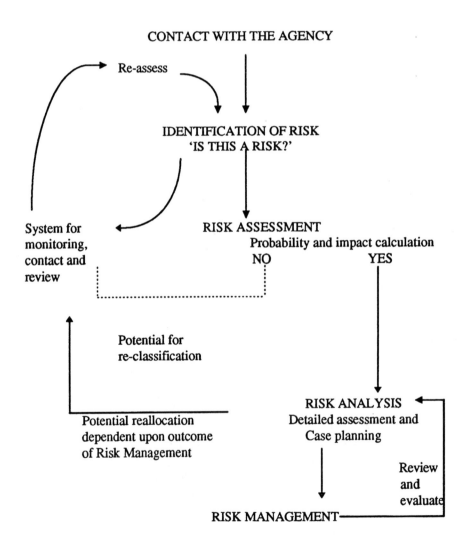

Training in risk work will also have to be explicitly linked to effectiveness training and development of motivational interviewing skills. Again this will require a strategic approach in which key connections across training events can be made. The process assumes that training should be integral to the communication and implementation of policy, and not approached as a substitute for policy communication or as a mechanism for dealing with staff resistance. The following example from West Glamorgan (Rolt 1997) illustrates a more interactive relationship between policy development and training, and highlights the constructive use of a training strategy (see Figure 10.5).

This model presumes that all managers have a responsibility to be well informed about local risk policies, and that probation committees, senior and middle managers are appropriately briefed prior to the implementation risk policies and procedures. This should be paralleled by appropriate training, for example the regional Home Office/ACOP training for senior managers, and in local services the training of middle managers and management teams (for example Berkshire, Durham, Hertfordshire, Inner London, West Midlands).

Senior probation officers in particular occupy a crucial position in the implementation of any risk management system. Their training should focus upon the skills and knowledge necessary to appropriately supervise staff, quality assure risk work, and appropriately allocate resources (see appendix four for the programme commissioned by Inner London and other services). This has subsequently been followed up by a questionnaire to participating Senior Probation Officers in order to evaluate the longer term impact of the training upon their management practice (Kemshall 1998a). The following results are of note:

- More vigorous communication of risk issues in both team meetings and individual supervision.

- Use of staff supervision to review risk assessments of team members.

- Use of staff supervision to monitor risk management.

- Use of staff supervision to evaluate the effectiveness of interventions.

- Notion of the 'defensible decision' a helpful management and practice tool.

Figure 10.5 Training Strategy

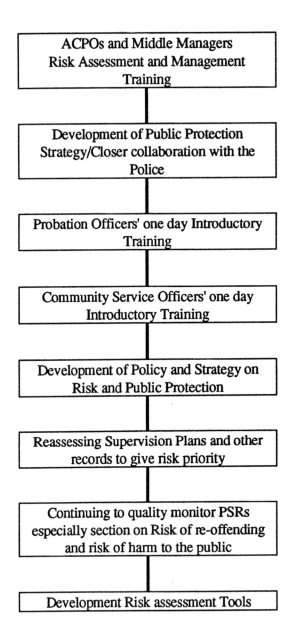

ACPOs and Middle Managers Risk Assessment and Management Training
Development of Public Protection Strategy/Closer collaboration with the Police
Probation Officers' one day Introductory Training
Community Service Officers' one day Introductory Training
Development of Policy and Strategy on Risk and Public Protection
Reassessing Supervision Plans and other records to give risk priority
Continuing to quality monitor PSRs especially section on Risk of re-offending and risk of harm to the public
Development Risk assessment Tools

(Rolt 1977)

Significant issues in fully implementing the area risk policy were:

- Resources, particularly time for middle managers.

- Staffing levels, for example vacancies in particular settings.

- Poor communication within and without the organisation.

- Lack of crucial information at the appropriate time, for example antecedents.

This strongly suggests that an integrated approach of policy development/implementation, training, and organisational change is likely to provide the most success.

The precautionary principle in action

In her paper Flynn (1978) identified the key principles which any risk system operating in criminal justice should have. In addition to their predictive, administrative and management functions, risk assessment instruments should also be judged on their contribution to these underlying principles. Primary amongst these are:

(1) the preservation of equity and justice in criminal justice; (2) the protection of individual liberties; (3) the recognition for the need to protect members of society from crime and violence... (Flynn 1978, p.133).

Clearly instruments which net widen, or which produce too many false positives do not meet these criteria. Conversely, instruments which produce too many false negatives cannot meet the protective criterion. In addition Flynn argued that risk based systems should also:

- Clearly and accurately identify high and low risk offenders and distinguish between them.

- Identify risky behaviour which should be a 'clear and present danger to members of society' (p.133).

- Contribute to decarceration of the less risky and that the system should be evaluated on its success in this regard.

- Not encourage preventative sentencing.

Present systems and their attendant risk instruments do not adequately meet these criteria. Procedures for adequately identifying and distinguishing high and low risk are embryonic. This is supported by the volume of serious incidents amongst those classified as medium or low risk (Probation Circular 36/97), the failure to classify out low risk, by the volume of offenders classified as high risk who do not reoffend harmfully (Brown 1996), and a suspicion that this is not necessarily due to the quality of risk management:

> SPO 1 (Inner London Probation Service): I increasingly ask the question what extra is being done to reduce risk? Are people doing anything 'deeply meaningful' with those registered people? Regrettably the answer is often 'no'.

This is supported by the seniors' view that risk management strategies are largely comprised of liaison and collaborative working with others. In effect, officers describe the process of their activities in staff supervision but not their content. Few specific intervention strategies could be discerned by seniors (Kemshall 1998a).

The precautionary principle has shifted the emphasis from proof and evidence to fears of 'what if'. Distinguishing between recidivists and those who 'commit serious predatory crimes and violence' (Flynn 1978, p.133) continues to plague both service managers and workers, particularly in the absence of reliable actuarial methods for violence prediction, and the lack of integration of current violence predictors into the assessment practice of the service.

The predominance of the precautionary principle is also evidenced by the lack of decarceration and the use of preventative sentencing. 'Classifying out' appears to have been overlooked, and in some instances local risk management systems can be better characterised as systems which 'classify up':

> SPO 1 (Inner London Probation Service): Have we got it right? We are so overworked that spending increasing amounts of time on a percentage of offenders whose predicted dangerousness has not come true seems strange.

In effect, this senior is questioning both whether the precautionary principle is delivering, and the underpinning rationality of risk based penalty.

The precautionary principle of a risk based penalty necessarily leads to the broader issue of the relationship between risk management systems, social regulation and principles of penalty. In 1986 Reichman noted the growing insurance approach to crime control, and that this implied a 'particular form of social arrangement organised around a set of procedures for allocating risk across a community of risk takers' (Reichman 1986, p.151).

Reichman characterised the increased dependence upon probability or actuarial calculations of crime risks; an increased emphasis upon 'opportunity reduction' (i.e. crime reduction); and 'loss prevention' as a 'trend toward an insurance or actuarial model of social control' (p.152). Other commentators have noted the rise of actuarial risk management in other walks of life (for example health care) (Simon 1987, 1988), and the increased impact of actuarial measures upon issues of social regulation. The implications of actuarial responses to social control, and the role of both criminal justice and probation within this will be discussed in the next chapter.

11. Risk and Social Regulation

Simon (1987) in a paper reviewing the growth and impact of actuarial practices argues that the increasing insurance approach to risk results in the objectification and aggregation of individuals, representing individuals as 'instances of a population' (p.62). Both the growth of commercial insurance and the collective insurance of the welfare state are rooted in the increased refinement of assessment tools for aggregating individuals and responding to them on the basis of this assessment. This has been combined with an increased political and economic preoccupation with safety and security (Simon 1987).

Simon traces this preoccupation through the development of accident insurance (for example workers insuring against the calamity of disabling accidents), welfare state provision to cover the risks of the general population, the legal liability of companies for their products, health care and medical malpractice, to more recent explosions in insurance for cars and credit cards, personal insurance and privately organised systems for guarding against crime risks.

His central tenet is that this risk society changes both social bonds and the sovereignty of the citizen. The former because individuals can be treated as little more than a collection of their risk indicators, labelled and located by their risk level, and not viewed as an individual with a distinct identity beyond the risk inventory. The 'cultural pattern of risk', defined by Simon as 'a cluster of knowledge and power practices' (p.63) disrupts sovereignty because the moral and political dimensions of people are devalued in favour of cost-benefit conceptualisations. In essence, the moral relationships of the sovereign state are supplanted by the aggregation and placing of individuals according to their risk.

Nowhere is this more clearly played out than in criminal justice where the disciplinary powers of the sovereign (e.g. ritual executions) have been replaced by institutional punishments (panopticons, prisons), and more recently by risk management techniques such as electronic tagging and close circuit television (Foucault 1977, Simon 1987, 1988). This has resulted in a dual and sometimes conflictual discourse in criminal justice. Garland has expressed this as the operation of an expressive rationality of punishment alongside an emerging economic rationality of risk (Garland 1997).

Expressive and Economic Rationalities of Risk

Garland defines expressive rationality as the 'need to express public sentiments about crime and criminals' (p.5), the state ritual expression of deterrence and retribution through the deployment of punishments. The White Papers 'Crime, Justice and Protecting the Public' (Home Office 1990a) and 'Protecting the Public: The Government's Strategy on Crime' (Home Office 1996b) along with the 1990s Conservative government emphasis upon 'prison works' are exemplars of this expressive rationality. The 1991 Criminal Justice Act marked a significant move towards economic rationality with its emphasis upon a bifurcatory sentencing approach and 'just deserts'. However, expressive rationality soon produced a turn around on some of the key areas of the act, resulting in significant amendments and a 'back to basics' approach to criminal justice in the Criminal Justice and Public Order Act 1994 (Wasik and Taylor 1995).

The more recent Crime Sentences Act 1997 (Home Office 1997a) and the proposed Crime and Disorder Bill (Home Office 1997b) clearly embody these twin rationalities. The Crime Sentences Act enables life sentences for violent or sexual offenders convicted for a second time and hospital direction for mentally disordered offenders. The Sex Offenders Act 1977 which came into force on the 1st September imposed the compulsory registration of sex offenders in the community (HOC 39/1997). These various pieces of legislation were recently described by a Home Office representative as 'a wide and comprehensive net' (Marriage 1998), and represent an extensive risk management system. In that it is predominantly directed at the 'monsters in our midst' (Witness, Channel 4, 1998) it is also a key mechanism for expressing public disgust, disquiet, and censure towards certain offenders. The proposed Crime and Disorder Bill proposes a Sex Offender Order under which those sex offenders deemed to present a continuing risk can be subject to a range of restrictions on their daily activities. Thus expressive rationality is used to justify ever increasing risk management strategies, and economic risk rationalities can be deployed to appease public expressions of punishment, deterrence and indeed demands for risk avoidance. In this sense, Garland (1997) is right to contend that expressive rationality often masquerades as economic risk rationality. In terms of probation practice, the preferred rhetoric of those wise enough to keep pace with the changing fortunes of criminal justice is of rehabilitation and 'what works' interventions as the vehicle of effective risk management (Garland 1997). In effect, to subsume a traditional penal rationality of welfarism and rehabilitation as a mechanism of social integration to a rationality of risk management and social control.

Risk and social control

The growth of actuarial practices has far reaching consequences. For Simon they result in the displacement of the individual from moral, rational agent, to a location in an actuarial table. The change from 'moral agent to actuarial subject' also transforms the mechanisms of power 'by the state and other large organisations' (Simon 1988, p.772).

From individual discipline to risk management

The major change is the shift from disciplinary attention to individual behaviour and its change (for example through treatment or rehabilitation), to the management of risk distribution, in effect to the management of 'the physical and social structures within which individuals behave' (for example restricting access, close circuit television, registers and surveillance nets) (Simon 1988, p.773). Reichman (1986) has called this an 'insurance concept of crime control' (p.153) in which the hazard reduction strategies of 'profiling', targetting, zero tolerance, surveillance and exclusion, and the work of 'Crime Concern' are prime examples. In this approach, individual motivation and responsibility for criminal acts are less important than actuarial factors of risk (such as previous criminality, age and gender), and restricting the opportunity of risky groups to offend is viewed as both economically more viable and effective than the pursuit of individual change (Reichman 1986, Shearing and Stenning 1981). In cost-benefit analyses, zero tolerance is a better bet than individualised programmes of rehabilitation.

In this approach, the results of criminal activity (and how they can be either reduced or more equitably shared), are the growing subject of attention rather than the offender per se. The offender is of interest only as a site for risk, and in a sense explanations (as opposed to predictions) of behaviour become redundant. This was given expressive ideological force by the then Home Secretary, Mr Howard in 1993 when he called for an abandonment of:

> ...trendy theories that try to explain away crime by blaming socio-economic factors. Criminals should be held to account for their actions and punished accordingly. Trying to pass the buck is wrong, counter-productive and dangerous. (Howard, 1993, cited in Wasik and Taylor 1995).

Prediction as the central tenet of risk management has replaced explanation. However, as Reichman notes this has resulted in a focus upon certain types of crime and certain types of offenders. Risk management requires prediction, and this in turn requires repetition and visibility. Probabilities calculated upon low base rates are notoriously unreliable. The effectiveness of any risk management system is dependent upon low uncertainty, high reliability and high predictability in its assessment procedures. It is therefore no coincidence that risk management in criminal justice has found it easier to focus upon recidivist crimes and the consequent development of predictive tools in which a limited number of variables can be identified and weighed. The prediction of low frequency activities presenting high danger remains elusive (Menzies et al 1994, Mulvey and Lidz 1995). In essence criminal risk management is based upon the prediction of habitual offenders, the prediction of the predictable.

Risk management or risk displacement

Whilst technologies of risk management have gained pace, for example encoding of credit cards, close circuit television, electronic tagging, encoding of goods and possessions, security screening etc., whether crimes are reduced or displaced onto those not able to take adequate risk precautions is a moot point. If such displacement takes place then risks are in effect transferred to those least able to insure against them. Targeted custody and preventative sentencing on those deemed most likely to compromise public safety are also significant risk management techniques, literally removing career criminals and those deemed 'intransigent' from circulation (Blumstein 1983, Blumstein et al 1986). However, as Reichman argues, transfer of risks rather than reduction can contain the seeds of its own downfall. Ironically for Reichman, spreading hazards breeds risk, for as more exposure to risk is experienced the 'incentives to protect against future losses are very much reduced.' (Reichman, 1986, p. 160).

The redistribution of property crime risks to insecure and impoverished neighbourhoods, or shoplifting costs to low income shoppers who then resort to crime themselves are obvious cases in point. More recently, the transfer of sex offenders to communities who resent their presence has created active vigilantes and on occasion perpetrators of violent crime (Witness, Channel 4, 1998).

Such an approach to risk is not merely a matter of new technologies (Reichman 1986, Simon 1988), but reflects wider changes in patterns of social regulation. As Pratt (1995) expresses it, there is a marked shift away from traditional disciplinary practices towards an 'informative' system in which the production of knowledge for the use of one set of people for the control of another is central:

> In relation to dangerousness, it can provide us with a profile...Not though so that we can change their behaviour...but...so that we can identify and contain such individuals. (Pratt 1995, p.26).

This can literally mean the prevention of certain individuals from entering into particular geographical or social spaces, gaining access to particular opportunities to offend, or preventing them entering into 'certain types of social relationships.' (Reichman 1986). The emphasis is upon prevention not action. Causes of behaviour and their eradication are not as important as the limitation of opportunities and the management of choice. This is most particularly evidenced by emphasis upon crime prevention as a risk management strategy (O'Malley 1992).

Technologies of social control

Other commentators have noted the application of insurance technologies to other social problems (Castel 1991, Donzelot 1979, 1991, Miller and Rose 1988, 1992, Rose 1993), and the shift from Foucault's disciplinary power (1977) to actuarial or 'risk-based technologies of power' (O'Malley 1992, p.252). The essence of Foucault's disciplinary power is normalisation, the specification of a norm against which individuals are both judged and if necessary corrected towards. The treatment or rehabilitation of delinquents is an example of this approach. In this technique problem individuals can be corrected or 'normalised' (O'Malley 1992). Actuarial systems however, do not concentrate upon the 'coercion of individuals' (O'Malley 1992, p.254). Rather variations from the norm are identified and the threat neutralised through tactics of redistribution, limitation, and control. Criminal intransigents for example are identified for increased control and limited access to offending opportunities by preventative and extended sentencing.

Simon (1987, 1988) amongst other commentators (Castel 1991, Cohen 1979, 1985, Donzelot 1979) has argued that the technologies of the 'risk society' have greater power and economy than the preceding disciplinary technique. Whilst it would be too simplistic to contend that technologies of power have a Darwinian predisposition towards unilinear progression (O'Malley 1992, Simon 1988), actuarial technologies certainly meet Foucault's criteria of progression; that is, high power for low cost, high intrusion with low visibility, and progressive extension of the system (Foucault 1977). Simon (1988) has concluded that one result of such a technology of power is that traditional social relations and communities are dispersed. In essence, individuals are categorised according to group risks which effectively ascribe them a group categorisation and location which may bear little relation to the group networks experienced in daily life (O'Malley 1992). This makes resistance to risk categorisations difficult to orchestrate, even when those categorisations are known. As Simon expresses it, as traditional understandings of self and group are fractured by risk classifications, sites for recognising and achieving 'common goals or purposes are removed' (Simon 1988, p.774).

In considering the form of classification used by actuarial practices, Simon goes further by asserting that the traditional 'dialectic of power/resistance' and their attendant ideological effects are displaced. For Simon, risk 'de-centres' individuals, eliminating the subjective identity into anonymous sites of risk:

> Actuarial   classification,   ...seems   to   eliminate...the   possibility   of
> identity...Rather than making people up, actuarial practices unmake them
> (Simon 1988, p. 792).

The actuarial future suggested by Simon (1988) is potentially bleak, with traditional sites of resistance such as class and gender fragmented, with new enforced collectivities of risk replacing them. For Simon (1988) risk replaces traditional identities and the political power organised around them, and diminishes the possibility of political change. He suggests that:

> Barricades are useless against a power that operates in the abstract space of
> actuarial tables (Simon 1988, p.798).

However, all may not be lost. Simon (1988) suggests that attention to the ideological effects of actuarial practices may provide a mechanism for not only understanding the impact of such practices but for resisting them. However, how such resistance will be possible is not entirely explained. O'Malley (1992) is more hopeful, and rejects the relentless move towards risk technologies. The transition is more subtle for O'Malley. He argues that there is no overarching 'logic of power', rather technologies of power cannot be divorced from the 'substantive political programs' which deploy them (O'Malley 1992, p.257). This shifts the emphasis from abstract conceptions of power to its use.

Following Miller and Rose (1990), O'Malley argues that technologies of power are developed with 'specific purposes in mind' (p.258), although this does not preclude their eventual deployment in other fields. This defines risk technologies as political as well as technological instruments, techniques instrumental in the implementation of specific political programmes:

> The history of the prison or of actuarial techniques in crime prevention...is not to be understood as the gradual encroachment of a more efficient technology of power, but the uneven and negotiated...implementation of a political program and the consequent...installation of appropriate techniques (O'Malley 1992, p.258. Reproduced with the permission of Routledge).

O'Malley reviews situational crime prevention as a case in point. Following Cohen (1985), O'Malley argues that crime prevention eschews concern with correction or behaviour. The agenda is clearly stated by the National Crime Prevention Institute (1986, p. 18, cited in O'Malley 1992), in which prevention rather than rehabilitation is prioritised; the effective rehabilitation of offenders is doubted; punishment, community corrections, and imprisonment are seen as effective controls for some offenders; crime can be reduced by altering the environment, for example by limiting opportunities in high crime areas; and that crime should be prevented before it occurs. In the intervening period this has received greater emphasis through 'Crime Concern', zero tolerance policing, targetting, preventative sentencing, and the prolonged incarceration of intransigents.

The new right programme of crime control

O'Malley identifies the preoccupation with situational crime risk management not as merely a question of economy, but importantly as the product of an 'economic rationalist, neo-conservative and New Right' crime programme (p.263). This approach has gained much ground in America, Britain and Australia (Henham 1997, Pratt 1995, Pratt 1996). O'Malley argues that the result is a recasting of both offenders and victims in line with New Right ideological conceptions of the individual. That is, 'homo prudens' or 'homo economicus', the rationally driven individual whose choice of action will be subject to cost-benefit analyses. Such an individual is of course essential to insurance based approaches to risk. The presumption is that given the correct cost-benefit information offenders will desist and victims will choose to protect themselves better. Theories of constraint, such as sociologically based explanations of crime causation (for example strain theory), are dismissed as indulgent excuses resulting in social dependency (Howard 1993). Whilst the public is promised increased protection, this is a double edged sword as public and individuals are also made increasingly responsible for their own protection, in terms of where they go, the precautions taken, the steps taken by property owners to protect their goods, and last but by no means least the move towards privatised security. Crime control itself can be subject to the 'free market' and the rational, economic choice of individuals.

This is not to dismiss the fact that individuals and communities can benefit from such practices (Teeside's zero tolerance policing for example, 'Crime Concern' in Bradford). However, these benefits should not be mistaken for the promotion of social justice (although O'Malley notes some non-British examples). It cannot necessarily be assumed that such measures either reduce risk or redistribute it away from those least able to tolerate it. Repeat victimisation studies suggest otherwise (Karmen 1990, National Board for Crime Prevention 1994, Walklate 1997). Crime risks may not necessarily be more equitably distributed throughout the population but rather may be increasingly managed in place, or at worst displaced to other sites of vulnerability rather than reduced (Barr and Pease 1992). Crime 'opportunity management' in particular runs the risk of focusing upon displacement rather than reduction (Barr and Pease 1992, Walklate 1997). The result may be high risk victims and locals as well as high risk offenders. The separation of risk concerns from social justice ones not only makes it 'respectable to regard criminals as unconstrained agents' (O'Malley 1992, p.265), but enables both the allocation of blame and the absolution of central government from responsibility for either social justice or crime causation.

From risk to dangerousness

Pratt (1995) notes that the 'rational choice' approach to crime risk management marks a significant departure from the previous dependency upon government for 'protection, security and regulation' (p.26). He argues that:

> ...only where the risk is most minimal and unknowable the threat from dangerous offenders - that governments are currently prepared to increase their insurantial responsibilities (Pratt 1995, p.26).

Whilst constituting a minimal risk, dangerous behaviour is unpredictable. It is exactly this combination of low frequency and randomness which makes dangerous behaviour difficult for the ordinary citizen to protect themselves against. In Pratt's words, 'citizens cannot insure themselves' against such an unpredictable threat (p.18). It is a danger which can arise anywhere from potentially anyone (Dunblane for example). Whilst other crime risks are amenable to situational risk management strategies (for example neighbourhood watch schemes and security systems to deal with burglary), dangerousness is not. Situational risk management systems are dependent upon highly predictable, repeat offences, often targeted to particular locales and victims. However, the dangerous offender is not so easily identified. Despite significant work to identify the offence patterns of sex offenders, and to translate the broader concept of dangerousness into violence risk (Duckitt 1988) or harm (Brooks 1984), the ability to accurately predict dangerous people remains problematic (Walker 1996).

Responses to dangerousness

It is in response to this 'uninsurable' difficulty that much government activity on dangerousness can be understood. In particular the use of legislation to provide the public with a 'guarantee' against dangerousness, for example section 2 (2) b in the Criminal Justice Act 1991, the Crime Sentences Act

1997, and the proposed Crime and Disorder Bill. In these cases the state is prepared to infringe traditional rights and tolerate a higher level of false positives in order to offer protection to its citizens. However, this protection is most often retrospective, dangerous offences have already occurred. However, the legislation is framed towards a concern with future acts. This framing itself is problematic, requiring accurate predictions to justify its use and results in significant tensions with established principles of proportionality (von Hirsch and Ashworth 1996).

Whilst actuarial practices are now more prominent in dangerous assessments, the reputation of dangerousness prediction is poor (Monahan 1981). This may partially explain the reluctance with which dangerous legislation has traditionally been used (Pratt (1995) for example notes the meagre use in New Zealand, six sentences of preventive detention between 1982-1986, with an average of 5.5 per annum since 1988). Whilst it is a little early to draw conclusions from the English context, it is clear that the legislative concept of dangerousness and its proof have been subject to Appeal Court challenge.

Whilst in America the predictive vacuum has been filled by the rise of actuarial methods for dangerousness, in particular for violence prediction (Menzies et al 1994, Monahan and Steadman 1994, Mulvey and Lidz 1995) as a means to make a rather nebulous concept calculable, a British resolution to this problem has yet to be found. The reaction of central policy makers to this issue has been the devolution of this difficult issue to local policy makers who, in the absence of predictive methods, have implemented a wide and diverse array of checklists and questions to structure decision making. The emphasis has largely been upon control rather than identification mechanisms, with attention to multi-agency risk management arrangements to limit the risk of harm (Home Office Special Conferences 1997). The responsibility for prevention and protection is firmly located with professionals as the public cannot self insure. Information exchange and surveillance nets are seen as the major mechanisms of ensuring protection. Whilst highlighted by numerous inquiries as a fault in risk management (Blom-Cooper et al 1995 for example), the actual contribution of such approaches to the reduction of dangerousness requires further evaluation (Hebenton and Thomas 1996).

Risk and social regulation: implications for the Probation Service

In 1977 Bottoms noted that as the objectives of penal policy change so do the tasks, roles and responsibilities of criminal justice workers. Recent years have seen increasing activity on the part of Probation senior managers to adapt to the new winds of penal change. This has not been a matter of simply adapting to 'Howard's Way', recent signs from the Straw office indicate little change (National Probation Convention 1997). The economic rationality of the New Right has not abated, and the Service has accepted this as a legitimate part of its accountability. The Service now expects to provide value for money and to account for the rational use of its resources. In addition to the embracing of this economic rationality, the Service has had to acknowledge the rather more unpredictable expressive rationality of punishment and being 'tough on crime'. To a large extent effectiveness has been proffered as a mechanism for bridging these two rationalities (Raynor 1997a), particularly of the targeted cognitive behavioural type.

However, even the newly cast rehabilitation of effectiveness is being supplanted by a more 'security-oriented model of crime control' (Garland 1997, p.9). This is reflected in the twin -preoccupations of the risk of recidivism and the tools to both assess and manage it (of which effectiveness is a part), and the risk of 'dangerousness'. It is also reflected in the economic rational that resources should follow risk and the various instruments currently being pursued to classify offenders for level of service (Home Office 1997, Home Office Special Conferences 1998). Both these difficult areas have been largely devolved to local area managers to solve (for example through the adoption of LSIR, or the development of Warwickshire's Assessment Case-Recording and Evaluation Model (ACE)). In addition, penal management is increasingly driven by economic concerns resulting in higher levels of accountability, fiscal control, and rational resourcing (Christie 1993, Humphrey et al 1993). The 'risk principle' is intrinsic to such decision making, providing a rational mechanism for targetting, resource allocation, and accountability. The principle can also serve expressive rationality, with high media coverage of risky cases going hand in hand with populist political pronouncements to 'get tough on crime' (the Jamie Bulger murder case and the attendant media coverage for example).

The recent address of the current Home Secretary Jack Straw to the National Probation Convention suggests that it is 'business as usual' as he asked the Service to work with the government on its 'modernisation agenda'. The emphasis was upon the punitive content of community penalties, gaining public confidence through a 'get tough' agenda, enforcement, but also effectiveness:

> Community supervision has to be credible as punishment but it also has to be effective if the public is to be protected. It has to reduce repeat offending and protect the public from harm (Straw, 1997).

These two sentences bring together both the expressive and economic rationalities underpinning current penal logic into a risk agenda; risk of recidivism and risk of harm. The agenda for the Probation Service as it moves into the 21st century is clear: effectiveness, public protection and risk management. In meeting this agenda the Service will need to consider and resolve the following:

- Probation services are now risk management systems. Which type of risk management system is likely to provide the most risk reduction and the most protection?

- The long term impact of insurance approaches to crime control, particularly for the rights and needs of offenders.

- The balance between rights, risks and responsibilities to various users which the Service can realistically pursue.

- The extent to which a risk based penality is compatible with social justice.

On a more practical level the following key issues will require attention:

- The choice of assessment tools for both the risk of recidivism and the risk of harm.

- The development of an effective agenda for risk management *in practice*.

- The development of evaluation tools to determine the outcome of risk management interventions.

- Management strategies to achieve the 'resources follow risk' principle.

- The development of adequate knowledge and skill within the whole work force.

Rationalisation and social regulation

On a broader level the Service will need to review its place within a risk based penality and the contribution of such a penality to social regulation. To this end, the increased rationalisation of the Probation Service has already begun with the adoption of a broadly Taylorist approach to management (Taylor 1911, Lash and Urry 1994), combined with a Weberian bureaucratic rationality (Weber 1976) in which institutionalised rules and regulations are enforced as the best means to achieve desired ends. The formal elements of such a bureaucratic rationality are already there: formalisation of rules, systems and tasks; a stress upon formal rules and tasks as the best means of achieving efficiency; highly predictable rule dependent operations; highly predictable services and tasks; quantification of all outcomes and all tasks exactly calculable; high control of tasks, staff and users. This has been unkindly but perhaps correctly described as the 'McDonaldisation of the Probation Service' (Oldfield 1994), and as part of a greater 'McDonaldisation of Society' (Ritzer 1993). In this world risk is construed as a 'product', and both the assessors and perpetrators of risk are subject to a pervasive economic utilitarianism.

Even the very processes of risk assessment and management may serve to objectify and distance both those subject to them and those using them. Standardised actuarial measures both hide the people to whom they are applied, and disguise the intentions of those who use them (Crivisqui 1993, Simon 1987, 1988). Such reification processes may be helpful to the bureaucrats who administer the system (for example in solving resource problems), but may prove disastrous for those affected by them. The repercussions of a numerical risk weighting or of a particular label could be great indeed.

The 'modernisation agenda' appears relentless, especially to busy managers and hard pressed practitioners. In a climate made fearful by cuts and a mentality of retrenchment it is difficult to pause for reflection and to consider the real nature of the crime risks debate. The real debate may not be about the choice of risk assessment tools, but about the type of society we are creating and in which we are prepared to live. As Douglas expresses it, risk is about blame, the identification of 'opponents' and the reinforcement of social solidarities (Douglas 1992). It is also about fear (Furedi 1997). In this sense risk is pervasive to all our lives, carrying with it great potential for accountability and blame, and for stigmatisation and exclusion. There is also potential for an inexorable widening of the risk net as those held accountable for risk attempt to reduce its inherent uncertainty through the use of precautionary techniques and invasive systems of information collection. Such a system can potentially treat everyone as 'at risk', but more importantly as a potential source of some risk. The possibility of an extended carceral net combined with fragmented social relations produces the spectre of isolated, uncertain and highly anxious individuals. In our attempt to 'colonise the future' through risk (Kemshall et al 1997) we may make that future very bleak indeed.

Part Four: Appendices

Appendix one: Vignettes of risk

Jason is 23 years old. He is currently serving a sentence of 4 years for arson with intent to endanger life, and 3 months for criminal damage. The probation officer involved in the case has to prepare a parole report. The offence was committed in the family home whilst the rest of the family were on holiday.

Jason expresses his wish in interview to return home on parole. It is the first parole review.

What should the officer do next?

The probation officer does pursue other arrangements for parole, and Jason is released to his elder sister's home. She has agreed to accommodate him and to provide support, this includes an undertaking not to leave Jason alone in the home. However, the officer discovers in supervision that Jason frequently returns to the family home, and has gained access to the house while the occupants were out at work. Jason blames his parents for his prison sentence, accepts little responsibility for the offence and has been assessed as having learning difficulties.

What should the officer do next?

Jason is in fact moved to a hostel for offenders in the area, he is also given a verbal and written warning by the officer. However, Jason continues to contact his family, by telephone and by visits. He continues to maintain that he is not to blame for the fire, he sees it as a natural response to his parents going on holiday without him - a means of 'getting even with them'. His attitude to the offence has remained unchanged since sentence. Warnings have had little effect.

What should the officer do next?

Vignette 2

John is 18 years old. He is currently subject to a one year Probation order for offences of burglary and theft. He reports regularly and is co-operative in supervision. The probation officer supervising the case learns from another probationer that John has started to do voluntary with the elderly.

What should the officer do next?

In fact, John is asked by the probation officer to disclose his convictions to the voluntary organisation before continuing to work. John is angered by this, he feels he will be prevented from working and that he is getting little credit for "going straight". He also states that as a black offender he does not expect to be fairly treated by the organisation when he does disclose.

What should the officer do next?

In fact, John agrees to tell the voluntary organisation that day and the probation officer will check this out with his work supervisor before John's next probation appointment. John fails to attend his next appointment, and upon checking the officer discovers that John has not attended for voluntary work either. John subsequently fails his next two appointments.

What should the officer do next?

Vignette 3

Joan is a white 33 year old woman currently on probation for one year for offences of theft and DSS fraud. She is a single parent with 3 children under the age of 10. She has recently lost a part-time job and the extra income this provided. She is waiting for the DSS to process her benefit claims. During a home visit the officer notices an Invalidity Claim book made out to someone else.

What should the officer do next?

In fact, the officer questions Joan who states that the book belongs to an infirm neighbour and she is going to the post office to cash it for them. Joan points out the neighbour's house, and offers to take the officer over to check.

What should the officer do next?

In fact the officer accepts Joan's statement. Some 2 months elapse. The officer attends a case conference in respect of Joan and her children. At the conference the police express their suspicions that Joan is continuing with DSS fraud and is in fact part of a small 'gang' operating locally.

What should the officer do next?

Vignette 4

Michael is a 44 year old white man, subject to an 18 month Probation Order for criminal damage x 2, BGH x 2 and theft. He is often argumentative and angry in interview, and has threatened reception staff when kept waiting. He inadvertently discloses in interview that he is working but also 'signing on'.

What should the officer do next?

Michael is in fact warned by his probation officer. He threatens her to 'mind her own business' and then he leaves.

What should the officer do next?

Two weeks elapse and Michael fails to attend two interviews. The officer contacts the DSS and Michael is still claiming.

What should the officer do next?

Vignette 5

Paul is a white 17 year old youth. The probation officer is currently preparing a pre-sentence report on Paul for offendencess of TWOC, TADA, driving whilst disqualified, and driving with no insurance. During interview Paul displays little remorse for his offending, does not seem to recognise the possible danger to others, and is unconvincing about not driving again. However, the offence seriousness score could just place Paul in the top area of the community sentence band.

What should the officer do next?

In fact the probation officer does cautiously propose a community sentence, and a Combination Order is imposed. After some weeks, the Community Service supervisor reports to the probation officer that Paul is attending irregularly, and that a sessional worker observed him in town driving a car.

What should the officer do next?

In fact there is a delay in breach proceedings. Before action can be investigated Paul is arrested for TADA, driving whilst disqualified, driving with no insurance and reckless driving. The probation officer has to present a further pre-sentence report.

What should the officer do next?

Vignette 6

Malcolm is a white 42 year old male. He is currently on a Probation Order with a condition of both residence and treatment for offences of indecent assault against his daughter. He has been the subject of probation for some weeks. He reports regularly, but avoids engaging in any discussion of the offences. The officer was informed by the hostel that Malcolm has broken the hostel 11.00 p.m. curfew.

What should the officer do next?

In fact the officer warns Malcolm but does not take breach action at this stage. A further two weeks elapse. Malcolm is reported again for breaking the curfew, and is reported by his ex-partner for approaching the family home.

What should the officer do next?

In fact Malcolm fails to report and leaves the accommodation at which he was conditionally residing prior to the instigation of breach proceedings.

What should the officer do next?

Appendix two: Risk interview schedule

Preamble

Thanks for co-operation. Purpose of this interview is to discuss how they think about, respond to and work with risk in their work There are a series of topic areas to be covered, but the questions aren't set. Can discuss in as much detail as they wish. Their views are very important.
Confidentiality rule as previously. Use of data collected etc. OKAY?

Description of who they are as per card

Language and Definitions of Risk

What do you understand by the term risk? Follow up as required, examples?

Who is a risk in Probation work? Examples?
Probe as to why, to whom, what is risky about them?

What concerns you most about their behaviour? What is it that they might do that you think is so risky? Probe.

Are some offenders more risky than others? Who, to whom and why?

Is the Service more concerned about some offenders than others? Are you?
Do you agree with this? Probe.

Which risky offenders get the most resources? Is this appropriate? What do you think, what would you do?

Knowledge of Risk

How do you know who or what is risky? Where does this knowledge come from? How was it acquired? Probe on training, experience, literature, use of other sources and other information. Do they use any criminological or other studies into offender risk? If yes, Probe.

Use of previous cases or dealings with risk.

Has the Service provided risk indicators for your use? Checklists or anything else? Would they help? Probe.

Risk Assessments

How do they do risk assessments? Use of techniques, instruments, checklist, intuition, what? Probe for clarification.

What are the signs or indicators they use? Why? What is their source? How do they know they are accurate/ useful?

Do they ever not classify as risky when perhaps they should? Probe, why examples.

Describe last risk assessment done.

What is a good decision on risk, what is a good risk assessment?

The Role and Use of Information

What information do you think is important in risk assessment and why?

How do they use it, collect it, why do they want it, why does it make a difference?

How do they check the validity or reliability of it?

Have you ever made a decision to ignore information, not to ask about something, or not to pass on information?

Circumstances and why?

Policies and Risk

What policies are in existence on risk? Probe on type.

What do they say? Do they get followed? Probe on the answers.

How do these policies influence the recording of risk? Probe.

How are these policies managed?

Are they effective in responding to risk? Probe answer.

Have you ever broken/ failed to follow such a policy? Probe.

Agency, Management, Expectations and Risk

What role do you think managers have in dealing with risk?

Do they fulfil it? Quality of supervision on the issue for example, guidance, systems for review.

What does the agency mean by risk, managers mean, and is it different to you and other officers? Probe and examples. What are the agency's priorities on risk and are they different to yours?

Is there a difference in the toleration of risk at different levels in the agency? Probe. Is there a hierarchy of risk when dealing with cases? Whose is it and where does it come from?

What happens if things go wrong? Probe on responses to blame.

Role, Responsibility and Risk

Risks prepared and/or allowed to take in present role.

If you were a manager would you take more/less risks, be more/ less worried by...?

What do you think worries managers most? (The SPO, ACPO CPO for example)

Risk and Resource

Has the existence or non-existence of a resource/s ever affected your assessment and subsequent decision on a risk? Probe on examples and why.

Hypothetical situation if required.

Being at Risk

In what situations do you consider yourself to be at risk? Probe, examples.

What did/ do you and others do about this? Probe.

Policies and guidance?

Role of Attitudes and Beliefs

Do you think that...?

How, examples.

Who, what concerns/worries you most? Why do you think this is?

Probe.

Anything else?

CLOSE.

Appendix three: Improving risk decisions: using critical path analysis

9.30   Arrival and coffee

9.45   Introduction and objectives

10.00   What is risk?
What are we assessing?
Calculating probability
Calculating impact

Exercise -
Your last risk decision:
how did you calculate probability?
how did you calculate impact?

11.00   Coffee

11.30   Risk assessment 'faults'
Cognitive bias and heuristics
Values versus indicators

Exercise -
Identify in your last risk assessment the:
heuristics, values and indicators you used
With hindsight bias how might your assessment
change between the use of heuristics, values
and indicators (Use the vignettes if time)
Feedback
Applying regularly to our practice

1.00   Lunch

2.00   Improving decision making - (Defensible decisions)

Using CPA (Input)

Exercise -   on own cases
other cases (vignettes)

3.15   Tea

3.30   Applying CPA to own practice setting
(i)   Improving my assessment decisions
(ii)   Improving assessment decisions of others
(iii)   Reviewing current assessment procedures

4.00   Review and Feedback

Appendix four: Identification and management of risk and dangerousness - Training for Senior Probation Officers

Day One

9.45	Coffee
10.00	Introduction and objectives
10.15	Definitions of risk and dangerousness The context of risk and dangerousness concerns Exercise and discussion
11.15	Coffee
11.30	The assessment of risk and dangerousness Introduction to assessment methods The role of the senior Exercise and discussion
1.00	Lunch
2.00	Sources of bias and error Mis-clarification and the potential for discrimination The balance of risks, rights and responsibilities
3.15	Tea
3.30	The development of best supervisory practice guidance for seniors
4.15	Plenary discussion
4.30	Close

Day Two

9.15	Coffee
9.30	Developing the concepts of risk, harm and dangerousness Further assessment techniques The role of the senior in supervision Allocating time and resources
11.15	Coffee
11.30	Strategies for risk management Matching interventions to risk 'What Works' for risk? Issues of evaluating practice Exercise and discussion
1.00	Lunch
2.00	The possibilities and pitfalls of inter-agency working Exercise and discussion
3.15	Tea
3.30	Putting it all together: Developing and supporting staff
4.15	Close

Identification and management of risk and dangerousness - Training for Senior Probation Officers

Training Objectives

1. To provide operational definitions of risk and dangerousness. To distinguish between these two terms and how they should be understood and used.

2. To examine the relevance of research findings on risk and dangerousness for probation work.

3. To provide an introduction to the two main assessment methods: clinical and actuarial.

4. To examine the role of the senior in the supervision of staff assessments of risk and dangerousness.

5. To explore the sources of bias and error in assessment.

6. To examine the potential for discrimination.

7. To examine strategies for risk management.

8. To examine the issues in multi-agency work in this area.

9. To develop some best practice guidance for seniors.

Note: This training will not address issues of registration raised by the policies of individual service areas. The focus of this training is upon the knowledge and skills required by seniors in order to appropriately supervise the risk practice of staff.

Competences: M3.1, M3.2, M3.3.

Bibliography

Adam, S., Moss, L. and Pleasance, G. (1980), 'Who makes Policy: Why and How?' *Probation Journal*, 27, 4, pp. 118-124.

Adams, J. (1995), *Risk,* University College, London.

Adamson, C. (1997), 'Existential and clinical uncertainty in the medical encounter: an idiographic account of an illness trajectory defined by Inflammatory Bowel Disease and Avascular Necrosis', *Sociology of Health and Illness*, 19, 2, pp. 133-159.

Andrews, D.A. (1982), *A Personal, Interpersonal and Community-reinforcement Perspective on Deviant Behaviour (PIC-R),* Ontario Ministry of Correctional Services, Toronto.

Andrews, D.A. (1995), 'The Psychology of Criminal Conduct and Effective Treatment', in J. McGuire (ed.), *What Works: Reducing Offending, Guidelines from Research and Practice,* John Wiley and sons, Chichester.

Andrews, D.A., Bonta, J. and Hoge, R.D. (1990), 'Classification for effective rehabilitation', *Criminal Justice and Behaviour*, 17, pp. 19-51.

Andrews, D.A. and Bonta, J. (1994), *The Psychology of Criminal Conduct,* Anderson, Cincinatti.

Andrews, D.A. and Bonta, J. (1995), *The Level of Supervision Inventory - Revised,* Multi-Health Systems Inc, Toronto.

Ansell, J. and Wharton, F. (eds) (1992), *Risk: analysis, assessment and management,* John Wiley and sons, Chichester.

Association of Chief Officers of Probation (ACOP). (1994), *Guidance on the Management of Risk and Public Protection. Position Statement,* Association of Chief Officers of Probation, Wakefield.

Association of Chief Officers of Probation (ACOP). (1995), *ACOP and Reconviction,* Association of Chief Officers of Probation, Wakefield.

Aubrey, R. and Hough, M. (1997), *Assessing Offenders' Needs: Assessment Scales for the Probation Service,* A report for the Home Office Research and Statistics Directorate, Home Office, London.

Audit Commission. (1989), *Promoting Value for Money in the Probation Service,* HMSO, London.

Bale, D. (1987), 'Uses of the risk of custody scale', *Probation Journal*, 34, 4, 127-131.

Bale, D. (1990), *Cambridge Risk of Custody Score, version 3,* Cambridge

Probation Service.

Barr, R. and Pease, K. (1992), 'The problem of displacement', in D.J. Evans, N.R. Fyfe, and D.T. Herbert (eds), *Crime, Policing and Place: Essays in Environmental Criminology*, Routledge and Kegan Paul, London.

Bartlett, H. (1970), *The Common Base of Social Work Practice*, NASW, Washington.

Battersby, A. (1964), *Network Analysis for Planning and Scheduling. Studies in Management*, MacMillan, London.

Bean, P. (1976), *Rehabilitation and Deviance*, Routledge and Kegan Paul, London.

Bean, P. (1997), 'Paedophiles and the Proposed Register', *Justice of the Peace and Local Government Law*, 22nd March, pp. 293-284.

Beck, U. (1992), *Risk Society - Towards a New Modernity*, Sage Publication, London.

Beck, U., Giddens, A. and Lash, S. (1994), *Reflexive Modernization*, Polity Press in association with Blackwell Publishers, Oxford.

Bell, D. Wallace, (1979), *Industrial Participation*, Pitman.

Bellaby, P. (1987), 'The perpetuation of a folk model of the life cycle and kinship in a pottery factory', in A. Bryman, W. Bytheway, P. Allatt and T. Keil (eds), *Rethinking the Life Cycle*, MacMillan, London.

Bellaby, P. (1990), 'What is genuine sickness? The relationship between work-discipline and the sick role in a pottery factory', *Sociology of Health and Illness*, 12 (1), pp. 47-68.

Bellaby, P. (1990a), 'To risk or not to risk? Uses and limitations of Mary Douglas on risk acceptability for understanding health and safety at work and road accidents', *Sociological Review*, 30, (3), pp. 465-483.

Benner, P. and Tanner, C. (1987), 'Clinical judgement: how expert nurses use intuition', *American Journal of Nursing*, 87 (1), pp. 23-31.

Berger, P and Luckmann, T. (1967), *The social construction of reality*, Penguin, Harmondsworth.

Bewley, M. (1996), 'A Comparative Study of Reconviction Rates in Cleveland', *Justice of the Peace and Local Government Law*, 9th November, p. 986.

Bines, H. (1992), 'Issues in course design', in H. Bines and D. Watson (eds), *Developing Professional Education*, Society for Research into Higher Education and Open University Press, Buckingham.

Blagg, H. and Smith, D. (1989), *Crime, Penal Policy and Social Work*, Longman, Harlow.

Blaxter, M. (1983), 'The cause of disease: women talking', *Social Science and Medicine*, 17, pp. 59-69.

Blom-Cooper, L., Hally, H. and Murphy, E. (1995), *The Falling Shadow: One Patient's Mental Health Care*, Duckworth, London.

Bloomsbury Conference (1995), *Managing What Works*, Home Office/ Association of Chief Officers of Probation/Central Probation Council, London.

Bloor, M. (1978), 'On the analysis of observational data: a discussion of the worth and uses of inductive techniques and respondent validation', *Sociology*, 12 (3), pp. 545-557.

Bloor, M. (1995), 'A user's guide to contrasting theories of HIV-related risk behaviour', in J. Gabe (ed.), *Medicine, Health and Risk: Sociological Approaches*, Sociology of Health and Illness Monograph 1. pp 19-30, Blackwell, Oxford.

Bloor, M. (1995a), *The Sociology of HIV Transmission*, Sage, London.

Blumstein, A. (1983), 'Prisons: population, capacity and alernatives', in J.A. Wilson (eds), *Crime and Public Policy*, Institute for Contemporary Studies, San Francisco.

Blumsteim, A., Cohen, J., Roth, J. and Visher, C. (eds) (1986), *Criminal Careers and 'Career Criminals'*, National Academy of Sciences, Washington D. C.

Borum, R. (1996), 'Improving the Clinical Practice of Violence Assessment" *American Psychologist*, 51 (9), pp. 945-956.

Bottoms, A. (1977), 'Reflections on the Renaissance of Dangerousness', *Howard Journal*, 16 (2), pp. 70-96.

Bottoms, A. and McWilliams, W. (1979), 'A Non-Treatment Paradigm for Probation Practice', *British Journal of Social Work*, 9, (2), pp. 159-202.

Bottoms, A. and Preston, R.H. (eds) (1980), *The Coming Penal Crisis: A Criminological and Theological Exploration,*. Scottish Academic Press, Edinburgh.

Bottoms, A. and Stelman, A. (1988), *Social Inquiry Reports*, Wildwood House, Aldershot.

Box, S. (1987), *Recession, Crime and Punishment*, MacMillan, London.

Boyd, E.M. and Fales, A.W. (1983), 'Reflecting learning: key to learning from experience', *Journal of Humanistic Psychology*, 23 (2), pp. 99-117.

Boyd Report, Steering Committee of the Confidential Inquiry into Homicides and Suicides by Mentally Ill Persons (1994), *A Preliminary Report on Homicide*. London: Steering Committee of the Confidential Inquiry into Homicides and Suicides by Mentally Ill Persons, London.

Bradshaw, J. (1972), 'The Concept of Social Need', *New Society*, vol. 19, pp. 640-643.

Brearley, C. P. (1979), 'Gambling with their lives?' *Community Care*, 8th November, 289, pp. 22-23.

Brearley, C.P. (1982), *Risk and Social Work: Hazards and Helping*, Routledge and Kegan Paul, London.

Brearley, C.P. (1983), *Risk and Ageing*, Routledge and Kegan Paul, London.

British Nuclear Fuels (1997), *Channel Four Advertisement*.

Brooks, A.D. (1984), 'Defining Dangerousness of the Mentally Ill: Involuntary Commitment', in M. Craft and A. Craft (eds), *Mentally Abnormal Offenders*, Balliere Tindall, London.

Brown, M. (1996), 'Serious offending and the management of public risk in New Zealand', *British Journal of Criminology*, 36 (1), pp. 18-36.

Bruner, J.S., Goodnow, J.J., and Austin, G.A. (1956), *A Study of Thinking*, Science Editions, New York.

Bulmer, M. (1979), 'Concepts in the analysis of qualitative data', *Sociological Review*, 27 (4), pp. 651-677.

Burgess, E.W. (1928), 'Factors making for success or failure on parole', *Journal of Criminal Law and Criminology*, 19 (2), pp. 239-306.

Burgess, E.W. (1929), 'Is prediction feasible in social work?' *Social Forces*, 7, pp. 533-545.

Burgess, E.W. (1936), 'Protecting the public by parole and parole prediction', *Journal of Criminal Law and Criminology*, 27, pp. 491-502. As reprinted in L.S. Cottrell, Jr., A. Junter and J.F. Short, Jr. (eds) (1973), *Ernest W. Burgess on Community, Family, and Delinquency*, Universtiy of Chicago Press, Chicago.

Burgess, R.G. (1982), *Field Research: A Sourcebook and Field Manual*, Allen and Unwin, London.

Burgess, R.G. (1984), *In the Field, An Introduction to Field Research*, Allen and Unwin, London.

Burnett, R. (1996), *Fitting Supervision to offenders: assessment and allocation decisions in the Probation Service*, Home Office Research Study 153, A Research and Statistics Directorate Report, Home Office, London.

Burney, E. (1985), *Sentencing Young People: What Went Wrong with the Criminal Justice Act 198*, Gower, Aldershot.

Burnstein, B. and Walters, J. (1996), 'Forward: Setting the Context', in Middlesex Probation Service, *Managing Dangerousness and Protecting the Public*, Middlesex Probation Service Committee, Middlesex.

Bush, J. (1995), 'Teaching Self-risk Management to Violent Offenders', in J. McGuire (ed.), *What Works: Reducing Reoffending: Guidelines from*

Research and Practice, John Wiley and sons, Chichester, pp. 139-154.

Butler Committee (1975), *Committee on Mentally Abnormal Offenders*, Home Office and Department of Health and Social Security, Cmnd. 6244, HMSO, London.

Butler-Schloss (Lord) (1988), *Report of the Committee of Inquiry into Child Sexual Abuse in Cleveland 1987*, Presented to the Secretary of State for Social Services by the Right Honorable Lord Butler-Schloss DBE, Cm 412, HMSO, London.

Carew, R. (1979), 'The Place of Knowledge in Social Work Activity', *British Journal of Social Work*, 9 (3), pp. 349-364.

Carlisle, Rt. Hon Lord of Bucklow (1988), *The Parole System in England and Wales. Report of the Review Committee*, HMSO, London.

Carper, B. (1978), 'Fundamental patterns of knowing in nursing', *Advances in Nursing Science*, 1, pp. 13-23.

Carroll, J.S. (1977), 'Judgements of recidivism: conflicts between clinical strategies and base-rate information', *Law and Human Behaviour*, 1 (2), pp. 191-198.

Carroll, J.S. and Payne, J.W. (1976), 'The psychology of the parole decision making process: a joint application of attribution theory and information processing.', in J. Carroll and J. Payne (eds), *Cognition and Social Behaviours*, Erlbaum, Hillsdale, NJ.

Carson, D. (1994) 'Dangerous People; through a broader conception of 'risk' and 'danger' to better decisions', *Expert Evidence*, 3, (2), pp. 51-69.

Carson, D. (1995) 'Calculated Risk', *Community Care*, 26th October, pp. 26-27.

Carson, D. (1996), 'Risking Legal Repercussions', in H. Kemshall and J. Pritchard (eds), *Good Practice in Risk Assessment and Risk Management, Volume 1*, Jessica Kingsley Publishers, London, pp. 3-12.

Carson, D. (1997), 'Risk Policies, Risk Management and Risk Strategies', in *Identifying dangerous carers in child protection work, European Experts' Seminar, 17th-18th January 1997*, The Bridge Child Care Project, London.

Castel, R. (1991), 'From dangerousness to risk', in G. Burchell, C. Gordon and P. Miller (eds), *The Foucault Effect. Studies in Governmentality*, Harvester Wheatsheaf, London.

Cavadino, M. and Dignan, J. (1992), *The Penal System: An Introduction*, Sage, London.

Cavadino, M. and Wiles, P. (1994), 'Seriousness of Offences: The Perceptions of Practitioners', *Criminal Law Review*, pp. 489-498.

Central Council for Education and Training in Social Work (1996), *Rules and Requirements for the Diploma in Social Work*, Second Revision, CCETSW, London.

Chapman, T. (1995), 'Creating a Culture of Change: A Case Study of a Car Crime Project in Belfast', in J. McGuire (ed.), *What Works: Reducing Reoffending: Guidelines from Practice and Research*, John Wiley and sons, Chichester, pp. 127-138.

Chappelow, J. (1994), 'Psychology and safety in aviation', in J. Secker-Walker (ed.), *Quality and Safety in Anaesthesia*, BMJ Publishing Group.

Christie, N. (1993), *Crime Control and Industry*, Routledge, London.

Cicourel, A. (1964), *Method and Measurement in Sociology*, Free Press.

Clark, D.A., Fisher, M.J. and McDougall, C. (1993), 'A New Methodology for Assessing the Level of Incarcerated Offenders', *British Journal of Criminology*, 33 (3), pp. 436-448.

Clarke, J., Cochrane, A. and McLaughlin, E. (eds) (1994), *Managing Social Policy*, Sage, London.

Clarke, S. (1995), *Strategic Decision Making: Implications for Risk Management*, paper for the Economic and Social Research Council 'Risk in Organisational Settings' conference at the White House, Regents Park, London, 16th-17th May 1995.

Coffey, A. and Atkinson, P. (1996), *Making Sense of Qualitative Data. Complimentary Research Strategies*, Sage, London.

Cohen, S. (1971), *Images of Deviance*, Pelican, London.

Cohen, S. (1979), 'The punitive city: Notes on the dispersal of social control', *Contemporary Crises* 3, pp. 339-363.

Cohen, S. (1985), *Visions of Social Control: Crime, Punishment and Classification*, Polity Press, London.

Cohen, S. (1994), 'Social Control and the Politics of Reconstruction', in D. Nelken (ed.) *The Futures of Criminology*, Sage, London.

Coleman Report (1989), *Review of Probation Training: Final Report*, Home Office, London.

Collingbridge, D. (1980), *The social control of technology*, Open University Press, Milton Keynes.

Collingbridge, S. (1983), *Technology in the policy process: controlling nuclear power*, Pinter, London.

Collingbridge, S. (1992), *The management of scale: big organisations, big decisions, big mistakes*, Routledge, London.

Collingbridge, S. (1996), 'Resilience, Flexibility, and Diversity in Managing the Risks of Technologies', in C. Hood, and D.K.C. Jones (eds), *Accident and Design: contemporary debates in risk management*,

University College London, London, pp 40-45.

Combs, B. and Slovic, P. (1979), 'Causes of Death: Biased Newspaper Coverage and Biased Judgements', *Journalism Quarterly*, 56, pp. 837-843.

Compton, B. and Gallaway, B. (1994), *Social Work Processes*, 5th edition, Brooks/Cole, Pacific Grove, CA.

Concise Oxford Dictionary (1995), Oxford University Press, Oxford.

Copas, J. (1995), *Some Comments on Meta-Analysis*, Department of Statistics, University of Warwick.

Copas, J., Ditchfield, J. and Marshall, P. (1994), *Development of a new reconviction score*, Research Bulletin 36, HMSO, London.

Copas, J., Marshall, P. and Tarling, R. (1996), *Predicting Reoffending for Discretionary Conditional Release*, Home Office Research Study 150, HMSO, London.

Cornish, B. and Clarke, R. (eds) (1986), *The Reasoning Criminal: Rational Choice Perspectives on Offending*, Springer Verlag, New York.

Cornwell, J. (1984), *Hard earned lives: accounts of health and illness from East London*, Tavistock Publications, London.

Cousins, M. and Hussein, A. (1984), *Michel Foucault*, MacMillan, London.

Cox, E. W. (1877), *The Principles of Punishment as Applied in the Administration of the Criminal Law by Judges and Magistrates*, Times Law Office, London.

Crivisqui, E. (1993), 'Statistics as a Tool in the Reform of Health Structures', *International Social Science Journal*, 135, XLV, i, pp. 67-82.

Cullen, Lord. (1990), *The Public Enquiry into the Piper Alpha Disaster*, HMSO, London.

Daily Record (1997), 'Face Your Failures', 12th November, p.1.

Dalgleish, L.I. (1991), *Assessment of perceived risk in child protection: A model, some data and implications for practice*, Paper presented to Child Maltreatement Conference, Sydney, Australia, 11th-12th April.

Davies, M. (1974), *Social Work in the Environment*, Heinemann, London.

Davies, M., Boswell, G. and Wright, A. (1989), *Skills, Knowledge and Qualities in Probation Practice*, Research Reports 1-4, Social Work Monographs, University of East Anglia, Norwich.

Davies, M. (1986), *The Essential Social Worker*, Gower, Aldershot.

Davis, A. (1996), 'Risk Work and Mental Health', in H. Kemshall and J. Pritchard (eds) *Good Practice in Risk Assessment and Risk Management, Volume 1*, Jessica Kingsley Publishers, London, pp. 109-120.

Denman, G. (1982), *Intensive Intermediate Treatment with Juvenile Offenders: A Handbook of Assessment and Groupwork Practice*, Centre of Youth, Crime and Community, Lancaster.

Denzin, K. (1978), *The Research Act*, McGraw-Hill, New York.

Department of Transport (1990), *Report on the collision that occurred on 4th March 1989 at Purley*, HMSO, London.

Dewey, J. (1933), *How we Think*, D.C. Heath and Co, Boston.

Dey, I. (1993), *Qualitative Data Analysis: A User-Friendly Guide for Social Scientists*, Routledge, London.

Dingwall, R. (1970), 'Some problems about predicting child abuse and neglect', in O. Stevenson (ed.), *Child Abuse: Public Policy and Professional Practice*, Harvester Wheatsheaf, Hemel Hempstead.

Dingwall, R., Eekelaar, J., and Murray, T. (1983), *The Protection of Children: State Intervention and Family Life*, Basil Blackwell, Oxford.

Ditchfield, J. (1997), 'Actuarial Prediction and Risk Assessment', *Prison Service Journal*, 113, pp. 8-13.

Donzelot, J. (1979), 'The poverty of political culture', *Ideology and Consciousness*, 5, pp. 73-87.

Donzelot, J. (1991), 'Pleasure in work', in G. Burchell, C. Gordon and P. Miller (eds), *The Foucault Effect. Studies in Governmentality*, Harvester Wheatsheaf, London.

Douglas, J.D. (1971), *Understanding Everyday Life*, Routledge and Kegan Paul, London.

Douglas, J.D. (1976), *Investigative Social Research*, Sage, Beverley Hills CA.

Douglas, M. (1966), *Purity and Danger: Concepts of Pollution and Taboo*, Routledge and Kegan Paul, London.

Douglas, M. (1972), 'Environments at Risk', in J. Benthall (ed.), *Ecology: The Shaping Inquiry*, Longman, London.

Douglas, M. (1973), *Natural symbols: exploration of cosmology*, 2nd edition, Barrie and Jenkins, London.

Douglas, M. (1986), *Risk Acceptability According to the Social Sciences*, Routledge and Kegan Paul, London.

Douglas, M. (1992), *Risk and Blame*, Routledge, London.

Douglas, M. (1992a), 'Institutions of the Third Kind: British and Swedish Labour Markets Compared', in M. Douglas, *Risk and Blame*, Routledge, London, pp. 167-186.

Douglas, M. and Wildavsky, A. (1982), 'How Can We Know the Risks We Face? Why Risk Selection is a Social Process', *Risk Analysis*, 2 (2), pp. 49-51.

Douglas, M. and Wildavsky, A. (1983), *Risk and Culture*, University of California Press, London.

Douglas, M. and Calvez, M. (1990), 'The Self as Risk Taker: A Cultural Theory of Contagion in Relation to AIDS', *Sociological Review*, 38 (3), pp. 445-466.

Duckitt, J. (1988), 'The prediction of violence', *South African Journal of Psychology*, 18, pp. 10-16.

Dunsire, A. (1978), *Control in a bureaucracy: the execution process*, volume 2, Martin Robertson, Oxford.

Dunsire, A. (1990), 'Holistic governance', *Public Policy and Administration* 5 (1), pp. 4-19.

Dunsire, A. (1992), 'Modes of governance', in J. Kooiman (ed.), *Modern governance*, Sage, London, pp. 21-34.

Durham Probation Service (1997), *Risk Policy and Procedures*, Durham Probation Service.

Economic and Social Research Council (1993), *Risk and Human Behaviour*, Briefing notes for applicants, ESRC, Swindon.

Einhorn, H.J. (1986), 'Accepting error to make less error', *Journal of Personality Assessement*, 50 (3), pp. 387-395.

Evening Mail, (1996), 'We're Sick of these Outrageous Decisions', M. Messant, 25th October, p.15.

Evening Mail, (1996), 'Shocking Cruelty of Unfit Mother',31st October, p.9.

Evening Mail, (1997), 'Action to Stop Probation Scandal', M. Messant, 16th July, p.6.

Everitt, A. and Hardiker, P. (1996), *Evaluating for Good Practice*, MacMillan Press, London.

Farrington, D.P. and Tarling, R. (1985), *Prediction in Criminology*, Albany State University Press, Albany, NY.

Faulkner, D. (1989), 'The Future of the Probation Service: A View from Government', in R. Shaw and J. Haines (eds), *The Criminal Justice System: A Central Role for the Probation Service*, Cambridge Institute of Criminology, Cambridge.

Feaviour, P., Peacock, D., Sanderson, H., Bontoff, C. and Wightman, S. (1995), 'Risk management: score values', *Community Care*, 2-8 Novermber, pp. 28-29.

Feeley, M. and Simon, J. (1992), 'The New Penology: Notes on the Emerging Strategy of Corrections', *Criminology*, 30 (4), pp. 449-475.

Feeley, M. and Simon, J. (1994), 'Actuarial Justice: The Emerging New Criminal Law', in D. Nelken (ed.), *The Futures of Criminology*, Sage, London.

Fennell, D. (1988), *Investigation into the Kings Cross Underground Fire*, Department of Transport. HMSO, London.

Fielding, N. and Fielding, J. (1986), *Linking Data*, Sage, London.

Finch, J. (1987), 'The vignette technique in survey research', *Sociology*, 21 (1), pp. 105-114.

Finch, J. and Mason, J. (1993), *Negotiating Family Responsibilities*, Tavistock/Routledge, London.

Fischoff, B. (1975), 'Hindsight does not equal foresight: The effects of outcome knowledge on judgement under uncertainty', *Journal of Experimental Psychology, Human Performance and Perception*, 1, pp. 299-299.

Fischoff, B., Slovic, P., Lichtenstein, S., Read, S. and Combs, B. (1978), 'How safe is safe enough? A psychometric study of attitudes towards technological risks and benefits', *Policy Studies*, 9, pp. 127-152.

Fischoff, B., Slovic, P. and Lichtenstein, S. (1983), The public vs. 'the experts', in V.T. Covello, W.G. Flamm, J.V. Rodricks and R.G. Tardiff (eds), *The Analysis of Actual vs Perceived Risks*, Plenum, New York, pp. 235-249.

Flanagan, J. (1954), 'The Critical Incident Technique', *Psychological Bulletin*, 51 (4), pp. 327-358.

Fletcher, H. (1995), 'New Reconviction Scale', *NAPO News*, September, 72, p.1, National Association of Probation Officers, London.

Floud, J. and Young, W. (1981), *Dangerousness and Criminal Justice*, Howard League for Penal Reform, Heinemann, London.

Flynn, E. (1978), 'Classifications for Risk and Supervision', in J. Freeman (ed.), *Prisons Past and Future*. Cambridge Studies in Criminology, Cambridge.

Flynn, N. (1993), *Public Sector Management*, Harvester Wheatsheaf, Hemel Hempstead.

Folkard, M.S., Smith, D.E. and Smith, D.D. (1976), *IMPACT Vol. II: The Results of the Experiment*, HMSO, London.

Foucault, M. (1977), *Discipline and Punishment*, Allen Lane, London.

Foucault, M. (1980), 'The eye of power', in C. Gordon (ed.), *Michel Foucault, Knowledge/Power*, Harvester, Brighton.

Frake, C. (1964), 'Notes on queries in ethonography', *American Anthropologist*, 66, pp. 132-145.

Freudenberg, W. R. (1988), 'Perceived risk, real risk: social science and the art of probabilistic risk assessment', *Science*, 242, October, pp. 44-49.

Freudenburg, W.R. (1993), 'Risk and recreancy: Weber, the division of labor, and the rationality of risk perception', *Social Forces*, 71, pp. 909-

932.

Fullbrook, D. (1998), 'The Warwickshire Probation Service/Oxford University ACE model', in *Home Office Special Conference Unit: Inter-Agency Work with Potentially Dangerous Offenders and Risk/Needs Tools*, Home Office Special Conferences Unit, London.

Furedi, F. (1997), *Culture of Fear: Risk-Taking and the Morality of Low Expectation*, Cassell, London.

Garfinkel, E. (1967), *Studies in Ethnomethodology*, Prentice-Hall, Englewood Cliffs, N.J.

Garfinkel, E., Lynch, M. and Livingston, E. (1981), 'The Work of a Discovering Science Construed with Materials from the Optically Discovered Pulsar', *Philosophy of Social Science*, 11 (1), pp. 131-158.

Garland, D. (1990), *Punishment and Modern Society*, Clarendon Press, Oxford.

Garland, D. (1997), 'The Social and Political Context', in R. Burnett (ed.), *The Probation Service: Responding to Change. Proceedings of the Probation Studies Unit First Annual Colloquium*, December 1996, Probation Studies Unit, Oxford.

Gaylin, W. (1978), *Doing Good: The Limits of Benevolence*, Pantheon Books, New York.

Gelsthorpe, L., Raynor, P. and Tisi, A. (1992), *Quality Assurance in Pre-Sentence Reports. Report to the Home Office Research and Planning Unit*, Home Office, London.

Genders, E. and Morrison, S. (1996), 'When violence is the norm', in N. Walker (ed.), *Dangerous People*, Blackstone Press, London.

Gendreau, P., Cullen, F.T. and Bonta, J. (1994), 'Intensive rehabilitation supervision: The next generation in community corrections?' *Federal Probation*, 58, pp. 72-78.

Gendreau, P., Coggin, C., and Little, T. (1995), *A Meta-Analysis of the Predictors of Adult Offender Recidivism: Assessment Guidelines for Classification and Treatment*, Report submitted to the Corrections Branch, Ministry Secretariat, Solicitor General Canada.

Giddens, A. (1976), *New Rules of Sociological Method*, Hutchinson, London.

Giddens, A. (1979), *Central Problems in Social Theory: Action, Structure and Contradiction in Social Analysis*, MacMillan Press, London and Basingstoke.

Giddens, A. (1984), *The Constitution of Society: Outline of the Theory of Structuration*, Polity Press, Cambridge.

Giddens, A. (1990), *Consequences of Modernity*, Stanford University

Press.

Giddens, A. (1991), *Modernity and Self Identity*, Polity Press in association with Blackwell Publishers, Oxford.

Giddens, A. (1995), *Politics, Sociology and Social Theory*, Polity Press, Cambridge.

Glaser, B. and Strauss, A. (1965), *Awareness of Dying*, Aldine, Chicago.

Glaser, B. and Strauss, A. (1967), *The Discovery of Grounded Theory*, Aldine, Chicago.

Glaser, B. and Strauss, A. (1968), *Time for Dying*, Aldine, Chicago.

Glaser, D. (1955), 'The efficacy of alternative approaches to parole prediction', *American Sociological Review*, 20, pp. 283-287.

Glaser, D. (1962), 'Prediction tables as accounting devices for judges and parole boards', *Crime and Delinquency*, 8 (3), pp. 239-258.

Glaser, D. (1973), *Routinizing Evaluation*, National Institute of Mental Health, Rockville Maryland.

Gottfredson, S.D. and Gottfredson, D.M. (1985), 'Screening for risk among parolees: policy, practice and research', in D.P. Farrington and R. Tarling (eds), *Predicting Crime and Delinquency*, Albany State University Press.

Gottfredson, S.D. and Gottfredson, D.M. (1986), 'Accuracy of Prediction Models', in A. Blumstein et al (eds), *Criminal Careers and 'Career Criminals'*, National Academy of Sciences, Washington, D. C.

Gottfredson, S.D. and Gottfredson, D.M. (1993), 'The Long-Term Predictive Utility of the Base Expectancy Score', *Howard Journal*, 32 (4), pp. 276-290.

Gottfredson, S.D. and Gottfredson, D.M. (1994), 'Behavioural Prediction and the Problem of Incapacitation', *Criminology*, 32, pp. 441-474.

Green, J. (1997), *Risk and Misfortune: The Social Construction of Accidents*, UCL Press, London.

Grinyer, A. (1995), 'Risk, the real world and naive sociology', in J. Gabe (ed.), *Medicine, Health and Risk: Sociological Approaches*, Sociology of Health and Illness Monograph 1, Blackwell, Oxford, pp. 31-51.

Gross, J. and Rayner, S. (1985), *Measuring Culture: A Paradigm for the Analysis of Social Organisation*, Columbia University Press, New York.

Habermas, J. (1976), *Legitimation Crisis*, Heinemann, London.

Ham, C. (1981), *Policy-Making in the National Health Service: A Case Study of the Leeds Regional Hospital Board*, MacMillan, London.

Ham, C. and Hill, M. (1993), *The Policy Process in the Modern Capitalist State*, Harvester Wheatsheaf, Hemel Hempstead.

Hammersley, M. (1990), *Reading Ethnographic Research: A Critical*

Guide, Longman, London.

Hammersley, M. (1992), *What's Wrong with Ethnography*, Routledge, London.

Hammond, D. (1993), 'Book review: Risk and Blame: Essays in Cultural Theory, Mary Douglas', *Anthropos*, 88 (4-6) pp. 5-8.

Hampshire Probation Service (1995), *Recognising and Reducing Risk. Improving the quality of decisions in situations which threaten harm. An interim report of the Risk Management Working Party.* Hampshire Probation Service.

Hardiker, P. (1977), 'Social Work Ideologies in the Probation Service', *British Journal of Social Work*, 7 (2), pp. 131-154.

Hardiker, P. and Webb, D. (1979), 'Explaining deviant behaviour: The social context of 'action' and 'infraction' accounts in the probation service', *Sociology*, 13 (1), pp. 1-17.

Hardiker, P. and Curnock, K. (1984), 'Social Work Assessment Processes in Work with Ethnic Minorities-the Doshi Family', *British Journal of Social Work*, 14 (1), pp. 23-48.

Harris, P. (1994), 'Client Management Classification and Prediction of Probation Outcomes', *Crime and Delinquency*, 40 (2), pp. 154-174.

Harris, R. and Webb, D. (1987), *Welfare, Power and Juvenile Justice*, Tavistock, London.

Haxby, D. (1978), *Probation: a changing service*, Constable, London.

Hay, W. and Sparks, R. (1993), 'Vulnerable Prisoners: Risk in Long-Term Prisons', in K. Bottomley, (ed.), *Criminal Justice: Theory and Practice*, British Society of Criminology Conference 1991, British Society of Criminology/Institute for the Study and Treatment of Delinquency, London.

Health and Safety Executive (1988), *Blackspot Construction*, HMSO, London.

Hebenton, B. and Thomas, T. (1996), ''Tracking' Sex Offenders', *Howard Journal*, 35 (2), pp. 97-112.

Hendry, E. and Lewis, P. (1990), 'Risk and Child Abuse', *Practice*, 4, (3), pp. 146-155.

Henham, R. (1997), 'Anglo-American Approaches to Cumulative Sentencing and the Implications for UK Sentencing', *Howard Journal*, 36, 3, pp. 263-283.

Her Majesty's Inspectorate of Probation (HMIP) (1988), *Performance Indicators for the Probation Service*, Home Office, London.

Her Majesty's Inspectorate of Probation (HMIP) (1995), *Dealing with Dangerous People: The Probation Service and Public Protection*,

Report of a Thematic Inspection, Home Office, London.

Her Majesty's Inspectorate of Probation (HMIP) (1996), *Assessment and Management of Risk: Draft Guidance*, Home Office, London.

Her Majesty's Inspectorate of Probation (HMIP) (1997), 'Risk Management Guidance', in Home Office/Association of Chief Officers of Probation: *The Assessment and Management of Risk*, Home Office/Association of Chief Officers of Probation, London.

Heyman, B. (1997), *Risk, Health and Health Care: A Qualitative Approach*, Edward Arnold, London.

Hidden, A. (1989), *Investigation into the Clapham Junction Railway Accident*, HMSO, London.

Hill, M. (1993), 'The exercise of discretion in the National Assistance Board', in C. Ham and M. Hill (eds), *The Policy Process: A Reader*, Harvester Wheatsheaf, Hemel Hempstead.

von Hirsch, A, and Ashworth, A. (1996), 'Protective Sentencing Under Section 2 (2) (b): The Criteria for Dangerousness', *Criminal Law Review*, pp. 173-183.

Hollin, C. (1995), 'The Meaning and Implications of 'Programme Integrity'', in J. McGuire (ed.), *What Works: Reducing Reoffending. Guidelines from Research and Practice*, John Wiley and sons, Chichester.

Home Office (1977), *A Review of Criminal Justice Policy 1976*, HMSO, London.

Home Office (1984), *Probation Service in England and Wales: Statement of National Objectives and Priorities*, Home Office, London.

Home Office (1988), *Home Office Letter to Chief Probation Officers July 1988: The Registration and Review of Serious Offenders*, Home Office, London.

Home Office (1988a), *Punishment, Custody and the Community*, Cm. 424, HMSO, London.

Home Office (1990), *The Victims Charter*, HMSO, London.

Home Office (1990a), *Crime, Justice and Protecting the Public*, Cm. 965, HMSO, London.

Home Office (1992), *Three Year Plan for the Probation Service, 1993-1996*, HMSO, London.

Home Office (1992a), *National Standards for Supervision in the Community*, HMSO, London.

Home Office (1995), *National Standards for the Supervision of Offenders in the Community*, Home Office, London.

Home Office (1996), *The Victim's Charter: A Statement of the Rights of Victims of Crime*, HMSO, London.

Home Office (1996a), *Three Year Plan for the Probation Service 1996-1999*, HMSO, London.

Home Office (1996b), *Protecting the Public: The Government's Strategy on Crime in England and Wales*, HSMO, London.

Home Office (1997), 'Risk/Needs Assessment', in *The Management and Assessment of Risk in the Probation Service, part one*, Home Office/ Association of Chief Probation Officers, London.

Home Office (1997a), *The Crime Sentences Act*, HMSO, London.

Home Office (1997b), *The Crime and Disorder Bill*, HMSO, London.

Home Office Circular 39 (1997), *The Sex Offender Act*, Home Office, London.

Home Office and Scottish Home Department (1962), *Report of the Departmental Committee on the Probation Service*, Cmnd. 1650, HMSO, London.

Home Office Special Conferences Unit (1995), *Managing What Works*, Home Office Special Conferences Unit, London.

Home Office Special Conferences Unit (1997), *Criminal Justice Conference: Inter-Agency Work with Dangerous Offenders: Sharing Information to Manage Risk*, Home Office Special Conferences Unit, London.

Home Office Special Conference Unit (1998), *Inter-Agency Work with Potentially Dangerous Offenders and Risk/Needs Tools*, Home Office Special Conferences Unit, London.

Hood, C.C. (1976), *The limits of administration*, John Wiley and sons, Chichester.

Hood, C.C. (1996), 'Where Extremes Meet: 'Sprat' versus 'Shark' in Public Risk Management', in C. Hood and D.K.C. Jones (1996), *Accident and Design: contemporary debates in risk management*, University College London, London, pp 208-227.

Hood, C. and Jones, D.K.C. (1996), *Accident and Design: contemporary debates in risk management*, University College London, London.

Hood, C., Jones, D., Pidgeon, N., Turner, B. and Gibson, R. (1992), 'Risk Management', in *The Royal Society: Risk: analysis, perception and management*, Report of a Royal Society Study Group, pp. 135-192.

Hood, R. and Sparks, R. (1970), *Key Issues in Criminology*, Weidenfeld, London.

Horlick-Jones, T. (1996), 'The Problem of Blame', in C. Hood and D.K.C. Jones (eds), *Accident and Design: contemporary debates in risk management*, University College London, London, pp. 61-71.

Horlick-Jones, T., Fortune, J. and Peters, G. (1993), 'Vulnerable systems, failure and disaster', in F, Stowell, D. West, and J. Howell (eds), *Systems science addressing global issues*, Plenum, New York, pp. 559-564.

Howard, M. (1993), 'Speech in Basingstoke, November 1993', cited in: M. Wasik and R.D. Taylor (1995), *Blackstone's Guide to the Criminal Justice and Public Order Act 1994*. Blackstone Press, London.

Howe, D. (1994), 'Modernity, postmodernity and social work', *British Journal of Social Work*, 24 (5), pp. 513-532.

Howells, K. and Hollin, C. R. (1989), *Clinical Approaches to Violence*, John Wiley and sons, Chichester.

Howlett, M. (1997), 'Community Care Homicide Inquiries and Risk Assessment', in H. Kemshall and J. Pritchard (eds), *Good Practice in Risk Assessment and Risk Management: Protection, Rights and Responsibilities, Volume 2*, Jessica Kingsley Publishers, London.

Huberman, A.M. and Miles, M.B. (1994), *Qualitative Data Analysis*, Sage, London.

Hudson, B. (1987), *Justice Through Punishment: A Critique of the 'Justice Model' of Corrections*, MacMillan, Basingstoke.

Hudson, B. (1993), *Penal Policy and Social Justice*, MacMillan, Basingstoke.

Hudson, B. (1996), *Understanding Justice*, Open University Press, Buckingham.

Humphrey, C. (1991), 'Callling on the Experts: The Financial Management Initiative (FMI): Private Sector Consultants and the Probation Service', *Howard Journal*, 30, pp. 1-18.

Humphrey, C., Carter, P. and Pease, K. (1992), 'A Reconviction Predictor for Probationers', *British Journal of Social Work*, 22, pp. 33-46.

Humphrey, C., Carter, P. and Pease, K. (1993), *Changing Notions of Accountability in the Probation Service*, The Institute of Chartered Accountants, London.

Hunt, A. W. (1964), 'Enforcement in probation casework', *British Journal of Criminology*, 4, pp. 239-252.

Independent (1995), 'Home Office's calculated crime just doesn't add up', 24th July, p.1.

Independent (1997), 'Beef on the bone is banned in new scare', 4th December, p.1.

Inner London Probation Service (1995), *Policy Statement on the Identification and Management of Risk and Dangerousness*, Inner London Probation Service, London.

Inside Story, Megan's Law, BBC, 4/2/1997.

Jackall, R. (1988), *Moral mazes: the world of corporate managers*, Oxford

University Press, New York.

Jackson, N. and Carter, P. (1992), 'The perception of risk', in J. Ansell and F. Wharton (eds), *Risk: analysis, assessment and management,* John Wiley and sons, Chichester, pp. 41-54.

James. A. (1994), 'Reflections on the Politics of Quality', in A. Connor and S. Black (eds), *Performance Review and Quality in Social Care,* Jessica Kingsley Publishers, London.

Jarvis, F. V. (1980), *Probation Officers' Manual,* 3rd edition, Butterworth, London.

Jasanoff, S. (1993), 'Bridging the Two Culture of Risk Analysis', *Risk Analysis,* 13 (2), pp. 123-129.

Jayyusi, L. (1984), *Categorization and the Moral Order,* Routledge and Kegan Paul, London.

Jenkins, S. (1989), 'It's the doers wot get the blame', *The Sunday Times,* 20th August, Section B, p.1.

Johns, C. (1994), 'Guided Reflection', in A.M. Palmer, S. Burns and C. Bulmer (1994), *Reflective Practice in Nursing: The Growth of the Professional Practitioner,* Blackwell Scientific Publications, Oxford.

Johnston, A. N. (1996), 'Blame, Punishment and Risk Management', in C. Hood and D.K.C. Jones (eds), *Accident and Design: contemporary debates in risk management,* University College London, London, pp. 72-83.

Johnston, P. (1997), 'Throughcare Practice, Risk and Contact with Victims', in H. Kemshall and J. Pritchard (eds), *Good Practice in Risk Assessment and Risk Management: Protection, Rights and Responsibilities, Volume 2,* Jessica Kingsley Publishers, London, pp. 288-300

Joint Negotiating Committee (1980), *Report of the Working Party on Management Structure in the Probation and After-Care Service,* Joint Negotiation Committee for the Probation Service, London.

Jones, S. and Joss, R. (1995), 'Models of Professionalism', in M. Yelloly and M. Henkel (eds), *Learning and Teaching in Social Work,* Jessica Kingsley Publishers, London.

Kahneman, D. and Tversky, A. (1973), 'On the Psychology of Prediction', *Psychological Review,* 80, pp. 237-251.

Kahnemann, D. and Tversky, A. (1984), 'Choices, values and frames', *American Psychologist,* 39 (4), pp. 341-350.

Kahneman, D., Slovic, P. and Tversky, A. (1982), *Judgement Under Uncertainty: Heuristics and Biases,* Cambridge University Press.

Karmen, A. (1990), *Crime Victims: An Introduction to Victimology,* Brooks Cole, Pacific Grove, CA.

Karpf, M. (1931), *The Scientific Basis of Social Work*, Columbia Press, New York.

Kemshall, H. (1984), *Defining Clients' Needs in Social Work*, Social Work Monographs: University of East Anglia, Norwich.

Kemshall, H. (1986), 'The Justice Model in Warwickshire', *Probation Journal*, 33 (3), pp. 106-108.

Kemshall, H. (1993), 'Are We All Accountants Now? Financial Management in the Probation Service', *Probation Journal*, 40, pp. 2-8.

Kemshall, H. (1993), 'Quality: Friend or Foe?' *Probation Journal*, 40, pp. 122-126.

Kemshall, H. (1993), 'Assessing Competence: Scientific Process or Subjective Inference? Do we really see it?' *Social Work Education*, 12, (1), pp. 36-45.

Kemshall, H. (1995), 'Risk in Probation Practice: The Hazards and Dangers of Supervision', *Probation Journal*, 42, (2), pp. 67-72.

Kemshall, H. (1996), *Reviewing Risk: A review of research on the assessment and management of risk and dangerousness: implications for policy and practice in the Probation Service*, A report for the Home Office Research and Statistics Directorate, Home Office, London.

Kemshall, H. (1996a), 'Offender Risk and Probation Practice.', in H. Kemshall and J. Pritchard (eds), *Good Practice in Risk Assessment and Risk Management, Volume 1*, Jessica Kingsley Publishers, London.

Kemshall, H. (1996b), *Risk Assessment and Risk Management Senior Manager Workshops*, Home Office Probation Training Section/ Association of Chief Officers of Probation, London.

Kemshall, H. (1997), 'The dangerous are always with us: dangerousness and the role of the probation service', *VISTA*, 2, (3), pp. 136-153.

Kemshall, H. (1997a), 'Risk in Probation Practice Training Issues', in *Management and Assessment of Risk in the Probation Service, part 2*, Home Office/Association of Chief Officers of Probation, London.

Kemshall, H. (1997b), 'Training Materials for Risk Assessment and Risk Management', in *Management and Assessment of Risk in the Probation Service, part 3*, Home Office/Association of Chief Officers of Probation, London.

Kemshall, H, (1997c), 'Do Sleep Safely: Crime Risks May Be Smaller than You Think', *Social Policy and Administration*, 31 (3), pp. 247-259.

Kemshall, H. (1997d), 'Risk and Parole: Issues in Risk Assessment for Release', in H. Kemshall and J. Pritchard (eds), *Good Practice in Risk Assessment and Risk Management: Protection, Rights and Responsibilities, Volume 2*, Jessica Kingsley Publishers, London.

Kemshall, H. (forthcoming 1998), 'Enhancing Risk Decision Making Through Critical Path Analysis', *Social Work Education.*

Kemshall, H. (1998a), *Risk Training for Senior Probation Officers: An Evaluation Report for Inner London Probation Service*, Inner London Probation Service, London.

Kemshall, H. and Pritchard, J. (1996), *Good Practice in Risk Assessment and Risk Management, Volume 1*, Jessica Kingsley Publishers, London.

Kemshall, H. and J. Pritchard: (1997) (eds), *Good Practice in Risk Assessment and Risk Management: Protection, Rights and Responsibilities*, Volume 2, *Jessica Kingsley Publishers, London.*

Kemshall, H., Parton, N., Walsh, M. and Waterson, J. (1997), 'Concepts of Risk in Relation to Organisational Structure and Functioning within the Personal Social Services and Probation', *Social Policy and Administration*, 31 (3), pp. 213-232.

King, M. (1991), *How the Law Thinks About Children*, Tavistock, London.

Kirk, J. and Miller, M. (1986), 'Reliability and Validity in Qualitative Research', *Qualitative Research Methods Series*, Sage, London.

Kitzinger, J. (1994), 'The methodology of focus groups', *Sociology of Health and Illness*, 16, pp. 103-121.

Knott, C. (1995), 'The STOP Programme: Reasoning and Rehabilitation in a British Setting', in J. McGuire (ed.), *What Works: Reducing Reoffending. Guidelines from Practice and Research*, John Wiley and sons, Chichester, pp. 115-126.

Krimsky, S. (1992), 'The Role of Theory in Risk Studies', in S. Krimsky and D. Golding (eds) (1992), *Social Theories of Risk*, Praeger, Westport, USA, pp. 3-22.

Krimsky, S. and Golding, D. (eds) (1992), *Social Theories of Risk*, Praeger, Westport, USA.

Kuhn, T. S. (1970), *The Structure of Scientific Revolutions*, University of Chicago Press, Chicago.

Lash, S. and Urry, J. (1994), *Economies of Signs and Space*, Sage, London.

Law, K. M. (1993), *A Retrospective Study Looking at the Efficacy of the HMP Wakefield Risk Assessment Proforma with Life Licencees*, Unpublished dissertation for MSc in applied criminal psychology, The Prison Service.

Lawrie, C. (1996), *Dealing with Dangerous People: The Probation Service and Public Protection*, paper to Public Protection Conference, Her Majesty's Inspectorate of Probation, Daventry, 27th-29th March.

Lawrie, C. (1997), 'Risk: The Role and Responsibilies of Middle Managers', in H. Kemshall and J. Pritchard (eds), *Good Practice in Risk Assessment and Risk Management: Protection, Rights and Responsibilities, Volume 2*, Jessica Kingsley Publishers, London, pp. 301-311.

Lawson-Cruttenden, T. and Addison, N. (1997), 'Harassment and Domestic Violence', *Journal of Family Law*, June, pp.429-431.

Leiss, W. and Chociolko, C. (1994), *Risk and Responsibility*, McGill-Queen's University Press, Montreal and London.

Lewis, P. (1991), 'Learning from Industry: Macho Management or Collaborative Culture', *Probation Journal*, 31, pp. 147-191.

Lidz, C.W., Mulvey, E.P. and Gardner, W. (1993), 'The accuracy of predictions of violence to others', *Journal of the American Medical Association*, 269, 8, pp. 1007-1011.

Limandri, B. J. and Sheridan, D. J. (1995), 'The prediction of intentional interpersonal violence: An introduction', in J. Campbell (ed.), *Assessing Dangerousness: Violence by Sexual Offenders, Batterers, and Child Abusers*, Interpersonal Violence: The Practice Series, Sage, London.

Lipsky, M. (1980), *Street Level Bureaucracy*. Russell Sage, London.

Litwack, T. R. (1994), 'Assessments of Dangerousness: Legal, Research and Clinical Developments', *Administration and Policy in Mental Health*, 21 (5), pp. 361-377.

Lloyd, C., Mair, G. and Hough, M. (1994), 'Explaining reconviction rates: a critical analysis', *Home Office Research Study No 136*, HMSO, London.

Lloyds List (1994), 'Massive improvement in Shell tanker safety record', 25th January.

London Borough of Brent (1985), *A Child in Trust: the Report of the Panel of Inquiry into the circumstances surrounding the death of Jasmine Beckford*, presented to the Brent Borough Council and to Brent Health Authority by members of the Panel of Inquiry, London Borough of Brent.

Losel, F. (1995), 'The efficacy of correctional treatment: A review and synthesis of meta-evaluations', in J. McGuire (ed.), *What Works: Reducing Offending*, John Wiley and sons, London, pp.79-111.

Lupton, D. (1993), 'Risk as a moral danger: the social and political functions of risk discourse in public health', *International Journal of Health Services*, 23, pp. 425-435.

Lupton, D. (1994), *Medicine as Culture. Illness, Disease and the Body in Western Societies*, Sage, London.

Lynch, M.A. (1976), 'Child Abuse: The Critical Path', *Journal of Maternal and Child Care*, July, pp. 25-29.

Mair, G. (ed.) (1990), *Risk Prediction and Probation*, Home Office

Research and Planning Unit, London.

Mair, G. (1996), 'Intensive Probation', in G. McIvor (ed.), *Working with Offenders*, Jessica Kingsley Publishers, London.

Mair, G. (1997) (ed.), *Evaluating the Effectiveness of Community Penalties*, Avebury, Aldershot.

Mannheim, K. (1970), 'The Sociology of Ideas and Interests', in H.H. Gerth and C. Wright Mills (eds), *From Max Weber: Essays in Sociology*. Routledge and Kegan Paul, London.

Mannheim, K. (1976), *Ideology and Utopia*, Routledge and Kegan Paul, London.

Mannheim, K. (1982), *Structures of Thinking*, Routledge and Kegan Paul, London.

Mannheim, H. and Wilkins, L.T. (1955), *Prediction Methods in Relation to Borstal Training*, HMSO, London.

Marriage, H. (1998), 'Current Home Office initiatives on potentially dangerous offenders', in Home Office Special Conference Unit (1998), *Inter-Agency Work with Potentially Dangerous Offenders and Risk/Needs Tools*, Home Office Special Conferences Unit, London.

Marris, C., O'Riordan, T., Langford, I. and Simpson, A. (1995), *Redefining the Cultural Context of Risk Perception*, Unpublished paper presented at Network Meeting of the Economic and Social Research Council Risk and Human Behaviour Programme: 'Conceptualising Risk, Science, Technology and Society: A Discussion of Theoretical Frameworks.' Edinburgh, 23rd January 1995.

Martinson, R. (1974), 'What works?' *The Public Interest*, March, pp.22-54.

Maupin, J. (1993), 'Risk Classification Systems and the Provision of Juvenile Aftercare', *Crime and Delinquency*, 39, 1, pp. 90-105.

Maurino, D.E., Reason, J., Johnston, N. and Lee, R.B. (1995), *Beyond aviation human factors*, Avebury Gower, Aldershot.

May, T. (1991), *Probation: Politics, Policy and Practice*, Open University, Milton Keynes.

May, T. and Vass, A, (1996) (eds), *Working with Offenders: Issues, Contexts and Outcomes*, Sage, London.

Mayhew, P. and Aye Maung, N. (1992), *Surveying Crime: findings from the 1992 British Crime Survey*, Research Findings No. 2, Home Office Research and Statistics Department, London.

Maynard-Moody, S., Musheno, M. and Palumbo, D. (1990), 'Street wise Social Policy: Resolving the Dilemma of Street-Level Influence and Successful Implementation', *Western Political Quarterly*, 43, pp.831-848

McEwan, S. and Sullivan, J. (1996), 'Sex Offender Risk Assessment', in H. Kemshall and J. Pritchard (eds), *Good Practice in Risk Assessment and Risk Management, Volume 1*, Jessica Kingsley Publishers, London, pp. 146-158.

McGuire, J. (1995), *What Works: Reducing Reoffending: Guidelines from Research and Practice*, John Wiley and sons, Chichester.

McGuire. J. (1997), 'A short introduction to meta-analysis', *VISTA*, 2 (3), pp. 163-176.

McGuire, J. and Priestley, P. (1985), *Offending Behaviour*, Batsford, London.

McGuire, J. and Priestley, P. (1995), 'Reviewing 'What Works': Past, Present and Future', in J. McGuire (ed.), *What Works: Reducing Reoffending: Guidelines from Research and Practice*, John Wiley and sons, Chichester, pp. 3-34.

McIvor, G. (1990), *Sanctions for Serious or Persistent Offenders*, Social Work Research Centre, Stirling.

McIvor, G. (1997), 'Evaluative research in probation: progress and prospects', in G. Mair (ed.), *Evaluating the Effectiveness of Community Penalties*, Avebury, Aldershot.

MacKenzie, G. (1996), *Danger, Necessity and Tribulation: A Theme for Reason*, paper presented to The Public Protection Conference, Her Majesty's Inspectorate of Probation, Daventry, 27th-29th March 1996.

McNeil, D.M. and Binder, R. (1987), 'Predictive validity of judgements of dangerousness in emergency civil commitments', *American Journal of Psychiatry*, 144, pp. 197-200.

McPhee, P. (1997), *Address to middle manager risk training event*, Unpublished Durham Probation Service.

McWilliams, W. (1981), 'The probation officer at court: from friend to acquaintance', *Howard Journal*, 20, pp. 97-116.

McWilliams, W. (1983), 'The mission to the English police courts 1876-1936', *Howard Journal*, 22, pp. 129-147.

McWilliams, W. (1985), 'The mission transformed: professionalisation of probation between the wars', *Howard Journal*, 24, (4), pp. 257-274.

McWilliams, W. (1986), 'The English Probation Service and the diagnostic ideal', *Howard Journal*, 26, (2), pp. 241-260.

McWilliams, W. (1987), 'Probation, pragmatism and policy', *Howard Journal*, 26, pp. 97-121.

McWilliams, W. (1989), 'An expressive model for evaluating probation practice', *Probation Journal*, 36 (2), pp. 58-64.

McWilliams, W. (1990), 'Probation practice and the management ideal',

Probation Journal, 37, (2), pp. 60-67.

McWilliams, W. (1992), 'Statement of Purpose for the Probation Service: A Criticism', *NAPO News*, 39, pp. 8-9.

McWilliams, W. (1992a), 'The rise and development of management thought', in R. Statham and P. Whitehead (eds), *Managing the Probation Service*, Longman, Harlow.

Megargee, E.I. (1976), 'The prediciton of dangerous behaviour', *Criminal Justice and Behaviour*, 3, pp. 3-22.

Menzies, R., Webster, C.D., McMain, S., Staley, S., and Scaglione, R. (1994), 'The Dimensions of Dangerousness Revisited', *Law and Human Behaviour*, 18, (1), pp. 1-28.

Merrick, D. (1996), *Social Work and Child Abuse*, Routledge, London.

Messant, M. (1996), 'We're Sick of these Outrageous Decisions', *Evening Mail*, 25th October, p. 15.

Messant, M. (1997), 'Action to Stop Probation Scandal', *Evening Mail*, 16th July, p. 6.

Meyer, H. K. (1959), 'Professionalization and social work', in A. Kahn, (ed.), *Issues in American Social Work*, Columbia University Press, New York.

Middlesex Probation Service (1996), *Assessment and Management of Risk and Dangerousness and Protection of the Public*, Middlesex Probation Service.

Miller, D. and Reilly, J. (1996), 'Mad Cows and Englishmen', *Planet: The Welsh Internationalist*, 117, June, pp. 118-119.

Miller, W.R. and Rollnick, S. (1991), *Motivational Interviewing: Preparing People to Change Addictive Behaviour*, The Guildford Press, London.

Miller, P. and Rose, N. (1988), 'The Tavistock Programme: The Government of Subjectivity and Social Life', *Sociology*, 22, (2), pp. 171-192.

Miller, P and Rose, N. (1990), 'Governing economic life', *Economy and Society*, 19, pp. 1-13.

Miller, P. and Rose, N. (1992), 'Political power beyond the state: problematics of government', *British Journal of Sociology*, 43, (2), pp. 173-205.

Minghella, E. and Benson, A. (1995), 'Developing reflective practice in mental health nursing through critical incident analysis', *Journal of Advanced Nursing*, 21, pp. 205-213.

Minichiello, V., Aroni, R., Timewell, E. and Alexander, L. (1990), *In-depth Interviewing: Researching People*, Longman Cheshire, Australia.

Mirlees-Black, C., and Maung, N.A. (1994), *Fear of Crime: Findings from the British Crime Survey*, Home Office, London.

Monahan, J. (1981), *The Clinical Prediction of Violence*, Sage, Beverley Hills, CA.

Monahan, J. (1992), 'Mental disorder and violent behaviour: perceptions and evidence', *American Psychologist*, 47, (4), pp. 511-521.

Monahan, J. (1993), 'Limiting Therapist Exposure to Tarasoff Liability: Guidelines for Risk Containment', *American Psychologist*, 48, pp. 242-250.

Monahan, J. and Steadman, H. (1994), *Violence and Mental Disorder: Developments in Risk Assessment*, Univeristy of Chicago Press, Chicago.

Mulvey, E.P. and Lidz, C.W. (1984), 'Clinical considerations in the prediction of dangerousness in mental patients', *Clinical Psychology Review*, 4, pp. 379-401.

Mulvey, E. P. (1994), 'Assessing the Evidence of a Link Between Mental Illness and Violence', *Hospital and Community Psychiatry*, 45 (4), pp. 663-668.

Mulvey, E.P. and Lidz, C.W. (1995), 'Conditional Preditction: A Model for Research on Dangerousness to Others in a New Era', *International Journal of Law and Psychiatry*, 18, (2), pp. 129-143.

Munro, E. (1996), 'Avoidable and Unavoidable Mistakes in Child Protection Work', *British Journal of Social Work*, 26, pp. 793-808.

Murphy, K. and Atkins, S. (1994), 'Reflection with a Practice-Led Curriculum', in A.M. Palmer, S. Burns and C. Bulmer, (1994), *Reflective Practice in Nursing: The Growth of the Professional Practitioner*, Blackwell Scientific Publications, Oxford.

National Crime Prevention Insititute (1986), *Crime Prevention*, Louisville.

National Board for Crime Prevention (1994), *Wise After the Event: Tackling Repeat Victimization*, 2nd May.

National Institute of Corrections (1981), *Model Probation and Parole Management Systems*, National Institute of Corrections, Washington, D.C.

National Probation Convention, (November 1997), Association of Chief Probation Officers and Central Probation Council.

National Probation Research and Information Exchange (1995), *Briefing on Reconviction*, N.P.R.I.E.

Nelkin, D. (1974), *Technological Decisions and Democracy: European Experiments in Public Participation*, Sage, Berkeley, California.

Nellis, M. (1993), 'Criminology, crime prevention and the future of probation training', in K. Bottomley, T. Fowles and R. Reiner (eds), *Criminal Justice: Theory and Practice: British Criminology Conference 1991 Selected Paper, Volume 2*, British Society of Criminology/ISTD, London.

Nellis, M. (1995), 'Probation values for the 1990s', *Howard Journal*, 34, (1), pp. 19-44.

Nisbett, R., Borigda, E., Crandall, R. and Reed, H. (1976), 'Popular induction: Information is not necessarily informative', in J. Carroll and J. Payne (eds), *Cognition and Social Behaviour*, Erlbaum, Hillsdale, N.J.

Nisbett, R. and Ross, L. (1980), *Human Inference: strategies and shortcomings of social judgement*, Prentice Hall, Englewood Cliffs, N.J.

Norman, I., Redfern, S., Toamlin, D. and Oliver, S. (1992), 'Developing Flanagan's critical incident technique to elicit indicators of high and low quality nursing care from patients and their nurses', *Journal of Advance Nursing*, 17, pp. 590-600.

Novaco, R.W. (1976), 'The function and regulation of the arousal of anger', *American Journal of Psychiatry*, 133, pp. 1124-1128.

Novaco, R. W. (1994), 'Anger as a Risk Factor for Violence among the Mentally Disordered', in J. Monahan and H.J. Steadman (eds), *Violence and Mental Disorder: Developments in Risk Assessment*, University Press, Chicago, pp. 21-60.

Nuffield, J. (1982), *Parole Decision Making in Canada: Research Towards Decision Guidelines*, Ministry of the Solicitor General, Communications Division, Ottawa.

Nuttall, C.P., with Barnard, E.F., Fowles, A.J., Frost, A., Hammond, W. H., Mayhew, P., Pease, K. Tarling, R. and Weatheritt, M.J. (1977), *Parole in England and Wales*, Home Office Research Study No. 38. HMSO, London.

Ohlin, L.E. and Duncan, O.D. (1949), 'The efficiency of prediction in criminology', *American Journal of Sociology*, 54, pp. 441-451.

Oldfield, M. (1994), 'Talking Quality: Meaning Control: McDonalds, the Market and the Probation Service', *Probation Journal*, 41, (4), pp. 186-192.

O'Malley, P. (1992), 'Risk, power and crime prevention', *Economy and Society*, 2, (3), pp. 252-275.

Orme, L. and Maggs, C. (1993), 'Decision making in clinical practice: how do expert nurses, midwives and health visitors make decisions?' *Nurse Education Today*, 13, pp. 270-276.

Parton, N. (1986), 'The Beckford Report: A Critical Appraisal', *British Journal of Social Work*, 16 (5), pp. 531-556.

Parton, N. (1994), 'Problematics of government, (post) modernity and social work', *British Journal of Social Work*, 24 (1), pp. 9-32.

Parton, N, (1994a), 'The Nature of Social Work under Conditions of (Post) modernity', *Social Work and Social Science Review*, 5 (2), pp. 93-112.

Parton, N. (1996), 'Social work, risk and the blaming system', in N. Parton (ed.), *Social Theory, Social Change and Social Work*, Routledge, London, pp.98-114.

Parton, N., Thorpe, D. and Wattam, C. (1997), 'Child Protection and the Moral Order', MacMillan Press, Basingstoke.

Patton, M. Q. (1980), *Qualitative Evaluation Methods*, Sage, London.

Pawson, R. and Tilley, N. (1994), 'What works in evaluation research', *British Journal of Criminology*, 34, pp. 291-306.

Payne, M. (1997), *Modern Social Work Theory*, MacMillan Press, London.

Perrow, C. (1984), *Normal Accidents: Living with High-Risk Technologies*, Basic Books, New York.

Pitts, J. (1992), 'The end of an era', *Howard Journal*, 31, pp. 133-149.

Pollock, N., McBain, I, and Webster, C. D. (1989), 'Clinical Decision Making the Assessment of Dangerousness', in K. Howells and C. Hollin (eds), *Clinical Approaches to Violence.* John Wiley and sons, Chichester, pp.89-115.

Polvi, N. and Pease, K. (1991), 'Parole and its problems: A Canadian-English comparison', *Howard Journal*, 30 (3), pp. 218-230.

Power, M. (1994), *The Audit Explosion*, Demos, London.

Power, M. (1994a), 'The Audit Society', in A.G. Hopwood and P. Miller (eds), *Accounting as Social and Institutional Practice*, Cambridge University Press, Cambridge.

Pratt, J. (1989), 'Corporatism: the third model of juvenile justice', *British Journal of Criminology*, 29, pp. 236-254.

Pratt, J. (1995), 'Dangerousness, Risk and Technologies of Power', *Australian and New Zealand Journal of Criminology*, 28, (1), pp. 3-31.

Pratt, J. (1996), 'Governing the Dangerous: An Historical Overview of Dangerous Offender Legislation', *Social and Legal Studies*, 5, pp. 21-36.

Priestley, P. (1977), *Social Skills and Personal Problem Solving: A Handbook of Methods*, Routledge and Kegan Paul, London.

Prins, H. (1988), 'Dangerous Clients: Further Observations on the Limitation of Mayhem', *British Journal of Social Work*, 18, pp. 593-609.

Prins, H. (1995), 'Risk Assessment: Seven Sins of Omission', *Probation Journal*, 42 (4), pp. 199-201

Probation Circular PC/84 (1994), *Risk Assessment for Temporary Release Prisoners*, Probation Service Division, London.

Probation Circular PC/96 (1994), *Risk Assessment for Temporary Release of Prisoners*, Probation Service Division, London.

Probation Circular PC/63 (1996), *Guidance to the Probation Service on the Offender Group Reconviction Scale (OGRS)*, Probation Service Division, Home Office, London.

Probation Circular PC/36 (1997), *Serious Incident Reports: Analysis*, Probation Unit, Home Office, London.

Prochaska, J.O. and DiClemente, C.C. (1986), 'Toward a comprehensive model of change', in W.R. Miller and N. Heather (eds), *Treating addictive behaviours: Processess of change*, Plenum Press, New York, pp. 3-27.

Prottas, J. M. (1979), *People Processing. The Street Level Bureaucrat in Public Service Bureaucracies*. D.C. Heath.

Polvi, N. and Pease, K. (1991), 'Parole and its problems: A Canadian-English comparison', *Howard Journal*, 30 (3), pp. 218-230.

Raine, J. and Wilson, M. (1993), *Managing Criminal Justice*, Harvester Wheatsheaf, Hemel Hempstead.

Rasmussen, J. (1990), 'Human error and the problem of causality in analysis of accidents', *Philosophical Transactions of the Royal Society of London*, 327B, pp. 449-462.

Rayner, S. (1986), 'Management of Radiation Hazards in Hospitals: Plural Rationalities in a Single Institution', *Social Studies of Science*, 16, pp. 573-591.

Rayner, S. (1992), 'Cultural Theory and Risk Analysis', in S. Krimsky and D. Golding (eds), *Social Theories of Risk*. Praeger, Westport, USA, pp. 83-116.

Rayner, S. and Cantor, R. (1987), 'How Fair is Safe Enough? The Cultural Approach to Societal Technology Choice', *Risk Analysis*, 7 (1), pp. 3-13.

Raynor, P. (1980), 'Is there any sense in social inquiry reports?' *Probation Journal*, 27, (3), pp. 78-84.

Raynor, P. (1985), *Social Work, Justice and Control*, Blackwell, Oxford.

Raynor, P. (1988), *Probation as an Alternative to Custody*, Avebury, Aldershot.

Raynor, P. (1997), *Implementing the 'Level of Service Inventory-Revised' (LSI-R) in Britain: Initial results from five probation areas*, The Cognitive Centre Foundation, Swansea.

Raynor, P. (1997a), 'Some Observations on Rehabilitation and Justice', *Howard Journal*, 36, (3), pp. 248-262.

Raynor, P., Smith, D. and Vanstone, M. (1994), *Effective Probation Practice*, MacMillan, Basingstoke.

Raynor, P. and Vanstone, M. (1992), *Straight Thinking on Probation: First Interim Report of the evaluation study*, Mid-Glamorgan Probation Service and Centre for Applied Social Studies, Swansea.

Raynor, P. and Vanstone, M. (1994), *STOP (Straight Thinking on Probation)*, Third Interim Evaluation Report, Mid Glamorgan Probation Service.

Raynor, P. and Vanstone, M. (1994a), 'Probation Practice, Effectiveness and the Non-Treatment Paradigm', *British Journal of Social Work*, 24, pp. 387-404.

Raynor, P., Gelsthorpe, L. and Tisi, A. (1995), 'Quality Assurance, Pre-Sentence Reports and the Probation Service', *British Journal of Social Work*, 25, pp. 477-488.

Reason, J. (1990), *Human Error*, Cambridge University Press, Cambridge.

Reder, P., Duncan, S. and Gray, M. (1993), *Beyond Blame: Child Abuse Tragedies Revisited*, Routledge, London.

Reddy, S. G. (1996), 'Claims to expert knowledge and the subversion of democracy: the triumph of risk over uncertainty', *Economy and Society*, 25, May, pp. 222-254.

Reichman, N. (1986), 'Managing Crime Risks: Toward an Insurance Based Model of Social Control', *Research in Law, Deviance and Social Control*, 8, pp. 151-172.

Report of the Presidential Commission on the Space Shuttle Challenger Accident, Government Printing Agency, 1986, Washington DC.

Rhodes, T. (1997), 'Risk theory in epidemic times: sex, drugs and the social organisation of 'risk behaviour'', *Sociology of Health and Illness*, 19 (2), pp. 208-227.

Ritzer, G. (1993), *The McDonaldization of Society*, Pine Forge Press.

Roberts, C. (1989), *Hereford and Worcester Probation Service Young Offenders Project: First Evaluation Report*, Department of Social and Administrative Studies, Oxford University, Oxford.

Roberts, C., Burnett, R., Kirby, A. and Hamill, H. (1996), *A System for Evaluating Probation Practice. Report of a method devised and piloted by the Oxford Probation Studies Unit and Warwickshire*, Centre for Criminological Research, Oxford.

Roberts, C. and Robinson, G. (1997), *A Comparative Study of Assessment Tools to Aid the Preparation of Pre-Sentence Reports: A Summary Report for the Greater Manchester Probation Service*, Centre for Criminological Research, Oxford.

Roder, W. (1961), 'Attitudes and Knowledge on the Topeka Flood Plain', in G.F. White (ed.), *Papers on Flood Problems*, Research Paper 700, Department of Geography, University of Chicago, Chicago.

Rolt, P. (1997), *West Glamorgan Probation Service Training Strategy*, West Glamorgan Probation Service, Swansea.

Rorty, R. (1980), *Philosophy and the Mirror of Nature*, Blackwell, Oxford.

Rose, N. (1990), *Governing the soul: The Shaping of the Private Self*, Routledge, London.

Rose, N. (1993), 'Government, authority and expertise in advanced liberalism', *Economy and Society*, 22, pp. 283-299.

Rose, N. (1996), 'Psychiatry as a political science: advanced liberalism and the administration of risk', *History of the Human Sciences*, 9, (2), pp. 1-23.

Rose, N. (1996a), 'The death of the social? Re-figuring the territory of government', *Economy and Society*, 25, (3), pp. 327-356.

Ross, R.R. and Fabiano, E.A. (1985), *Time to Think: A Cognitive Model of Delinquency Prevention and Offender Rehabilitation*, Institute of Social Sciences and Arts, Johnson City.

Ross, R. R., Fabiano, E. A. and Ewles, C. D. (1988), 'Reasoning and Rehabilitation', *International Journal of Offender Therapy and Comparative Criminology*, 32, pp. 29-35.

Ross, R.R., and Fabiano, E.A. and Ross, R. (1989), *Reasoning and Rehabilitation: a handbook for teaching cognitive skills*, Cognitive Centre, Ottawa.

Rowe, M.D. (1977), *An Anatomy of Risk*, John Wiley and sons, Chichester.

Royal Society (1992), *Risk: Analysis, Perception and Management*, Report of a Royal Society Study Group, London.

Runciman, W.B. (1993), 'System Failure: An Analysis of 2000 Incident Reports', *Anaesthesia and Intensive Care*, 21, (5), October, pp. 684-695.

Rutherford, A. (1993), *Criminal Justice and the Pursuit of Decency*, University of Oxford Press, Oxford.

Rushton, A. and Nathan, J. (1996), 'The Supervision of Child Protection Work', *British Journal of Social Work*, 26, pp. 357-374.

Russo, J. Edward and Shoemaker, Paul J.H. (1992), *Confident Decision Making*, Piaktus, London.

Ryan, T. (1996), 'Risk Management and People with Mental Health Problems', in H. Kemshall and J. Pritchard (eds), *Good Practice in Risk Assessment and Risk Management, Volume 1*, Jessica Kingsley Publishers, London, pp.93-108.

Sagan, S. (1993), *The limits of safety: organisations, accidents and nuclear weapons*, Princeton University Press, Princeton, New Jersey.

Satayamurti, C. (1981), *Occupational Survival*, Blackwell Publishers, Oxford.

Schon, D.A. (1983), *The Reflective Practitioner*, Basic Books, New York.

Schon, D.A. (1987), *Educating the Reflective Practitioner*, Jossey-Bass. in the Jossey-Bass Higher Education Series, San Francisco; London.

Schon, D.A. (1991), *The Reflective Practitioner: How Professionals Think in Action*, Arena, Ashgate Publishing, Aldershot.

Schon, D.A. and Argyris, C. (1978), *Organisational Learning: A Theory of Action Perspective*, Addison-Wesley, New York.

Schon, D.A. and Argyris, C. (1996), *Organisational Learning 2: Theory, Method, and Practice*, Addison-Wesley, New York.

Schutz, A. (1970), *On Phenomenology and Social Relations*, Uiversity of Chicago Press, Chicago and London.

Schutz, A. (1976), *The Phenomenology and the Social World*, Heinemann, London.

Schwing, R.C. and Albers, W.A. (eds) (1980), *Societal risk assessment: how safe is safe enough?* Plenum, New York.

Scott, P. (1977), 'Assessing dangerousness in criminals', *British Journal of Psychiatry*, 131, pp. 127-142.

Scottish Social Work Inspectorate (1998), *Risk Assessment*, Scottish Office, Edinburgh.

Seatrade Review (1994), 'Legs to stand on', 29th-31st March.

Secretary of State for Social Services (1974), *Report of the Inquiry into the Care and Supervision Provided in Relation to Maria Colwell*, HMSO, London.

Sellafield Visitor Centre (1997), Public displays.

Shah, S. (1978), 'Dangerousness: a paradigm for exploring some of the issues in law and psychology', *American Psychologists*, 33, pp. 224-238.

Shaw, R. (1991), 'Supervising the Dangerous Offender: Communication the vital but often missing factor', *NASPO News*, 10, p. 4.

Shaw. R. (1996), 'Supervising the Dangerous in the Community', in N. Walker (ed.), *Dangerous People*, Blackstone Press, Oxford, pp. 154-178.

Shearing, C.D. and Stenning, P. (1981), 'Private security: its growth and implications', in M. Tonry and M. Norval (eds), *Crime and Justice: An Annual Review of Research, 3*, University of Chicago Press, Chicago.

Sheen, Mr Justice. (1987), *MV Herald of Free Enterprise. Report of Court*

No. 8074 Formal Investigation, Department of Transport, London.

Sheldon, B. (1978), 'Theory and Practice in Social Work: A Re-examination of a Tenuous Relationship', *British Journal of Social Work*, 8 (1), pp. 1-25.

Sheldon, B. (1982), *Behaviour Modification: Theory, Practice and Philosophy*, Tavistock Publications, London.

Sheppard, D. (1996), *Learning the Lessons: Mental Health Inquiry Reports published in England and Wales between 1969-1996 and their Recommendations for Improving Practice*, Second edition, Zito Trust, London.

Sheppard, M. (1995), 'Social Work, Social Science and Practice Wisdom', *British Journal of Social Work*, 25, pp. 265-293.

Shrader-Frechette, K.S. (1991), *Risk and rationality: philosophical foundations for populist reforms*, University of California Press, Berkeley.

Shrivastava, P. (1987), *Bhopal: Anatomy of a Crisis*, Ballinger, Cambridge.

Silverman, D. (1985), *Qualitative Methodology and Sociology*, Gower, Aldershot.

Silverman, D.(1993), *Interpreting Qualitiative Data: Methods for Analysing Talk, Text and Interaction*, Sage, London.

Simon, J. (1987), 'The emergence of a risk society: Insurance, law, and the state', *Socialist Review*, 95, pp. 61-89.

Simon, J. (1988), 'The Ideological Effects of Actuarial Practices', *Law and Society Review*, 22, (4), pp. 772-800.

Sims, A. (1976), 'The critical incident technique in evaluating nursing performance', *International Journal of Nursing Studies*, 13, pp. 123-130.

Singleton, W.T. and Hoyden, J. (1994), *Risk and Decisions*, John Wiley and sons, Chichester.

Slovic, P. (1987), 'Perception of Risk', *Science*, 236, pp. 280-285.

Slovic, P. (1992), 'Perception of Risk: Reflections on the Psychometric Paradigm', in S. Krimsky and D. Golding (eds) (1992), *Social Theories of Risk*, Praeger, Westport, USA, pp. 117-152.

Slovic, P., Fischoff, B. and Lichtenstein, S. (1980), 'Facts and Fears: Understanding Perceived Risk', in R.C. Schwing and W.A. Albers (eds), *Societal Risk Assessment: How Safe is Safe Enough?*, Plenum Press, New York.

Slovic, P., Fischoff, B. and Lichtenstein, S. (1985), 'Regulation of risk: a psychological perspective', in R.G. Noll (ed.), *Regulatory Policy and the*

Social Sciences, University of California Press, Berkeley.

Smith, D. (1980), 'Individualisation and Justice', *Probation Journal*, 27, (4), pp. 111-134.

Smith, D. (1996), 'Developments in Probation in England and Wales 1984-1993', in G. McIvor (ed.), *Working with Offenders*, Jessica Kingsley Publishers, London, pp. 6-24.

Smith, G. (1980), *Social Need: Policy, Practice and Research*, Routledge and Kegan Paul, London.

Smith, Graham. (1996), *Dealing with Dangerous People: The Probation Service and Public Protection*, paper to The Public Protection Conference, Her Majesty's Inspectorate of Probation, Daventry, 27th-29th March.

Smith, G. and Harris, R. (1972), 'Ideologies of Need and the Organisation of Social Work Departments', *British Journal of Social Work*, 1 (1), pp. 27-45.

Social Work Services Inspectorate (Scotland) (1998), *Risk and Needs Assessment: A Supplement to the National Objectives and Standards for Social Work in the Criminal Justice System*, The Scottish Office, Edinburgh.

South East London Probation Service (1996), *Assessment and Management of Risk Policy*, South East London Probation Service.

Sparks, R. (1992), *Television and the Drama of Crime*, Open University Press, Buckingham.

Spooner, P. (1992), 'Corporate responsibility in an age of deregulation', in D. Parker and J. Handmer (eds), *Hazard management and emergency planning*, James and James, London, pp. 95-108.

Stanley, L. (1990), 'Doing Ethnography, Writing Ethnography: A Comment on Hammersley', *Sociology*, 24 (4), pp. 617-627.

Starbuck, W.H. and Milliken, (1988), 'Challenger: Fine tuning the odds until something breaks', *Journal of Management Studies*, 25 (4), pp. 319-340.

Steadman, H.J., Monahan, J., Appelbaum, S., Grisso, T., Mulvey, E.P., Roth, L H., Robbins, P.C. and Klassen, D. (1994), 'Designing a New Generation of Risk Assessment Research', in J. Monahan and H.J. Steadman (eds), *Violence and Mental Disorder*, University of Chicago Press, Chicago and London, pp. 297-318.

Stevenson, O. (1970), 'Knowledge for social work', *British Journal of Social Work*, 1 (2), pp. 225-237.

Strachan, R. and Tallant, C. (1997), 'Improving Judgement and Appreciating Biases Within the Risk Assessment Process', in H. Kemshall and J. Pritchard (eds), *Good Practice in Risk Assessment and*

Risk Management: Protection, Rights and Responsibilities. Volume 2, Jessica Kingsley Publishers, London, pp. 15-26.

Strauss, A. and Corbin, J. (1990), *Basics of Qualitative Research: Grounded Theory Procedures and Techniques,* Sage, London.

Strauss, A. and Corbin, J. (eds) (1997), *Grounded Theory in Practice,* Sage, London.

Straw, J. (1997), 'Address to National Probation Convention', in *NAPO News,* 95, 7-9, National Association of Probation Officers, London.

Sumner, C. (1994), *The Sociology of Deviance: An Obituary,* Open University Press, Buckingham.

Sutton, D. and Davies, P. (1996), *Evaluating Probation Practice - A Way Forward: Developing Procedures to Evaluate Overall Practice Performance Whilst Contributing to Practitioner Effectiveness,* The Cognitive Centre Foundation.

Tait, E.J. and Levidow, L. (1992), 'Proactive and reactive approaches to risk regulation: the case of biotechnology', *Futures,* 24 (April), pp. 219-231.

Taylor, F.W. (1911), *The Principles of Scientific Management,* Harper and Row, New York.

Thompson, M. (1980), 'The aesthetics of risk: culture of conflict', in R.C. Schwing and W.A. Albers (eds), *Societal Risk Assessment: How Safe is Safe Enough?,* Plenum Press, New York.

Thompson, M. (1991), 'Plural Rationalities: The Rudiments of a Practical Science of the Inchoate', in J.A. Hansen (ed.), *Environmental Concerns: An Interdisciplinary Exercise,* Elsevier, London, pp. 241-254.

Thompson, M. and Wildavsky, A. (1982), 'A Proposal to Create a Cultural Theory of Risk', in H.C. Kunreuther and E.V. Ley (eds), *The Risk Analysis Controversy: An Institutional Perspective,* Springer-Verlag, New York, pp. 145-161.

Thorpe, D. and Pease, K. (1976), 'The relationship between recommendations made to the court and sentences passed', *British Journal of Criminology,* 12, (3), pp. 230-249.

Thorpe, D., Smith, D., Green, C. and Paley, J. (1980), *Out of Care: The Community Support of Juvenile Offenders,* Allen and Unwin, London.

The Times (1997), 'Blunders lead to reform of smear testing', 21st October, p.6.

Toft, B. and Reynolds, S. (1994), *Learning from disasters: a management approach,* Butterworth-Heinemann, Oxford.

Tonry, M. (1995), *Malign Neglect - Race, Crime and Punishment in America,* Oxford University Press, New York.

Towl, G.J. and Crighton, D.A, (1997), 'Risk assessment with offenders', *International Review of Psychiatry*, 9, pp. 187-193.

Turner, B.A. (1978), *Man-made disasters*, Wykeham Press, London.

Turner, S., Petersilia, J. and Deschenes, E.P. (1992), 'Evaluating intensive supervision probation/parole (ISP) for drug offenders', *Crime and Delinquency*, 38 (4), pp. 539-556.

Tutt, N. and Giller, H. (1984), *Social Inquiry Reports*, Audiotape: Lancaster Information Systems, Lancaster.

Tversky, A. and Kahnemann, D. (1973), 'Availability: a heurisitic for judging frequency and probability', *Cognitive Psychology*, 4, pp. 207-232.

Tversky, A. and Kahnemann, D. (1974), 'Judgement under uncertainty: Heuristics and biases', *Science*, 185, pp. 1124-1131.

USSR State Committee on the Utilization of Atomic Energy (1986), *The Accident at Chernobyl Nuclear Power Plant and Its Consequences*, information compiled for the IAEA Experts' Meeting, 25th-29th August, Vienna: IAEA.

Vennard, J. (1996), 'Evaluating the effectiveness of community programmes with offenders', *VISTA*, 2 (1), pp. 15-27.

Vickers, G. (1978), *Unpublished memorandum*. MIT, cited in Schon, (1983).

Vincent, C., Ennis, M. and Audley, R. (1993), 'Safety in Medicine', in Vincent, C., Ennis, M. and Audley, R. (eds), *Medical Accidents*, Oxford University Press, Oxford.

Wagenaar, W. and Groenewold, J. (1987), 'Accidents at sea: mulitple causes and impossible consequences', *International Journal of Man-Machine Studies*, 27, pp. 587-598.

Walker, J.C. (1992), *Standards and Partnerships in Teaching and Teacher Education: USA and UK Experience*, Centre for Research in Professional Education, University of Canberra.

Walker, N. (1991), 'Dangerous Mistakes', *British Journal of Psychiatry*, 158, pp. 752-757.

Walker, N. (1996), *Dangerous People*, Blackstone Press, London.

Walklate, S. (1997), 'Risk and Criminal Victimization', *British Journal of Criminology*, 37, (1), pp. 35-45.

Ward, D. and Spencer, J. (1994), 'The Future of Probation Qualifying Training', *Probation Journal*, 41, (2), pp. 95-98.

Ward, D. and Spencer, J. (1997), 'New Labour-New Training?', *Probation Journal*, 44 (3), pp. 128-129.

Warwickshire Probation Service (1995), *The Assessment and Management of Risk*, Warwickshire Probation Service, Warwick.

Wasik, M. and Taylor, R.D. (1991), *Blackstone's Guide to the Criminal Justice Act*, Blackstone Press, London.

Wasik, M. and Taylor, R.D. (1995), *Blackstone's Guide to the Criminal Justice and Public Order Act 1994*, Blackstone Press, London.

Wason, P.C. and Johnson-Laird (1972), *Psychology of Reasoning: Structure and Content*, Batsford, London.

Waters, R. (1980), 'The Management Structure Review', *Probation Journal*, 27, (4), pp. 126-131.

Wattam, C. (1992), *Making a Case in Child Protection*, NSPCC/Longman, London.

Webb, B. (1982), 'The art of note-taking', in R.G. Burgess (ed.), *Field Research: Sourcebook and Field Manual*, Allen and Unwin, London.

Weber, M. (1949), *The Methodology of the Social Sciences*, Translated and edited by E.A. Shils and H.A. Finch, The Free Press, New York.

Weber, M. (1976), *The Protestant Ethic and the Spirit of Capitalism*, George Allen and Unwin, London.

Webster, C.D., Dickens, B.M. and Addario, S. (1985), *Constructing Dangerousness: Scientific, Legal and Policy Implications*, University of Toronto Centre of Criminology, Toronto.

Weist, J. (1981), 'Treatment of violent offenders', *Clinical Social Work Journal*, 9, (4), pp. 271-281.

Wells C. (1996), 'Criminal Law, Blame and Risk: Corporate Man-slaugher', in C. Hood, and D.K.C. Jones (eds), *Accident and Design: contemporary debates in risk management*, University College London, London.

West Midlands Probation Service (1993), *Training in Finance Management*, provided by H. Kemshall and M. Willis, Department of Social Policy and Social Work, Birmingham University.

West Midlands Probation Service (1997), *Risk: Practice Guidance for the Assessment and Management of Risk*, West Midlands Probation Service.

Weston, W.R. (1973), 'Style of management in the probation and aftercare service', *Probation Journal*, 20, pp. 69-73.

White, S. (1998), 'Analysing the Content of Social Work: Applying the Lessons from Qualitative Research', in J. Cheetham and M. Kazi (eds), *The Working of Social Work*, Jessica Kingsley Publishers, London.

Wildavsky, A. (1985), *Trial without error: anticipation versus resilience as strategies for risk reduction*, Centre for Independent Studies, Sydney.

Wildavsky, A. (1988), *Searching for Safety*, Transaction Books, New Brunswick.

Wilkinson, J. (1994), 'Using a reconviction predictor to make sense of reconviction rates in the probation service', *British Journal of Social Work*, 24 (4), pp. 461-473.

Wilkinson, A.J. (1997), 'Improving Risk Based Communications and Decision Making', *Journal of Petroleum Engineers*, 949, pp. 936-943

Witness (1998), 'The Monsters in Our Midst', Channel 4.

Wynne, B. (1982), *Rationality and Ritual: The Windscale Inquiry and Nuclear Decisions in Britain*, The British Society for the History of Science: 168.

Wynne, B. (1982a), 'Institutional Mythologies and Dual Societies in the Management of Risk', in E. Ley and H. Kunreuther (eds), *Risk Assessment: An Institutional Approach*, Springer-Verlag, New York, pp. 127-143.

Wynne, B. (1986), 'Public Perceptions of Nuclear Risks: Technological Treadmill or Institutional Development', in L.E. Roberts (ed.), *Nuclear Power and Public Acceptance*, University of East Anglia, Norwich.

Wynne, B. (1987), 'Risk Perception, Decision Analysis and the Public Acceptance Problem', in B. Wynne (ed.), *Risk Assessment and Hazardous Waste Management: Implementation and the Dialectics of Credibility*, Springer-Verlag, London.

Wynne, B. (1988), 'Unruly Technology', *Social Studies of Science*, 18, pp. 155.

Wynne, B. (1989), 'Sheepfarming after Chernobyl', *Environment*, 31, (11-15), pp. 33-39.

Wynne, B. (1989a), 'Frameworks of Rationality in Risk Management-Towards the Testing of Naive Sociology', in J. Brown (ed.), *Environmental Threats: Perception, Analysis, and Management*, Belhaven, London, pp. 33-45.

Wynne, B. (1992), 'Risk and Social Learning: Reification to Engagement', in S. Krimsky and D. Golding (eds) (1992), *Social Theories of Risk*, Praeger, Westport, USA, pp. 275-297.

Wyre, R. (1997), 'Marked for Life', *Community Care*, 20th-26th February, pp. 26-27.

Index